ARTIFICIAL INTELLIGENCE APPLICATIONS FOR HEALTH CARE

Edited by
Mitul Kumar Ahirwal, Narendra D. Londhe,
and Anil Kumar

CRC Press
Taylor & Francis Group
Boca Raton London New York

CRC Press is an imprint of the
Taylor & Francis Group, an **informa** business

First edition published 2022
by CRC Press
6000 Broken Sound Parkway NW, Suite 300, Boca Raton, FL 33487-2742

and by CRC Press
4 Park Square, Milton Park, Abingdon, Oxon, OX14 4RN

CRC Press is an imprint of Taylor & Francis Group, LLC

Library of Congress Cataloging-in-Publication Data
Names: Ahirwal, Mitul Kumar, editor. | Londhe, Narendra D., editor. |
Kumar, Anil, 1980- editor.
Title: Artificial intelligence applications for health care / edited by
Mitul Kumar Ahirwal, Narendra D. Londhe, Anil Kumar.
Description: First edition. | Boca Raton : Taylor and Francis, 2022. |
Includes bibliographical references and index.
Identifiers: LCCN 2021052132 | ISBN 9781032148465 (hardback) |
ISBN 9781032148472 (paperback) | ISBN 9781003241409 (ebook)
Subjects: LCSH: Artificial intelligence--Medical applications. | Medical informatics.
Classification: LCC R859.7.A78 A74 2022 | DDC 610.285--dc23/eng/20220110
LC record available at https://lccn.loc.gov/2021052132

ISBN: 978-1-032-14846-5 (hbk)
ISBN: 978-1-032-14847-2 (pbk)
ISBN: 978-1-003-24140-9 (ebk)

DOI: 10.1201/9781003241409

Typeset in Times
by MPS Limited, Dehradun

Dedication

This is dedicated to our parents and family members.

Contents

Foreword

This book is edited by three authors having expertise in different domains. Dr. Mitul Kumar Ahirwal is working with Computer Science and Engineering department, MANIT Bhopal, India and has expertise in computational intelligence techniques and Python. Dr. Narendra D. Londhe is working with Electrical Engineering department, NIT Raipur, India and has expertise in biomedical signal/image processing. Dr. Anil Kumar is working with Electronics and Communications Engineering department, PDPM-IIITDM Jabalpur, India and has expertise in digital signal processing and digital filter design for biomedical signals.

This book is a very good choice for the readers who wish to continue their studies and research in interdisciplinary areas of artificial intelligence and biomedical signal/image processing.

Preface

At present, the health care industry is growing at a very fast rate. This is because of requirements and development of high precision and modern equipment/instruments as well as diagnosis methods. These requirements are fulfilled by research and studies conducted over different databases and subjects. The role of biomedical signals and images are very important in these studies. These research and studies also make use of artificial intelligence techniques. To understand and apply artificial intelligence techniques, sufficient skills are required. Hence, the objective of this book is to explore the applications of artificial intelligence techniques in the field of health care and provide a good understanding of technique used.

Artificial intelligence mainly includes the techniques that are iterative in nature. These techniques may help in optimization of solution or in learning/training for a predication and classification of model. Since the past decade, applications of these techniques are providing promising results in biomedical engineering and healthcare industry. Biomedical signal/image processing is one of the important fields that is currently playing a vital role in the healthcare industry.

This book has been edited by three experts from different domains, first editor is from computer science domain, second editor is from electrical engineering domain, and the third editor is from electronics & communication domain. Hence, the scope of book is wide and it covers paradigms of Computer Science, Electrical, and Electronics Engineering fields.

Therefore, this book will help readers working in the field of artificial intelligence and biomedical signal/image processing. Readers of artificial intelligence field will get the idea and basic implementation for applications of their expertise in biomedical signal/image processing field. On the other hand, readers of biomedical signal/image processing field will get familiar with the topics of artificial intelligence, machine learning, and optimization fields.

Acknowledgement

First of all we thank our parents for all the things that we have today. We would like to thanks our supervisors. We also express thanks to our family members for their support and sacrifices. Special Thanks to Dr. N.S. Raghuvanshi (Director, MANIT Bhopal), Dr. A.M. Rawani (Director, NIT Raipur), and Dr. Sanjeev Jain (Director, PDPM-IIITDM Jabalpur) for their encouragement and support. Thanks for all the authors/contributors for their valuable contribution in this book. Thanks for research labs/institutes for uploading their datasets for public usage in research and academics. Many thanks for CRC Press and Taylor & Francis Group for accepting the book proposal and their continuous support. At last, but not least, we thank almighty god for giving us strength to complete this book as a mission.

Editors Biographies

 **Dr. Mitul K. Ahirwal** received his B.E. in Computer Science & Engineering from SATI, Vidisha, (M.P) (Affiliated to RGPV, Bhopal, India) in 2009 and completed his M.Tech. in Computer Technology from National Institute of Technology, Raipur, India in 2011. He completed his Ph.D. in the Computer Science and Engineering Department, PDPM IIITDM, Jabalpur, India. Presently, he is Assistant Professor in the Department of Computer Science and Engineering at Maulana Azad National Institute of Technology, Bhopal, India. He has several national and international publications in his credit. He is also working on several research projects funded by different agencies. His research area is biomedical signal processing, swarm optimization, brain–computer interface, and healthcare system. He has been involved as a reviewer with various reputed journals.

Institute webpage: http://www.manit.ac.in/content/dr-mitul-kumar-ahirwal

Google Scholar: https://scholar.google.co.in/citations?user=fWgOgcIAAAAJ&hl=en

 **Dr. Narendra D. Londhe** has completed his M.Tech and Ph.D. in the year of 2004 and 2011, respectively from Indian Institute of Technology, Roorkee, Uttarakhand, India. Currently he is working with National Institute of Technology, Raipur as an Associate Professor in Department of Electrical Engineering. His area of research includes image and signal processing, soft computing, biometrics, ultrasound imaging, IVUS imaging, brain–computer interface, pain assessment, and psoriasis severity detection. He has more than 40 publications in SCI indexed journals, more than 30 peered reviewed reputed national and international journal publications, and approximately 35 national and international reputed conferences. Moreover, he is member of many technical communities and societies such Senior member of IEEE, Member of IET, Life Member of The Institution of Engineers (India), Life Member of Ultrasonic Society of India, Life Member of Acoustical Society of India, Life Member of Biomedical Engineering Society of India, Life Member of Telemedicine Society of India, Life Member of Instrument Society of India, and Life Member of Institution of Engineers.

Institute webpage: http://www.nitrr.ac.in/viewdetails.php?q=ee.ndlondhe

Google Scholar: https://scholar.google.co.in/citations?user=7bH2p9oAAAAJ&hl=en

 **Dr. Anil Kumar** has completed a B.E. from Army Institute of Technology (AIT), Pune, Pune University in Electronic & Telecommunication Engineering and M.Tech and Ph.D. from Indian Institute of Technology, Roorkee, India in 2002, 2006, and 2010, respectively. After doctoral work, he joined as an Assistant Professor in the Electronics & Communication Engineering Department, Indian Institute of Information Technology Design and Manufacturing, Jabalpur, India since 2009 to July 2016. His academic and research interest is in designing Digital Filters & Multirate Filter Bank, Multirate Signal Processing, Biomedical Signal Processing, Image Processing, and Speech Processing.

Institute webpage: http://faculty.iiitdmj.ac.in/faculty/anilk

Google Scholar: https://scholar.google.co.in/citations?user=Xqz4P2AAAAAJ& hl=en

Contributors

Nikhil Agrawal
Indian Institute of Information Technology
Nagpur, India

Mitul Kumar Ahirwal
Maulana Azad National Institute of
    Technology
Bhopal, India

Mithilesh Atulkar
National Institute of Technology
Raipur, India

Ashwini M. Bakde
Department of Radio-Diagnosis
All India Institute of Medical Sciences
Nagpur, Maharashtra, India

Vikramjit Banerjee
International Institute of Information
    Technology
Pune, India

Chaithra Bhat
International Institute of Information
    Technology
Pune, India

Narendra Kuber Bodhey
Department of Radiodiagnosis
All India Institute of Medical Sciences
Raipur, India

Sanjay Chitnis
Dayananda Sagar University
Bangalore, India

Manisha Das
Department of Electronics and Communi-
    cation Engineering Visvesvaraya
National Institute of Technology
Nagpur, Maharashtra, India

Manoranjan Dash
Electrical Engineering Department
National Institute of Technology
Raipur, India

P. Chaya Devi
Anil Neerukonda Institute of Technology
    & Sciences, Visakhapatnam
Andhra Pradesh, India

Prashant Gadakh
International Institute of Information
    Technology
Pune, India

Kuldeep Kumar Gautam
Maulana Azad National Institute of
    Technology
Bhopal, India

Subhojit Ghosh
Electrical Engineering Department,
National Institute of Technology
Raipur, India

R. Goswami
Anil Neerukonda Institute of Technology
    & Sciences, Visakhapatnam
Andhra Pradesh, India

A. Govardhan
JNTUH College of Engineering
Hyderabad, India

Deep Gupta
Department of Electronics and Communi-
    cation Engineering Visvesvaraya
National Institute of Technology
Nagpur, Maharashtra, India

Akshansh Jaiswal
International Institute of Information
  Technology
Pune, India

Manali Kaswa
International Institute of Information
  Technology
Pune, India

Jaskirat Kaur
Chandigarh Group of Colleges Jhanjeri
  Mohali Chandigarh
Chandigarh, India

Ramanpreet Kaur
Chandigarh Group of Colleges Jhanjeri
  Mohali Chandigarh
Chandigarh, India

Mangesh Ramaji Kose
National Institute of Technology
Raipur, India

Madhusudan G. Lanjewar
School of Physical and Applied Sciences
Goa University
Goa, India

Ganesh Laveti
Gayatri Vidya Parishad College of
  Engineering for Women
Visakhapatnam, Andhra Pradesh, India

Narendra D. Londhe
Electrical Engineering Department
National Institute of Technology
Raipur, India

G. Madhu
VNR Vignana Jyothi Institute of Enginee-
  ring and Technology
Hyderabad, India

Deepti Mittal
Thapar Institute of Engineering and
  Technology
Patiala, Punjab, India

G. Nagachandrika
VNR Vignana Jyothi Institute of Enginee-
  ring and Technology
Hyderabad, India

Jivan S. Parab
School of Physical and Applied Sciences
Goa University
Goa, India

Rajesh K. Parate
Department of Electronics
S. K. Porwal College
Kamptee, India

Avani Pathak
International Institute of Information
  Technology
Pune, India

Sandeep Patil
National Institute of Technology
Silchar, India

Petia Radeva
Department of Mathematics and Computer
  Science
Universitat de Barcelona
and
Computer Vision Center
Barcelona, Spain

Rajeev Ramesh
International Institute of Information
  Technology
Pune, India

S. Sathyanarayanan
Sri Sathya Sai University for Human
  Excellence
Gulbarga, India

Shubhi Sharma
University of Petroleum and Energy
  Studies
Uttrakhand, India

Siddharth Sharma
Indian Institute of Technology Roorkee
Uttrakhand, India

Vipul Sharma
Maulana Azad National Institute of
  Technology
Bhopal, India

Aman Shinde
International Institute of Information
  Technology
Pune, India

Ravi Singh
Maulana Azad National Institute of
  Technology
Bhopal, India

Siddhant Singh
International Institute of Information
  Technology
Pune, India

Rajendra Sonawane
Psoriasis Clinic and Research Centre,
  Psoriatreat Pune
Maharashtra, India
and
National Institute of Technology
Raipur, India

K. Lakshman Srikanth
Legato Health Technologies LLP
Bangalore, India
and
GAR Infobahn
Telangana, India

Sajedul Talukder
Southern Illinois University
Carbondale, IL, USA

Hitesh Tekchandani
National Institute of Technology
Raipur, India

Shrish Verma
National Institute of Technology
Raipur, India

1 A Survey of Machine Learning in Healthcare

S. Sathyanarayanan
Sri Sathya Sai University for Human Excellence, Gulbarga, India

Sanjay Chitnis
Dayananda Sagar University, Bangalore, India

CONTENTS

1.1 INTRODUCTION

The advanced medical equipment used in secondary and tertiary healthcare centres is considerably expensive, and obtaining quality healthcare has become difficult and unaffordable for majority of the population. Hence, the application of Machine Learning (ML) in healthcare domains to automate various procedures is expected to help accelerate diagnostic procedures, reduce cost and increase access to quality care for general population. ML can be used in the analysis of healthcare data for faster diagnosis. ML-enabled systems can also be used for prediction by analysing the vast amount of healthcare data to enable preventive measures in time. ML in biomedical technologies will help in the development of smaller, portable, easy-to-use, cloud-enabled and affordable devices, which can be used by the medical staff at primary healthcare centres; thereby, reducing the workload of doctors and eliminating the need for advanced diagnostic equipment for most of the patients. This will also make expensive resources more easily available for people in need. Thus, ML in healthcare could provide greater access to quality care with minimal hindrances.

This chapter reviews some of the ongoing research in this area after a brief tutorial of ML and also briefly describes few ML-enabled devices already in use.

1.2   ARTIFICIAL INTELLIGENCE

Traditionally, computers had to be programmed by humans. This limited its application in areas with set rules and specific protocols. John McCarthy, an American computer scientist, defined AI as the science and engineering of making intelligent machines [1]. AI is used to describe systems that mimic "cognitive" functions that are associated with humans, such as problem-solving skills and learning [2]. *Narrow AI* systems are those that carry out specific tasks, for example the AI systems currently being used in healthcare domain. These systems are common, for example virtual assistants on smart phones and recommendation systems. *Artificial General Intelligence* (AGI) systems are capable of learning different tasks like humans. However, such systems do not exist as of now. The different types of AI systems based on the type of work they accomplish are briefly discussed here and depicted in Figure 1.1.

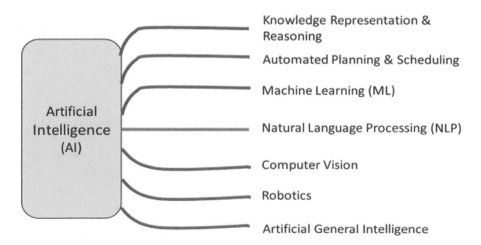

FIGURE 1.1   Types of AI.

Knowledge Representation and Reasoning (KR & R or KR): This is a type of AI wherein knowledge representation deals with representing information in the form of symbols and propositions. It makes use of reasoning as the method of deducing facts from the data, for example, computer-aided diagnosis.

Automated Planning and Scheduling: This is also called AI planning. It considers the time and resource constraints and generates a series of actions in sequence to achieve the objective.

Machine Learning: This gives computers the capability to learn from data without being programmed manually.

Natural Language Processing (NLP): This aims to build systems that can make sense out of the raw natural language data as input. An example is Siri in Apple devices.

Computer Vision: This enables computers to process image and video data and see, observe and make sense out of it. For example, computer vision helps in detecting patterns in various medical imaging data to help in diagnosing diseases.

Robotics: A robot is an autonomous system or a system with external control with the capability to perceive its environment, make decisions and perform actions in the real world. Robotics is a field that makes use of various branches of science and engineering to build autonomous robots.

Artificial General Intelligence: The goal of AI as a field is to move towards Artificial General Intelligence (AGI). A system having AGI implies that the system can match humans in intellectual capacity. The examples considered so far are examples of narrow AI.

1.2.1 MACHINE LEARNING

ML is a subfield of computer science that provides computers the ability to learn to perform a task on its own from experience without being explicitly programmed. Tom Mitchell defined learning precisely with the following definition [3]: "A computer program is said to learn from experience E with respect to some class of tasks T and performance measure P, if its performance at tasks in T, as measured by P, improves with experience E".

Such systems learn from the data provided and give a prediction for new data. The conventional ML algorithms are dependent on the availability of data for effectiveness. For example, a price prediction algorithm for houses may give a prediction for the house if the location, size, etc. are given. Each information included in the representation of the house for sale is known as a feature. The ML system learns how each of these features of the house correlates with various outcomes. The conventional programming systems give output based on the program and input data. The ML system gives a model as its output based on the input data and the various outcomes which is fed to it. This is illustrated in Figure 1.2.

1.2.1.1 Steps in Developing an ML System

A project to develop an ML-enabled system involves multiple phases before it can be put to use.

Data Collection and Labelling: The first step in ML is the collection of data, including the detailed description of the data involved that will help in

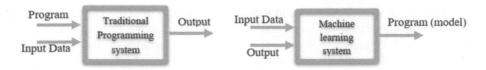

FIGURE 1.2 Difference between traditional programming system and machine learning system.

understanding and identifying the type of data required for the ML model. The process of detecting and tagging data samples is called data labelling.

Pre-processing: After data is collected, it has to be pre-processed, which may involve deduplication, normalisation and error correction to make the data suitable for use.

Feature Engineering: A *feature* is an attribute or a measurable property shared by all the independent units of the data on which analysis or prediction is to be done [4].

For example, in property prices data, the area of the house, the number of rooms and the age of the property can be considered as features. The collection of data of all the houses sold may be considered as a dataset. If the dataset is represented in a tabular format with each row providing information about one house, features appear as columns in the dataset. *Feature engineering* is the process of extracting features from raw data to increase the prediction capability or the accuracy of the ML model.

Selection of Algorithm: There are multiple algorithms for ML and selection of a suitable algorithm based on the input data format and the prediction expected of the model is an important component of an ML system.

Training: This is the next step in ML model in which input is given to the ML algorithm, which detects patterns on its own to build a model that will be used later for prediction.

Evaluation: The model is then evaluated with test data, that is, data that is not used for training, but whose output values are known. If the test result is not satisfactory, the previous step of training the model is repeated to get satisfactory results.

Prediction: The model thus evaluated and found to be satisfactory is then used to give a prediction for actual use cases after integrating it in a system.

Figure 1.3 shows the various steps in the production of an ML model.

1.2.1.2 Types of Machine Learning

ML can be broadly categorised into four types – supervised, unsupervised, semi-supervised and reinforcement learning. Figure 1.4 depicts the types of ML and the most common application for which the type is used.

FIGURE 1.3 Steps in the production of an ML model.

(*Source*: https://www.pcictx.org/).

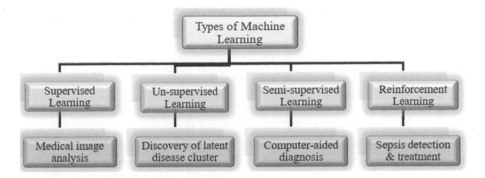

FIGURE 1.4 Types of machine learning.

Supervised Learning: In this subset of ML, the input of a dataset, as well as the corresponding known output, is fed to the algorithm. The algorithm then builds a model by finding a function to map the set of input data to its known output by using a set of assumptions. The algorithm predicts the output for the known dataset, compares its predicted output to the known output and tries to minimise the error by changing the initial set of assumptions in an iterative process until the model attains sufficient accuracy in its prediction. The data used for the above process is called the training data.

When the output of a model is a category or a class and not a numeric value, the method is called a *classification technique*. In this technique, the model gives output by recognising patterns in the input dataset. When the output of a model is a continuous value, then the method is called the *regression technique*.

Unsupervised Learning: Unsupervised learning techniques are used to work with a dataset whose output values or labels are unknown. The algorithm is given only inputs. The model identifies hidden patterns and extracts insights from the input without supervision, which are then incorporated into its learning. Unsupervised learning uses two methods: clustering and dimensionality reduction. Analysing the data and grouping them based on the similarity of the characteristics into different clusters or classes is called *clustering*. The extraction of information from the data and leaving out less relevant features is called dimensionality reduction. It is used when the number of features (or dimensions) of the input dataset is very large. The redundant features and features with minimal impact on the output of the model are removed to make the number of features more manageable.

Semi-supervised Learning: The cumbersome stage in supervised learning is data preparation. A semi-supervised learning method could be used to reduce the amount of work in the data preparation stage. First, a small amount of labelled data is used to partially train an ML model like in supervised learning and it is then used to label the large amount of unlabelled data. This procedure is called *pseudo-labelling*. The mix of the labelled and pseudo-labelled data is then used to train the model [5].

Reinforcement Learning: In Reinforcement Learning (RL), the software agent performs actions and learns from the rewards and penalties for its actions in an interactive environment and strives to maximise the cumulative rewards. Gaming and self-driving cars are examples where RL has been used. RL has also been used for detecting and treating sepsis.

1.2.2 Deep Learning

Artificial Neural Networks (ANN): A neuron is the fundamental component of the brain. A human brain contains around 100 billion neurons. Each neuron is connected to around 100,000 other neurons, enabling communication between them. If the signal received by a neuron is above a certain value called the threshold value, the neuron sends signals to the other neurons to which it is connected. The neurons are nonlinear in their behaviour and the transmitting of signals is controlled by the biochemistry [6].

ANN is inspired by the brain's structure and its functioning. ANN is a computing system made up of a very large number of simple elements that are highly interconnected and each of the elements process information by responding to inputs [7]. Dr. Robert Hecht-Nielsen, the inventor of one of the first neurocomputers, defined an *artificial neural network as* [7]

> *"...a computing system made up of a number of simple, highly interconnected processing elements, which process information by their dynamic state response to external inputs."*

An ANN is made up of a series of layers. Each layer consists of an array of processing units called nodes or artificial neurons. The neurons receive input from the neurons in the preceding layer and give output to the neurons of the succeeding layer. The input to each neuron is a set of feature values multiplied by their corresponding weights, which is then summed up to determine the weighted evidence. This value is processed by an activation function, a nonlinear function in the neuron, to determine the output. The activation functions are nonlinear. The various weights of the input are adjusted during training to get the accurate output. The first and the last layers are the input layer and the output layer, respectively. The middle layers are called "hidden" layers since they are not seen by the interfaces to the network and perform the computation. The hidden layer nodes consist of *activation functions*. A simple ANN with the input layer, hidden layer and the output layer is depicted below in Figure 1.5.

Deep learning (DL): DL is a subset of ML, built using ANN where the number of middle or hidden layers is more than one. The word "deep" is due to the number of the layers in the middle being more than one and hence DL is also called Deep Neural Networks (DNNs). The word "learning" is used because as the model processes more data the accuracy or its prediction power increases; therefore it is said to be learning from its experience. The relationship between AI, ML and DL is illustrated in Figure 1.6.

Feature Hierarchy: Raw data like images or videos are fed as input to a DL algorithm. As the raw data is processed, each layer extracts features from the raw data and passes it on to the next layer. The succeeding layers process the basic features from the preceding layers and identify more complex features. As the data

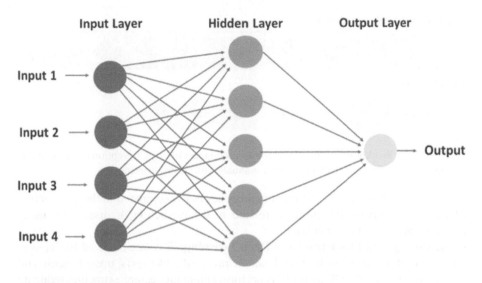

FIGURE 1.5 Artificial neural networks.

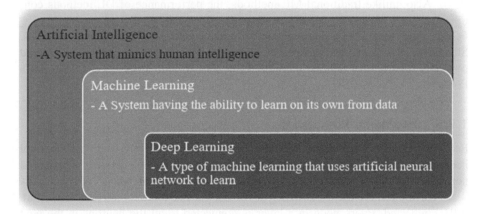

FIGURE 1.6 Difference between artificial intelligence, machine learning and deep learning.

progresses through the layers, increasingly complex features are identified by the network on its own. This is called feature hierarchy.

Representation Learning: This is a technique by which a DL algorithm is given raw data as input and the algorithm automatically discovers the representations [8] of the data on its own and allows the system to learn on its own [9]. DL methods perform representation learning by having multiple layers of simple nonlinear activation functions in the nodes of each of the layers that transform the input it receives into a representation at a more abstract higher level [8]. That means that for an image, for example, the input might be a matrix of pixels, then the first layer might detect the edges, then the next layer might detect an arrangement of edges, then the next layer might detect nose, ears, mouth and so on and then the next layer might identify a face, and so on.

Conventional Machine Learning

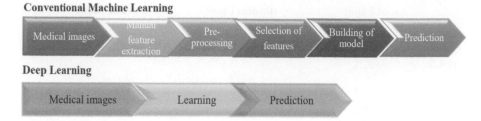

FIGURE 1.7 Workflow of AI systems for prediction models: a) Conventional ML, with the various steps involving selecting features manually, b) DL by learning.

Figure 1.7 illustrates the different approaches in DL compared to the approach in ML to solve a particular problem related to the prediction of disease by using medical images as the input data.

Advantages and Constraints of Deep Learning: The data received for input to a DL algorithm can be unstructured data or raw media like texts, images, audio and video recordings [10]. DL algorithms perform automatic feature extraction reducing the need for supervision and reducing the time taken in the data pre-processing stage. Also, unlike traditional ML methods, the performance of DL methods continues to improve as the size of the input data increases.

DL algorithms need a huge amount of data to learn and take correct decisions. Since the DL algorithms perform a very large amount of processing, they need powerful systems, which is possible now due to the emergence of Graphics Processing Units (GPUs).

1.2.3 THE MAJOR TYPES OF DL

Feedforward neural networks, recurrent neural networks (RNN) and convolutional neural networks (CNN) are supervised ML algorithms. Generative adversarial networks (GAN) is an example of unsupervised ML algorithms.

Feedforward Neural Networks: In feedforward neural networks, the nodes are fully connected. Every node in a layer is connected to all the neurons in the next layers. Such structures are called multilayer network of neurons (MLN) [11]. The flow of information is from the input layer to the output layer through the hidden layers without any feedback [12].

Autoencoder: An autoencoder network has an input layer, an output layer and one or more hidden layers connecting them, but the output layer has the same number of units as the input layer [12]. Its purpose is to reconstruct its inputs. Therefore, autoencoders are unsupervised learning models used for dimensionality reduction and for learning generative models of data [12].

Convolutional Neural Networks: In the CNN model, the neurons are connected to only some of the next layer neurons. The learned features are convolved with the input data using 2D convolutional layers. This algorithm is suitable for processing images. Here, convolution is a mathematical operation on two functions that produces a third function expressing how the shape of one is modified by the other and refers to both the result function and to the process of computing it.

Recurrent Neural Networks: RNN are used in applications where the output depends on the previous results. Hence, RNN are said to have memory.

Generative Adversarial Networks: GAN are used when the training data is not sufficient. These are used to generate new data to supplement the training data. They consist of the generator and the discriminator. The generator creates fake data based on the real training data it receives. The discriminator analyses the data and tries to distinguish the genuine data from the fake data [13]. GAN can be used to create training datasets for other applications by generating realistic fake data.

1.3 APPLICATIONS OF ML IN HEALTHCARE

As in all other domains, there is a lot of hype about what ML can do in the field of healthcare. Though the hype over the past few years about ML replacing doctors is not justified, technology will increasingly outperform human physicians at specific tasks. AI starts to integrate in the following way. In the first phase, AI augments healthcare practitioners. For example, a chatbot allows doctors to query other cases, context-sensitive AI assistant reminds doctors of appointments, tasks, etc. In the second phase, AI starts to play an increasingly important role and practitioners rely on it. For example, AI-based workflows suggest next steps to doctors based on case history, sometimes even automatically invoking other workflows and tests. Healthcare delivery is accelerated due to automation. In the third step (not implemented commonly as of now), AI will drive healthcare and healthcare practitioners will augment AI (reverse of step 1). For example, diagnosis and treatment recommendations would be done by AI and doctors merely validate the diagnosis and the recommended treatment. Some of the healthcare domains in which ML has been used are heart diseases, medical imaging and electronic health record (EHR).

Figure 1.8 illustrates the benefits of a healthcare model integrated with AI compared to the traditional healthcare model. The advantages of an AI-integrated healthcare model are low cost, improved prediction and greater accuracy, a proactive system with less physical interaction compared to the traditional model which is reactive, requires physical presence of patients, is less accurate and expensive.

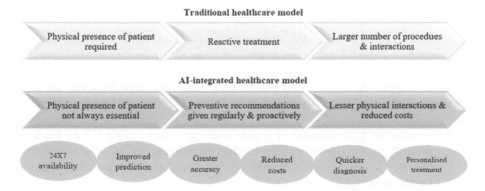

FIGURE 1.8   Comparison of traditional and AI-integrated healthcare models.

(*Source*: Aite group).

1.3.1 CARDIOVASCULAR DISEASES

Cardiovascular diseases (CVDs) are one of the main causes of mortality. Some aspects of the CVD epidemic in developing countries are the early age that it affects and the high fatality rate. Congenital heart disease (CHD) affects one in every hundred children born across the world [14].

Heart sound auscultation using a stethoscope is the primary method of detecting any abnormalities in the heart. Years of experience are required to diagnose heart murmurs correctly. Hence, further tests that require expensive medical resources could be used inefficiently.

Consider a similar scenario, with one change that the paramedic staff working in a primary healthcare centre has access to an electronic stethoscope with a recording facility and could connect to a cloud server for analysing the heart murmurs and receive response within a few seconds. Further, these devices save the time of doctors, who are expensive resources.

Heart Auscultation: Cardiac disorders can be diagnosed using heart auscultation with high accuracy. Cardiac auscultation is a procedure that involves listening and analysing heart sounds using an electronic stethoscope, a device that records heart sounds digitally. The recording is called a phonocardiogram (PCG). Several digital signal processing and ML techniques could be used to study the PCG and diagnose heart disorders. Automated heart sound analysis is called computer-aided auscultation (CAA). CAA is being applied for development of affordable tools for diagnosis.

1.3.2 MEDICAL IMAGING

Medical images are analysed by radiologists who are constrained by human factors. Hence, it is an ideal case for automation. The data is relatively organised in the domain of medical imaging due to which it is one of the domains in which ML is being applied. Different ways of digital medical images include magnetic resonance imaging (MRI) scans, X-rays, retinal photography and histology slides. Some of the domains in which ML systems have been applied are discussed below. The workflow of an AI-integrated medical image analysis system is depicted in Figure 1.9.

Radiology: Research on AI in radiology has seen some success as DL-based algorithms equalled or exceeded humans in several tasks, such as the detection of pneumonia on a chest X-ray or the analysis of white matter lesions on MRI scans of the brain [16].

Several efforts have compared DL methods with ML algorithms and the performance of DL techniques is found to be better [17]. The performance of radiologists has been equalled or is better by DL-based algorithms for both detection and segmentation. Classification of lymph node metastasis in PET-CT by DL had lower specificities, but higher sensitivities than the radiologists [18]. The integration of ML/AI into clinical practice will reduce the workload of radiologists and increase their effectiveness.

Diabetic Retinopathy: Diabetic retinopathy (DR) causes damage to the retina and timely treatment can reduce the risk of blindness [19]. The time-consuming

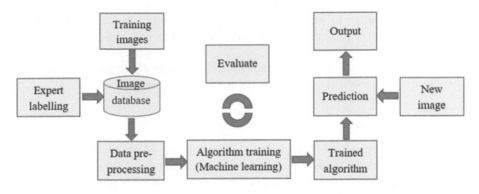

FIGURE 1.9 Applying ML/DL in the workflow of medical image analysis [15].

(*Source*:   https://www.researchgate.net/figure/The-workflow-for-training-and-evaluation-of-the-supervised-machine-learning-model-The_fig1_343306473).

manual process to detect DR, the expensive equipment and the high level of expertise required for diagnosis delay early detection. CNN have been used to diagnose DR. The clinician can use an AI-enabled system for fundus image analysis so that the next step for the treatment can be performed quickly.

Oncology: Early detection of cancer could help increase the chances of survival. The healthcare data is usually obtained for research are from "omics" like metabolomics or genomics, and research. These data are mostly incompatible. These data could be utilised for drug discovery and biomarker identification by applying DL algorithms like DNN and RNN to achieve high accuracy in diagnosing cancer.

Identification of Biomarker: The human genome is an extremely complicated sequence of nucleic acids. The expression of genes changes according to the situation and many biological functions are regulated by these changes. Biomarkers for a specific tumour are the specific genes that change due to a particular pathological condition. These could be identified by the DL approach to diagnose breast cancer [20].

Cancer Detection from Gene Expression Data: A group of researchers developed DeepGene, which classified cancer based on DL that addresses the challenges in existing somatic point mutation-based cancer classification (SMCC) studies by extracting high-level features between combinatorial somatic point mutations and specific cancer types [21].

Tumour Segmentation: DL has been used to segment brain tumours in MR images and it provided better results as compared to segmenting the brain tumours manually.

Tracking Tumour Development: The size of tumours and detection of new metastases that could have been overlooked were detected by DL techniques [22]. Researchers at Google developed DL tools to complement the workflow of pathologists.

Prognosis Detection: South Korean researchers developed a prediction model using DL for the prognosis of patients affected by gastrectomy and received superior results as compared to other prediction models [23].

Feature Detection in MRI: Tumour images obtained by non-invasive medical technologies have been used to measure tumour growth in patients affected by using the CNN method of DL.

The use of DL in oncology for early cancer detection and prognosis increases the chances of providing early treatment, saving both time and cost.

1.3.3 Drug Discovery/Manufacturing

Researchers are applying ML algorithms in the discovery of new drugs as ML helps detect new patterns in the data. Researchers have started using DL in drug discovery as it is possible to create an NN architecture customised for a problem [24]. The properties of a molecule can be predicted using the CNN method of DL [25].

Researchers are turning to AI to improve clinical trials due to a large number of failures [26]. Attempts have been made to help patients look for clinical trials on their own by using AI, like the open-source web tool DQueST, developed by Weng and colleagues. They also developed a software called Criteria2Query that uses NLP to help researchers search databases easily for people who are eligible to take part in clinical trials [26].

Clinical trials are now being designed using AI. The ultimate possibility of AI is to eliminate clinical trials by conducting virtual clinical trials using the vast electronic health records to see how the population would respond [26]. The cost of clinical trials could be reduced by analysing the biomedical data generated from research experiments to predict the effects and side effects of a drug [27].

1.3.4 Electronic Health Records

EHRs are systems that enable healthcare personnel and patients to access all the medical data of the patient instantly after authentication of identity. They allow tools that help in decision-making and thus enable automating and streamlining of workflows in healthcare.

The use of ML-enabled EHR enables more effective care by giving relevant information in real time to improve interaction with the patient. The system can remember what works for each user. ML helps in predictive, diagnostic and prescriptive analysis, thus, helping in the personalisation of the treatment, which was difficult earlier since each outcome needed a custom dataset.

NLP allows the DL algorithm to process free text that is generated. Rajkumar et al. proposed a new format based on the Fast Healthcare Interoperability Resources (FHIR, it is a standard for exchanging healthcare information electronically) for representing patients' entire raw EHR records and showed that DL methods using this format can predict medical events from different centres accurately without having to customise the system for a particular site [28]. These models outperformed earlier models built without ML in all cases. Figure 1.10 depicts the processing of data by an ML-enabled EHR system that can process different types of structured as well as raw data. The system can analyse images using AI and also using NLP for processing clinical notes.

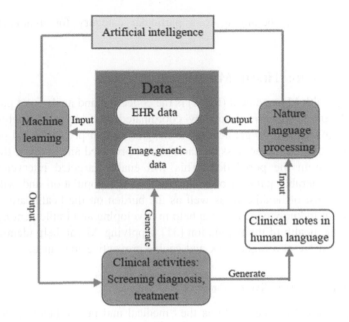

FIGURE 1.10 Machine learning in the healthcare sector [29].

(*Source*: https://medium.com/sciforce/top-ai-algorithms-for-healthcare-aa5007ffa330).

1.3.5 CLINICAL DECISION SUPPORT SYSTEM

Clinical decision support (CDS) provides filtered information of a person and knowledge at appropriate times, to improve the outcome by enabling the streamlining of the workflow. Alert fatigue of doctors can be reduced by incorporating ML into the CDS design to filter the alerts [30].

1.3.6 SURGICAL ROBOTICS

Robotic surgery or robotics-assisted-surgery (RAS) is minimally invasive surgery using a robotic arm with small tools. DL uses CNN for computer vision to enhance the robustness and adaptability of RAS to perceive the environment and RL techniques to learn from a surgeon's physical motion. Researchers are trying to improve surgical workflow through automation.

1.3.7 PRECISION MEDICINE

Precision medicine aims to enhance healthcare by personalising treatment and prevention in a person by studying the effect of the environment and lifestyle of the person along with the person's genes to give a unique treatment or prevention which suits that person. This is because each person's susceptibility to a particular disease is different due to several factors, which the traditional methods did not consider.

Using ML to analyse the large genomic datasets that are available now will help in identifying a combination of genes whose expression can help in classifying a group of patients as belonging to a particular category for treatment and or prevention.

1.3.8 POPULATION HEALTH MANAGEMENT

Population Health Management (PHM) is the collection and analysis of patient data across different healthcare sectors by coordinated steps by all stakeholders including the government to get actionable insights so that proactive and preventive measures can be taken to address the lack of care provided and increase the general level of health in the population. This will enable targeted intervention after identifying vulnerable patients or a subgroup of the population and will help in reducing the cost of healthcare as well as the burden on the healthcare system. It will also result in knowledge that can help in developing and implementing policies to improve the health of the population [31]. Applying AI can help identify groups of patients that are at a higher risk and enable preventive measures.

1.3.9 mHEALTH AND SMART DEVICES

mHealth is defined by the WHO as the "medical and public health practice supported by mobile devices, such as mobile phones, patient monitoring devices, personal digital assistances and other wireless devices" [32]. The significant increase in computing power in mobile and Internet connectivity has resulted in mobile health technologies that can improve the quality of healthcare and research. mHealth integrated with AI can predict and prevent conditions and diseases.

An example is eKidneyCare (details in Table 1.1), an interactive smartphone app that synchronises data with the pharmacies and prompts chronic kidney disease (CKD) patients to review medications every month. The app was designed to help patients adhere to medication and to improve patient safety [33].

Smart wearable devices including smartwatches with sensors for measuring various health parameters, including pulse rate and ECG, are increasingly becoming available and are expected to become as common as the cell phone. These devices with increasing functionality may change the way the healthcare system functions.

1.3.10 AI FOR TACKLING PANDEMIC

AI tools can be used in different areas for early alerts, predictions, detection, tracking and monitoring, managing the population and development of cures and vaccination [34]. Early warnings about pandemics can help nations take precautionary measures. ML and DL in particular can be used to analyse the huge and varied type of data.

AI tools can also be used for the detection of affected people as well as their tracking. Several researchers are using AI for discovering drugs to fight the pandemic. Some researchers have used ML models to identify existing drugs that could treat COVID-19 [34].

The recent research efforts to implement Ml in various areas of the heathcare domains and their performance are given in Table 1.1.

TABLE 1.1

ML Performance Summary in Some of the Healthcare Domains

S. No.	ML method used	Healthcare domain	Result	Discussion
1	CNN	DR	Accuracy = 75%	Classified images of the fundus of the eye into 5 groups based on the severity of DR after training the CNN model on 90,000 fundus images [35]
2	CNN	DR	F-score = 0.95 compared to F-score of 0.91 by ophthalmologists	Detection of DR in retinal fundus photographs [36]
3	NLP	Clinical trials	Increased enrolment of patients by 80%	IBM's Watson to match participants for clinical trials [27]
4	NLP	Clinical trials	Identified 16 participants in 1 hour compared to 2 participants in 6 months	Developed by Deep 6 AI, an AI-based trial recruitment company [26]
5	DL-	Oncology	Localisation score = 89% compared to 73% by pathologists	Identification of breast cancer tumours that have spread to adjacent lymph nodes. Use of a tool developed by Google to complement pathologist's workflow [23] resulted in an 85% reduction in human error rate. Used algorithm Inception (GoogLeNet)
6	CNN	Surgical robotics	Success rate = 87%	Berkeley researchers developed an algorithm for automated suturing [37]
7	CNN	Surgical robotics	Reduced complications due to suturing by at least 20%	A robotic surgical system called STAR was developed to guide the suturing process [38, 39]
8	mHealth App	mHealth	Adverse drug reactions reduced by 32%	eKidneyCare, an mHealth app used for storing and sharing medical and health information was installed on the phone of chronic kidney patients [33, 40]
9	CNN	Oncology	Accuracy = 93%	Tumour segmentation – Differentiate between malignant and benign breast tumours in the elastogram images of more than 200 patients [41]

(Continued)

TABLE 1.1 (Continued)

ML Performance Summary in Some of the Healthcare Domains

S. No.	ML method used	Healthcare domain	Result	Discussion
10	CNN	Oncology	Reduced false-positive findings	Detection in MRI image – CNN applied on diffusion-weighted MRI [22].
11	DNN	Oncology	A classifier was built to detect malignant cancer cells	The University of Wisconsin provided the data for breast cancer [20]
12	DNN	Sickel cell disease	Classified the different RBC types and could distinguish between oxygenated and deoxygenated RBCs	Datasets from 7,000 images of single red blood cells (RBCs) from 8 patients with sickle cell disease were investigated [20].
13	NLP	Spread of pandemic	BlueDot predicted the spread of the COVID-19 virus accurately	BlueDot used NLP based tool to analyse social media, Web searches, news and health reports and predicted based on flight paths [42]
14	CNN	Pathology	Prostate cancer was identified immediately. 30% of normal slides of breast cancer could be identified	prostate cancer and micro-and macro-metastases of breast cancer were immediately-identified; 30% of the normal and benign tissue slides need not be processed further [43]
15	DL	AI for pandemic	Prediction of the protein structure of COVID19	Google's DeepMind was used for analysis [34]
16	RL	Sepsis	Value of the software's selected treatment more than clinicians	RL agent called AI Clinician developed to suggest treatment for sepsis patients in ICU dynamically [44]
17	Unsupervised Learning	EHR	Discovery of latent disease clusters	Detection of disease clusters and patient subgroups using EHR [45]

1.4   ML USE CASES IN HEALTHCARE

Breast Cancer Detection: Around 95% of women who are asked to undergo further tests after the first test is done by the conventional method are false-positive cases [46]. These people have to undergo advanced tests unnecessarily. Therapixel, a start-up, is using AI to analyse mammograms, which reduces the number of women called for further testing [46].

Sophia Genetics of Switzerland is using AI to identify mutations of the genes [47] causing cancer to aid doctors in selecting the treatment. This product is being used by around 970 hospitals across the world [46].

IDx-DR: The first FDA-approved AI algorithm is the IDx-DR for detecting DR [48]. It is the first AI-based autonomous medical diagnostic system [49].

Arterys Medical Imaging Platform: One of the first ML applications approved by the FDA is Arterys medical imaging platform to diagnose heart problems. Arterys takes 10 seconds to differentiate the two ventricles compared to a clinician who takes around 60 minutes to do the same. The patient examination time is also reduced from 71 minutes to around 52 minutes. This model has now been extended to analyse other body parts.

BenevolentAI: BenevolentAI, an AI start-up in London, used their AI-based systems to search the scientific literature and identified a possible treatment for the coronavirus with an existing drug within a few days [50]. BenevolentAI, in collaboration with AstraZeneca, has identified a key molecule that plays a key role in chronic kidney disease (CKD) by using AI to comb through the literature.

SPOT: Around 270,000 people die every year in the USA due to sepsis progressing to sepsis shock. The SPOT (Sepsis Prediction and Optimization of Therapy) system by HCA healthcare is a real-time predictive analytics system integrated with AI to detect sepsis up to 20 hours earlier than the conventional methods [51].

InnerEye: InnerEye, a software developed by Microsoft and approved by the FDA, can identify and display possible tumours and other anomalies from the 3D patient scan in X-ray images and helps to do radiotherapy 13 times faster [52].

AirStrip: The AirStrip is a mobile app facilitating the exchange of data by allowing sharing of EHRs between various devices to improve the workflow [52] and is particularly useful during an emergency.

Thermalytix: It is an ML-enabled portable and lightweight computer-aided diagnostic tool, developed by a Bangalore-based start-up named Niramai, to detect breast cancer at very early stages without invading privacy and without using harmful radiations. It is more accurate than physical examination. The system is coupled with a web interface software called SMILE to upload patient information to enable the software solution running on the server to generate a report after analysing it based on the Software as a Service (SaaS) model [53].

1.5 LIMITATIONS AND CHALLENGES IN ADOPTION OF AI IN HEALTHCARE

There are major challenges that healthcare entities face regarding the adoption of AI-enabled systems that are preventing quicker implementation of these systems.

Limited Data: Limited availability of datasets is the biggest challenge for DL. The development of a huge training dataset is a time-consuming task for medical experts and data scientists.

Black Box Issue: A major issue is the inability to explain the logic used by a DL system to give its output. Beyond a few layers, even experts who designed the DL system may not be able to explain the logic used by the system. In the healthcare domain, the interpretation of the diagnosis or recommendation is important for all the stakeholders. The General Data Protection Regulation (GPDR) makes the "right to explanation" mandatory. Explainable AI (XAI) is a recent area of research and refers to methods that result in solutions to the system being understood by human experts and will help produce more explainable models.

Security and Privacy of Data: Healthcare entities collect very sensitive information, which is required to be safeguarded from unauthorised access. HIPAA (Health Insurance Portability and Accountability Act, passed by US Congress in 1996) laws protect medical records of patients. ML in healthcare must completely align with the data protection requirements.

Regulatory Issues: The recent GDPR rules in Europe are the main hindrance to the advancement of AI. The GDPR requires informed consent from the person and also allows the person to seek removal of his data [54]. The regulatory bodies, in general, approve static software. The algorithm in the static software does not change with use. But the AI/ML algorithms learn from more data as it is used and evolves. The regulatory cycle must address the issue of such "adaptive algorithms" [55]. Another legal issue is accountability in case the ML system makes a harmful recommendation. Is it the company that has produced the ML system, the doctor or the researchers/engineers who developed the system?

1.6 CONCLUSION

This chapter introduced AI, ML and DL, the different types of AI and the various methods of ML and DL and the relationship between AI, ML and DL. DL is more powerful and yields higher accuracy, but requires large data and powerful systems. ML could be applied even when there is less data and is sufficient for many applications.

The chapter then discussed the research being done to apply ML in different areas of healthcare, including cardiac care, medical imaging, drug discovery, surgical robotics and EHR.

ML has the potential to reduce or eliminate the routine manual workflows in healthcare by automation, help in prevention by prediction due to its capacity to analyse enormous amounts of data and also aid in diagnosis by detecting diseases early and accurately so that timely treatment can be initiated. The use of ML in medical imaging has been demonstrated and has shown better performance than the physicians in the diagnosis and will increasingly be used by physicians as a tool to increase their effectiveness. ML is also being used for surgery and suturing and is expected to be more widely used in the near future. Physicians are overworked and have very little time and information about the history of the patient when treating any patient. The use of EHR and precision medicine will help physicians in giving a better treatment by providing them with timely information and quicker diagnosis.

The ultimate result of integrating ML in the healthcare system will be to make healthcare cheaper, more accessible and faster. It is leading to the development of portable biomedical devices, which will enable healthcare to be accessible for patients and reduce the care gap. Combining this with mHealth will change the way the healthcare system functions. In short, ML is transforming healthcare.

ACKNOWLEDGEMENTS

I am grateful to Dr Girish S, Dr R. Anand and Mr Ganesh Kumar for their valuable feedback after reviewing the draft and Mrs Shobha Sathyanarayanan for drawing the figures.

REFERENCES

[1] McCarthy, J. "WHAT IS ARTIFICIAL INTELLIGENCE?," 12 November 2007. [Online]. Available: http://www-formal.stanford.edu/jmc/whatisai.html.

[2] Wikipedia. "Artificial intelligence," [Online]. Available: https://en.wikipedia.org/wiki/Artificial_intelligence.

[3] Mitchell, T. Machine Learning, McGraw Hill, 1997.

[4] Wikipedia. "Feature engineering," [Online]. Available: https://en.wikipedia.org/wiki/Feature_engineering.

[5] Heath, N. "What is machine learning? Everything you need to know," 14 September 2018. [Online]. Available: https://www.zdnet.com/article/what-is-machine-learning-everything-you-need-to-know/.

[6] Kailas, A. K. B. Vodrahalli, "3D computer vision based on machine learning with deep neural networks: A review," *Journal of the Society for Information Display* 25.11 (25 January 2018): 676–694.

[7] Ray, T. "Demystifying neural networks, deep learning, machine learning, and artificial intelligence," 29 March 2018. [Online]. Available: https://www.stoodnt.com/blog/ann-neural-networks-deep-learning-machine-learning-artificial-intelligence-differences/.

[8] LeCun, Y., Bengio, Y., Hinton, G. "Deep learning," *Nature*, 521 (28 May 2015): 436–444.

[9] Wikipedia. "Feature learning," [Online]. Available: https://en.wikipedia.org/wiki/Feature_learning.

[10] Nicholson, C. "A beginner's guide to neural networks and deep learning," [Online]. Available: https://pathmind.com/wiki/neural-network.

[11] Karagiannakos, S. "Deep learning algorithms: The complete guide," 26 February 2020. [Online]. Available: https://theaisummer.com/Deep-Learning-Algorithms/.

[12] Wikipedia. "Types of artificial neural networks," [Online]. Available: https://en.wikipedia.org/wiki/Types_of_artificial_neural_networks.

[13] Developers.google.com. "Generative adversarial networks - introduction," [Online]. Available: https://developers.google.com/machine-learning/gan.

[14] Saxena, A. "Congenital heart disease in India: A status report," *Indian Pediatric, 55* (2018): 1075–1082.

[15] Ranschaert, E. "Artificial intelligence in radiology: Hype or hope?," *Journal of the Belgian Society of Radiology* 47 (17 November 2018): 1–2.

[16] Choudhary, A. K., Jansche, A., Schneider, G., Bernthaler T . "Machine learning for microstructure quantification of different material classes," *Practical Metallography* 57 (July 2020).

[17] Paul, R., Hawkins, S. H., Balagurunathan, Y., Schabath, M., Gillies, R. J., Hall, L. O., Goldgof, D. B. "Deep feature transfer learning in combination with traditional features predicts survival among patients with lung adenocarcinoma," *Tomography* 2 (December 2016): 385–395.

[18] Wang, H., Zhou, Z., Li, Y., Chen, Z., Lu, P., Wang, W., Liu, W., Yu, L. "Comparison of machine learning methods for classifying mediastinal lymph node metastasis of non-small cell lung cancer from 18F-FDG PET/CT images," *EJNMMI Research* 7.1 (2017).

[19] Padhy, S. K., Takkar, B., Chawla, R., Kumar, A. "Artificial intelligence in diabetic retinopathy: A natural step to the future," *Indian Journal of Ophthalmology* 67 (July 2019): 1004–1009.

[20] Software.intel.com. "Deep learning for cancer diagnosis: A bright future," 24 January 2018. [Online]. Available: https://software.intel.com/en-us/articles/deep-learning-for-cancer-diagnosis-a-bright-future. [Accessed June 2021].

[21] Yuan, Y., Yi, S., Li, C., Kim, J., Cai, W., Feng Z. H., Dagan, D. "DeepGene: An advanced cancer type classifier based on deep learning and somatic point mutations," *BMC Bioinformatics* 17 (2016).

[22] Jäger, P., Bickelhaupt, S., Laun, F. B., Lederer, W., Heidi, D., Kuder, T. A., Paech, D., Bonekamp, D., Radbruch, A., Delorme, S., Schlemmer, H.-P., Steudle, F., Maier-Hein, K. H. "Revealing hidden potentials of the q-Space signal in breast cancer," in Bildverarbeitung für die Medizin 2018, Springer Berlin Heidelberg, 2018, pp. 664–671.

[23] Stumpe M., Peng, L. "Assisting pathologists in detecting cancer with deep learning," 3 March 2017. [Online]. Available: https://ai.googleblog.com/2017/03/assisting-pathologists-in-detecting.html.

[24] Chen, H., Engkvist Ola, Wang, Y., Olivecrona, M., Blaschke, T. "The rise of deep learning in drug discovery," *Drug Discovery Today* 23.6 (June 2018): 1241–1250.

[25] Budek, K. "Machine learning in drug discovery," 28 February 2019 [Online]. Available: https://deepsense.ai/machine-learning-in-drug-discovery/.

[26] Woo, M. "Trial by artificial intelligence," *Nature* 573 (26 September 2019): S100–S102.

[27] Microsoft, "Project Hanover - Machine reading for precision medicine," 2019. [Online]. Available: https://www.microsoft.com/en-us/research/project/project-hanover/.

[28] Rajkomar, A., Oren, E., Dean, J. "Scalable and accurate deep learning with electronic health," *npj Digital Medicine* 1 (8 May 2018):1–10.

[29] Sciforce, "Top AI algorithms for healthcare," Medium.com, 24 April 2019. [Online]. Available: https://medium.com/sciforce/top-ai-algorithms-for-healthcare-aa5007ffa330.

[30] Heringa, M., van der Heide, A., Floor-Schreudering, A., De Smet, P. A. G. M., Bouvy, M. L. "Better specification of triggers to reduce the number of drug interaction alerts in primary care," *International Journal of Medical Informatics* 109 (12 November 2017): 96–102.

[31] Healthcatalyst.com. "Population health management -- An example of why it really matters," [Online]. Available: https://www.healthcatalyst.com/Population-Health-Management-Outcomes.

[32] Moyle, S. "What is mHealth?," Ausmed, 26 March 2015. [Online]. Available: https://www.ausmed.com/cpd/articles/what-is-mhealth.

[33] Nelson, H. "mHealth App improves kidney medication adherence, engagement," 22 March 2021. [Online]. Available: https://mhealthintelligence.com/news/mhealth-app-improves-kidney-medication-adherence-engagement.

[34] Kambli, R. "Examining the true potential of AI tools in tackling COVID-19 crisis," 30 April 2020. [Online]. Available: https://www.expresshealthcare.in/covid19-updates/examining-the-true-potential-of-ai-tools-in-tackling-covid-19-crisis/419594/.

[35] HarryPratt, F., Coenen, D. M., Broadbent, S. P., Harding, Zheng, Y. "Convolutional neural networks for diabetic retinopathy," in 20th Conference on Medical Image Understanding and Analysis, 2016.

[36] Gulshan, V., Peng, L., Coram, M. "Development and validation of a deep learning algorithm for detection of diabetic retinopathy in retinal fundus photographs," *JAMA* 316 (2016): 2402–2410.

[37] Schulman, J., Gupta, A., Venkateshan, S., Tayson-Frederick, M. "A case study of trajectory transfer through non-rigid registration for a simplified suturing scenario," in IEEE/RSJ International Conference on Intelligent Robots and Systems, 2013.

[38] Sennaar, K. "Machine learning in surgical robotics – 4 applications that matter," emerj, 3 February 2019. [Online]. Available: https://emerj.com/ai-sector-overviews/machine-learning-in-surgical-robotics-4-applications/.

[39] Shademan, A., Decker, R. S., Opfermann, J. D., Leonard, S., Krieger, A., Kim, P. C. W. "Supervised autonomous robotic soft tissue surgery," *Science Translational Medicine* 8.337 (04 May 2016).

[40] Ong, S. W., Jassal, S. V., Porter, E. C., Min, K. K., Uddin, A., Cafazzo, J. A., Rac, V. E., Tomlinson, G., Logan, A. G. "Digital applications targeting medication safety in ambulatory high-risk CKD patients: Randomized controlled clinical trial," *Clinical Journal of the American Society of Nephrology* 16.4 (18 March 2021): 532–542.

[41] Zhang, Q., Xiao, Y., Suo, J., Shi, J., Yu, J., Guo, Y., Wang, Y., Zheng, H. "Sonoelastomics for breast tumor classification: A radiomics approach with clustering-based feature selection on sonoelastography," *Ultrasound in Medicine and Biology* 43.5 (21 February 2017): 1058–1069.

[42] Chen, J., See, K. C. "Artificial intelligence for COVID-19: Rapid review," *Journal Of Medical Internet Research* 22.10 (27 October 2020): 12.

[43] Litjens, G., Sánchez, C. I., Timofeeva, N., Hermsen, M., Nagtegaal, I., Kovacs, I., Kaa, C. H. v. d., Bult, P., Ginneken, B. v., Laak, J. v. d. "Deep learning as a tool for increased accuracy and efficiency of histopathological diagnosis," *Scientific Reports* 6 (23 May 2016):1–11.

[44] Komorowski, M., Celi, L. A., Badawi, O., Gordon, A. C., Faisal, A. A. "The artificial intelligence clinician learns optimal treatment strategies for sepsis in intensive care," *Nature Medicine* 24 (November 2018): 1716–1720.

[45] Wanga, Y., Zhaoa, Y., Therneaub, T. M., Atkinson, E. J., Tafti, A. P., Nan, Zhang, Shreyase, Amin, Limper, A. H., Khosla, S., Liu, H. "Unsupervised machine learning for the discovery of latent disease clusters and patient subgroups using electronic health records," *Journal of Biomedical Informatics* 102 (February 2020).

[46] Cynober, T. "Artificial intelligence in oncology: Fantasy or reality?," Labiotech.eu, 17 June 2019. [Online]. Available: https://www.labiotech.eu/ai/artificial-intelligence-oncology/.

[47] Smith, J. "Swiss multi-cancer diagnostic test approved in Europe," 11 April 2019. [Online]. Available: https://www.labiotech.eu/medical/sophia-genetics-cancer-ai/.

[48] FDA. "FDA permits marketing of artificial intelligence-based device to detect certain diabetes-related eye problems," 11 April 2018. [Online]. Available: https://www.fda.gov/news-events/press-announcements/fda-permits-marketing-artificial-intelligence-based-device-detect-certain-diabetes-related-eye.

[49] Vidal-Alaball, J., Fibla, D. R., Zapata, M. A., Marin-Gomez, F. X., Fernandez, O. S. "Artificial intelligence for the detection of diabetic retinopathy in primary care: Protocol for algorithm development," *JMIR Research Protocols* 8 (1 February 2019):e12539.

[50] Metz, C. "How AI steered doctors toward a possible Coronavirus treatment," 1 May 2020. [Online]. Available: https://economictimes.indiatimes.com/small-biz/startups/newsbuzz/how-ai-steered-doctorstoward-a-possible-coronavirus-treatment/articleshow/75484021.cms.

[51] CDC. "Sepsis data and reports," CDC, 14 February 2020. [Online]. Available: https://www.cdc.gov/sepsis/datareports/index.html.

[52] Beaton, T. "Top 10 healthcare mobile apps among hospital, health systems," mhealthintelligence.com, 6 July 2017. [Online]. Available: https://mhealthintelligence.com/news/top-10-healthcare-mobile-apps-among-hospital-health-systems.

[53] Niramai. "Introduction," Niramai, [Online]. Available: https://www.niramai.com/about/overview/. [Accessed 9 July 2021].

[54] He, J., Baxter, S. L., Jie Xu, J. X., Zhou, X., Zhang, K. "The practical implementation of artificial intelligence technologies in medicine," *Nature Medicine* 25 (7 January 2019):30–36.

[55] Newsfortomorrow.com. "Reducing risk in AI and machine learning-based medical technology," [Online]. Available: https://newsfortomorrow.com/index.php/2019/12/06/reducing-risk-in-ai-and-machine-learning-based-medical-technology/.

2 A Review on Biomedical Signals with Fundamentals of Digital Signal Processing

Mangesh Ramaji Kose and Mithilesh Atulkar
National Institute of Technology, Raipur, India

Mitul Kumar Ahirwal
Maulana Azad National Institute of Technology, Bhopal, India

CONTENTS

2.1 Introduction..24
2.2 Biomedical Signals..25
    2.2.1 Electrocardiogram (ECG) Signal....................................25
        2.2.1.1 ECG Terminology and Recording.....................25
        2.2.1.2 Different Types of Recording Techniques.........28
        2.2.1.3 ECG Processing..29
        2.2.1.4 Common Problems...29
        2.2.1.5 Common ECG Applications.................................30
    2.2.2 Electroencephalogram (EEG) Signal...............................31
        2.2.2.1 Basic Terminology and Recording.....................33
        2.2.2.2 Types of EEG Signals..35
        2.2.2.3 EEG Processing..36
        2.2.2.4 Common Problems...37
        2.2.2.5 EEG Applications...39
    2.2.3 Electromyography (EMG)..39
        2.2.3.1 EMG Signal Recording.......................................40
        2.2.3.2 EMG Signal Processing.......................................41
        2.2.3.3 Common Problems...42
        2.2.3.4 EMG Applications...42
    2.2.4 Electro-Oculogram (EOG)..43
        2.2.4.1 EOG Signal Recording..44
        2.2.4.2 EOG Processing..45

DOI: 10.1201/9781003241409-2

2.1 INTRODUCTION

Signals are a unique way of representing data. Signals are mainly captured through sensory devices/sensors from environment like speech, images, seismic ways, and bioelectric potentials. A branch that deals with concepts, mathematics, techniques for manipulation and analysis of digital signals is known as Digital Signal Processing (DSP). DSP is applicable in various fields as shown in Figure 2.1. It includes various areas of science and engineering [1,2]. The digital signal is a sequence of discrete values carrying some information. Generally, the real-world signals are analog by nature. Digital signals are constructed from analog signals using sampling and quantization process. The sampling process means retaining the value of original analog signal at certain time. The quantization process is used to represent the value of amplitude using finite level. Each of the above process decides the amount of information in digital version of the signal. The length of digital signal obtained from analog signal depends on the sampling frequency. Sampling frequency of the signal is the numbers of samples recorded in the duration of 1 second. For example, if

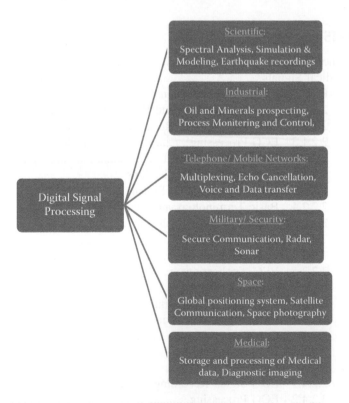

FIGURE 2.1 Various application of DSP in real world.

20 samples are recorded in a second, it means 20 Hz is the sampling frequency (fs) of recorded signal. Sampling interval (T) is defined as T = 1/fs. The signal gets corrupted with various noise signals or gets distorted during recording. Here, noise is nothing but any unwanted signal apart from the signal of interest. Digital filters play an important role in eliminating the noise signals and restoring the original signal. Digital filter consists of several coefficients obtained through filter design algorithm for specification provided as per application and requirement of filtering process. Many filter design algorithms exist, wherein each algorithm has its merits and demerits. Biomedical signal faces problem of interference. Interference is nothing but a signal other than signal of interest, which gets introduced/mixed into original signal while recording. For example, during EEG (electroencephalogram-electrical activity of brain) recording the electrodes are placed over the scalp. These electrodes may capture EOG (Electrooculogram signals generated due to eye movement) signals in addition to the EEG signals. Here, EOG signal is considered as noise signal. Characteristics of the noise signal needs to be considered while designing the digital filter to remove it from acquired EEG signal. Three types of filters are commonly used for this purpose, that is, low-pass (LP) filter, high-pass (HP) filter and band-pass (BP) filter. LP filter blocks the specific frequencies that are higher than the specified cut-off frequency. HP filter is used to block the specific frequency lower than the specified cut-off frequency. BP filter is used to block the specific range of frequency in between the lower and higher limit of threshold frequency. Various types of biomedical signals are discussed further with their process of recording, applications, and their common problems.

2.2 BIOMEDICAL SIGNALS

2.2.1 Electrocardiogram (ECG) Signal

ECG signal represents the electrical activity of the heart; it is recorded by placing electrodes on the skin near the chest region. Analysis of ECG signals helps detect various cardiovascular diseases like atrial fibrillation, ischemia, or arrhythmia. Accurate analysis of ECG is essential for a cardiologist and a physician to characterize the ECG signal corresponding to certain disease condition, so that the patient receives proper treatment. The ECG signal has specific structural pattern that gets distorted or changed in the diseased condition. The below figure presents the structure of ECG signal recorded from a healthy person. The waveform shape of an ECG signal is shown in Figure 2.2(a). ECG signal consists of repetition of this waveform, including P wave, QRS complex wave, and T wave. Figure 2.2(b) is a plot of original/real signal sample for ECG database [2–4]. ECG waveform repeats its shape after approx 0.8 seconds; it is a standard time for healthy person. Intervals among different waves are shown in Figure 2.2(a), such as PR, ST, and QT interval, etc.

2.2.1.1 ECG Terminology and Recording

There are different configurations of an ECG recording machine; having 3, 6, or 12 electrodes for monitoring the heart condition. In the standard 12-lead ECG instrument, 10 electrodes are placed on different body parts as shown in Figure 2.3 [3–5]. In Figure 2.4, different heart locations are shown with their role in providing

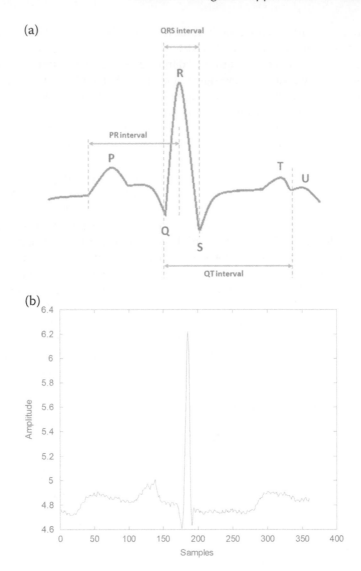

FIGURE 2.2 (a) ECG waveform including different waves and their intervals and (b) plot of original ECG signal.

the waveform shape of ECG signal. Ionic activities are controlled by sinoatrial (SA) node in heart. In SA node, the process of depolarization takes place and also spreads across the atrium. Atrial depolarization gives the shape of P wave with duration of approx 80 ms. Depolarization goes down up to ventricles from atrioventricular (AV) node. Depolarization of left and right ventricles gives the shape to QRS complex with duration of approx 80 to 100 ms. Then repolarization of atria and QRS complex are overlapped, therefore atrial repolarization remains hidden in QRS complex. Ventricular repolarization for duration of around 160 ms results in generation of T wave. The U wave in ECG signal is generated because of repolarization

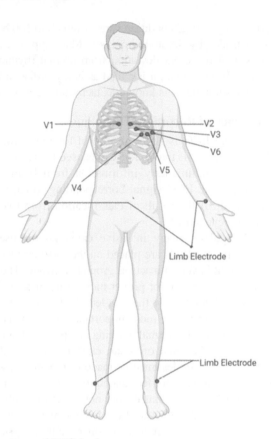

FIGURE 2.3 Locations of ECG leads.

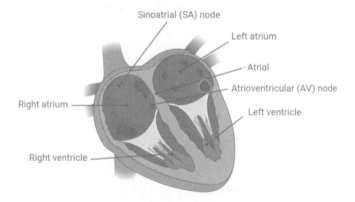

FIGURE 2.4 Human heart anatomy and ECG cyclex.

of papillary muscle, which can be ignored [5,6]. Characterization of heart diseases can be easily done on the basis of intervals of different waves in ECG signal.

A heartbeat represents one complete cycle of P wave, QRS complex, T and wave. The heart rate of a person is calculated based on these beats. The common/standard value of heart rate in healthy/normal condition varies from 60 to 100 beats/minute [5,6]. Rhythm of heart is controlled by SA node impulses. Many types of arrhythmia occur due to heart disorders, which present deviation from normal rhythm of heartbeat. If heart rate goes below 60 beats/minute, it is called as bradycardiac arrhythmia. If heart rate goes above 100 beats/minute, it is known as tachycardiac arrhythmia [5,6].

2.2.1.2   Different Types of Recording Techniques

Two-lead ECG: Two-lead ECG is generally useful for long time ECG recording using portable ECG recorder. This two-lead ECG is used for Holter monitoring. The two-lead ECG captures complimentary information from heart by being placed orthogonal to each other. The ECG signal corresponding to each lead must show similar classification result. If the result of classification from two channels is not same then that signal is rejected [7].

Five-lead ECG: Nowadays, many intensive care systems use five-lead ECG monitoring systems, where four leads are placed on the torso corresponding to limbs. The electrode placed at right lower limb acts as ground electrode. The fifth electrode is placed on the standard chest location for proper monitoring of arrhythmia. Figure 2.5 presents the placement configuration of the five-lead ECG recorder [8].

Wearable ECG Electrodes: The most important aspect in the construction of a wearable ECG recorder is that the normal working of a person should not be affected. Wearable electrodes need to be fixed on smart cloth to measure the ECG through human body surface. These electrodes must be made from soft and washable material so that a person wearing them does not feel uncomfortable. The number of electrodes on the smart clothes must be less so that it does not affect the daily life of a person. Most importantly it should be able to record the ECG signal. Figure 2.6 presents the configuration of a wearable ECG recorder using smart clothing system.

Figure 2.6 presents three-electrode ECG recorder integrated with smart cloth. The electrodes 1 and 2 are used to record ECG signals whereas the electrode 3 is

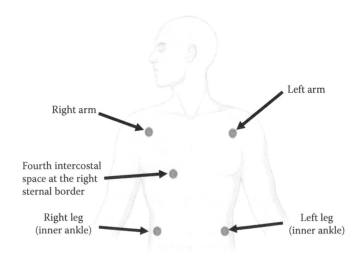

FIGURE 2.5   Five-lead ECG recorder placement configuration.

FIGURE 2.6   Wearable ECG recorder.

used as a reference electrode. The device labeled number 4 is connected to the electrodes, receives signals from the electrodes, and sends it to smartphones [9].

2.2.1.3   ECG Processing

An ECG signal carries information of electrical activities/functioning of heart. There are various signal-processing techniques applied on ECG signal to extract the information. Different stages of ECG signal processing techniques include signal preprocessing, analysis of heart rate variability, and ECG signal compression [10,11]. ECG signals get contaminated with various noise signals during ECG recording process. Signal preprocessing includes elimination of noise to obtain ECG signals of interest. Noise in ECG signal may be of different types, such as low or high frequency unwanted signals. Therefore, a band pass filter is frequently used. After the filtering process of ECG signal, generally, heart rate variability (HRV) analysis is performed. HRV analysis gives information about the various heart disorders and diseases.

In simple terms, HRV is nothing but variation in the intervals between heartbeats. Heart rate or beats depend on the intervals and difference in QRS segments. For HRV analysis, QRS complex detection is must. The patient suffering from cardiac problems needs to determine the heart rate variability. Bradycardic arrhythmia is characterized by long R-R interval and tachycardiac arrhythmia is characterized by short R-R interval [10]. Thus, in diagnosis of cardiac disease, the analysis of HRV is essential and this is globally accepted by the doctors/practitioners. In some of the cases, long ECG signals are not required for extraction of clinically significant information, then compression techniques are also used to reduce the storage size of clinical ECG database.

2.2.1.4   Common Problems

The ECG signal gets contaminated by various artifacts/noises due to which the information in the ECG signal gets hampered. The ECG signal most commonly gets contaminated by baseline wander, powerline interference, and electromyogram signals. Figure 2.10 presents visualization of ECG and artifacts. To extract accurate information from ECG signals, it is required to eliminate noises. The preprocessing step of signal processing includes signal filtration, which filters out the noises from ECG signals [12–14]. Pure ECG is shown in Figure 2.7(a). Figure 2.7(b) represents the baseline wander noise, which is a low frequency artifact contaminating the pure ECG. Figure 2.7(c) presents ECG signal contaminated with muscle noise, which is caused due to muscle contraction. Figure 2.7(d) presents ECG signal with electrode motion

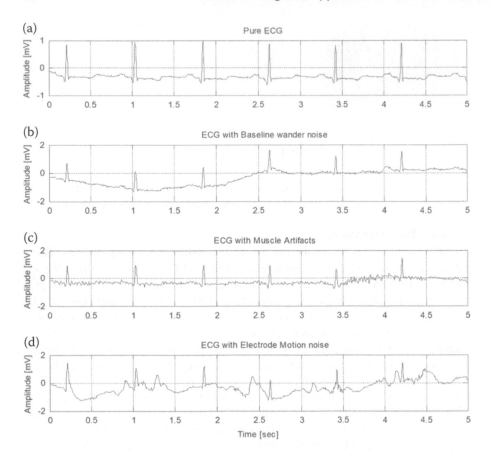

FIGURE 2.7   Visualization of pure ECG and noisy ECG.

noise, which is the result of skin stretching and change in resistance of skin that is near the ECG leads. Hence, design of filter is dependent on the type of noise/artifacts.

Sometimes, improper grounding of the ECG recording instrument generates power line interference and also due to the electromagnetic interference and noise from nearby instruments.

2.2.1.5 Common ECG Applications
- Analyzing the functionality of heart
- Useful in monitoring patients under stress
- As part of general health check-up in patients above 40 years
- Useful in identifying irregular heartbeats
- Checking if implanted pacemaker is working properly

2.2.1.5.1 Review of Recent and New Applications of ECG
- ECG signal-based identification of emotional condition
- ECG signal as a biometric identifier
- ECG signals for detecting drowsiness in drivers

2.2.2   Electroencephalogram (EEG) Signal

Human brain is a complex and an important organ. It consists of millions of in-terconnected neurons sharing information to generate cognitive activity. The working of human brain is not yet completely explored. EEG signal presents non-invasive, cheaper, and easier neuroimaging techniques used to analyze brain functionality. EEG signal presents electrical functionality of human brain, which gets recorded using electrodes. There are many other techniques available for analysis of brain functionality, such as Functional Magnetic Resonance Imaging (FMRI) and Computer Tomography (CT), but they are costlier than EEG. EEG signals are non-stationary and non-linear by nature, because their generation is complex [15–17]. The electrical potential is generated due to transfer of collective or combined neural information between the groups of neurons. EEG electrodes are used to record these potential by placing them on the scalp [17]. The visualization of multichannel EEG is presented in Figure 2.8. The EEG signal corresponding to channel number 1, 2, 3, and 32 from total 32-channel EEG data is plotted.

Event-related potentials (ERPs) are the type of EEG signals that represent brain response to some event or action performed by a person. It occurs for a very short

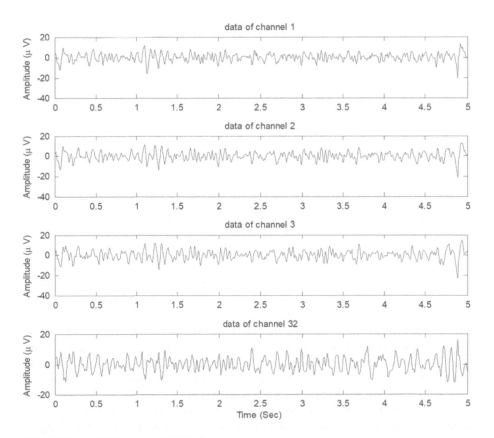

FIGURE 2.8   Multi-channel EEG signal.

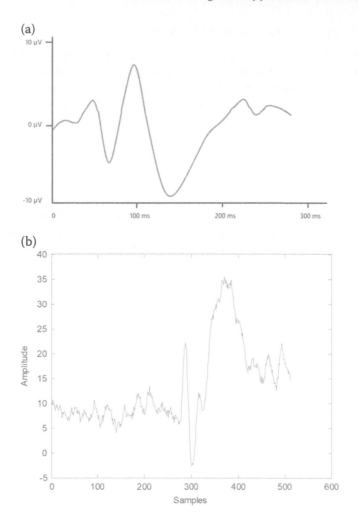

FIGURE 2.9　(a) P100 wave ERP and (b) real visual-event-related (VEP) wave.

duration in the form of spikes. Depending on the task being performed and person who is performing the task, the characteristics of ERP vary [18,19]. Illustration of ERP signal is presented in Figure 2.9. Figure 2.9(a) presents P100 wave of ERP signal, which is interpreted as a peak of positive amplitude after 100 ms of event [20]. The plot of visual-evoked potential (VEP) capture from left occipital region of human brain is presented in Figure 2.9(b) [21]. The pattern is extracted by averaging the data from 30 trials of same events. These ERP signals play an important role in brain–computer interface (BCI) systems. These ERP signals may be generated using time locked or non-time locked approach. Time locked approach means the response to an event must be noticed within a specified time whereas in case of non-time locked approach the response of an event will be noticed at any time. The ERPs can also be characterized on the basis of phase value of signal called as phase lock approach.

2.2.2.1 Basic Terminology and Recording

The EEG potential is defined as V(x, y, t), which is interpreted as the recording of voltage value at time t from the EEG channel placed at locations (x, y) on the human scalp. Human brain is broadly divided into two regions – left hemisphere and right hemisphere, each of these hemispheres are further divided into four regions called lobes, shown in Figure 2.10(a). The four lobes are frontal lobe, temporal lobe, parietal lobe, and occipital lobe. These lobes perform various functions as given in Figure 2.10(b).

The cerebrum cortex is the outer layer of the cerebellum. It is a folded structure of 2 to 5 mm varying thickness. It consists of 1010 (approx 10 billions) of interconnected neurons and has a surface area of near about 2000 cm^2. The EEG electrodes are placed according to 10–20 system of electrode placement during EEG recording. It is an international standard of EEG electrodes placement. It also has some variations depending on the number of electrodes. The EEG recording with 21 to 64 channels (electrodes) is performed by using 10–20 system of electrode placement. For EEG recording using 128 channels the 10–10 system of electrode placement is used. Higher number of electrodes results in higher spatial resolution [2,15,16]. Figure 2.11 illustrates the 10–20 electrode placement system.

The electrode placements are named according to the name of brain lobes as depicted in Figure 2.11(a) and 2.11(c). For example, F (frontal lobe), P (Parietal lode), C (central lobe), T (temporal lode), O (occipital lode), and A (earlobes for reference electrodes). The numbers are also associated with these labels depending on the hemisphere on which that lobe is present. Odd numbers are associated to the label from left hemisphere and even numbers are associated with the label from right side of hemisphere. For example, O1 is interpreted as the occipital lobe from left hemisphere. The common values of sampling frequency while EEG recording range from 256 to 512 Hz, which can vary up to 20 kHz for research purpose. Various referencing styles are also used while EEG recording. Some of them are:

  i. **Sequential Montage**: In this type of referencing style, each electrode is presented as the difference of readings from adjacent electrodes. For example, channel "F3-F5" represents the difference of reading from F3 and F5 channels.
  ii. **Referential Montage**: Here, each electrode is presented as the difference between readings from the current electrode and readings from reference electrode. In general, the ear lobe position is considered as reference location as there is no standard position for reference electrode.
  iii. **Average Reference Montage**: In this, the recordings average of the channels is taken as reference channel.
  iv. **Laplacian Montage**: Here, each electrode is presented as the difference between the electrode and a weighted average of all the neighboring electrodes.

Sometimes the invasive approach of EEG recording is used for clinical purpose and critical cases, where electrodes are placed inside the scalp using surgical operations. The invasive approach of EEG recording provides spatial resolution and higher amplitude.

(a)

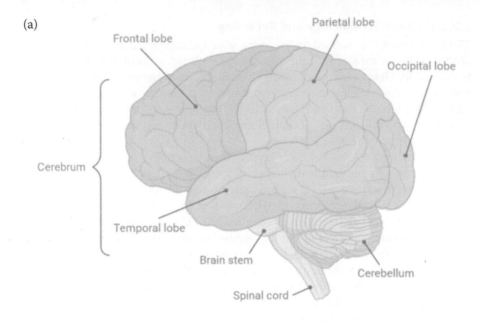

(b)

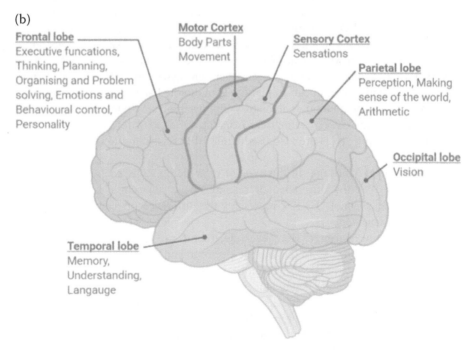

FIGURE 2.10 Anatomy of human brain (a) four brain lobes and (b) brain lobes with their functions.

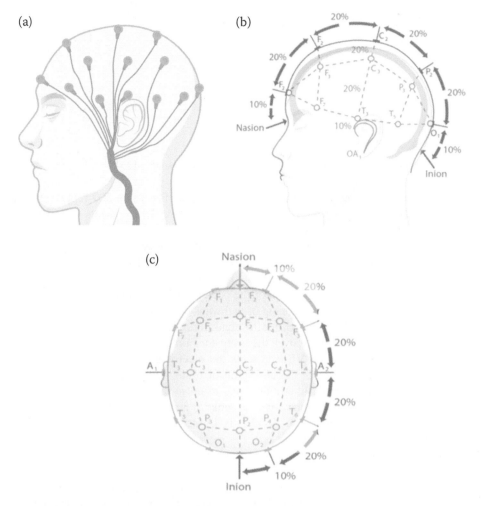

FIGURE 2.11 EEG electrode placement over scalp and their positions according to 10–20 electrode placement system, (a) normal side view, (b) side view with position of electrode, and (c) top view with position of electrode.

2.2.2.2 Types of EEG Signals

i. **ERP:** It represents a voltage fluctuation that is time locked to an event recorded from scalp. The event represents a stimulus caused by cognitive operations, sensory-related operation, memory-related operation, and affective operation. ERP signal components are classified according to polarity of signal, timing, sensitivity to manipulation of task, scalp distribution, etc. These components are represented by P300, contingent negative variation, and complex of long and middle latency evoked potential. The P300 wave is most prominent and vastly studied positive deflection in ERP signal. The letter "P" represents the positive potential,

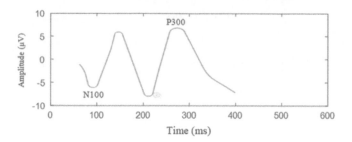

FIGURE 2.12   ERP signal representing N100 and P300 potential [23].

whereas "N" represents the negative potential. The value 300 represents that it is the wave with 300 ms latency. Figure 2.12 presents the ERP signal showing P100 and N300 potential [22].

ii. **VEP:** The visual evoked potential presents the electrical potential captured from the scalp over the visual cortex. The VEPs can be extracted from EEG by averaging the signal. To record the VEP signals, electrodes are placed at midline location of the occipital brain region. The VEPs are used to analyze the functioning of pathways or nerves to the visual cortex. The VEP can be affected due to abnormality in the visual cortex. The VEP distributed widely over the scalp for normal subject.

iii. **SSVEP:** Steady state VEP presents the electrical potential experienced over the occipital and parietal region of brain. SSVEP has a certain attractive characteristic like high signal to noise ratio and robustness. The SSVEP is generated when a person looks at a source of light flickering at persistent frequency. The SSVEP is limited to the region lateral and anterior to the striate cortex.

iv. **Sleep EEG:** Sleep EEG represents the recording of electrical activity in the brain while the person is awake or in sleep, recorded using electrodes placed on scalp. There are different types of sleep EEG recording: (i) sleep deprivation EEG and (ii) natural sleep EEG. The sleep EEG is used to analyze sleep disorder in a person.

2.2.2.3   EEG Processing

The EEG processing basically consists of two steps, that is, EEG filtering and signal analysis. The EEG filtering is responsible for noise removal and separation of different frequency components called EEG bands. In the analysis step, statistical properties of EEG are observed for feature extraction and classification purposes [2,16].

EEG signal is split into its conventional frequency components with their associated mental states. The range of frequency from 0.5 to 35 Hz represents spectrum of EEG signal with around 100 microvolts amplitude. The frequency bands that can be extracted from EEG signal are as follows:

1. The frequency band lower than 4 Hz represents Delta (δ) band – Deep sleep

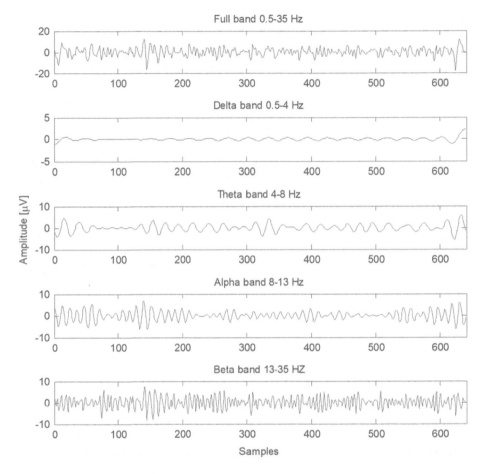

FIGURE 2.13 Full band EEG with conventional EEG frequency bands.

2. The frequency range in between 4 and 8 Hz represents Theta (θ) band – Meditation
3. The frequency range in between 8 and 13 Hz represents Alpha (α) band – Relaxed state
4. The frequency range between 13 and 30 Hz represents Beta (β) band – Active or Working
5. The frequency value greater than 30 Hz represents Gamma (γ) band – Higher-level meditation and Hyperactivity of brain.

The illustration of full band EEG and its component frequency bands is presented in Figure 2.13.

2.2.2.4 Common Problems

The EEG signal gets contaminated with biological and environmental artifacts, which corrupts pure EEG. The biological artifacts include bioelectric signals other

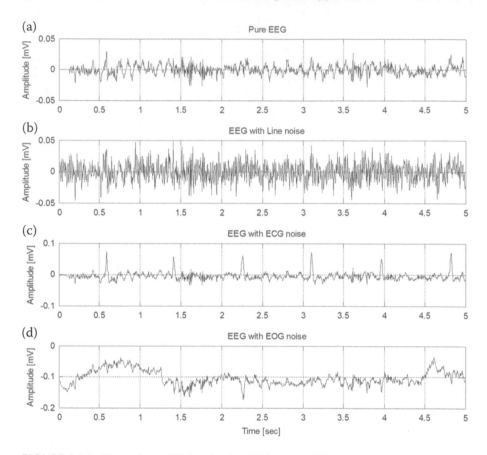

FIGURE 2.14   Plots of pure EEG and noisy EEG due to different types of noises.

than EEG, like electrooculogram (EOG) signal, introduced due to blinking, movement of eyes and extra-ocular muscle activity, artifacts due to ECG, and electromyogram (EMG) signal generated from muscle activity. Environmental artifacts include powerline noise, electromagnetic potential from other machines, movement of EEG cables, application of too much gel while EEG recording. Various filters can be designed to eliminate these artifacts from EEG signal [24–27]. Figure 2.14 presents pure EEG as well as EEG signal contaminated with ECG, EOG, and line noise. Figure 2.14(a) presents a pure EEG; EEG contaminated with line noise is presented in Figure 2.14(b). EEG signals contaminated with ECG and EOG signals are presented in Figure 2.14(c) and (d).

There is another serious problem in EEG signal called self-interference. The electrical potential from one electrode creates interference to the nearby electrodes as the EEG recording is performed on whole brain. The removal of self-interference can be performed using the technique called blind source separation. Identification of accurate source of signal is difficult as it is potential generated from a group of neurons.

2.2.2.5   EEG Applications

i. **Conventional applications:**
- Brain disease detection
- Identification of mental condition in different situations
- Quantification of emotion, stress, and mental workload
- Brain–computer interface for entertainment purpose

ii. **Recent EEG applications:**
- **Neurogaming and entertainment:** In this type of application the EEG signals are used to control the games.
- **Neuromarketing or consumer neuroscience:** It is the recent application of EEG signal that makes use of the EEG signals to analyze the psychological and emotional conditions of a consumer while purchasing any product. This is the recent branch of advertisement field.
- **Biometrics:** Emotional and cognitive status can be used to identify a person, hence EEG signals also found its application in biometrics.
- **Custom solutions and neurofeedback:** Monitoring the status of health and quality of life with the help of brain activity during meditation or exercise.

2.2.3   Electromyography (EMG)

EMG is a type of biomedical signal that represents the electrical potentials possessed by muscle tissue. The electrical potential is generated through the flow of ions across the muscle tissues. Electromyography is a technique used to record the electrical potential information from these muscle tissues and analyze them. The device used to record the EMG signal is called as myograph. All the physical activities of human body are controlled by central nervous system (CNS). After the receipt of stimuli, brain sends signal to the particular muscle that is to be recruited for physical activity using CNS. Muscles are acted in a group called motor units. Motor unit presents an intersection center where muscle fibers connect to the motor neuron. Activation of motor unit results in Motor Unit Action Potential (MUAP). The repeated activation from CNS results in MUAP trains, which produces the resultant EMG signal. The motor unit is depicted in Figure 2.15.

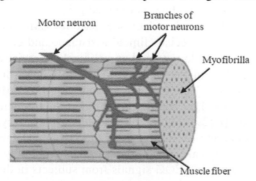

FIGURE 2.15   Motor unit consist of motor neuron and muscle fiber.

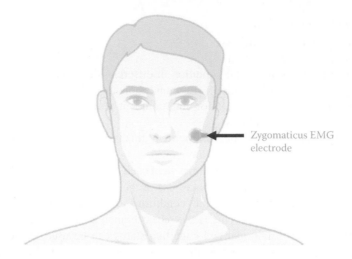

Zygomaticus EMG
electrode

FIGURE 2.16   Non-invasive electrode for zygomaticus EMG recording.

A muscle consists of a collection of cells, having capability of contraction and relaxation. Muscle tissues are able to receive and act according to the stimuli. There are basically three types of muscle tissues depending on the control mechanism, structure, and contractile property: (i) cardiac muscle, (ii) skeletal muscle, and (iii) smooth muscle. The EMG signal is associated with the skeletal muscle. Skeletal muscles contain large number of neurons for contraction.

2.2.3.1   EMG Signal Recording

EMG signals are generally recorded using two types of electrodes, namely invasive and non-invasive [23]. The non-invasive approach of EMG recording is conducted by placing electrodes on the skin. Figure 2.16 depicts the non-invasive electrode for zygomaticus EMG recording.

The EMG signal is recorded using non-invasive approach is composite in nature, containing action potential from all the muscle fibers present under the skin. During the invasive approach of EMG recording the wire or needle electrodes are placed directly in the muscle. The invasive approach of EMG recording is useful when the potential from particular muscle fiber is required [28].

Figure 2.17 depicts the invasive electrodes used for EMG recording. The wire and needle electrode needs precise clinical assistance and certification whereas the non-invasive electrodes do not need any clinical supervision. The amplitude value for EMG signal is in the range from 1 to 10 mV, due to which it is significantly weak signal. The frequency range for the EMG signal lies in range between 0 and 500 Hz. The dominant range of frequency for EMG lies between 50 and 150 Hz [29]. Figure 2.18 depicts a plot of zygomaticus major EMG signal corresponding to subject 1 of the DEAP (Database for Emotion Analysis Using Physiological Signals) dataset. It is a publicly available dataset consisting of EEG, EMG, and EOG signals from subjects in different emotional condition [30].

(a)

(b)

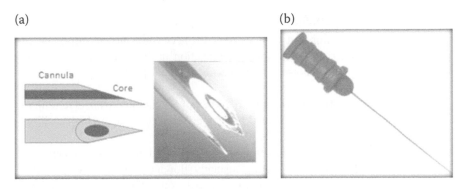

FIGURE 2.17 Invasive electrodes for EMG recording: (a) needle electrode and (b) wire electrode.

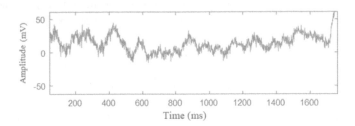

FIGURE 2.18 Raw zygomaticus major EMG signal.

2.2.3.2 EMG Signal Processing

The EMG signal in its raw form is useless for any analysis; it needs to be quantified to get useful information from it. The EMG signal processing steps are broadly divided into three parts: (i) signal filtration and smoothing (ii) feature extraction, and (iii) classification.

Signal filtration and smoothing: The EMG filtration can be performed using low pass Butterworth filter having threshold frequency of 10 Hz. After the filtration of EMG, the next step is smoothing of EMG. The EMG is smoothed by calculating the mean of the upper and lower values of the envelope of the filtered version of EMG.

Feature extraction: After getting the pure form of EMG signal, the next step is to extract the features that will enable the classifier to improve prediction. The features can be extracted from EMG in different domains, that is, frequency domain, time domain, and time-frequency domain. The time domain features include mean absolute value (MAV), MAV slope, zero crossing, length of waveform, etc. Frequency domain features include mean frequency, median frequency, mean peak frequency, time to peak force, spectral moments, frequency ratio, power spectrum ratio, central frequency variance, etc. [29].

Classification: The classification of EMG signal is important to diagnose the person with neurologic movement disorder. The EMG signals from healthy subjects are different than the EMG signals from neurological movement deficient person. Various classification algorithms like support vector machine, ANN, random forest, naïve bayes, wavelet neural network, etc., have been applied to classify EMG signals based on extracted features.

2.2.3.3   Common Problems

EMG signal gets contaminated with various artifacts while flowing through multiple tissues. The electrical noise causes degradation in the quality of the recorded signal. Following types of noises affect the EMG signal [31]:

i.   **Noise from electronics equipment:** The noise generated from electronics equipment cannot be eliminated but can be reduced by using high-quality equipment.
ii. **Ambient noise:** This kind of noise is generated from electromagnetic radiations. Human bodies are constantly flooded with electromagnetic radiations and it is not possible to avoid exposure. The ambient noise has amplitude greater than the magnitude of EMG by order of three.
iii. **Motion artifact:** The motion artifact noise gets induced into EMG signal by electrode cables and electrode interface. The motion artifact induces distortion in EMG signal. It can be get reduced by proper arrangement of the electronics equipment and setup.
iv. **Inherent instability of signal:** Firing rate of motor unit affects the EMG signal. The motor unit fires in **frequency** range of 0–20 Hz. This type of artifact is unwanted and it is important to remove it.

There are many other factors required to be considered while recording and processing EMG signal. These factors are classified as follows:

*   **Causative factors**: There are basically two types of causative factors affecting the EMG signal: (i) extrinsic and (ii) intrinsic. Extrinsic factors include structure of electrode being used for recording signal, placement of electrodes on skin, and EMG electrode location with respect to motor unit. The intrinsic factors include anatomical and physiological factors caused due to fiber diameter, blood flow, and type of fiber composition.
*   **Intermediate factors**: These include psychological and physiological factors that get triggered due to causative factors. The interference from the neighboring muscle can induce intermediate factors.
*   **Deterministic factors**: These factors get influenced by the intermediate factors. The rate of motor firing and active motor units directly affect the EMG signal.

2.2.3.4   EMG Applications

EMG signal has been used for variety of applications as follows:

*   EMG signal is used as a diagnostic tool in medical field
*   Human–machine interface uses EMG signal to interact with machine
*   Isometric muscle activity sensing can be performed using EMG
*   Used for interactive gaming applications
*   Can be used for unvoiced speech identification
*   Human emotion recognition

2.2.4 ELECTRO-OCULOGRAM (EOG)

EOG signal represents the corneoretinal potential that gets recorded by placing electrodes on the skin near eyes. Corneoretinal potential is nothing but the electrical potential present between the retina and cornea of human eye. EOG signal presents the location of eye, it is used to identify the eye movement. The typical value for EOG amplitude ranges in between 250 and 1000 μV and the approximate frequency range of 0–30 Hz.

The range of EOG amplitude is greater than that of the electroencephalogram signal. EOG signals are easily detected than that of the EEG signal. It can be detected even though eyes are closed. Figure 2.19 presents that the cornea and retina of human eye is positively and negatively charged, respectively. Figure 2.20 depicts the plot of vertical and horizontal EOG signal corresponding to subject 1 from the DEAP (A Database for Emotion Analysis Using Physiological Signals) dataset. It is a publicly available dataset that consists of EEG, EMG, and EOG signals from subjects under different emotional condition [30].

+
Cornea   Retina

FIGURE 2.19 Corneoretinal potential (CRP).

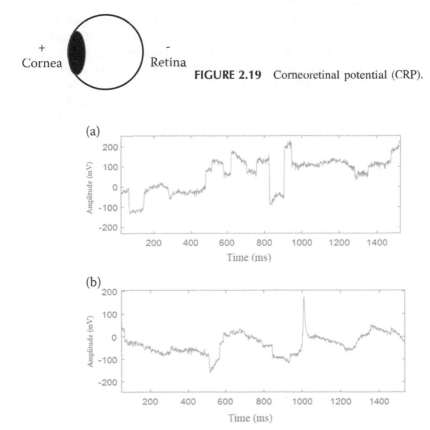

FIGURE 2.20 EOG signal (a) horizontal EOG (b) vertical EOG.

The signal presented in Figure 2.20(a) is the horizontal EOG obtained by calculating the difference in signal from electrode placed on left and right side of the eye. Figure 2.20(b) presents vertical EOG obtained by calculating the signal difference between the top and bottom electrode signals [22,31]. The classification of EOG has been performed for the clinical purposes.

The eye movement can be identified using EOG signal by evaluating the increase or decrease in its amplitude. Any event in EOG is generated by two eye movements, where one movement creates the event and the other movement is used to return a neural position. During the eye movement three different steps are identified using EOG signals, that is, rise in EOG amplitude from low to high level, stabilizing at the high level of amplitude, and fall in amplitude from high to low level. Therefore, the four different characteristics can be obtained from EOG signal, that is, starting edge, ending edge, area within two edges, and error. To classify and remove the eye blink, the area between two edges is utilized. The width of area is much smaller for the eye blink condition. In general if the width of area is smaller than 250 ms then it is considered as eye blink event [32].

2.2.4.1 EOG Signal Recording

The EOG signal recording can be performed independently on both eyes, but for vertical direction both eyes move in conjunction, hence, for vertical EOG single eye can be used. Figure 2.21 presents EOG recording approach using five surface channels placed on the skin around eyes. The vertical EOG is captured using two channels (Ch.+ and Ch. V–) placed above and below of right eye. The horizontal EOG is recorded using two electrodes (Ch. H+ and Ch. H–) placed at right and left side of outer canthi. The electrode (G) placed on forehead presents the reference channel.

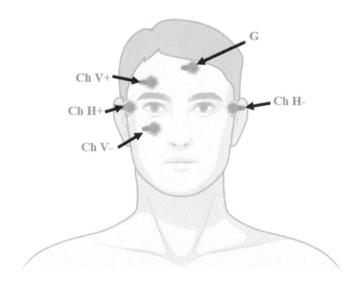

FIGURE 2.21 Electrode placement for EOG signal recording.

2.2.4.2   EOG Processing

Although EOG does not directly perform detection of human behavior or physical state, it provides information that is utilized to perform classification. For example, the frequency of eye blinking can predict the fatigue or anxiety status of human being. The classification using EOG signal requires certain processing steps to be performed. The EOG processing includes signal filtration, feature extraction, and classification.

EOG signal gets contaminated with muscle noise and electromagnetic interference from the cables and equipment used to record EOG. These noises need to be eliminated to get pure EOG signal. There are various filters available in literature, such as low pass filter, high pass filter, notch filter, etc. The features extracted from filtered EOG improve the prediction performance.

i. Feature extraction

   Feature extraction is an important processing step that affects the classification performance. Various time domain features extracted from EOG
   include [33]:

   • Peak amplitude from EOG signal
   • Maximum valley amplitude from EOG signals
   • Position value of maximum peak amplitude
   • Position value of maximum valley amplitude
   • Summation of absolute value in both negative and positive value of
     amplitude
   • EOG signal variance

ii. Classification

   EOG classification is the final step used for prediction of different types of
   signal based on the input features. The classes to be predicted depend on
   the field of application. Various classification algorithms like SVM, ANN,
   naïve bayes, etc., can be used for the classification.

2.2.4.3   Common Problems

EOG signals gets contaminated with different noises while recording it. The main sources of noise contaminating the EOG signal are as follows

   • Electromagnetic noise from the powerline near the recording device
   • Internal noise gets added into EOG generated from measurement device
   • Noise generated due to improper contact between skin and EOG electrode
   • The noises from EMG signal
   • The noise in the form of EEG signal

2.2.4.4   Applications of EOG Signal

The EOG signal has a variety of applications in different field of research [23].

   • Electrical wheelchair control
   • Mobile robot control

- Mouse cursor control
- Eye writing recognition
- Emotional condition recognition
- Sleep stage detection
- Fatigue state detection

REFERENCES

[1] Smith, S. W. The scientist and engineer's guide to digital signal processing, 1997. https://doi.org/(http://www.dspguide.com/).

[2] Ahirwal M. K., Kumar A., Singh G. K. Biomedical signals, in: Computational Intelligence and Biomedical Signal Processing. SpringerBriefs in Electrical and Computer Engineering. Springer, Cham, 2021. 10.1007/978-3-030-67098-6_1.

[3] B.C.O. Textbooks. 19.2 Cardiac muscle and electrical activity, 2018, 1–22. https://openstax.org/books/anatomy-and-physiology/pages/19-2-cardiac-muscle-and-electrical-activity (accessed August 16, 2021).

[4] Plawiak, P. ECG signals (744 fragments), Mendeley Data, V3. 3, 2017. https://data.mendeley.com/datasets/63zm778szb/3.

[5] Malmivuo, J., Plonsey, R. Bioelectromagnetism: Principles and applications of bioelectric and biomagnetic bields, Oxford University Press, USA, 1995.

[6] Silva, H., Lourenço, A., Canento, F., Fred, A., Raposo, N. ECG biometrics: Principles and applications, in: BIOSIGNALS 2013 - Proceedings of the International Conference on Bio-Inspired Systems and Signal Processing, SciTePress - Science and and Technology Publications, 2013, 215–220. 10.5220/0004243202150220.

[7] Ye, C., Coimbra, M. T., Kumar, B. V. K. V. Investigation of human identification using two-lead Electrocardiogram (ECG) signals, in: 2010 Fourth IEEE International Conference on Biometrics: Theory, Applications and Systems (BTAS), IEEE, 2010, 1–8. 10.1109/BTAS.2010.5634478.

[8] Drew, B. J., Califf, R. M., Funk, M., Kaufman, E. S., Krucoff, M. W., Laks, M. M., Macfarlane, P. W., Sommargren, C., Swiryn, S., Van Hare, G. F. Practice standards for electrocardiographic monitoring in hospital settings: An American Heart Association scientific statement from the councils on cardiovascular nursing, clinical cardiology, and cardiovascular disease in the young, *Circulation* 110, 2004, 2721–2746. 10.1161/01.CIR.0000145144.56673.59.

[9] Li, M., Xiong, W., Li, Y., Wearable measurement of ECG signals based on smart clothing, *International Journal of Telemedicine and Applications* 2020. 10.1155/2020/6329360.

[10] Navin, O., Kumar, G., Kumar, N., Baderia, K., Kumar, R., Kumar, A. R-peaks detection using shannon energy for HRV analysis, in: *Lecture Notes in Electrical Engineering*, 2019, 401–409. 10.1007/978-981-13-2553-3_39.

[11] Anand, R. S., Kumar, V. Efficient and reliable detection of QRS-segment in ECG signals, in: IEEE/ Engineering in Medicine and Biology Society Annual Conference, 1995. 10.1109/rcembs.1995.511734.

[12] Ahirwal, M. K., Janghel, R. R., Kose, M. R. Descendant adaptive filter to remove different noises from ECG signals, *International Journal of Biomedical Engineering and Technology,* 33, 2020, 258. 10.1504/ijbet.2020.10029989.

[13] Moody, G. B., Mark, R. G. The impact of the MIT-BIH arrhythmia database, *IEEE Engineering in Medicine and Biology Magazine* 20, 2001, 45–50. 10.1109/51.932724.

[14] Moody, G. B., Muldrow, W. K., Mark, R. G. Noise stress test for arrhythmia detectors, *Computers in Cardiology* 11, 1984, 381–384.
[15] Sanei, S., Chambers, J. A. EEG signal processing, John Wiley & Sons, 2013.
[16] Shanbao, T., Thankor N. V. Quantitative EEG analysis methods and clinical applications, Artech House, 2009.
[17] Collura, T. F., History and evolution of electroencephalographic instruments and techniques, *Journal of Clinical Neurophysiology* 10, 1993, 476–504. 10.1097/00004 691-199310000-00007.
[18] Teplan, M. Fundamentals of EEG measurement, *Measurement Science Review*, 2, 2002, 1–11.
[19] Pfurtscheller, G., Lopes Da Silva, F. H. Event-related EEG/MEG synchronization and desynchronization: Basic principles, *Clinical Neurophysiology* 110, 1999, 1842–1857. 10.1016/S1388-2457(99)00141-8.
[20] Odom, J. V., Bach, M., Barber, C., Brigell, M., Marmor, M. F., Tormene,A. P., Holder, G. E., Vaegan, A. Visual evoked potentials standard, *Documenta Ophthalmologica* 108, 2004, 115–123. 10.1023/B:DOOP.0000036790.67234.22.
[21] Kropotov, J. D. Functional neuromarkers for psychiatry: Applications for diagnosis and treatment, 2016. 10.1016/C2012-0-07144-X.
[22] Quian Quiroga R., EEG, ERP and single cell recordings database free EEG data database freely ERP data publicly available (ucsd.edu)[https://sccn.ucsd.edu/~arno/ fam2data/publicly_available_EEG_data.html]
[23] Kim, M. R., Yoon, G. Control signal from EOG analysis and its application, *Electronic and Communication Engineering* 7, 2013, 1352–1355.
[24] Ahirwal, M. K., Kumar, A., Singh, G. K. Descendent adaptive noise cancellers to improve SNR of contaminated EEG with gradient-based and evolutionary approach, *International Journal of Biomedical Engineering and Technology* 13, 2013, 49–68. 10.1504/IJBET.2013.057713.
[25] Ichimaru, Y., Moody, G. B. Development of the polysomnographic database on CD-ROM, *Psychiatry and Clinical Neurosciences* 53, 1999, 175–177.
[26] Goldberger A. L., Amaral L. A. N., Glass L., Hausdorff J. M., Ivanov P. C., Mark R. G., Mietus J. E., Moody G. B., Peng C.-K., Eugene Stanley H. PhysioBank, PhysioToolkit, and PhysioNet: Components of a new research resource for complex physiologic signals, *Circulation* 101, 2000, e215–e220. https://www.ncbi.nlm.nih. gov/pubmed/10851218.
[27] Levens, A. J. Muscles alive. Their functions revealed by electromyography, *Military Medicine* 145, 1980, 262–262. 10.1093/milmed/145.4.262a.
[28] Zahak, M. Signal acquisition using surface EMG and circuit design considerations for robotic prosthesis, in: *Computational Intelligence in Electromyography Analysis - A Perspective on Current Applications and Future Challenges*, 2012, 13. 10.5 772/52556.
[29] Chowdhury, R. H., Reaz, M. B. I., Bin Mohd Ali, M. A., Bakar, A. A. A., Chellappan, K., Chang, T. G. Surface electromyography signal processing and classification techniques, *Sensors (Switzerland)* 13, 2013, 12431–12466. 10.3390/ s130912431.
[30] Koelstra, S., Muhl, C., Soleymani, M., Jong-Seok Lee, A., Yazdani, T., Ebrahimi, T., Pun, A., Nijholt, I. P. DEAP: A database for emotion analysis; using physiological signals, *IEEE Transactions on Affective Computing* 3, 2012, 18–31. 10.11 09/T-AFFC.2011.15.
[31] Godana, B., Leus, G., Barroso, A. Estimating indoor walking velocity profile using a software radio-based radar, in: Proceedings - 1st International Conference on Sensor Device Technologies and Applications, SENSORDEVICES 2010, 2010, 44–51. 10.1109/SENSORDEVICES.2010.16.

[32] Aungsakul, S., Phinyomark, A., Phukpattaranont, P., Limsakul, C. Evaluating fea-
     ture extraction methods of electrooculography (EOG) signal for human-computer
     interface, in: Procedia Engineering, 2012, 246–252. 10.1016/j.proeng.2012.01.12
     64.
[33] Tibarewala, D. N., Banerjee, A. S., Paul, S. Emsotional eye movement analysis
     using electrooculography signal, *International Journal of Biomedical Engineering
     and Technology* 23, 2017, 59. 10.1504/ijbet.2017.10003041.

3 Images in Radiology: Concepts of Image Acquisition and the Nature of Images

Narendra Kuber Bodhey
All India Institute of Medical Sciences, Raipur, India

CONTENTS

3.1 INTRODUCTION

Radiology is an important aspect in the field of medicine due to its diagnostic and therapeutic roles. The former comes under diagnostic radiology and the latter is termed as interventional radiology. Since the discovery of X-rays, radiology has been growing in leaps and bounds and it not only acquires the images but also provides a substrate as well as the potential for technologies to be innovated for all other branches. Robotic surgeries or intraoperative use of navigation tools are based on obtaining images.

DOI: 10.1201/9781003241409-3

In any branch of medicine it, and inclusive of radiology, doctors have a data repository of normal conditions or images stored in memory obtained throughout his/her practice. Any deviation from reference imaging is considered to be a pathologic condition. This is a concept of human intelligence that got translated into artificial intelligence. The algorithms, as one would know from other chapters from this book, learn from data and then any recognizes any deviation. Also, the imaging patterns of a particular type of disease can be categorized as per clinical requirements. Hence, if a person is trying to develop some AI algorithms for radiology or non-radiology clinical applications, it is of utmost importance to understand the concepts of various types of images with their sources. This chapter intends to take the reader through the basic ideas of the images and their modalities without actually dwelling on the intricate details. Those interested in the details of particular aspects are recommended to go through the dedicated material available in the literature.

The information that radiologists see is all about the images, which display different shades of grey between black and white. The radiologist was also termed as "photographer" not so long before; a photographer who could see through the body especially in terms of X-ray images. Then came the ultrasound images followed by the CT scan, MRI, and others. The images still were in the shades of grey. Later, the Doppler effect was put into use along with the ultrasound, which imparted color to these images. Some colorful images are also seen in CT or MRI scans. However, the original images from these are still in shades of grey, and it is the post-processing that can color these images for better understanding the anatomy.

It was in 1895 when Sir Wilhelm Roentgen on the 8th of November accidentally discovered X-rays, which marks the birth of radiology.

- What are the modalities and their images in radiology?
- What does the radiologist do when he evaluates the images for particular diagnosis?
- What is the potential work that can be done in the field of imaging from a technology point of view?

Radiology images are pictorial outputs of imaging equipment. The type of imaging equipment is termed as a *modality* in radiology. The radiology images use a common format known as *Digital Imaging and Communication in Medicine* (DICOM). DICOM is initiated by the National Electrical Manufacturers Association (NEMA) and as quoted by Bidgood WD Jr. "specifies a non-proprietary data interchange protocol, digital image format and file structure for biomedical images and image-related information". DICOM, thus, is a common language platform for all radiology images across the globe (Figure 3.1).

Various types of imaging equipment that are used for acquiring a specific type of image are called as radiological modalities. The modalities used in radiology are:

    i. Radiography – termed as X-ray in common usage
       a. General radiography
       b. Fluoroscopy
       c. Mammography

 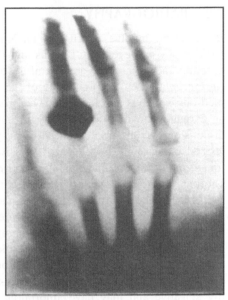

FIGURE 3.1 The first radiograph was the hand of the wife of Sir Roentgen shot to fame as "hand mit ringer", i.e., hand with the ring. She commented "I have seen my death".

    d. Dental radiography
    e. Dual-energy X-ray absorptiometry scan (DEXA)
  ii. Ultrasonography (USG) with or without color Doppler
 iii. Computed Tomography (CT)
    a. Noncontrast and contrast-enhanced CT (NCCT and CECT)
    b. High-resolution CT (HRCT)
    c. CT angiography
    d. Cardiac/Coronary CT angiography
    e. CT perfusion
    f. CT colonoscopy (virtual colonoscopy)
  iv. Magnetic resonance imaging (MRI)
    a. Conventional MRI
    b. Advanced MRI
       • Diffusion-weighted MRI
       • Perfusion MRI – Contrast perfusion and noncontrast perfusion (ASL)
       • MR spectroscopy (MRS)
    c. Special MRI investigations
       • MR myelography
       • MR cystography
       • MR cholangiopancreatography
       • Fetal MRI
       • Cardiac MRI
   v. Digital subtraction angiography (DSA)

3.2   RADIOGRAPHY

Radiography involves the use of an X-ray tube that is the heart of all forms of radiography and even in CT scans and DSA. Thus, it is a modality that produces ionizing radiations that are harmful for patients. Radiography is *conventional radiography* when the processing of the X-ray plate after exposure is by chemical methods, which is also termed as wet processing. The radiography output is termed as a radiograph or also as X-ray in common usage. This radiograph is a two-dimensional image printed on an x-ray plate/film. Then came the era of compu-terized radiography in the mid-1980s with the concept of converting an analog image into a digital image using a phosphor plate that can be stimulated by light photons [1]. Also known as CR, the technology involves the use of the same X-ray machine, but the exposure is of a CR imaging plate is then read on a digitizer or CR reader. The image is then displayed directly on the computer and thereafter it is printed on a film by a dry printer. The imaging plates/cassettes need to be taken to and from the digitizer to the X-ray room for exposing and reading. The next technology of *digital radiography* (DR) brought in more ease by introducing the use of a flat panel detector installed in the X-ray machine itself. These detectors are X-ray sensitive and may have amorphous silicon or amorphous selenium as their content. The mechanical carrying of the cassettes of conventional radiography or computed radiography is done away with as also the digitizer or the CR reader. Thus, the footprint of the space required, and the throughput time also significantly decreased. The material used in the CR imaging plate and the detector of the DR is specific for the sensitivity to the X-rays and the details of the same can be found elsewhere [1–3].

Since we are dealing with images, we need to understand only the basics of these technologies at this point. There is a definite difference between an image from a conventional radiography system and the subsequent CR or a DR image. The la-titude of the greyness or the contrast in an image from conventional radiography depends on the quantum of X-rays allowed to pass and the chemical processing in the darkroom. Once the image is taken on an X-ray film, this contrast is fixed. The only way to digitize this image is by scanning this film or taking a photograph of this film, which can then be stored in the form of non-DICOM type of format (jpeg, png, etc.) that generally would be termed as a lossy type. The images from a CR and DR are already in the computer system in the DICOM format. Some degree of contrast adjustment can be done on the computer for the desired appearance on the film before printing with both the CR and DR images. The added advantage of the DR is that the image resolution is far better than that of CR or conventional radiography.

This same technology of conventional, CR, or digital radiography can be ex-tended beyond the routine X-ray of the body for a special type of radiography. When it is used for breast imaging it is called mammography [4], dental radio-graphy when used for the dental, and DEXA scan [5] for the bone density mea-surement. When used for imaging all the jaw components in a straightened plane, it is termed as an orthopantomography (OPG) [6]. The radiography as mentioned earlier has only a two-dimensional output and gives a relative panoramic idea of the exposed part to the radiologist only at a specific time point. When the third dimension of time is added to it, it becomes a technology called as *fluoroscopy*. The concept was introduced to depict the dynamic physiology of various organs so that continuous radiography can be possible, and the series of images thus stored can be viewed as a video-like loop. It then gives radiologists information about the physiology of the movement function. Radio-opaque contrast is introduced into an organ of interest and monitored for various abnormalities of flow/movement/leak/reflux. The investigations that a radiologist can perform using this technique are barium swallow (esophagogram), barium meal, barium enema, cystography, sinogram, cavitogram, cholangiography, angiography, fistulography, venography, and others. It could also be used as image guidance for treatment procedures in certain cases.

The image output of the radiography is described by a radiologist as radio-opaque or radiolucent. When the CR or DR is used, the images are stored always in a DICOM format and can be retrieved in the same format for viewing, printing, and analysis (Figures 3.2 and 3.3).

3.3 ULTRASONOGRAPHY

Ultrasonography (USG) is a modality that makes use of a piezoelectric crystal in its probe, which is moved mechanically on the patient's body surface [7]. The probe emits the ultrasound waves that are then transmitted through the body, and it also receives them back as a modified signal. The difference in the emitted waves and the received waves is what constitutes an image of a grey spectrum. Thus, it is an echo of the transmitted waves, and hence the terminology as echogenic (bright) or echo poor or echolucent (dark) is used for describing the appearances. Sometimes the terminology used is hyperechoic (bright), anechoic (completely dark), hypoechoic (relatively dark), or isoechoic (the same echogenicity as that of the organ in reference) (Figure 3.4).

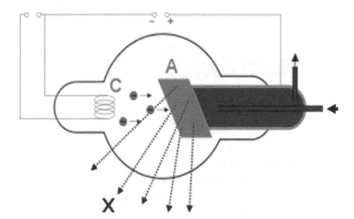

FIGURE 3.2 Schematic diagram of the X-ray tube. *C* denotes the cathode which emits the electrons that travel to anode *A* at a high speed and resultant X-rays (*X*) are emitted.

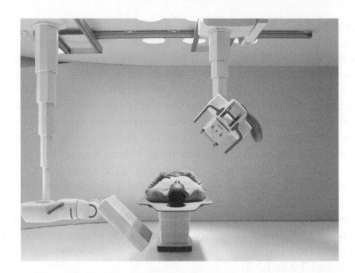

FIGURE 3.3   Digital radiography set up – X-ray tube to the top right of the patient, the detector to the left and below indicating an oblique view of X-ray being taken.

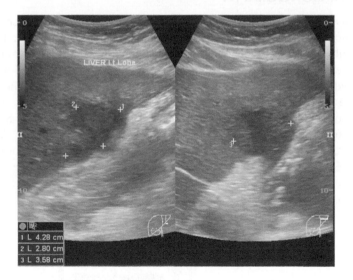

FIGURE 3.4   USG of the liver showing a relatively darkish appearing area marked at its boundaries by electronic calipers "+". This disease or lesion will be termed as hypoechoic to the rest of the liver.

While most of the information given by the ultrasound or ultrasonography is about the structure status of the internal organs, the addition of Doppler gives information about the flow function inside a blood vessel and or the heart. The basic concept is of a Doppler effect. The blood flowing towards the probe is denoted in red and that flowing away from the probe is blue. (Do not take it as a blanket understanding of red is arterial and blue is venous flow.) The information from the vascular Doppler could be in the form of uniform laminar flow or a turbulent flow or no flow. The color pattern also correlates with the spectrum and the radiologist gets the information about the actual velocity in the sampled area. Nowadays, there is an auto-estimation of the vessel wall thickness as an indicator of atherosclerosis. The term is "intimo-medial thickness (IMT)". The velocity of the blood across an arterial segment could be translated by auto-computation that helps detect stenosis (narrowing) of the vessel. Sometimes the radiologist also would prefer to mention the pressure gradient across the narrowed segment, which is given by the modified Bernoulli's equation [8] represented by Equation (3.1).

$$\Delta P = 4c^2 \tag{3.1}$$

where; ΔP is the pressure gradient and c is the velocity of the blood at the place of narrowing.

In Figure 3.5(a), color Doppler activation over a greyscale image shows the incoming blood labeled as red, outgoing blood as blue, and the admixture of red and blue signifying multidirectional flow suggestive of turbulence. Figure 3.5(b) illustrates the red flow in the artery and the spectrum of the flow. The early part of the spectrum seen as a peak is during the contraction phase of the cardiac cycle and the later phase is the waning down of the peak during the relaxation phase of the cycle that is also termed as systole.

There are different kinds of Doppler ultrasounds, the hardware of which generally depends on the application for which it is used. Handheld Doppler is a small instrument that is used in the outpatient clinic for peripheral vessels; transcranial Doppler for use in the evaluation of intracranial vascular spectrum and the intravascular ultrasound (IVUS). In IVUS, a special type of probe is inserted into the vessel, which gives information about the vessel from its internal surface. Figure 3.6 shows the IVUS image of the interior of a blood vessel. It is revealing a trough-like area of the luminal surface which is an important fact to know for a physician to decide about medication and further treatment.

The echocardiography is also an extended version of the ultrasound. The ultrasound evaluation of the heart is termed as echocardiography and the rest of the

(a)   (b)

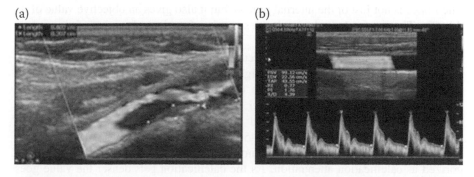

FIGURE 3.5   (a) Color Doppler activation over a greyscale image and (b) red color and spectrum flow in the artery.

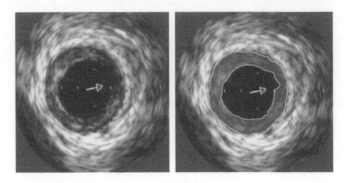

FIGURE 3.6   IVUS image.

applications are almost similar. Since it does not make use of ionizing radiation it is considered to be quite safe even for a pregnant female.

3.4   COMPUTED TOMOGRAPHY

Computed Tomography (CT) was invented by Hounsfield and Cormack with the first commercial CT scanner available in 1972 [9]. The "tomos" denotes slicing and that's the reason it is called tomography. CT scan houses the X-ray tube and detectors at the other end, which move at a 180° toward each other around the patient. The X-ray beam is a highly collimated fan beam and can see the internal organs as per the slice or section. Interested readers can go through the details of the equipment's hardware elsewhere in the literature. However, it should be noted in this place that a patient is put in the CT scanner after complying with the pre-requisites for a clinical diagnosis. The radiologist then selects the appropriate protocol for that part and the type of scan is done as per the clinical question that needs to be answered. The use of an X-ray tube entails the patient getting the ionizing radiation the way they get it with radiography. However, the image is not a panoramic two-dimensional but a section of two dimensions. After taking an initial scout or a localizer image, the scanner slices the body into a transverse or an axial image due to which it was initially termed as Computed Axial Tomography (CAT). The image is not just of the internal organs, but it also gives an objective value of its density. The image thus obtained gives a mix of various densities of the organs (Figure 3.7).

Like USG, here also we have different terminologies used for the description of the organ structure. Hyperdense (bright), hypodense (dark), isodense, or iso-attenuated (same density as reference organ) are the terms used in the relative description of image details. However, the objective density can be denoted as Hounsfield Units (HU) or also called attenuation values. The value of zero to +15–20 is termed as fluid density, 20–50 soft tissue density, 50–70 HU is thicker soft tissue, 70–100 HU as blood attenuation values, more than 120 HU is categorized as calcification attenuation. As the calcification gets denser the value goes on getting higher and the bone attenuation is more than 800 HU. If the attenuation is below zero upto −100 HU, the tissue is that of fat and if the value is less than minus

(a)   (b)

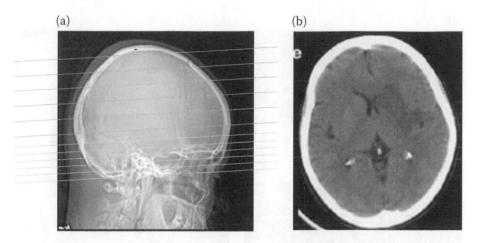

FIGURE 3.7   (a) Localizer or scout on which the images are planned and (b) brain slice in an axial plane or a transverse plane.

700 to 800 then it is of air. It is this objectivity in measuring the X-ray attenuation by a tissue and sections of desirable thickness that is the advantage of CT scan technology.

Figure 3.8 shows the axial slice of the brain of a patient who had a brain hemorrhage. The hemorrhage or an area of bleed is identified as a bright or hyperdense appearance. The area immediately around this is slightly darker termed as hypodense and is darker than the similar area on the opposite side. This signifies that there is an accumulation of water which brings the Hounsfield units down in the number. The three blackest pockets are termed the ventricles of the brain that

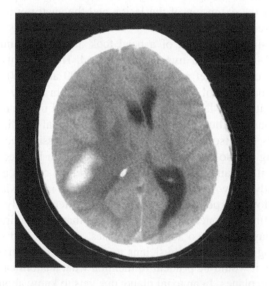

FIGURE 3.8   Brain axial slice of a patient having a brain hemorrhage.

(a)   (b)

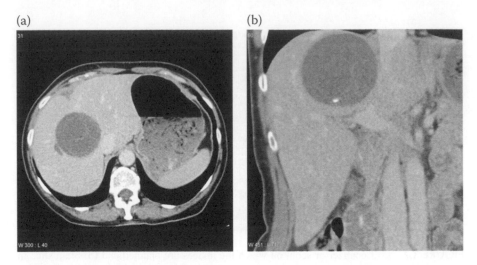

FIGURE 3.9   (a) Axial section CT image of the upper abdomen and (b) its coronal reformatted image.

contain cerebrospinal fluid (CSF). The outermost bright and thick boundary of the brain denotes the skull bone, which as per the HU scale is always normally bright (hyperdense).

Similarly, Figure 3.9(a) shows an axial section of the upper abdomen at the level of the liver where a round darker area is seen in the background of a normal grey appearance of a liver. So the lesion here would be described as hypodense to the rest of the liver. If it would have been bright or white we would have termed it as hyperdense to the rest of the liver. Figure 3.9(b) shows a coronal reformatted image of Figure 3.9(a). The advantage of seeing in another orthogonal plane is that it gives information about the extension of the lesion and the anatomy in the head to foot (craniocaudal) direction.

Previously, a simple CT scan of a head took almost 10 minutes that yielded approximately 12–15 sectional images of the head. However, using an advanced multidetector CT one can get anywhere between 700 and 3000 sectional images depending upon the protocol applied and that too within a very short time. These high-speed acquisitions of large image data have opened up the doors for multiple clinical applications and thus also the potential for artificial intelligence. The higher number of images has also allowed a host of post-processing techniques.

Post-processing is also one of the ingredients that can be incorporated into the different AI algorithms and hence it is essential to know certain aspects associated with it. We already know that the images acquired are in an axial or a transverse plane. It takes a lot of expertise and experience to interpret only the axial images and come to a definitive conclusion. These images that are acquired by the scanner can now be displayed into two additional planes – coronal and sagittal, thus, enabling the radiologist and other physicians to assess the same structure in all three dimensions. Here, it would be prudent to mention what anatomical information can we obtain from the planes. In an axial plane, one gets to know about the structure in anteroposterior and right to left direction; the sagittal plane reconstruction gives information about the craniocaudal and anteroposterior direction and the coronal plane gives the details in right-left and craniocaudal direction.

3.4.1 NONCONTRAST AND CONTRAST-ENHANCED CT

Non-contrast CT (NCCT) and contrast-enhanced CT (CECT) are important data acquisitions that have extensive clinical applications. The physics behind this is also interesting. CECT is a CT scan acquisition after administration of iodine-based contrast/dye. This contrast increases the density or attenuation in all those tissues which are alive or viable. The dead/pus/necrotic tissue will not show any change in the attenuation. All the vessels will take up the contrast with an exorbitant increase in their attenuation values. The increase in the vessel attenuation due to presence of a contrast in them will also depend upon the time at which the scan was performed after the start of administration of the contrast. So, if it is an early phase, the artery will show increase in density, and if later it is the venous opacification that will increase in attenuation.

With the newer scanners, the post-processing workstation also yields a three-dimensional volume reconstruction of the acquired data. Various such reconstruction techniques that can be applied (after acquiring continuous axial sections with zero distance between them) are *maximum intensity projection, minimum intensity projection, volume rendering technique, endovascular view, endoscopic view,* and others. These could be applied to imaging of specific organ systems wherein nowadays there is an auto-reporting card available with certain applications. Due to ultrafast scanners giving a huge data acquisition and the available post-processing tools as described by the ordinary CT scan now gives a variety of applications, namely HRCT, CT angiography/venography, CT perfusion, CT colonoscopy, cardiac/coronary CT angiography, and others. The details of each of these applications are not under the purview of this chapter for now, but a basic conceptual idea would help the readers to understand and plan their algorithms for their own AI programs [10].

In Figure 3.10, the colon or the large intestine is distended with air through an enema tube. After that, axial images with zero spacing are taken and then we get the

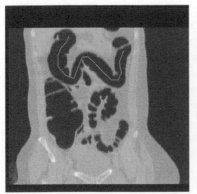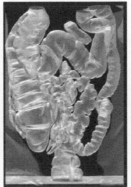

FIGURE 3.10   CT colonoscopy/colonography images.

first image as the coronal reformation of the axial acquisition. The second and third images are 3D reconstructions only of the colonic lumen filled with air. This post-processing is done whenever that software package is available with that scanner. This technique helps in identifying pathologies present in the lumen or arising from the luminal surface of the intestine. Examples could be any foreign body or sometimes even packets of drugs used by drug peddlars.

3.4.2   HIGH-RESOLUTION CT

High-Resolution CT (HRCT) scan has a thickness of 1 millimeter or less and it uses a higher quantum X-rays, with a smaller field of view (FOV) and reconstruction kernel as per the organ imaged. When performed for the temporal bone the reconstruction is done in a bone kernel and gives the details about the inner and middle ear structures, which are not so easily discernible on a routine scan of the head. The direct clinical applications of this HRCT temporal bone are for trauma or infection involving this area or involving the adjacent area with suspected extension into this area. An important application is in deaf-mutism when the child is being planned for a cochlear implant, wherein the HRCT temporal bone, MRI of posterior fossa, and the other investigations are evaluated in combination to plan the best candidate for cochlear implant surgery and to prognosticate the outcome of the surgery.

3.4.3   CT ANGIOGRAPHY/VENOGRAPHY

CT angiography/venography (CTA/CTV) represents the depiction of the vascular tree (arterial or venous) using the CT technique. Again, it is the high-speed acquisition of the data that is helping in looking at the opacified arteries or the veins with far better spatial resolution than the dynamic or catheter angiography (DSA). In this protocol, the acquisition is by bolus track technique that tracks the arrival of contrast bolus by continuous monitoring of the attenuation of the desired artery. Once it detects contrast in the tracked artery, the scanner starts acquiring very thin millimeter or submillimeter slices for the desired region. This gives the radiologist a picture of the arteries because the fast scanners scan the complete area while the contrast is still in the artery. These images are then post-processed to give angiographic pictures in various planes.

The major drawback that was there with initial scanners was the slower speed of acquisition and their inability to have thinner slices. The thick slices gave a stair-step artifact to the contour of a structure when viewed in any plane other than the axial plane. The thinner slices, zero-gap (no loss of data in between the slices), and the spiral acquisition of a large volume of data in the present-day scanners due to their multiple detectors have now enabled the data viewing in any plane with minimal or no distortion.

CAD tools (which is also considered to be an initial type of AI) now enable radiologists to have automated views of the artery in different planes, straightening of that vessel to have a clear picture, auto calculations of the percentage stenosis (narrowing), presence or absence of the calcification in the atheromatous plaque of the stenosis. When this technique is extended for primary visualization of the venous system, it would be termed as CT venography. The areas for which the technique is deployed will give the specialized name for the CTA or CTV. The greatest advantage of CTA over a DSA is that one can see the vessel and its wall along with the organ that is associated with it, unlike the DSA which depicts only the luminal portion of the vessel. The CTA of the extracardiac vessels is relatively less challenging technically as well as clinically compared to the CTA of the heart or the coronary CT angiography.

Figure 3.11 illustrates the abdominal aorta and its branches by suppression of the background tissues. The calcium deposition on the arterial walls is seen as a far brighter focus compared to the contrast-filled artery. This technique uses the thresholding technique where all the structures above a particular attenuation threshold are seen.

3.4.4 CARDIAC CT/CORONARY CT ANGIOGRAPHY

Cardiac CT/Coronary CT angiography is a specialized CT angiography and is different from the latter due to various reasons. The extracardiac structures are generally not mobile, however, the heart and the coronary vessels move with the cardiac beats and hence crisp and unblurred images are not possible with all CT scanners. The CT scanner should be enabled with a cardiac-gated CT. What is cardiac gating? For this, one should first understand the need for gating. As we already know that images of any moving object will be blurred, hence we make sure that the object is first made immobile and then a picture is taken. Similarly, while taking a chest radiograph we ask the patient to hold their breath to nullify the

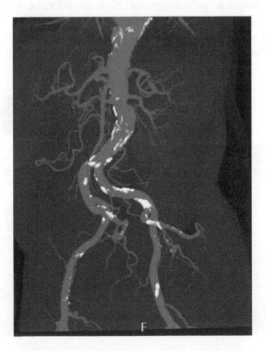

FIGURE 3.11 Greyscale 3D reconstruction displayed as a coronal plane projection of CT angiography images acquired in the axial plane.

movement blur because of respiratory movement. However, we cannot stop the heart to get clearer pictures. Hence, the scanner is made to rotate the gantry (assembly of the X-ray tube and the detector) at the speed of the heartbeat to make the relative motion between them equal to zero. This matching of the rotation speed of the gantry with that of the heart contraction is termed as "cardiac gating".

The gating is done by simultaneously acquiring the ECG data. This gating technique could be either prospective or retrospective. The prospective gating means that the data is acquired only during the stable portion of the cardiac cycle wherein the heart is relatively immobile and that is generally during the late diastole. The retrospective gated cardiac CT means that the data acquisition is occurring throughout the cardiac cycle. Thus, it is evident that the quantum of data acquired from the retrospective gated cardiac CT is huge. Further heart rate of the patient will also quantify the amount of data that is acquired in this retrospective scan. The higher the heart rate larger will be the data and the more will be the radiation to the patient during such scans. So if there is no contraindication, then the radiologist would prefer the heart rate to be slightly lower (around 60–65 beats per minute).

Nowadays, the CAD/AI-governed post-processing tools are available in the workstation supplied with the scanner that can determine calcium scoring (to see the overall calcium deposits in the branches of the three coronary arteries), auto analysis of the coronary arterial narrowing, etc. Coronary CT angiography is one of the good noninvasive techniques of assessing the status of the coronary arteries in a certain group of patients. The cardiac CT is also useful in chamber assessment in various other intracardiac pathologies or even to delineate the abnormalities of congenital heart disease.

Figure 3.12(a) shows a MIP image of cardiac-gated coronary CTA, which represents the origin of the coronary artery from the aorta and its continuation.

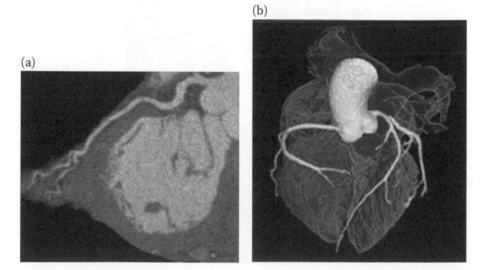

FIGURE 3.12   (a) MIP image of cardiac-gated coronary CTA and (b) post-processed 3D rendered image.

Figure 3.12(b) is the post-processed 3D volume-rendered image to show the aorta and the coronary tree for easy understanding of physicians.

3.4.5 CT Perfusion

CT perfusion is a technique of CT scan where the scanner takes continuous images in a given area of coverage for a defined period with simultaneous injection of contrast media [11]. The perfusion technique gives information about the blood perfusing the tissue (brain) and the post-processing tools give information about the physiological parameters like relative cerebral blood flow (rCBF), cerebral blood volume (CBV), mean transit time (MTT), etc. These parameters give a fair idea about a decreased perfusion in cases of stroke when the regular CT brain is yet to show any changes in the parenchyma. The information that the radiologist obtains is the DICOM images of that area for which the CT perfusion was performed as the acquisition data and the time-signal intensity curve which yields the values of rCBF, rCBV, and MTT. Thus, the data obtained with this technique has a time dimension to it as well as yielding physiological information. So this data could also be analyzed as a signal rather than a DICOM or any other image format. However, for the ready interpretation, the scanners that are supplied with this technique are also equipped with post-processing software. This enables to mark an ROI and the values of rCBF, rCBV, and MTT are readily displayed.

Likewise, when the CT scan is exploited to image the intricate details of a particular organ either by altering the slice thickness or repeating the scan concerning time, the imaging procedure could be labeled as *CT colonoscopy*, *CT cystography*, etc.

3.5 MAGNETIC RESONANCE IMAGING (MRI)

Magnetic Resonance Imaging (MRI) is one of the versatile imaging modalities that has revolutionized radiology [12]. It utilizes the magnetic properties of the tissues and their resonance and hence there is no damage caused by ionizing radiations to the body. Originally called as Nuclear Magnetic Resonance in 1945 when it was found that the nucleus of atoms resonate in a magnetic field when a second oscillating magnetic field is applied. The hypothesis of the use of these properties was proposed by Raymond Damadian in 1969 and later published in 1971 by Paul Lauterbur and Peter Mansfield and all three developed various technical aspects of MR imaging. Damadians method developed the human scanner, Lauterbur created the projection reconstruction method, and Mansfield's method was called as line scanning and involved scanning of the pieces of the structure. Only the basics of the principle are discussed here to understand the concept; however, the interested readers are directed to the physics of MR imaging elsewhere in the literature. The multiplanarity of the images during the acquisition phase and the characterization of the tissue is the hallmark of MRI, which is quite a leap above that by the CT scan. The magnetic interaction of the RF pulse and the gradients in the MRI gives a set of various images and of course, all of them are also in a DICOM format.

TABLE 3.1

Effect of TR and TE on MR Image Contrast

Parameter	T1WI	PD	T2WI
TR	Low	Intermediate	High
TE	Low	Low	High

These images in conventional MR imaging are T1 weighted images (T1WI), T2 weighted images (T2WI), proton density (PD) images, gradient-echo (GRE) images, fluid-attenuated inversion recovery (FLAIR) images, and many others. With these as the base, many more advanced sequences have been developed having different names with different vendors. However, the basic T1WI, T2WI, FLAIR, PD have same names across the manufacturers. There are two basic technical parameters in the MR image acquisition that make T1/T2/PD weighted images – known as the time to repeat (TR) and time of echo (TE), and these times are measured in milliseconds (ms). Table 3.1 shows the effect of TR and TE on MR image contrast.

Figures 3.13(a) and 3.13(b) show that the fluid pockets inside the brain are hypointense on T1WI and hyperintense on T2WI, respectively, which means that they are fluid. Figure 3.13(c) is also T2WI showing a large tumor in the left hemisphere. This tumor is brighter than any of the brain parenchyma. That is why it is described as hyperintense to the brain parenchyma. But if you see that this tumor is less bright than the CSF pockets so it will be called hypointense to CSF.

The nature of the tissue character will dictate its appearance on T1 and T2 weighted images. The water or clear fluid looks dark on T1 and bright on T2WI, the fat or lipids appear brighter on T1 and variably bright on T2WI. The blood looks brighter on T1 and variably darker on T2WI, and that depends on the age and nature of the blood. So the terminology that is used in MR images is hypointense for dark, hyperintense for bright, and isointense if the area in question is the same as the

(a)   (b)   (c)

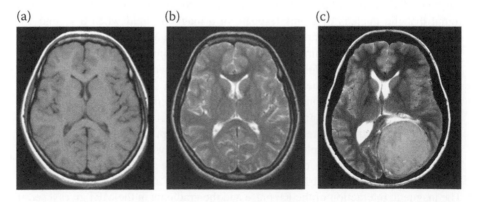

FIGURE 3.13 (a) T1, (b) T2 weighted image of the brain of a normal patient, and (c) T2 weighted axial image of a patient with intracranial tumor.

TABLE 3.2
Nature of the Tissue Character for MR Image of the Brain

	T1WI	T2WI	FLAIR
Cerebrospinal fluid (ventricle/ spaces)	Hypointense	Hyperintense	Hypointense
White matter	Hyperintense	Hypointense	Hypointense
Gray matter	Iso-Hyperintense	Iso-Hyperintense	Iso-Hyperintense
Fat of the scalp	Hyperintense	Iso-Hyperintense	Iso-Hyperintense
Patent blood vessel	Hypointense[*]	Hypointense[*]	Hypointense[*]

Note:
[*] is termed as flow voids for any blood vessel which has maintained flow.

reference structure. Thus, for the MR image of a brain, Table 3.2 can be kept as a reference for ease of understanding.

Therefore, whenever a radiologist comes across any structure or pathology, the basic appearances of water, fat, blood, etc. on these sequences are used to decipher about the organ in question for the normal structure or any pathology therein. The years of experience, permutation, and combination of appearances of an abnormality gives a radiologist an edge for a proper diagnosis.

Various applications are put to use with these basic concepts of MR image acquisition in mind. Certain changes are made to the basic sequences or certain new sequences are used to have these clinical applications. MR myelography uses heavily T2 weighted images to give a very bright signal to the CSF of the spine thus giving a picture like that of X-ray myelography. Similar such applications like magnetic resonance cholangio-pancreatico-graphy (MRCP) for the delineation of the hepatobiliary and pancreatic ducts and MR cystography are applied for the urinary bladder imaging. The fetal MRI is another special type of investigation which is performed whenever there is doubt regarding prenatal defect in the fetus.

3.5.1 CONTRAST-ENHANCED MRI

Contrast-enhanced MRI makes use of a contrast agent containing gadolinium chelates, which are injected intravenously while performing the T1WI [13]. This gadolinium-based contrast is given only to patients who have normal kidney function. The contrast makes certain structures look bright even if they were not bright in the first place in the precontrast T1WI. This change in appearance from not bright to a bright signal after administration of intravenous contrast is called post-contrast enhancement. Post-contrast enhancement of signal on T1WI signifies some sort of abnormality – in the brain, it is a sign of the breakdown of blood-brain barrier and neovascularization; in other areas of the body, it is a sign of abnormal vascularity of pathology in that particular tissue/organ. Sometimes the absence of normal tissue enhancement is also considered as a positive finding by the radiologist and is a sign of diminished normal vascularity, which is usually because of a block in the vessel supplying that organ.

This brings us to an MRI technique that gives us exclusive information about the blood vessel and is hence termed as *MR angiography* when evaluating an artery and *MR venography* when it shows the venous mapping [14,15]. As we know already that the MRI exploits the existing magnetic properties in the body and with the use of external RF pulse it excites the tissue and the relaxation properties of varying tissues, establishing the contrast between the adjacent structures. This concept holds true for stationary tissues. Although the same magnetic excitement does also happen for the blood vessel, because of the flow, the magnetized blood would have moved out of the slice of interest and hence they appear to be hypointense on all sequences. So it is termed as no signal or "signal void" as a normal finding for a blood vessel on conventional MRI sequences. MR angiogram is a technique that renders the blood vessels bright by a special technique of magnetic saturation of the background tissues [16].

Some of the techniques are *TOF (time of flight), MOTSA (Multiple overlapping thick slab acquisition), phase contrast, NATIVE, Inhance Inflow IR (IFIR), B-TRANCE (Balanced Triggered Angiography Non-contrast Enhanced).* All these techniques do not involve the use of contrast and hence can be performed even in patients with deranged renal functions. Depending upon the timing and the saturation bands that are used below the inflow with respect to artery or vein, one can get artery or vein as a mapped structure. A faster protocol is of a contrast-enhanced angiogram, which makes use of T1 relaxation properties and hence is faster than the non-contrast MR angiogram techniques. Recently used dynamic contrast MR angiogram gives a complete picture of inflowing contrast through the artery and its outflow through the draining vein. Thus, it gives all the phases similar to a digital subtraction angiogram and that too in a very short period. It is also named by certain suppliers as time-resolved imaging of contrast kinetics (TRICKS) [17].

3.5.2   MRI PERFUSION

MRI perfusion is another dynamic technique; however, it gives information about the flow properties inside the tissue with reference to inflow artery [18]. It is similar to that of CT perfusion described earlier in the section of CT scan. The images are multiple and have a time dimension added to the structural information. This information can then be displayed as a time-intensity graph similar to that described before. So if we perform an MR perfusion for the brain, then the parameters that we get are relative cerebral blood flow (rCBF), relative cerebral blood volume (rCBV), mean transit time (MTT). These parameters help to detect hypoperfusion in acute cases of stroke so that early treatment can be started and the damage due to stroke can be reduced. Extended application of MR perfusion is found in space-occupying lesions of tumors or infections, which helps differentiate between the two and between various grades of tumors also.

3.5.3   MR SPECTROSCOPY

MR spectroscopy (MRS) is also a technique that gives yield in the form of a signal [19]. Multiple metabolites are mapped in hydrogen spectroscopy. These metabolites have peaks at defined points in the axis also termed peaks at defined parts per million (ppm). The physics of acquisition of these images is not covered here and readers are suggested to refer dedicated literature on the same. The metabolites that the radiologists look for in MRS of the brain are choline, creatine, N-acetyl aspartate, lipid, lactate, and alanine of which the first three are the most common ones and the others are seen in different states of pathologies. Depending upon the peaks and their relative ratios, the radiologist interprets if it is a normal graph or an abnormal one. For a person in processing, the MRS is a signal and not a DICOM image.

3.5.4 DIFFUSION-WEIGHTED AND DIFFUSION TENSOR MRI

Diffusion-weighted imaging (DWI) and *Diffusion Tensor Imaging* (DTI) MR imaging technique [20,21] exploit the diffusion property of tissue while obtaining the image. The Brownian motion states that the molecular motion of diffusion is limitless if there is no constraint to the substance in question. However, the same diffusion gets limited if the substance is limited by the vessel in which the substance is kept. This concept is utilized in DW MRI. DWI yields two types of images – diffusion images and the ADC or apparent diffusion coefficient map. When a particular part appears bright on DWI and dark on ADC (ADC values are lowered) it is said to be having a restricted diffusion. The ADC map yields values which also help in obtaining objective information about the restricted diffusion.

Here, I would like to give an example of acute stroke. In acute stroke, a patient has neuro-deficit or paralysis to put it in a simplified manner. If this even is less than six hours, then the CT scan may not show any finding and could be essentially normal. In such a case, the MRI can show restricted diffusion, which is an early indicator of neuronal damage. However, this damage is still in its reversible stage and hence called ischemia and not an infarct. So if the CT scan is normal, the patient has come early on, the DWI shows restricted diffusion, and there is a defect on perfusion MRI (thus amounting to a diffusion perfusion mismatch), then such patient of stroke can benefit from the thrombolytic procedure (clot lysis) and with no permanent neuronal damage or paralysis. This DWI hardly takes 2–3 minutes as a sequence and a complete stroke imaging protocol in an acute setting including CT and MRI will take maximally 15–20 minutes if there is proper triaging. Likewise, there are lower ADC values in tumors also and the higher the grade of malignancy, the lower is the ADC value. This diffusion imaging is a faster imaging protocol because it gathers the diffusion information only in a few directions and hence there is no directional information (Figure 3.14).

Diffusion tensor imaging or DTI is an extended version of DWI. The diffusion information is gathered in multiple more directions because of which directional information of diffusion can be made available. Hence, it is also termed as a vector quantity. If one takes an example of a nerve to delineate diffusion by DTI, the diffusion will be less due to the cross-sectional restriction of its dimension. But the diffusion will keep on occurring along the length of the nerve, thus giving directional information about the nerve, yielding an image of a nerve – thus a neurography. Likewise, this can be done in the brain or spinal cord and giving the

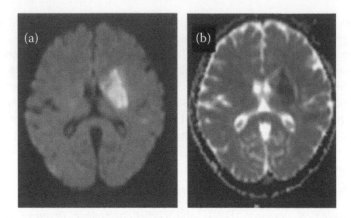

FIGURE 3.14 (a) DWI showing a bright signal on the left gangliocapsular region with the corresponding dark signal on an ADC map seen in (b). This is interpreted by a radiologist as restricted diffusion suggesting an acute stroke.

direction of the nerve fibers and hence called diffusion tensor fiber tracking. These fiber tracks are displayed as colored fibers. However, the images on which these fibers are tracked on a post-processing tool is called a fractional anisotropy map (FA Map) displayed in RGB color pattern. Each of the colors denotes the orientation of the fibers: Red – horizontal/right to left, Green – front-back/anteroposterior, and Blue – denotes the fibers that run vertically/from head to foot. This FA map enables radiologist to get an objective value of FA in a particular ROI. This also has a bearing either in the diagnosis per se of pathology or its severity grading for prognosis.

As discussed above, the diffusion is restricted along the cross-section of the nerve and is unrestricted along the length. Hence the diffusion value will be maximum along the length of the nerve and less along its cross-section. The diffusion along the length is the first eigenvector denoted as λ_1 and those two along the orthogonal cross-sections are second and third eigenvectors denoted as λ_2 and λ_3. Another information that one can get is either by manual or auto-calculation of mean diffusivity (MD), which incorporates all these three eigenvectors. Further details if required can be read in literature dedicated to diffusion tensor imaging. Although fiber tracking is mostly applied to the brain and spine, the other parameters of FA, MD, λ_1 λ_2 λ_3 can be calculated as a variable for other tissues like bone, muscles, etc.

3.5.5 CARDIAC MRI

Cardiac MRI is similar to cardiac CT in one aspect that it also uses cardiac gating during the image acquisition to get crisp clear images of that beating organ. It does not use any ionizing radiation. The initial technology of cardiac-gated MR images was only static T1/T2 WI. However, with newer advances that use the technique of K space segmentation [22], it is now possible to see the dynamic beating motions of the heart.

The basic images in cardiac MR imaging are:

i. *Black Blood images*: The blood in the cardiac chambers and the blood vessels appear dark whereas the walls appear grey. These images are used in the evaluation of the muscular tissue of the chambers, which could be for the congenital anomaly or to look for any infiltrative changes.

ii. *Bright Blood images*: True FISP/SSFP images render the blood as bright even without giving contrast to the patient. With the use of the K space segmentation technique, the beating heart can be seen objectively with reference to the ECG trace. The synchrony of the contraction and relaxation of the ventricular myocardium can be assessed. In a case of myocardial infarction, there could be a dyssynchronous contraction, incomplete emptying, thinning of the walls, etc. So the contraction is termed as mentioned below:

- Normokinesia: Normal ventricular contraction of all the walls of the ventricles.
- Hypokinesia: Slowing of the contracting movement of certain segments of the walls.
- Akinesia: No perceivable contraction of a particular myocardial segment.
- Dyskinesia: Usually during the contraction of the ventricular myocardium there is the inward movement of the walls of the myocardium. Instead of the inward movement during the contraction, if there is an outward movement of the myocardial segment during the contraction phase, then that segment is labeled as a dyskinetic segment.

One should understand certain terms here, such as systole – contraction and diastole – relaxation. The images through the complete cardiac or ECG cycle are loaded on a dedicated software available with the MRI scanners on an attached workstation. The system detects the images in diastole and systole and then allows for certain calculations from the clinical point of view. Thus, it enables the radiologist to calculate the ventricular function in the following parameters:

i. *End-diastolic volume* (EDV): The volume of the ventricular cavity at the end of the diastole (just before the start of the systole) expressed as milliliters.

ii. *End-systolic volume* (ESV): Ventricular cavity volume at the end of the systolic phase (just before the ventricle starts relaxing) expressed as milliliters.

iii. *Stroke volume* (SV): The volume of the blood that the ventricle ejects out and is essentially the difference of EDV and ESV and also expressed as milliliters.

$$SV = EDV - ESV \qquad\qquad (3.2)$$

iv. *Ejection fraction* (EF): The ratio of SV as toEDV and expressed as a percentage.

$$EF = \frac{SV}{EDV} \times 100 \qquad (3.3)$$

Various applications that can be dealt within the gamut of cardiac imaging by MRI are morphology and anatomy, cardiac function & flow, myocardial viability, myocardial tagging, myocardial perfusion with & without pharmacological stress, diffusion tensor imaging, MR spectroscopy, and BOLD imaging. There is a lot that can be discussed and talked about cardiac MRI concepts and potentials. The readers can search for them in the literature based on the applications mentioned. However, one should understand that the type of images that are derived are either static DICOM images or with an additional "time dimension" to them. There is a slight difficulty quotient attached with the cardiac MR images due to this time dimension. So if some post-processing has to be done to see a 3D reconstruction of a cine loop of bright blood images, it is four-dimensional information due to the time as the fourth dimension. Likewise, a lot of work has been done in terms of flow acquisition and its post-processing imparting objectivity to the information with direct clinical application for patient use. Hence, although one may get a lot to read about cardiac MR and its advanced protocols and post-processing tools available commercially as well as their alpha or beta versions of research, yet it lags behind its noncardiac applications for other organs.

3.6 DIGITAL SUBTRACTION ANGIOGRAPHY

Digital Subtraction Angiography (DSA) is an invasive radiology technique that breaches the normal continuity of the tissues and uses various other materials like catheters, tubes, wires, balloons, a stent for either diagnosis and or treatment of certain diseases entities [23]. It is an advanced version of fluoroscopy. In angiography, access to the vessel is established by a needle puncture and then tubes called sheath/catheters are advanced into the target vessels and then iodine-based dye called contrast is injected into the vessel to opacify the blood. This opacified blood is visualized on the DSA unit as a X-ray image. However, the system subtracts the first radiographic image from the subsequent images that result in visualization of only the vessels. The other tissues are digitally subtracted thus giving details of the angioarchitecture, that is, details of the vascular tree. These images are in the form of a cine run or a cine loop which is seen as if the bolus of contrast is running from the arterial through the capillary into the venous side. It can be visualized as a single frozen image to work on the post-processing. The post-processing can be done even on the cine loop. One of the advanced technology is to acquire a 3D rotational angiography which after acquisition gives a 3D view of the vascular tree thus making it very easy to navigate the catheter system. This unit can be used for diagnosis angiography but seems to have grossly decreased in the number of patients for this, because of the availability of noninvasive angiographic techniques by CT scan and MRI.

However, complex treatment procedures are being done under DSA. The vascular procedures done by an interventional radiologist are simulated like "plumbing the pipes". These procedures can be listed as:

i. Vessel opening procedures: Recanalization of blocked vessels; which is done to relieve the patient of the pain of tissue damage because of the blocked vessels.
   - Angioplasty
   - Stenting
   - Angioplasty with stenting
ii. Vessel closing procedures: Closing up of the leaking blood vessels, called embolization. The bleeding blood vessels could be in the form of enlarged vessels, abnormal vasculature like arteriovenous malformations or fistulae, aneurysms that could be life-threatening at times. Thus the embolization is a life-saving procedure in most such situations
iii. Vascular repair: Near normalization of the vascular flow; that is also called endovascular aneurysm repair.

Again, a lot can be said about these procedures which are beyond the scope of this chapter. We shall concentrate on the "Image" aspect at present. The images are of course in DICOM format but again there is a time dimension to it as mentioned above. The post-processing that can be done in DSA is from the simple measuring of the size of vascular abnormality, determining or predicting the path of the catheter. The algorithms could probably fuse the DSA images/loops with the images of CT scans or MRI. Certain cases of follow-up of pathologies could also benefit from CAD-like algorithms.

3.7   CONCLUSION

Overall, radiology has a lot of potential for using AI. It could be either the AI algorithm for images per se or one could combine various other factors about the patient, including either or all of the information. The information could contain general demographics of the patient like age, gender, socioeconomic status, blood reports, biopsy reports, previous surgeries if any, and more. For any AI algorithm to be effective as per the intended objective, it is mandatory to work as a team comprising members from different sectors. An AI for healthcare is best achieved with tandem well-coordinated teamwork between the healthcare providers and the developers.

REFERENCES

[1] Artz, D. S. "Computed radiography for the radiological technologist." *Seminars in Roentgenology* 32.1 (1997).
[2] Bansal, G. J. "Digital radiography. A comparison with modern conventional imaging." *Postgraduate Medical Journal* 82.969 (2006): 425–428.
[3] Cowen, A. R., Kengyelics, S. M., Davies, A. G. "Solid-state, flat-panel, digital radiography detectors and their physical imaging characteristics." *Clinical Radiology* 63.5 (2008): 487–498.

[4] Gold, R. H., Bassett, L. W., Widoff, B. E. "Highlights from the history of mammography." *Radiographics: A Review Publication of the Radiological Society of North America, Inc* 10.6 (1990): 1111–1131.

[5] Miller, P. D. "The history of bone densitometry." *Bone* 104 (2017): 4–6.

[6] Hallikainen, D. "History of panoramic radiography." *Acta Radiologica* 37.3 (1996): 441–445.

[7] Campbell, S. "A short history of sonography in obstetrics and gynaecology." *Facts, Views & Vision in ObGyn* 5.3 (2013): 213.

[8] Donati, F., et al. "Beyond Bernoulli: Improving the accuracy and precision of noninvasive estimation of peak pressure drops." *Circulation: Cardiovascular Imaging* 10.1 (2017): e005207.

[9] Lell, M. M., et al. "Evolution in computed tomography: The battle for speed and dose." *Investigative Radiology* 50.9 (2015): 629–644.

[10] Scalise, P., et al. "Computed tomography colonography for the practicing radiologist: A review of current recommendations on methodology and clinical indications." *World Journal of Radiology* 8.5 (2016): 472.

[11] Moraff, A., Jeremy, H., Max, W. "Stroke/Cerebral perfusion CT: Technique and clinical applications." Multislice CT. Springer, Cham, 2017: 133–143.

[12] Edelman, R. R. "The history of MR imaging as seen through the pages of radiology." *Radiology* 273.2S (2014): S181–S200.

[13] Lohrke, J., et al. "25 years of contrast-enhanced MRI: Developments, current challenges and future perspectives." *Advances in Therapy* 33.1 (2016): 1–28.

[14] Hartung, M. P., Grist, T. M., François, C. J. "Magnetic resonance angiography: Current status and future directions." *Journal of Cardiovascular Magnetic Resonance* 13.1 (2011): 1–11.

[15] Paoletti, M., et al. "Intra-and extracranial MR venography: technical notes, clinical application, and imaging development." *Behavioural Neurology* 2016 (2016).

[16] Cavallo, A. U., et al. "Noncontrast magnetic resonance angiography for the diagnosis of peripheral vascular disease." *Circulation: Cardiovascular Imaging* 12.5 (2019): e008844.

[17] Romano, A., et al. "The role of time-resolved imaging of contrast kinetics (TRICKS) magnetic resonance angiography (MRA) in the evaluation of head–neck vascular anomalies: A preliminary experience." *Dentomaxillofacial Radiology* 44.3 (2015): 20140302.

[18] Jahng, G.-H., et al. "Perfusion magnetic resonance imaging: A comprehensive update on principles and techniques." *Korean Journal of Radiology* 15.5 (2014): 554–577.

[19] Bradley, W. G. "MR spectroscopy of the brain for radiologists." *Biomedical Imaging and Intervention Journal* 3 (2007): 112–117.

[20] Lerner, A., et al. "Clinical applications of diffusion tensor imaging." *World Neurosurgery* 82.1–2 (2014): 96–109.

[21] Malayeri, A. A., et al. "Principles and applications of diffusion-weighted imaging in cancer detection, staging, and treatment follow-up." *Radiographics* 31.6 (2011): 1773–1791.

[22] Bluemke, D. A., et al. "Segmented K-space cine breath-hold cardiovascular MR imaging: Part 1. Principles and technique." *American Journal of Roentgenology* 169.2 (1997): 395–400.

[23] Crummy, A. B., Strother, C. M., Mistretta, C. A., "The history of digital subtraction angiography." *J Vasc Interv Radiol* 1 (2018): 1138–1141.

4 Fundamentals of Artificial Intelligence and Computational Intelligence Techniques with Their Applications in Healthcare Systems

Shubhi Sharma
University of Petroleum and Energy Studies, Uttrakhand, India

Siddharth Sharma
Indian Institute of Technology Roorkee, Uttrakhand, India

CONTENTS

DOI: 10.1201/9781003241409-4

4.1   INTRODUCTION

AI is a computer's ability to imitate or mimic human intelligence and falls under the branch of computer science. It is a multidisciplinary field that encompasses numerous professions and advanced methods of technology. AI contains a wide scope for areas involved in the process of decision-making. AI aids in the development of intelligent agents, which observe their surroundings and take specific actions to maximize their chances of success. It is more concerned in developing systems that illustrates some form of knowledge. The major goal of AI is to develop computer systems that can perform high-level intelligence tasks.

AI has its own importance as it has brought a great revolution in the field of computer science. This is the century's most important and recognizable development. Many of the world's leading countries realized the significance of AI since the year 1970. However, it started emerging as a separate field of study in the year 1940.

Healthcare is one of the important areas for the application of AI. Different types of healthcare data, i.e., structured and unstructured are available. Each data uses different machine learning algorithms, e.g., structured data use support vector machine (SVM) and neural network whereas unstructured data uses natural language processing. Different disease states in which AI tools are used are neurologic conditions, cardiac disorders, and cancer. By using appropriate algorithms AI can learn features from large healthcare dataset and can use it later to extract information that can assist clinical practitioners. Through AI system, we can reduce diagnosis errors, which can be missed by human clinical practitioners [1–7].

AI systems in healthcare applications are deployed by first training them through the clinical generated data, such as results of diagnosis, screening, etc. To make them learn the similarities among the data, features are then extracted by mapping the associations among the data. AI constitutes huge advantages in medical study [1,2,8].

Machine learning is a subfield of AI and has many applications in the field of healthcare. Figure 4.1 states different applications of AI. The reason behind the success of machine learning algorithms in healthcare is that they have the capability to attain great accuracy in diagnosing and processing patient information. This collaboration of machine learning and healthcare has advanced the medical treatment process. Figure 4.2 shows different fields of AI, such as machine learning, robotics, natural language processing, machine vision and automation.

This study provides an insight into the use of AI in healthcare. MEDLINE, National Library of Medicine created by the USA is an authorized database that contains biomedical and healthcare journals, citations, and abstracts. This database is in high demand among nurses, healthcare professionals, researchers, and clinicians. EBSCOhost is a great research platform used by healthcare companies and institutions for study of journals and researches done in the area of healthcare. The search on MEDLINE is also based on EBSCOhost. This platform uses the combination of two keywords for searching purposes. For example, to search for AI applications in healthcare the first keyword to be searched would be AI and then

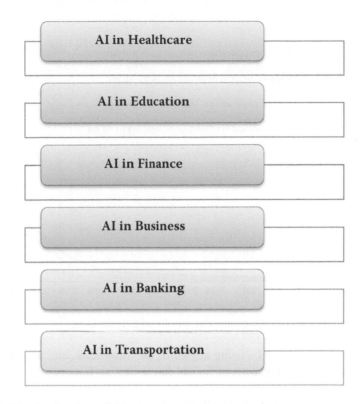

FIGURE 4.1 Applications of AI.

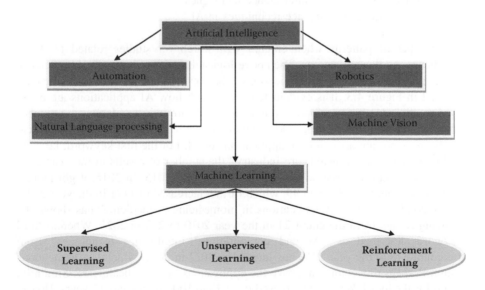

FIGURE 4.2 Different fields of AI.

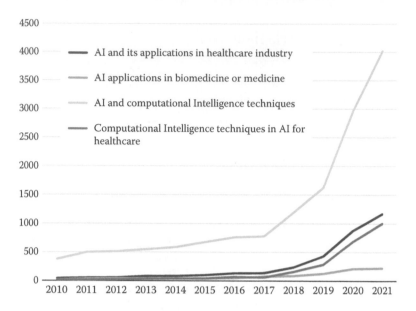

FIGURE 4.3   Year wise publication search results on Science Direct.

classification can be made by using keywords like healthcare, etc. Searching for a keyword is based on the pattern of logical linguistics, such as:

1. AI and its applications in healthcare industry
2. AI applications in biomedicine or medicine
3. AI and computational intelligence techniques
4. Computational intelligence techniques in AI

These types of patterns when entered will search for studies related to AI in healthcare and its applications. The above logical linguistics is searched on Science Direct platform for research publications. The obtained results from the search are showed in Figure 4.3. It is evident from the graph how AI applications are being used as clinical decision support systems in healthcare industry. Increasing number of publications in the past decade shows that healthcare industry and biomedical fields are important areas for the applications of AI. For the first keyword, i.e., "AI and its applications in healthcare industry" the number of results in the year 2010 were just 42 and it increased by 7 or 10 till the year 2015. In 2016, it got its first jump at the count of 133 from 99, which further increased to 1171 in the year 2021. The second keyword "AI applications in biomedicine or medicine" has shown the growing results from the count 21 in the year 2010 to 223 in 2021. Whereas third keyword described as "AI and computational intelligence techniques" from the count 378 in the year 2010 has jumped to 4022 in 2021, which is a tremendous count. Perhaps this count can prove the applications of AI in healthcare. Similarly, count for the fourth keyword increased from 19 to 1004 in the past 12 years. Hence, this study states that using a combination of keywords can be very helpful.

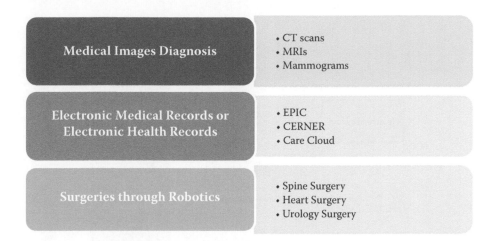

FIGURE 4.4 Machine learning in healthcare.

Similarly, using such combinations of patterns we can also find out the computational intelligence techniques used in biomedicines. For more computational technique-specific results we can type "artificial neural network in healthcare" or "fuzzy systems in healthcare" or "genetic algorithm and neural networks and fuzzy logics in healthcare". Hence, it's clear that using such logical linguistic pattern for search purpose will result in applicability and popularity of the combinations of methodologies [9,10]. Figure 4.4 shows the areas where machine learning is implemented in the healthcare sector.

4.2 HEALTHCARE DATA

Huge amount of patient health information is generated in the healthcare sector. To process this big data is a challenging task for humans. Therefore, AI provides several algorithms to recognize the similarity or patterns from this large dataset and to predict the result outcomes of patients. AI algorithms in healthcare help medical practitioners in diagnosing diseases, which is further helpful in identifying the best treatment for patients. Nowadays, different types of data are available in healthcare, which also includes sensor data, clinical data, omics data, etc. as shown in Figure 4.5. These data require different types of feature extraction techniques for further processing. Depending on the type of data different algorithms are available to extract relevant features. Also, different algorithms are used to train the AI system for future prediction. Let's discuss these different types of healthcare data [11].

4.2.1 CLINICAL DATA

Clinical data is gathered for research purposes in the biomedical field during patient treatment. It has wide applications in healthcare sector. For the collection of this data, the purpose and goal must be understood. It should be able to make the objective clear, i.e., for what purpose it is being collected. It includes Electronic Medical Record (EMR) that contains laboratory tests, radiology images, etc.,

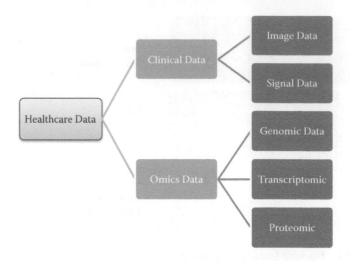

FIGURE 4.5   Types of healthcare data.

patient name, age etc. The Food and Drug Administration (FDA) states that there should be a proper data structure. The one specific data structure is Clinical Data Interchange Standards Consortium (CDISC) datasets. Clinical data manager captures the data and cleans it. He is responsible for the communication between statisticians and the programmers to make sure if the data collected is appropriate and unbiased. Clinical data has two forms; one is image and another is signal.

4.2.1.1   Image Data

This type of data is captured as MRI images, X-rays, mammography, etc. during the treatment. Large amount of data is available for public use as an open source data, such as The Cancer Imaging Archive (TCIA), GrepMed, Alzheimer's Disease Neuroimaging Initiative (ADNI), CI Machine Learning Repository, Mammographic Image Analysis Society (mini-MIAS) database, Kaggle, etc. Figure 4.6 shows images from different datsets. Some of the works done on clinical data are: the multilevel perception model defined by Dagli et al. [12] through which they predicted the survival rate of patients having non-small lung cancer for two years. Here, they collected samples of 559 patients and ranked the attributes using the RelifF feature selection method. They concluded that multi-layer neural network worked better in prediction model by showing promising results of area under curve of 0.75. Another work done was defined by Kayal et al. [13] where they proposed a new approach to classify the survival prediction rate of patients suffering from hepatocellular carcinoma (HCC). They collected 165 patient samples, where out of total 49 risk factors only 15 risk factors were identified as responsible factors for HCC. They have shown that accuracy achieved with deep neural network is much higher than supervised and unsupervised models. This type of data is available easily but not bounded to different forms like demographics, medical notes, and electronic recordings captured from physical examinations or by using medical devices [14].

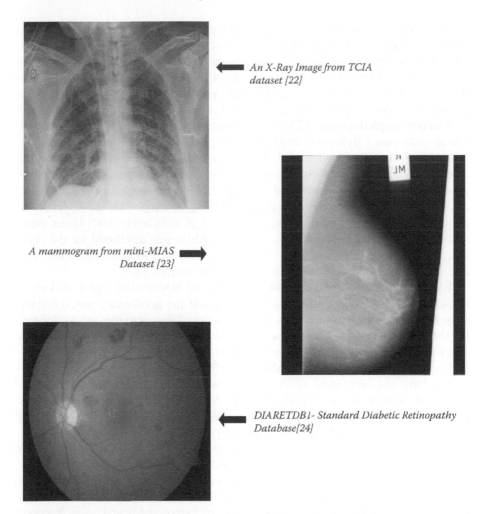

An X-Ray Image from TCIA dataset [22]

A mammogram from mini-MIAS Dataset [23]

DIARETDB1- Standard Diabetic Retinopathy Database[24]

FIGURE 4.6 Image data examples: (a) X-ray image from TCIA; (b) mammogram from mini-MIAS; (c) DLARETDB1-standard diabetic retinopathy.

4.2.1.2 Signal Data

Sensor data consists of data elements that are generated by sensors, such as signals generated by time series, explained as pair of sequence in ordered manner. Computing devices process these data elements and can be simple/complex value or more complex data. Following are the three important and different types of signals:

Electrocardiogram (ECG): An ECG is a test that is used to observe the heart rate at rest. This helps in identifying the risk of heart diseases. An AI-based ECG was developed to detect the presence of atrial fibrillation during the normal sinus rhythm. This was based on convolution neural network (CNN) and used 10-second and 12-lead ECGs as standard [15]. As we know that AI plays very important role when it comes to healthcare, therefore by applying deep learning-based algorithms on huge datasets, these models are enough to identify the heart rhythms as normal or abnormal [16]. Another work has shown great results by using an algorithm, where the issue of reducing computational burden was addressed succesfully. This work was completely based on a compression technique of linear approximation distance thresholding along with neural network (back propagation method). They made use of MIT-BIH database and found that this algorithm works faster with convergence and has promising accuracy in recognizing the features [17].

Electroencephalograph (EEG): The structure of human brain is complex and has non-stationary dynamics. EEG is a straight fit of cortical activity with the temporal resolution of millisecond. It's an electrical potentials record formed by cerebral cortex nerve cells. Scalp and intracranial are two types of EEG; this depends on signal captured in the head [18]. EEG has great contribution in the field of AI, such as an algorithm based on deep learning is developed for the detection of epileptiform EEG discharges automatically [19]. A completely ANN-based automatic system for analysis and classification of EEGs was developed for the classification of single epochs of trace on expert system. This work identified the time and space correlation between the neural network outputs [20].

Electromyogram (EMG): Another variation of bioelectrical signal is electromyography, i.e., developed in muscles throughout the involuntary and voluntary muscle activities, such as relaxation and contraction. These activities are disciplined by the nervous system. These type of signals are complicated in nature due to functional properties and riotous environment. To classify EMG signals for controlling multifunction prosthesis, ANNs are efficiently being used [21–24].

We have just seen some of the specific works based on the type of signals. Following are the works accomplished by authors on signal data. By using data streams collected from wearable sensors an algorithm was proposed by Luca et al. [25], which is able to detect Parkinson's disease (PD). They conducted experiments on 20 people and recorded the movement of each individual by using six sensors. There were total 13 tasks performed by each and every one in such a way where one experiment was conducted one day and then repeated two weeks later. This is how 41,802 data clips were taken to use. For training purpose convolution neural networks was used whereas random forest classifier was used to determine the tremor and bradykinesia. Random forest classifier has shown better results for detection of bradykinesia with 0.73 value of AUROC (area under the ROC curve) and 0.79 value for tremor.

To detect the risk caused by developmental arrays and typical development in infants David et al. [26] defined the classification of algorithms. By fixing Opal sensors on the infant's ankle, long-day inertial movement was recorded and the data was divided into two sets; one is from 0 to 6 months and other is from 6 to 12 months. Therefore, 19 movement features were extracted using some univariate feature selection methods. Three machine learning algorithms were used to obtain support vector and then classification was performed. This work was shown to have an accuracy of 90.

4.2.2 OMICS DATA

Collection of large amount of high and complex dimensional data, which consists of genomic, proteomics and transcriptomic data is called omics data. To handle this type of data various machine learning algorithms are used.

4.2.2.1 Genomic Data

Genome and DNA (deoxyribonucleic acid) data of an organism is genomic data. This is used in the field of bioinformatics. It is used for collecting, storing, and processing the genomes of living organisms. It requires huge amount of storage space and software to analyze.

4.2.2.2 Transcriptomic Data

Transcriptomic data is the data found in biological samples and is extracted from several mRNA transcripts. To create dataset these samples are analyzed. This technique of obtaining this data is called as transcriptomics.

4.2.2.3 Proteomic Data

This is a set of proteins presented as cells, tissues, or organisms. It is a representation of the cell's actual functional molecules.

4.3 DISEASES TARGETED BY AI

As we know, abundant literature is available related to the use of AI in healthcare and researches are focused on mainly few types of diseases, e.g., diseases related to nervous system, cancer, and heart disease. Implementing AI for cancer diagnosis requires unique and complex decision-making. It's not only about dealing with the type of disease but patient condition to get the treatment and how the patient is responding to the treatment is also important. Though the technology is improved but achieving accuracy in detecting, characterizing, and monitoring is still a challenge [27,28]. Enormous amount of work is done in the field of cancer; a few of them are: to identify skin cancer Esteva et al. [29] inspected the clinical images. For oncology, IBM Watson was determined as a reliable AI-based system for cancer diagnosis [30]. For heart disease the AI system application was discussed by Bouton et al. [31] where they used quadriplegia to restore the movement control. Man and machine interface power was tested by Farina et al. [32], which is based on the discharge timings of spinal motor neurons to control the upper-limb prostheses. In the field of cardiology, the US FDA provided clearance for marketing Cardio DL application [33]. Through cardiac images Siegel et al. [34] presented the capabilities of AI in the field of heart disease. All of these diseases are the reason behind the increasing mortality; therefore, it is very important to diagnose them at early stages. This early diagnosis is only possible to be achieved by using accurate analytical methods on medical images, EMR or EHR, which is the pillar of a successful AI system.

4.4 COMPUTATIONAL INTELLIGENCE TECHNIQUES AND THEIR APPLICATIONS

As we already know that size of healthcare data is very large. To analyze data with such huge dimensions and complexity is a challenging and nearly impossible task for humans. Therefore, a high-end intelligent data analysis technique is required,

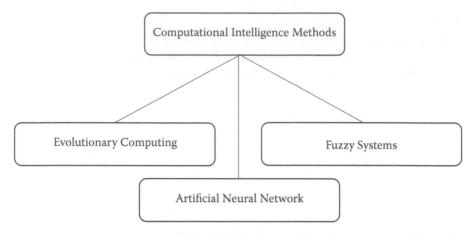

FIGURE 4.7 Computational intelligence methods.

which can extract useful information from data. However, the data analysis process faces some challenges due to following reasons [34]:

- If the data is of different types or heterogeneous data
- If the data size is too large (in terabytes or so)
- If the data is non-stationary

To address such issues, computational intelligence techniques are required to address such complexity and mismatch of data. Computational intelligence defines a community of computational systems that consists of learning, adaption, and heuristic optimization. These models are used to solve problems that are impossible to solve by using traditional computational algorithms. Figure 4.7 shows the three main strengths of computational intelligence; neural networks, evolutionary computation, and fuzzy systems. Let's discuss these computational intelligence techniques in the following sections.

4.4.1 ARTIFICIAL NEURAL NETWORK

Nowadays, ANN is considered as a potential tool for analyzing logs and predicting the properties of reservoir. Back propagation neural networks are more popular. An ANN is an important part of computational intelligence systems that simulates the way of analyzing and processing the information in a way as human brain does. It solves the problems that are impossible to solve by statistical standards. ANN structure is very similar to the structure of human brain where neuron nodes are interconnected in a web-like structure. It contains abundant cells called as neurons where each and every neuron is made up of a cell body, which is responsible for carrying information as an input and output from the brain to process it [34]. Figure 4.8 explains how step by step ANN is implemented in healthcare applications.

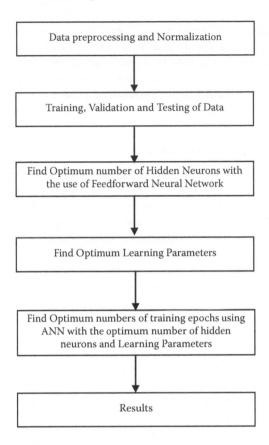

FIGURE 4.8   Flowchart for ANN methodology in healthcare.

The very first step is the collection of data and its preprocessing. Using noisy and unprocessed data can be an intensive task to perform that can affect the performance of the system. Therefore, preprocessing of data is a crucial step for any system. After preprocessing dataset is divided into training and testing sets into some predefined standard ratio. To avoid overfitting of data to adjust the classification parameter validation dataset is used in addition. Then for the given ANN model find out the optimum number of hidden neurons with the use of feedforward neural network. After this, optimal learning parameters are identified. Finally, using ANN optimum numbers of training epochs and hidden neurons and learning parameters are identified, which then determine the result of the system.

It is proved that the use of AI in medicine and biological research has great potential and trained ANN models to check the small biological neural cluster functionality. ANNs are now widely accepted in medical applications across a wide range of fields, particularly in cardiology. In diagnostics, electronic signal analysis, analysis of medical images, and radiography, ANNs have been widely used. Many authors have used ANNs for modelling in medical and clinical research. ANNs are progressively being used in pharmacoepidemiology and extraction of medical data [34].

Cancer was diagnosed using neural networks by Khan et al. where the tumor category outcomes are based on prinicpal components estimated from 6567 genes [35]. For breast cancer prediction, neural network is used where inputs are the textural features of mammographic images [36]. Also to diagnose Parkinson's disease where inputs are motor and non-motor symptoms and neuroimages, a neural network-based model was used by Hirchauer et al. [37].

4.4.2 EVOLUTIONARY COMPUTATION

Evolutionary computation is a branch of AI and machine learning and is an important part of computational intelligence. Evolutionary computation has several applications such as robot designing, training of neural networks, solving optimization problems, and tuning hyper parameters, etc. Search and optimization issues are solved using evolutionary algorithms through evolutionary computation.

In environmental and earth applications, for the purpose of optimization, scheduling, and time series approximation evolutionary computation has been used. Random choice is used by evolutionary algorithms to lead a high-end search towards the portions of search space that should be likely to improve. Here, chromosome represents an individual, who is made up of genes, and having a single point in the solution search space, e.g., land use pattern here is a single point in a land use optimization problem's search space where a land use pattern is a chromosome. Genes are essentially the problem parameters to be solved. Depending on how the problem is defined, a gene can take many different forms. A gene can be a land parcel with a specific land use and land qualities for the land use allocation problem. An objective or fitness function is used to assess a chromosome's fitness (survival strength). A fitness function is a metric for maximizing profit, usefulness, or goodness. A population is made up of all of the chromosomes that are being developed. Less fit chromosomes are replaced with newly generated chromosomes and then reinserted into the population, where only the fittest survived until the following generation takes place. The process of evolution takes place here, where the fitness of competing chromosomes is compared to pick the parent chromosomes for reproduction purpose [38].

Several types of evolutionary algorithms are available but the best known are genetic programming, genetic algorithms, evolutionary programming, evolutionary strategies, etc. All of these are based on same general principles but different in species [39].

Genetic algorithm: This algorithm was proposed in the year 1960 by John Holland [40,41]. It is the most well-known type of evolutionary algorithm. These algorithms were so widely used that the terms "genetic algorithms" and "evolutionary computation" are frequently interchanged (though, as noted, they should be considered distinct).

Genetic programming: This programming is a best version of genetic algorithms, which was created by John Koza [42,43]. Instead of providing encoded viable solutions as a fixed-length character string to a problem computer programmes are used in this technique. To put it another way, the people in the population are programmes that, when run, represent potential solutions (phenotypes) to the problem.

Evolution strategies: Ingo Rechenberg [44,45] and Hans Paul Schweffel [46,47] presented evolution methods as a way for tackling parameter-optimization problems in the 1960s.

Evolutionary programming: Fogel [48,49] defined evolutionary programming as a method for developing AI-based systems. He claimed that an intelligent conduct necessitates the capability to predict changes in the environment as well as the ability to translate such predictions into appropriate behaviors for achieving a goal. The environment can be characterized as a succession of characters drawn from a finite alphabet in its most basic form. With this expertise, the evolving creature is expected to create a symbol for output which is somehow related to the next symbol going to appear in the environment, based on its knowledge of the environment. The reward function, which quantifies the prediction rate accuracy, should be maximized by the output symbol. In evolutionary programming, finite state machines were chosen to represent individuals because based on symbol interpretation they prepare a purposeful representation of behavior.

In medicine, evolutionary computation is used to execute a variety of tasks. Whenever a decision is necessary in medicine, evolutionary approaches may typically be found in a niche. In the field of medicine, evolutionary algorithms execute three types of tasks: (I) data mining, mostly for diagnosis and prediction, (II) signal processing and medical imaging, and (III) scheduling and planning.

4.4.3 FUZZY SYSTEMS

This system is a collection of algebraic or differential equation having fuzzy numbers as parameters representing the vagueness in parameter values and rules implemented with fuzzy predicates. These systems comprise fuzzy inputs and fuzzy outputs. Figure 4.9 shows the general block diagram for fuzzy-based systems in healthcare. To deal with

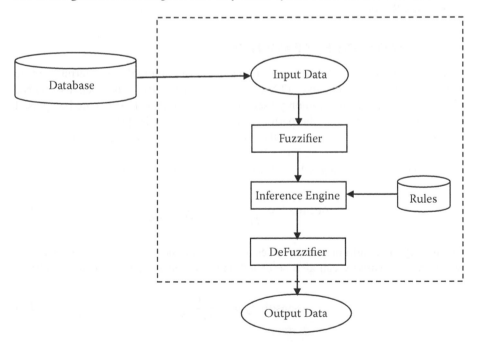

FIGURE 4.9 Flowchart for fuzzy-based systems in healthcare.

non-statistic unpredictability in applications, such as classification/clustering, function approximation, and prediction, fuzzy systems are frequently used. Fuzzy logic helps in getting logical and better assessments for values that are close to classification boundaries. For some challenges like interpretation of sets of medical results, it provides an appropriate and flexible base for developing knowledge-based systems in healthcare, in eastern medicine, differentiation of syndromes, in western medicine disease diagnosis, and mixed diagnosis for the western and eastern medicine combination. The best choice made was by combining the western and eastern medicine along with monitoring the patient data in real time [34,50].

4.5 NO-CODE AI TOOLS

To create AI-based models one must have adequate knowledge of coding, and should be a programmer or data scientist by profession. For researchers who are from non-computer background deployment of these machine learning-based models is quite difficult and challenging. But tech giants have made it easy by providing such development tools freely to ensure the promising results without the knowledge of coding or deep learning. Such tools have revolutionized the organizations. Following are some of the No-Code AI tools available online [51,52]:

- Create ML by Apple
- Teachable Machine
- Accelerate Share Insights by Amazon Web Services
- Google AI Platform
- Data Robot

4.6 PERFORMANCE PARAMETERS

When AI is used in healthcare applications the most commonly used terms are true positive (TP); true negative (TN); false positive (FP); false negative (FN). Following are the most commonly used performance parameters that are being used by researchers to evaluate the performance of the AI model [7]:

Accuracy: Accuracy is one of the most common performance parameters used. It is calculated as the ratio of correctly classified predictions to the total number of predictions. Its value ranges from 0 to 1 and calculated as Equation (4.1),

$$\text{Accuracy} = \frac{TP + TN}{TP + FN + TN + FP} \tag{4.1}$$

Sensitivity: The ratio of true positives to total actual positives in the data describes sensitivity. Sensitivity can also be called as recall, calculated as Equation (4.2),

$$\text{Sensitivity} = \frac{TP}{TP + FN} \tag{4.2}$$

Specificity: The ratio of true negatives is to total negatives in the data defines specificity. This will be calculated as Equation (4.3),

$$\text{Specificity} = \frac{TN}{TN + FP} \tag{4.3}$$

Precision: Precision can be calculated as the ratio of true positives versus total predicted positives. Precision will be calculated by Equation (4.4),

$$\text{Precision} = \frac{TP}{TP + FP} \tag{4.4}$$

F1 score: The F1-Score or F-Score or F-Measure is defined as Equation (4.5),

$$F1 = 2 * ((\text{precision} * \text{recall})/(\text{precision} + \text{recall})) \tag{4.5}$$

Basically, F-Score tries to convey the balance between precision and recall.

Area under curve: AUC can be defined between two points by finding the definite integral between these two points. For example to find the area under the curve y= f(x). The formula for AUC is given in Equation (4.6),

$$\text{AUC} = \int_a^b f(x) . \, d(x) \tag{4.6}$$

Where value of x lies between a and b.

As we have seen that different types of data are available in healthcare. To analyze this enormous amount of data different machine learning algorithms are used, such as supervised, unsupervised, and reinforced algorithms. Performance parameters like sensitivity, specificity, accuracy, AUC, etc. are used to evaluate the prediction rate of the system. In this study we have seen how different algorithms work for different types of healthcare data [7].

4.7 CHALLENGES

As technology always has scope for improvement. Similarly at present AI-based applications have lots of challenges and hence a scope of improvising the present techniques. One of the challenges presented in this study is that real-time implementation is facing some hurdles and this is due to lack of standards of regulations. The US FDA has taken an initiative to overcome this issue and has provided guidance for using such AI systems. Another challenge is exchanging of data, i.e., to make AI systems works smoothly and with remarkable accuracy they need to be trained (on regular basis) from clinical studies. However, if an AI system is installed once then continuous supply of data for further advancements of system is difficult. To resolve this issue a healthcare revolution is working on the same to encourage data sharing. So we will try to provide solutions and some more studies on these hurdles. Also we will look for some more advancements in using computational intelligence techniques to uprise the healthcare industry [53–55].

4.8 CONCLUSION

This study gives the overview of AI fundamentals along with the brief description about its history. Different types of healthcare data are presented in this chapter, such as clinical data, signal data, etc. The characteristics of AI revealed that different datasets require different algorithms to provide best results. A review of computational intelligence techniques like ANN, evolutionary computation, and fuzzy sets with their applications is also described. How AI developed successful models in healthcare by working on different datasets and different algorithms has also been discussed. Results of AI-based models are generated by using performance parameters, such as accuracy, sensitivity, AUC, etc. As of now it has been observed that AI is creating boom in healthcare sector; however, there is always a scope for improvement.

REFERENCES

[1] Dilsizian S. E., Siegel E. L. Artificial intelligence in medicine and cardiac imaging: Harnessing big data and advanced computing to provide personalized medical diagnosis and treatment. *Curr Cardiol Rep* 16 (2014): 441

[2] Patel V. L., Shortliffe E. H., Stefanelli M., et al. The coming of age of artificial intelligence in medicine. *Artif Intell Med* 46 (2009): 5–17.

[3] Pearson T. How to replicate Watson hardware and systems design for your own use in your basement. 2011. https://www.ibm.com/developerworks/community/blogs/InsideSystemStorage/entry/ibm_watson_how_to_build_your_own_watson_jr_in_your_basement7?lang=en (accessed 1 Jun 2017).

[4] Weingart S. N., Wilson R. M., Gibberd R. W., et al. Epidemiology of medical error. *BMJ* 320 (2000): 774–777.

[5] Graber M. L., Franklin N., Gordon R. Diagnostic error in internal medicine. *Arch Intern Med* 165 (2005): 1493–1499.

[6] Winters B., Custer J., Galvagno S. M., et al. Diagnostic errors in the intensive care unit: A systematic review of autopsy studies. *BMJ Qual Saf* 21 (2012): 894–902.

[7] Lee C. S., Nagy P. G., Weaver S. J., et al. Cognitive and system factors contributing to diagnostic errors in radiology. *AJR Am J Roentgenol* 201 (2013): 611–617.

[8] Jha S., Topol E. J. Adapting to Artificial Intelligence: Radiologists and pathologists as information specialists. *JAMA* 316 (2016): 2353–2354.

[9] Devi M., et al. A survey of soft computing approaches in biomedical imaging. *J Healthc Eng* 2021 (2021).

[10] Yardimci A. Soft computing in medicine. *Appl Soft Comput* 9.3 (2009): 1029–1043.

[11] Dhillon A., Singh A. Machine learning in healthcare data analysis: A survey. *J Biol Today's World* 8.6 (2019): 1–10.

[12] Dagli Y., Choksi S., Sudipta R. Prediction of two year survival among patients of non small cell lung cancer. Computer Aided Intervention and Diagnostics in Clinical and Medical Images. Springer, Cham (2019): 169–177.

[13] Kayal C. K., Bagchi S., Dhar D., Maitra T., Chatterjee S. Hepatocellular carcinoma survival prediction using deep neural network. Proceedings of International Ethical Hacking Conference. 2019: 349–358.

[14] Administration UFaD. Guidance for industry: Electronic source data in clinical investigations. 2013. https://www.fda.gov/downloads/drugs/guidances/ucm328691. pdf (accessed 1 Jun 2017).

[15] Attia Z. I., et al. An artificial intelligence-enabled ECG algorithm for the identification of patients with atrial fibrillation during sinus rhythm: A retrospective analysis of outcome prediction. *Lancet* 394.10201 (2019): 861–867.

[16] Mincholé A., Rodriguez B. Artificial intelligence for the electrocardiogram. *Nat Med* 25 (2019): 22–23. 10.1038/s41591-018-0306-1.

[17] Gang L., Wenyu Y., Ling L., Qilian Y., Xuemin Y. An artificial-intelligence approach to ECG analysis. *IEEE Eng Med Biol Mag* 19.2 (March–April 2000): 95–100. 10.1109/51.827412.

[18] Subasi A., Ercelebi E. Classification of EEG signals using neural network and logistic regression. *Comput Methods Programs Biomed* 78.2 (2005): 87–99.

[19] Fürbass F., et al. An artificial intelligence-based EEG algorithm for detection of epileptiform EEG discharges: Validation against the diagnostic gold standard. *Clin Neurophysiol* 131.6 (2020): 1174–1179.

[20] Castellaro, C., et al. An artificial intelligence approach to classify and analyse EEG traces. *Clin Neurophysiol* 32.3 (2002): 193–214.

[21] Wojtczak P., et al. Hand movement recognition based on biosignal analysis. *Eng Appl Artif Intell* 22.4–5 (2009): 608–615.

[22] Clark K., Vendt B., Smith K., Freymann J., Kirby J., Koppel P., Moore S., Phillips S., Maffitt D., Pringle M., Tarbox L., Prior F. The Cancer Imaging Archive (TCIA): Maintaining and operating a public information repository. *J Digit Imaging* 26.6 (2013 Dec): 1045–1057. 10.1007/s10278-013-9622-7.

[23] Suckling J., et al. The mammographic image analysis society digital mammogram database. *Int Congr* 1069 (1994): 375–378.

[24] Kauppi T., Kalesnykiene V., Kamarainen J.-K., Lensu L., Sorri I., Raninen A., Voutilainen R., Uusitalo H., Kälviäinen H., Pietilä J. DIARETDB1 diabetic retinopathy database and evaluation protocol. *Medical Image Understanding and Analysis* 2007 (2007): 61–71.

[25] Lonini L., et al. Wearable sensors for Parkinson's disease: Which data are worth collecting for training symptom detection models. *NPJ Digit Med* 1.1 (2018): 1–8.

[26] Goodfellow D., et al. Predicting infant motor development status using day long movement data from wearable sensors. *arXiv preprint arXiv:1807.02617* (2018).

[27] Zacharaki E. I., et al. Classification of brain tumor type and grade using MRI texture and shape in a machine learning scheme. *Magn Reson Med* 62.6 (2009): 1609–1618.

[28] Bi W. L., et al. Artificial intelligence in cancer imaging: Clinical challenges and applications. *CA Cancer J Clin* 69.2 (2019): 127–157.

[29] Esteva A., Kuprel B., Novoa R. A., et al. Dermatologist-level classification of skin cancer with deep neural networks. *Nature* 542 (2017): 115–118.

[30] Somashekhar S. P., Kumarc R., Rauthan A., et al. Abstract S6-07: Double blinded validation study to assess performance of IBM artificial intelligence platform. *Cancer Res* 77.4 Suppl (2017): S6–S7.

[31] Bouton C. E., Shaikhouni A., Annetta N. V., et al. Restoring cortical control of functional movement in a human with quadriplegia. *Nature* 533 (2016): 247–250.

[32] Farina D., Vujaklija I., Sartori M., et al. Man/machine interface based on the discharge timings of spinal motor neurons after targeted muscle reinnervation. *Nat Biomed Eng* 1 (2017): 0025.

[33] Marr B. First FDA approval for clinical cloud-based deep learning in healthcare. 2017. https://www.forbes.com/sites/bernardmarr/2017/01/20/first-fda-approval-for-clinical-cloud-based-deep-learning-inhealthcare/#7a0ed8dc161c (accessed 1 Jun 2017).

[34] Zhu X. Computational intelligence techniques and applications. Computational

Intelligence Techniques in Earth and Environmental Sciences. Springer, Dordrecht (2014): 3–26.

[35] Khan J., Wei J. S., Ringnér M., et al. Classification and diagnostic prediction of cancers using gene expression profiling and artificial neural networks. *Nat Med* 7 (2001): 673–679.

[36] Dheeba J., Albert Singh N., Tamil Selvi S. Computer-aided detection of breast Cancer on mammograms: A swarm intelligence optimized wavelet neural network approach. *J Biomed Inform* 49 (2014): 45–52.

[37] Hirschauer T. J., Adeli H., Buford J. A. Computer-aided diagnosis of Parkinson's disease using enhanced probabilistic neural network. *J Med Syst* 39 (2015): 179.

[38] Zhang B., et al. Evolutionary computation and its applications in neural and fuzzy systems. *Appl Comput Intell Soft Comput* 2011 (2011).

[39] Pena-Reyes C. A., Sipper M. Evolutionary computation in medicine: An overview. *Artif Intell Med* 19.1 (2000): 1–23.

[40] Holland J. H. Outline for a logical theory of adaptive systems. *JACM* 9.3 (1962): 297–314.

[41] Goldberg D. E., Holland J. H. Genetic algorithms and machine learning, Kluwer Academic Publishers, (1988).

[42] Koza J. R. Genetic programming: A paradigm for genetically breeding populations of computer programs to solve problems. Vol. 34. Stanford University, Department of Computer Science, Stanford, CA (1990).

[43] Koza J. R. Genetic programming: On the programming of computers by means of natural selection. Vol. 1. MIT Press (1992).

[44] Rechenberg I. Cybernetic solution path of an experimental problem. *Royal Aircraft Establishment Library Translation* 1122 (1965).

[45] Vent W. Rechenberg, Ingo, Evolutionsstrategie—OptimierungtechnischerSystemenach-Prinzipien der biologischen Evolution. 170 S. mit 36 Abb. Frommann-Holzboog-Verlag. Stuttgart 1973. Broschiert 62 (1975): 337–337.

[46] Schwefel H.-P. Kybernetische Evolution alsStrategie der experimentellenForschung in der Stromungstechnik. *Diploma thesis, Technical University of Berlin* (1965).

[47] Beyer H.-G., Schwefel H.-P. Evolution strategies–a comprehensive introduction. *Nat Comput* 1.1 (2002): 3–52.

[48] Fogel L. J. Autonomous automata. *Ind Res* 4 (1962): 14–19.

[49] Fogel L. J., Owens A. J. MJ Walsh artificial intelligence through simulated evolution. Wiley-IEEE Press (1962).

[50] Phuong N. H., Kreinovich V. Fuzzy logic and its applications in medicine.*Int J Med Informat* 62.2–3 (2001): 165–173.

[51] Thakkar M. Custom core ml models using create ml. Beginning Machine Learning in iOS. Apress, Berkeley, CA (2019): 95–138.

[52] Carney M., et al. Teachable machine: Approachable Web-based tool for exploring machine learning classification. *Extended abstracts of the 2020 CHI conference on human factors in computing systems.* (2020):1–8, https://doi.org/10.1145/3334480.3382839.

[53] Kayyali B., Knott D., Kuiken S. V. The big-data revolution in US health care: accelerating value and innovation. 2013. http://www.mckinsey.com/industries/healthcare-systems-and-services/our-insights/thebig-data-revolution-in-us-health-care (accessed 1 Jun 2017).

[54] Graham J. Artificial intelligence, machine learning, and the FDA. 2016. https://www.forbes.com/sites/theapothecary/2016/08/19/artificial-intelligence-machine-learning-and-the-fda/#4aca26121aa1. (accessed 1 Jun 2017).

[55] Alkan A., Günay M. Identification of EMG signals using discriminant analysis and SVM classifier. *Expert Syst Appl* 39.1 (2012): 44–47.

5 Machine Learning Approach with Data Normalization Technique for Early Stage Detection of Hypothyroidism

Madhusudan G. Lanjewar and Jivan S. Parab
Goa University, Goa, India

Ajesh K. Parate
S. K. Porwal College, Kamptee, India

CONTENTS

5.1   INTRODUCTION

The thyroid is a little gland in the neck region that produces thyroid hormones. It may produce hormones in large quantities or little. Hypothyroidism is a condition wherein the thyroid gland is unable to release sufficient amounts of thyroid hormones. These hormones help control the metabolism of the body and further affect how the body uses energy. Lacking the accurate amount of thyroid hormones, the body's normal functions start to impede, and the body faces changes each day. The symptoms are mood swings, happiness, sadness, fatigue, depression, constipation, feeling cold, weight gain, muscle weakness, dryness, thinning hair, and slowed heart rate. Hyperthyroidism is a situation when the thyroid gland makes excessive thyroid hormones [1]. Symptoms of hyperthyroidism are nervousness, restlessness, inability to concentrate, increased appetite, difficulty sleeping, itching, hair loss, nausea, and vomiting. For diagnosis, entire medical history and physical tests like free T4, T3, cholesterol, and TSH tests are required. As these tests produce a large amount of data, ML can be used for finding crucial features from a large amount of data. Due to this ML can be used in combination with medical science for accurate diagnosis of hypothyroidism disease [2].

ML is one of the automation methods that studies the function as well as structure of algorithms, which can learn, understand, and assess the disease using the given data [3]. The obtained medical care datasets plays a crucial role in detecting the ailment. In the patient laboratory, different features and records are analyzed for disease identification. Due to the analysis of the results, the severity of the disease can be estimated [4]. The automatic study will help precision medicine health analysts [4]. The data collected can be used from patient socioeconomics, medical records, and other sources to develop a suitable and efficient learning model. Various factors differentiate between the conventional and ML techniques for disease prediction. Conventionally, many of the crucial features were not considered for correct forecasting, whereas more features, which provide greater precision, were studied in ML techniques [5]. For different types of data, ML has enormous analytical, visual, and predictive capabilities.

The main objective of this chapter is to implement a software tool to assist doctors or physicians for identification of diseases. Python programming language was used to implement KNN, RF, and DT models. Experiment was conducted with multiple feature selection methods and data normalization techniques to isolate and recognize features that characterize hypothyroid type correctly. The results of the proposed ML models were assessed using a confusion matrix, cross-validated with k-fold method, and then compared the results of the models.

5.1.1 RELATED WORK

Several ML techniques have been evolved in literature to achieve the best accuracy and model ensembles are widely used [6]. A nonparametric test showed precise significant disparities in both parameters ($p < 0.05$) between the FV-PTC and conventional thyroid. These first results showed that phantom-based quantitative ultrasound imaging with ML is crucial for thyroid tumor administration [7]. The results show that, when compared to LD and contained with the confines of previous thyroid portrayals, the joint echogenicity texture (JET) model offered accurate illustrations of the thyroid glands [8]. Ozyilmaz et al. implemented several ANN, such as adaptive conic section function neural network (CSFNN), fast back-propagation (FBP), back-propagation (BP), and multilayer perceptron (MLP), for the detection of thyroid disorder [9]. Polat et al. considered an artificial immune-recognition system (AIRS) for thyroid detection and found 81% accuracy [10]. Shukla et al. presented the thyroid disease diagnosis with artificial neural networks (ANNs) such as the learning vector quantization networks (LVQ), radial basis function (RBFN), and the back-propagation algorithm (BPA) [11]. Varde et al. presented a clinical laboratory system for thyroid diagnosis [12]. Keles et al. proposed a special system using the neuro-fuzzy classification method for thyroid identification and found an accuracy of 95.33% [13]. Temurtas et al. proposed thyroid illness diagnosis using multi-layer perception (MLP) with Levenberg Marquardt-LM methods and found an accuracy of 93.19% [14]. Dogantekin et al. performed generalized discriminant analysis (GDA) and support vector machine (SVM) methods for thyroid illness classification and achieved 91.86% accuracy [15]. Chen et al. performed optimization using particle swarm algorithm for thyroid disease and found an accuracy of 97.49% [16]. Jaganathan et al. proposed C4.5 and MLP methods to classify thyroid disease and achieved 93.49% accuracy. This result was compared with the generalized discriminant analysis-wavelet support vector machine (GDA-WSVM) technique, which is 91.86% accurate and found that the proposed system performs well against the GDA-WSVM [17]. Hui-Ling et al. proposed Fisher score particle swarm optimization support vector machines (FS-PSO-SVM) to access the thyroid dataset [18]. Binary logistic regression (BLR), Naïve Bayes classifier (NB), SVM, and radial basis function neural network (RBFNN) models were used to analyze thyroid diagnosis [19,20]. Hayashi et al. proposed a J48 graft to classify thyroid ailment and achieved classification accuracy of 97.02% [21]. Saiti et al. suggested a probabilistic neural network (PNN) and SVM for the classification of hypothyroidism and hyperthyroidism disease [22]. Ordonez et al. proposed DT and associated rules for disease prediction and achieved the highest 80% accuracy with DT [23]. Ahmad et al. proposed linear discriminate analysis, KNN, and adaptive neuro-fuzzy inference (ADNFI) system to classify thyroid disease and achieved accuracy of 98.5% and sensitivity of 94.7% [24]. Furthermore, Ahmad et al. combined ADNFI and information gain technique and reduced computation time and complexity involved in classification [25]. They obtained classification accuracy (95.24%), sensitivity (96.17%), and specificity (91.7%). Ma et al. proposed a DT framework to classify thyroid and achieved the highest accuracy of 98.89% [26].

5.2 MATERIAL AND METHODS

5.2.1 SYSTEM FRAMEWORK

The objective of this chapter is to develop an ML-based method to classify hypothyroid disease. The proposed flow structure of system is shown in Figure 5.1,

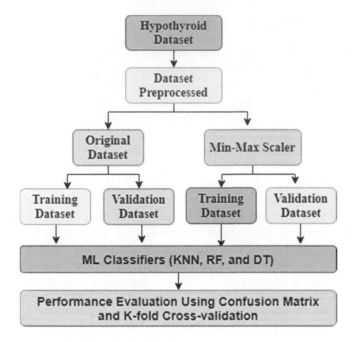

FIGURE 5.1 Framework of thyroid disease classification system.

and it is split into four steps – dataset collection, data preprocessing, classification, and performance evaluation.

In step 1, the dataset of thyroid diseases from UCI repository is selected. In step 2, the dataset attributes were preprocessed before applying them to the ML classifiers. This move is helpful in replacing the missing values, substitute numerical in place of a string, and change the numerical class into categorical. The Min-Max Scaler data normalization technique was applied to the dataset to improve the system performance. In step 3, ML models, namely, KNN, RF, and DT, were implemented using the Python programming language to classify thyroid disease. In step 4, the models were accessed using the confusion matrix technique to compare the model's performance.

5.2.2 Hypothyroid Disease (HD) Dataset

The dataset used for this work is taken from the website of UCI repository [27]. The dataset contains 3163 cases, of which 3012 are in the negative category, with 151 in the compensated hypothyroid category. There are a total of 25 features to categorize the information. The detail about dataset is tabulated in Table 5.1.

5.2.3 Min-Max Scaler Technique

Standard Scaler technique uses standard normal distribution (SND). Therefore, it makes distribution mean and the variance of data scaled to unity. Min-Max Scaler

TABLE 5.1
Hypothyroid Dataset Description

Dataset Attributes Description	Value Type
age	continuous
sex	Male (M), Female (F)
on_thyroxine	T, F
query_on_thyroxine	T, F
on_antithyroid_medication	T, F
thyroid_surgery	T, F
query_hypothyroid	T, F
query_hyperthyroid	T, F
pregnant	T, F
sick	T, F
tumor	T, F
lithium	T, F
goiter	T, F
TSH_measured	T, F
TSH	continuous
T3_measured	T, F
T3	continuous
TT4_measured	T, F
TT4	continuous
T4U_measured	T, F
T4U	continuous
FTI_measured	T, F
FTI	continuous
TBG_measured	T, F
TBG	continuous

escalades all the data features in the range 0 to 1 or else in the range -1 to 1. Min-Max Scaler may be used when the upper and lower boundaries are well known from domain knowledge. In the Min-Max Scaler technique, all the features will be represented into [0, 1] range. Variables determined at different levels do not equally accord to the model fitting and the model function learned and could result in a bias. Thus, Min-Max Scaling normalization is generally used before fitting the model to handle this problem. This method could be helpful for several ML models to stabilize the back propagation process even faster compared to original non-scaled data when the input features are scaled at a minimum and maximum [28]. The mathematical equation for data scaling is given in Equation (5.1).

$$x_{scaled} = \frac{x - min(x)}{max(x) - min(x)} \tag{5.1}$$

5.2.4   ML Classifiers

Classification is the process of predicting the class of given data points. A **classifier** in ML is an algorithm that automatically orders or categorizes data into one or more of a set of "classes". Identifying thyroid diseases using training and validation data is the main objective. Numerous applications like trade modeling, consumer segmentation, drug analysis, and loan analysis are found in the healthcare sector. There are numerous algorithms present for classification, such as LR, KNN, SVM, Naïve Bayes, J-48, etc. Three classifiers like KNN, RF, and DT are used for prediction of thyroid diseases. The following is a brief description of these three classifiers:

K-Nearest Neighbor (KNN): KNN is the simplest supervised ML technique used for both, classification as well as for regression. It is used for predictive classification problems in the industry. KNN uses similarities in features to estimate the values of latest data points, which also means that value will be given to new data points on the basis that it coincides closely. We must select the K (integer value), which is the closest point for the data. The distance of the test data from each training line is calculated using Euclidean, Manhattan, or Hamming methods for each point in the test data. Euclidean is the most frequently used distance calculation method. In this process, distances calculated are sorted in ascending order based on the value of the distance. Next, the upper K rows of the sorted panel will be selected followed by the class having the most common class of these rows assigned to the test point [29].

It is the algorithm used for classification; to determine if the attempts of the data groups fall in group A or it in group B. It is to look at the states of the points that may be nearest [222]. The range of arbitrarily is the point to take a sample of the patients data and analyze it. If there are many points in the group A, then it is likely that the data point will be grouped in A instead of B and vice versa.

Algorithm:
The KNN algorithm classifies data based on the majority of votes to its nearest neighbors, with the instance being named to the class, the most recurrent among its K nearest neighbors. Neighbors are found using distance function as shown in Equation (5.2). If the value of K is equal to 1, then the instance value is simply allocated to the class of its nearest neighbor. When the values are 0 and 1 it is used to bring the issue of standardization of numerical values as well as a combination of numerical and indubitably variables in the dataset.

$$(x + Sa)^n = \sqrt{\sum_{i=1}^{k} (xi - yi)^2} \qquad (5.2)$$

Random Forest (RF): RF is also an algorithm-based onsupervised/administered learning. The "forest" is a group of decision-making trees, normally trained by the "bagging" method. The common objective of the bagging procedure is to increase the overall result. The advantage of RF is the majority of current ML systems that can be used for both grading and regression problems. RF increases the randomness of the model as the trees grow. It seeks the best distinct feature among a certain number of features instead of finding for the most notable features while splitting a node. This produces a broad range that usually leads to a better model. Therefore, the algorithm for splitting a node takes into account only a random subset of characteristics in the random forest. We can randomize trees by using the random thresholds per feature instead of looking for the best possible threshold [30].

Random forest is type of an ensemble classifier based on the idea of randomization it develops a decision tree having a group of independent and non-identical data.

Random forest is contemplated as one of the ensemble learning technique in the correlative ensemble learning subsets. In random forest, every decision tree, or individual base learner, gets access to feature vectors of random subgroup. Hence the feature vector is described as shown in Equation (5.3).

$$X(\text{input}) = (x_1, x_2, x_3, \dots \dots, x_p) \tag{5.3}$$

Here p is the dimension property of the vector for the base learner. The main aim is to calculate the estimate function as $f(x)$ that estimates the Y variables. The prediction function isgiven in Equation (5.4).

$$M(Y, f(X)) \tag{5.4}$$

Here M is the loss function, and the main aim is to reduce the desired value of the loss. Application involving regression and classification, squared error loss and zero-one loss are ultimate choices, respectively. These functions are depicted in Equations (5.5) and (5.6), respectively.

$$M(Y, f(X)) = (Y - f(X)^2) \tag{5.5}$$

$$M(Y, f(X)) = I(Y = /f(X) = \{0, \text{ if } Y = f(X), 1 \text{ elsewise}\} \tag{5.6}$$

To make an ensemble, a group of base learners were brought together. If base learners are depicted as shown in Equation (5.7).

$$g1(x), g2(x), \dots, gj(x) \tag{5.7}$$

for application uses regression, the averaging will be calculated using Equation (5.8), and for classification, the polling will be based on Equation (5.9).

$$f(x) = 1/J \sum_{j=1}^{J} hj(x) \tag{5.8}$$

$$f(x) = \arg \max \sum_{j=1}^{J} I(y = hj(x)) \tag{5.9}$$

Decision Tree (DT): A DT is a flowdiagram-like structure of the tree, in which an inside node is a feature(s), and a branch depicts a decision rule. In the DT, the top node is also called the root node. The partition can be learned based on the value of the features. It remedies the tree by calling recursive partitioning. It helps decision-making in this flowchart-like structure. It is like visualizing a diagram that easily simulates thinking at the human level, hence decision-making trees are easy to understand. DT is a glass box-like ML algorithm. It shares interior decision-making logic that cannot be found in algorithms such as the neural network of the black-box type. Its training time is faster than the algorithm of the neural network. The time complexity of decision-making bodies depends on the number and attributes of the particular data. The DT is a method that does not depends on assumptions of the probability distribution, free of distribution, or a nonparametric method. High-dimensional data can be handled with good precision by DT. The first DT algorithm divides the records by choosing the best attribute with the attribute selection measures (ASM), makes these selected attributes a decision node, and breaks the data group into smaller subgroups. After that, it starts the creation of a tree by redoing this process recursively on every child until one of the conditions matches, such as all tuples belong to the same allocate value [31].

5.2.5 PERFORMANCE MEASURES

The confusion matrix is a common measure in solving problems of classification. The performance of binary and multi-class classification problems can be assessed with the confusion matrix. Matrices of confusion are counts of actual and estimated values. The TN output represents True Negative, and it indicates the number of negatives accurately classified. TP represents True Positive, which implies the correct classification of positive samples. The FP is False Positive and is classified as positive for actual negative. The FN is False Negative and categorized as a negative for actual positive value [32]. The following metrics of the confusion matrix are applied to evaluate the model or system.

Accuracy: It corresponds to the proportion of the total number of accurate estimates.

$$\text{Accuracy} = \frac{TP + TN}{TP + FP + TN + FN} \tag{5.10}$$

Precision: The precision metric demonstrates the specificity of the positive class. It tests if the positive class prediction is accurate. The precision is 1 when the classifier classifies all positive values perfectly.

$$\text{Precision} = \frac{TP}{TP + FP} \tag{5.11}$$

Sensitivity: It is sometimes called as True Positive Rate (TPR) or Recall. It calculates the correctly detected positive class ratio. This measure shows how strong the model to identify a positive class.

$$\text{Recall} = \frac{TP}{TP + FN} \tag{5.12}$$

F1-score: It is nothing but the weighted score average of precision and recall.

$$F1 - \text{score} = \frac{2}{\left(\frac{1}{\text{Recall}}\right) + \left(\frac{1}{\text{Precision}}\right)} \tag{5.13}$$

True negative rate (TNR): It is the proportion of negative cases classified correctly.

$$\text{TNR} = \frac{\text{TN}}{\text{TN} + \text{FP}} \tag{5.14}$$

5.3 RESULTS

This section includes the testing of the classification system of hypothyroid diseases with three ML classifiers. TD dataset is split into training (2530) and validation (633) datasets. The dataset has NULL values, missing values, and string values. These values were preprocessed before applying ML model on them. The "TBG" attribute or column was dropped from the dataset because it contains a large number of NULL values. In this work, 24 out of 25 attributes were used to train and validate the model. First, the models were trained with the original 24 attributes and then evaluated the performance of the models. Next, the Min-Max Scaler technique was applied to the dataset for data normalization. The models trained with these values and the model performance was evaluated. Finally, the model performances of both scenarios were compared. The efficiency of the models is assessed with a confusion matrix. Table 5.2 tabulates the model's name indication with and without the Min-Max Scaler technique for easy understanding.

The experiments were performed to find the model's performance after applying 24 attributes of the original dataset. The dataset was split into two parts with a ratio of 80:20. The dataset and ratios are common for all models. The models were trained with the training dataset and validate with the validation dataset. Figure 5.2 shows the confusion matrix of KNN, RF, and DT. The comparative performance analysis of all ML models was evaluated using a confusion matrix. The four metrics (Equations (5.2) to (5.6)) accuracy, precision, recall, and F1-score were used to check the performance of all models.

TABLE 5.2
Model Name Indication with and without Min-Max Scaler Technique

Models	Model without Min-Max Scaler	Model with Min-Max Scaler
KNN	KNN-A	KNN-B
RF	RF-A	RF-B
DT	DT-A	DT-B

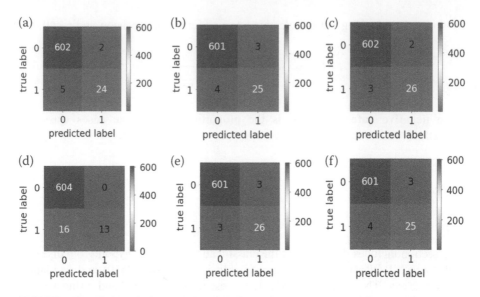

FIGURE 5.2   The confusion matrix a) KNN-A, b) RF-A, and c) DT-A models and d) confusion matrix of KNN-B, e) RF-B, and f) DT-B models.

Figure 5.2 shows the confusion matrix of all models. The KNN-A, RF-A, and DT-A models correctly predict 626, 626, and 628 instances, respectively, out of 633. The KNN-A and RF-A models predict most instances correctly and only seven instances wrongly, while DT-A model predict most instances correctly and only five instances wrongly. On the other hand, KNN-B, RF-B, and DT-B models correctly predict 621, 627, and 626, respectively, out of 633. RF-B and DT-B models wrongly predict only 6 and 7 instances, respectively, out of 633. This performance shows that the RF-B model outperformed all other models.

Figure 5.3 shows the bar charts of four performance measures like accuracy, precision, recall, and F1-score of all models with and without applying the Min-Max Scaler technique. The highest accuracy of 98% achieved by the KNN-A, RF-A, and DT-A models without the Min-Max Scaler technique. The accuracy performance of all models is good. The highest 94% precision was achieved by the KNN-A model, followed by RF-A (91%) and DT-A (89%). The recall of the RF-A and DT-A is 88%, followed by KNN-A (81%). The F1-score indicates the overall model performance, and the RF-A and DT-A models achieved the highest 91% F1-score among the models. This performance shows all three models are performing well to predict thyroid disease.

The Min-Max Scaler data normalization technique was applied to improve the model performance and achieved the highest accuracy of 99% by the RF-B and DT-B models. The accuracy performance of these models is excellent. The highest 99% precision was achieved by the KNN-B model, followed by RF-B (96%) and DT-A (90%). The highest recall achieved by DT-B (96%), followed by RF-B (94%) and KNN-B (74%). The highest F1-score achieved by RF-B (95%), followed by DT-B (92%) and KNN-B (82%). It is observed that the performance of the model

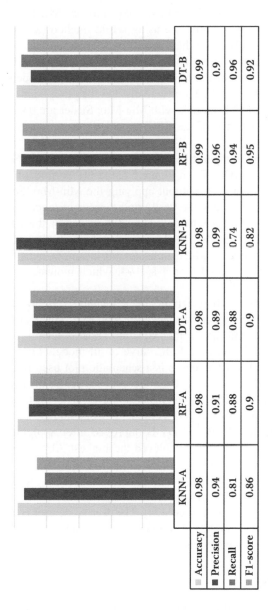

	KNN-A	RF-A	DT-A	KNN-B	RF-B	DT-B
Accuracy	0.98	0.98	0.98	0.98	0.99	0.99
Precision	0.94	0.91	0.89	0.99	0.96	0.9
Recall	0.81	0.88	0.88	0.74	0.94	0.96
F1-score	0.86	0.9	0.9	0.82	0.95	0.92

FIGURE 5.3 Comparison analysis of all models using confusion matrix measures.

improved after applying the Min-Max Scaler technique. This performance indicates all three models are performing well to predict thyroid disease. The RF-B has outperformed all other models in terms of the F1-scoremetric. Furthermore, these models were assessed with k-fold (k = 10) cross-validation method. Cross-validation is performance analysis method used to assess ML models. Figure 5.4 shows the cross-validation performance using k-fold method (k = 10).

From Figure 5.4, It is observed that the accuracy of all models with and without the Min-Max Scaler method is not changed, but the precision, recall, and F1-score are improved. The F1-score of the KNN-A, RF-A, and DT-A models without Min-Max Scaler are 0.9, 0.92, and 0.92, respectively. On the other hand, the F1-score of the KNN-B, RF-B, and DT-B models with Min-Max Scaler are 0.9, 0.94, and 0.92, respectively. The performance of the RF-B models improved after applying Min-Max Scaler.

Figure 5.5 shows the comparative analysis of LR, KNN, and SVM models in terms of TPR, TNR, and AUC. From Figure 5.5, the DT-A model has achieved the highest rate with a TPR of 0.96 without applying the Min-Max Scaler technique. The TPR value of 0.96 indicates the 96 thyroid disease instances out of 100 were predicted correctly by the DT-A model. The TPR values of the RF-A (0.88) followed by KNN-A (0.81) models. On the other hand, the highest TPR (0.96) was achieved by the DT-B model, which indicates 96 instances out of 100 predicted correctly. The TPR of the RF-B model is 0.94, which indicates the 94 instances predicted correctly out of 100.

The Receiver Operator Characteristic (ROC) analysis is an efficient way to measure ML and data mining performance [33]. The ROC curve of KNN-A, RF-A, and DT-A models without using the Min-Max Scaler technique is shown in Figure 5.6a. Figure 5.6b shows the ROC curve of all models after using the Min-Max Scaler technique. The ROC curve is a schematic plot used to illustrate binary classification diagnostic capabilities. The ROC curve is nearer the top left corner for better results in the classification problems. The performance of the RF-A model is good, while the performance of the DT-A model is worst and closer to the threshold line. The performance of RF-B and DT-B improved after applying the Min-Max Scaler technique. The DT-B model achieved the highest AUC score of 0.96, followed by RF-B (0.94), which shows the model performing well.

If the dataset has highly unbalanced data, then the F1-score metric is considered for model performance evaluation. The reason that these measurements are easier to interpret is also because of the F1-score [34]. The thyroid dataset is unbalanced, and this will help evaluate the models. The overall performance of the RF-B model is excellent compared to other models.

5.4   DISCUSSIONS

In the field of healthcare, all data are important for preventing and controlling the disease precisely and efficiently. Traditional procedures help diagnose diseases, but they take long time. In the literature, several computer-based solutions were already offered for solving the manual problem. Table 5.3 tabulates prediction accuracy of ML-based hypothyroid disease available in the literature.

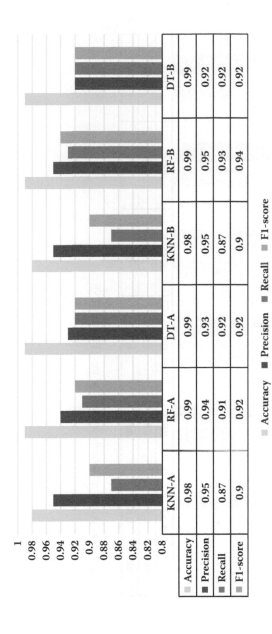

	KNN-A	RF-A	DT-A	KNN-B	RF-B	DT-B
Accuracy	0.98	0.99	0.99	0.98	0.99	0.99
Precision	0.95	0.94	0.93	0.95	0.95	0.92
Recall	0.87	0.91	0.92	0.87	0.93	0.92
F1-score	0.9	0.92	0.92	0.9	0.94	0.92

■ Accuracy   ■ Precision   ■ Recall   ■ F1-score

FIGURE 5.4   Cross-validation of the models using k-fold methods.

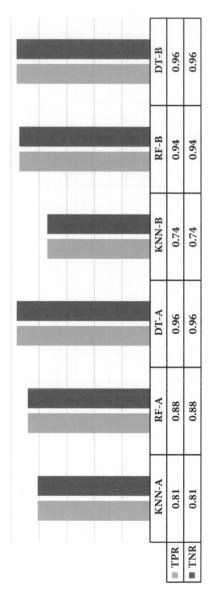

	KNN-A	RF-A	DT-A	KNN-B	RF-B	DT-B
TPR	0.81	0.88	0.96	0.74	0.94	0.96
TNR	0.81	0.88	0.96	0.74	0.94	0.96

FIGURE 5.5 Comparative analysis of all models in terms of the TPR, and TNR.

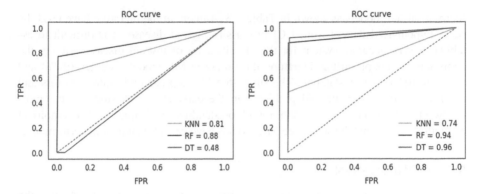

FIGURE 5.6   ROC curve for a) LR-C, KNN-C, and SVM-C models, b) LR-D, KNN-D, and SVM-D models, c) LR-E, KNN-E, and SVM-E models and b) LR-F, KNN-F, and SVM-F models.

TABLE 5.3
ML-Based Hypothyroid Disease Prediction System Available in the Literature with Accuracy

Authors	Methods	Cross-Validation (K- Fold)	Accuracy
Polat et al. [10]	AIRSTenfold		81%
Keles et al. [13]	Neuro-Fuzzy TenfoldTenfold		95.33%
Temurtas et al. [14]	MLPThreefold		93.19%
Dogantekin et al. [15]	SVM	Test Data	91.86%
Chen et al. [18]	Swarm optimizationTenfold		97.49%
Jaganathan et al. [17]	C4.5 and MLPTenfold		93.49%
Hayashi et al. [21]	J48Tenfold		97.02%
Ordonez et al. [23]	DT	Test Data	80%
Ahmad et al. [24]	KNN, ADNFITenfold		98.5%
Ahmad et al. [25]	combined ADNFI Tenfold and information gain		95.24%
Ma et al. [26]	DT	Test Data	98.89%.
Proposed work	**RF Tenfold**		**99.39%, F1-score = 0.94**

In this work, an ML-based system was presented to classify hypothyroid diseases. Two case studies were discussed with and without the Min-Max Scaler techniques. The literature review clarified various methods for identifying and classifying hypothyroid diseases, as tabulated in Table 5.3. Most of the authors presented papers in literature based on accuracy metrics, but this is an unbalanced dataset, and the accuracy metric is not suitable to evaluate the model. In this work, the authors evaluated the model's performances in terms of accuracy, F1-score, and AUC-ROC curve. The proposed ML models performed well compared to the literature-listed models as shown in Table 5.3. Authors in the literature have used the same hypothyroid dataset from UCI to classify thyroid disease. It is difficult to establish a very accurate system for the classification of thyroid disease. Among the approaches available in this literature, the proposed ML model accuracy (99%) and F1-score (0.94) are outstanding. The suggested ML approach will allow doctors and other users to identify thyroid problems in the early stages. A study of the most trustworthy technology tested and found outstanding performance. The empirical evaluation shows that the suggested ML models have exceptional overall performance.

5.5 CONCLUSION

The main goal here is to develop a tool that would allow doctors to identify the disease quickly. This chapter presented the ML-based approach to classifying hypothyroid condition successfully. Three classifiers, namely KNN, RF, and DT were successfully implemented using Python programming language. The 24 features selected from the original hypothyroid dataset successfully, and the RF and DT models achieved remarkable accuracy with the Min-Max Scaler technique. Min-Max Scaler was employed to increase the ability to normalize the dataset attributes to enhance the model performance. The Min-Max Scaler is applied successfully, and the performance of the model is significantly enhanced. Performances of all models were assessed with a confusion matrix. The authors will continue to extend this study to classify more types of thyroid diseases.

REFERENCES

[1] Peter Z. G., Berardi V. L. An investigation of neural networks in thyroid function diagnosis. *Health Care Management Science* 1.1 (Sep 1998).
[2] Godara S., Singh R. Evaluation of predictive machine learning techniques as expert systems in medical diagnosis. *Indian Journal of Science and Technology* 910 (March 2016).
[3] Kececi A., Yildirak A., Ozyazici K., Ayluctarhan G., Agbulut O., Zincir I. Implementation of machine learning algorithms for gait recognition. *Engineering Science and Technology* 23 (2020): 931–937.
[4] Dharavath R., Katheria Y. S. Ensemble method based predictive model for analyzing disease datasets: A predictive analysis approach. *Health and Technology* 9 (2019): 533–545. 10.1007/s12553-019-00299-3.
[5] Godara S., Singh R. Evaluation of predictive machine learning techniques as expert systems in medical diagnosis. *Indian Journal of Science and Technology* 9 (2016): 1–14. 10.17485/ijst/2016/v9i10/87212.
[6] Milan K., Godara S. Comparative study of data mining classification methods in cardiovascular disease prediction 1. *IJCST* 2 (2011): 2229–4333.
[7] Roberto J. L., Ridgway B., Sarwate S., Oelze M. Imaging of follicular variant papillary thyroid carcinoma in a rodent model using spectral-based quantitative ultrasound techniques. In IEEE 10th International Symposium on Biomedical Imaging (2013): 732–735.
[8] Savelonas A. M., Iakovidis D. K., Legakis I., Maroulis D. Active contours guided by echogenicity and texture for delineation of thyroid nodules in ultrasound images. *IEEE Transactions on Information Technology in Biomedicine* 13.4 (July 2009).

[9] Ozyilmaz L., Yildirim T. Diagnosis of thyroid disease using artificial neural network methods. In Proceedings of ICONIP (2002).

[10] Polat K., Seral S., Salih G. A novel hybrid method based on artificial immune recognition system (AIRS) with fuzzy weighted pre-processing for thyroid disease diagnosis. *Expert Systems with Applications* 32.4 (May 2007).

[11] Shukla A., Kaur P., Tiwari R., Janghel R. R. Diagnosis of thyroid disease using artificial neural network. In Proceedings of IEEE IACC (2009).

[12] Varde A. S., Massey K. L., Wood H. C. A clinical laboratory expert system for the diagnosis of thyroid dysfunction. In Proceeding of Annual International Conference of the IEEE Engineering in Medicine and Biology Society (1991).

[13] Keleş A. ESTDD: Expert system for thyroid diseases diagnosis. *Expert Systems with Applications* 34.1 (2008).

[14] Temurtas F. A comparative study on thyroid disease diagnosis using neural networks. *Expert Systems with Applications* 36.1 (2009).

[15] Dogantekin E., Dogantekin A., Avci D. An expert system based on generalized discriminant analysis and wavelet support vector machine for diagnosis of thyroid diseases. *Expert Systems with Applications* 38.1 (2011).

[16] Stegmayer G., Gerard M., Milone D. H. Data mining over biological datasets: An integrated approach based on computational intelligence. *IEEE Computational Intelligence Magazine* 7.4 (Nov 2012).

[17] Palanichamy J., Nallamuthu R. An expert system for optimizing thyroid disease diagnosis. In Proceedings of International Journal of Computational Science and Engineering (2012).

[18] Chen H.-L., Yang B., Wang G., Liu J., Chen Y., Liu D. A three-stage expert system based on support vector machines for thyroid disease diagnosis. *Journal of Medical Systems* 36.3 (2012).

[19] Young J., Ha E. J., Cho Y. J., Kim H. L., Han M., Kang S. Computer-aided diagnosis of thyroid nodules via ultrasonography: Initial clinical experience. *Korean Journal of Radiology* 19.4 (2018).

[20] Chen Shao-Jer, Chang C., Chang K., Tzeng J., Chen Y., Lin C., Hsu W. C., Chang-K. W. Classification of the thyroid nodules based on characteristic sonographic textural feature and correlated histopathology using hierarchical support vector machines. *Ultrasound in Medicine & Biology* 36.12 (2010).

[21] Hayashi Y. Synergy effects between grafting and subdivision in Re-RX with J48graft for the diagnosis of thyroid disease. *Knowledge-Based Systems* 131 (2017): 170–182.

[22] Fatemeh S., Mahdi A. Thyroid disease diagnosis based on genetic algorithms using PNN and SVM. In Proceedings of IEEE (2009).

[23] Ordonez C. Comparing association rules and decision trees for disease prediction. In Proceedings of International Conference of Information Knowledge Management (2006).

[24] Ahmad W., Ahmad A., Iqbal A., et al. Intelligent hepatitis diagnosis using adaptive neuro-fuzzy inference system and information gain method. *Soft Computing* 23 (2018): 1–8.

[25] Ahmad W., Ahmad A., Lu C., Khoso B. A., Huang L. A novel hybrid decision support system for thyroid disease forecasting. *Soft Computing* 22 (2018): 5377–5383.

[26] Ma C., Guan J., Zhao W., Wang C. An efficient diagnosis system for thyroid disease based on enhanced kernelized extreme learning machine approach. In International Conference on Cognitive Computing, Springer, Cham (2018): 86–101.

[27] UCI repository. https://archive.ics.uci.edu/ml/machine-learning-databases/thyroid-disease/.

[28] Loukas S. Everything you need to know about Min-Max normalization: A Python tutorial (2020). https://towardsdatascience.com/everything-you-need-to-know-about-min-max-normalization-in-python-b79592732b79.

[29] KNN algorithm - Finding nearest neighbors. https://www.tutorialspoint.com/machine_learning_with_python/machine_learning_with_python_knn_algorithm_finding_nearest_neighbors.htm

[30] Donges N. A complete guide to the random forest algorithm (2019). https://builtin.com/data-science/random-forest-algorithm.

[31] Navlani A. Decision tree classification in Python (2018). https://www.datacamp.com/community/tutorials/decision-tree-classification-python.

[32] Kulkarni A., Chong D., Batarseh F. A. 5 - Foundations of data imbalance and solutions for a data democracy. Editor(s): Feras A. Batarseh, Ruixin Yang, Data Democracy. Academic Press (2020): 83–106. 10.1016/B978-0-12-818366-3.00005-8,2020.

[33] Fawcett T. An introduction to ROC analysis pattern recognition. *Letters* 27.8 (2006): 861–874. 10.1016/j.patrec.2005.10.010.

[34] Czakon J. F1 Score vs ROC AUC vs accuracy vs PR AUC: Which evaluation metric should you choose? (2021). https://neptune.ai/blog/F1-score-accuracy-roc-auc-pr-auc.

6 GPU-based Medical Image Segmentation: Brain MRI Analysis Using 3D Slicer

Sajedul Talukder

Southern Illinois University, Carbondale, IL, United States

CONTENTS

6.1   INTRODUCTION

As a key component of both consumer and corporate computing, the graphics processing unit (GPU) is critical [1]. Originally intended to accelerate the rendering of 3D graphics [1], the GPU is used in a wide range of applications, including digital automation and video rendering [2,3]. GPUs are becoming more popular for use in artificial intelligence [4], cybersecurity [5–7], and medical image segmentation [8] despite their best-known uses in gaming and creative creation [9]. Image segmentation, or partitioning of an image into disjoint sections based on image characteristics such as color detail, strength, or texture, is critical for many applications, such as object detection, labeling, and recognition [10,11]. Image segmentation plays a significant role within imaging scans in the medical field, as semi-automated or automatic extraction of the area of interest (ROI) is regarded to be the most important medical imaging technique. The purpose of image segmentation is to divide an image into ROIs, which is primarily useful for segmenting body tissue/organs. Since the medical field offers wide applications for image processing

DOI: 10.1201/9781003241409-6

109

algorithms, there is a community dedicated to implementing more efficient and faster solutions.

The medical field is a perfect example of where imaging techniques need to be very fast and efficient. However, due to the huge three-dimensional medical data-sets that must be processed in real clinical applications, medical imaging processes are frequently computationally intensive. Since GPU computational speed has increased so rapidly over the recent years, when compared to traditional CPU-based computing frameworks, GPU provides a better platform for significant acceleration of many computationally intensive operations.

The previous research within this area of expertise suggests that GPU-based image segmentation and processing is much more efficient than conventional CPU (central processing unit) based computing frameworks. We focus on the benefits that GPU-based image processing can have when used within various applications for the medical field and offer quantitative reasoning to suggest the recommended approach, respectively. Also, pairing GPU-based computing with NVIDIA AI-Assisted Annotation (AIAA) [12], we adopt an extension for the program 3D Slicer [13], a free, open-source, and multi-platform software package widely used for medical, biomedical, and related imaging research to explore the capabilities of this computing framework.

This chapter presents the following contributions:

Survey Brain Image Segmentation: Reviews the literature on image segmentation within the medical field, considering the GPU as the primary computation brain.

Image Segmentation Approaches: Provides a comprehensive overview of the low-level and high-dimensional medical image segmentation approaches.

GPU Segmentation Demonstration: NVIDIA AIAA. Adopts an extension for the program 3D Slicer with AI-assistive technology (NVIDIA AIAA) to demonstrate the capabilities of GPU segmentation on a brain MRI consisting of a large brain tumor.

The rest of the chapter is organized as follows. Section 6.2 presents the literature review that closely relates and contributes to our research. Section 6.3 discusses the image segmentation approaches. Section 6.4 presents our demonstration of the GPU segmentation using NVIDIA AIAA. Finally, Section 6.5 concludes the chapter by highlighting the extent of future direction.

6.2   RELATED WORKS

There are lots of resources on image segmentation within the medical field, even when considering the GPU as the primary computation brain. The following are a few key examples that closely relate and contribute to our research. Sharma et al. [14] proposed automated medical image segmentation techniques. This related work deals with the differences, benefits, and limitations among MR (magnetic resonance) vs CT (computed topography) imaging and how they need to be effective for different types of application. Segmentation of a brain is much different from the segmentation of a thorax, so there needs to be clarity on which type of scan/segmentation method is used where and how the results will best reflect the desired outcome.

Taha and Hanbury [15] proposed to use metrics to evaluate 3D medical image segmentation. Since we are focusing on the efficiency of image segmentation algorithms, we need to clearly define ways in which to confirm quality. Image comparison for quality evaluation is vital for monitoring development within the space, and this study illustrates that perfectly. Challenges to measuring the effectiveness of medical segmentation include choosing the right metrics and defining them correctly in the literature, inefficient metric computation methods that lead to problems with huge amounts of data, and the absence of fuzzy segmentation using existing measures.

Di Salvo et al. [16] presented image and video processing on CUDA. The research proposed here argues for the use of CUDA for various applications of image and video processing. Fields such as the medical industry can take advantage of the vast amount of efficiency that the GPU platform offers due to its straightforward and highly multicore features. When used for time processing, CUDA provides very high efficiency while maintaining the same level of accuracy.

Eklund et al. [17] presented a survey of GPU mechanisms that deal with the processing of the medical image. There is a lot to learn about graphics processing units (GPUs) in this research. When it comes to the medical world, GPUs can play a significant role in enabling practical usage of computationally intensive techniques due to their ability to drastically accelerate parallel computing, as well as being inexpensive and using less power (specifically with imaging). This review not only covers common operations for the processing of images using GPU but also goes over how those algorithms are used toward individual scans.

Shi et al. [18] also published a review of GPU-based medical image processing methods. The purpose of this study was to create a complete reference source for everyone interested in GPU-based medical image processing, whether they are beginners or experts. This work goes over the conventional applications that include segmentation. It also covers the visualization as well as registration that spans all the key areas that are involved in the processing of the medical image. We have a discussion on the benefits of visualization tools implemented using GPU that are used in the medical field, as well as an overview of techniques employed in this area.

Bankman [19] provided an introduction to segmentation. Within the medical field, imaging algorithms need to be able to handle variability. The data collected is from real people each with a unique condition. That is precisely what this piece of research addresses and reveals techniques used to combat data variation. Fuzzy clustering, the use of deformable models, as well as volumetric data are discussed. Volumetric data deals specifically with 3D segmentation and material analysis which is useful for GPU-based imaging techniques.

An overview of methods for segmenting optical coherence tomography from the retina was provided by Kafieh et al. [20]. This research focuses on the different types of algorithms that can be used for the segmentation of optical coherence tomography. Optical coherence tomography (OCT) is a technique for describing and imaging distinct features of biological tissue and for describing diverse information about the interior structures of an object. This chapter reads the history of the algorithms used within the field and shows how the medical imaging field has grown over the years relating to the precision, abilities, and accuracy of their results.

Smistad et al. [8] provided a comprehensive review of how the GPU can solve problems with the segmentation of anatomical structures. Since segmentation of imaging from CT, MRI, and ultrasound are key for diagnostics, planning, and guidance, more efficient solutions become required as time goes on. This chapter goes over the essentials of GPU computing, segmentation algorithms, and a proposal of the future for GPU hardware manufacturers.

6.3 IMAGE SEGMENTATION TECHNIQUES

GPUs, although originally created for rendering graphics, have become popular for lots of high-performance computation due to the more recent programmability and low cost to performance. When compared to a CPU-based computing environment, theoretical performance might vary by a factor of 10 in favor of the GPU [17]. While both modern CPU and GPU can manage thousands of threads, the GPU executing a competent algorithm may process thousands of threads at the same time, while the CPU progresses over less than a dozen (generously). One of the fields of which capitalized upon this was the medical field within their medical image processing/segmentation. Since there is a strong nature of parallelism among GPU computation, performance often is tied to the implementation of parallelly adapted algorithms. This is advantageous since the algorithms that deal with the processing of the images are usually extremely parallel by design, making them easier to implement on a GPU [17]. Medical image processing runs based on the patient's available data, which is steadily increasing for each case, resulting in the need for fast algorithms that provide high accuracy as well as speed. Although there are many different types of algorithms involved in the processing of medical images [8], this chapter will focus mainly on the algorithms involved within image segmentation specifically. By defining level set segmentation as a sequence of image blending graphics operators, the first GPU-based medical image segmentation technique attempted to harness the high performance of graphics cards for various numerical computations [18]. Another technique, which used the then-recent programmable shader technology, used the enhanced flexibility to enable 3D image segmentation using curvature regularization to favor smooth ISO surfaces. Among other methods, including ones implemented with CUDA, we can generalize with two types of segmentation approaches: low and high-levels. Low-level methods, which rely on GPU implementations of watershed and region growth algorithms are in contrast to high-level segmentation frameworks, which do not directly manipulate the pixel/voxel information from the image. There has been work proposed in this area using geodesic active contours as well as contours with gradient vector flow [21] as well as CUDA-powered approaches. Since CUDA was released, there has been highly improved performance in terms of speedup concerning the sequential version of various image segmentation algorithms using CUDA and CUDA-enabled GPUs [16]. Since the medical field needs real-time, high dimension segmentation approaches, CUDA seems to be the go-to implementation going forward to deal with the very large data sets the medical imaging scans provide. CUDA does not operate proficiently without optimized algorithms though, so one needs to make the right decision with respect to choosing the most fitting algorithm for the application.

6.3.1 SEEDED REGION GROWING

As the name suggests, the seeded region approach for image segmentation takes either pixel or voxel regions as seeds that the user defines, which eliminates the need of using any tuning parameters. This method is one of the fastest and simplest ones for segmentation. To initiate this approach, the input is converted into a grayscale image. The pixels of the image that are chosen as seeds grow by connecting to their neighbors. Let h_{min} be the minimum gray value and h_{max} be the maximum gray value of a grayscale volume image. We can define the image as a digital cubic grid $G = (V, E)$, where the vertices are called voxels. The domain of the image is represented by the set of vertices $V \subseteq Z3$. The set of edges E defines the connectivity of the digital grid graph where any vertex q belongs to the neighborhood of a given vertex p, if the pair $e = (p, q) \in E$. A given vertex is said to have 6-Connectivity with connection to its front, back, vertical, and horizontal neighbors. If the vertex is connected to all its direct neighbors, we call this 26-Connectivity. Once the seeds are set, either using a GUI or automatically with prior knowledge, we use those seeds as start nodes to then grow our region of interest based on if neighboring pixels fit the criteria that were defined. These criteria use properties like the contrast of the pixel and the gradient to evaluate the current pixel against the seed or any previously included pixels (once the area has developed from seeds). As long as there are nearby pixels that meet these criteria, the area will expand (see Figure 6.1). The algorithm behaves comparably to a breadth-first search algorithm.

As one could imagine, the number of threads grows as the border of the region of interest expands. On CPU-based computing frameworks, changing the number of threads usually is done by restarting the kernel, which makes it so all values from global memory need to be read again. In each iteration, though, we may leverage the GPU by taking each pixel individually and creating one thread for each in the whole image. But doing this adds more computational work due to branch divergence as well as increasing memory usage [8]. Since the traditional CPU-based

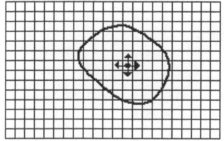 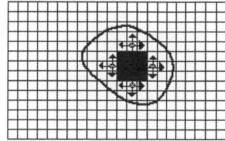

FIGURE 6.1   Seeded region growing from a seed pixel.

implementation has too high of a computational cost when images scale larger, CUDA and the GPU have been used to accelerate the seeded region growing approach. One notable approach, respective to this method, was proposed to exploit advanced functionality of the graphics hardware [22]. This method permits the users to draw on the volumes in order to paint expanding seeds interactively. In addition to visualization and interaction, this method also improves the execution time by utilizing the GPU's concurrent computational power. However, one has to draw a good number of seeds in order to utilize the full potential of GPU's parallelism.

6.3.2 WATERSHED

A watershed is a geographical area that aids in the drainage of water (typically rainfall) into a river or stream. It is a highland region through which water flows into a river or stream. Watershed transformation uses a similar concept to treat the picture as a topographic map, with the intensity of each pixel indicating the height. Dark regions, for example, are intuitively seen to be "lower" in height and can indicate troughs. Bright regions, on the other hand, might be regarded as "upper", functioning as hills or a mountain range. The watershed technique to image segmentation assumes that a picture is seen as a three-dimensional object. The height is determined from the intensity of the pixel/voxel (see Figure 6.2).

Once the generated landscape is complete, there are three types of points, categorized by how a drop of water would behave at the specific point. These three categories include scenarios in which a drop of water would:

- Stay at the point (local minima)
- Move downward to into one local minimum
- Move downward into > 1 local minimum

Points of the first category represent watersheds or catchment basins and points of third category represent watershed lines or divide lines since they split into more

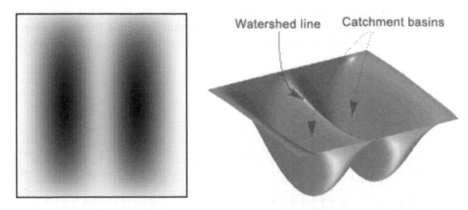

FIGURE 6.2   The watershed approach, where intensity is interpreted as a height within the topological representation.

than one local minimum. The distinction between types of points is important because the main purpose of this algorithm is to find watershed lines. This then begs the question; how does one find watershed lines? To answer this question, we must look to an analogy based on the topological representation. Suppose there are holes in all the places where a point of type 1 (local minimum) occurs. These perforations would allow water to flow through them. A consistent rate of flooding would then be applied to the watersheds within the topological representation. As a result, when two watersheds are ready to converge, something called a dam (which is exactly the same as a dam you think of holding back a large body of water) is built between them, with an increasing height with the rise of the water level. The height of the dam continues to increase until it is the same as the highest represented point within the topological landscape. These dams that were created are the watershed lines.

As far as acceleration with parallelism on the GPU, we see an obstacle in constructing good multi-threaded algorithms. The watershed approach has an inherent sequential nature. However, the topological landscape has been successfully transformed into a graph, the picture has been subdivided, and each local minimum has been flooded in parallel. Overall, these speedups are reported to be only within the range of 2–7x faster. One notable attempt, by Kauffmann and Piche in 2008 [23], demonstrated the execution of watershed segmentation utilizing a cellular automation technique using a weighted graph. They used the Bellman-Ford algorithm to calculate a weighted cost of the shortest path from all pixels to each local minimum. Thus, the shortest path will then always lead downwards. By using this approach, they established a method that can process all of the pixels/voxels of an image in parallel using the same instruction, boasting speedups of 2.5x.

Wagner et al. [24] presented a parallel watershed algorithm that takes a gray value gradient image g: $\Omega \rightarrow [h_{min},..., h_{max}]$ as input and computes a label image l: $\Omega \rightarrow N$ which contains the segmentation result. For each gray level h, starting at the global minimum h_{min}, new basins are created according to the local minima of the current level h. Already existing basins, are expanded if they have adjoining pixels of the gray value h. The procedure stops when the maximum gray value h_{max} is reached. This implementation was 5–7x faster than serial implementation on 3D images [22].

6.3.3 LEVEL SET APPROACHES/METHODS

The level set approaches to segmentation are based on spreading a contour within the input images. We define a scalar function with positive values inside the current segmentation and having negative values outside, thus defining the segmentation boundary by the function's zero level set. An additional dimension is added to the contour when using this level-set feature, which means that we can start with 2D images, define a boundary at the start, and then propagate along the z-axis, almost creating a 3D object out of slices, much like a 3D printer works. We can intuitively understand the idea of the level set method from a simple example. Let's say there is an active volcano that will erupt at any moment. Once the lava starts to come out from the top of the volcano, it will start to move down the surface of the volcano. Suppose we want to track the frontier of the lava. How do we model this scenario?

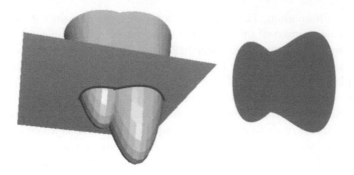

FIGURE 6.3 The level-set approach showing the movement through the image plane, which shows two merged circles that will grow over time.

The level set method works by imagining the frontier growth of the lava as a 3D surface. The surface will grow in height which is corresponding to the time. For any given time, t, if we intersect the 3d surface with a plane, we will get a contour that gives us a curve. This curve is known as our level set at time t. During the start of the eruption at t = 1, the height of the surface is 0. The contour at this point is a zero-level set. As time passes, the contour of the surface will grow in the z-direction. The level set method is represented by a mathematical function that takes as the parameter the position and time and returns the height. Figure 6.3 shows an example of the level-set approach.

GPU implementations of the level-set approach have been proposed as early as 2001, where Rumpf and Strzodka [25] exploited the performance benefits of high memory bandwidth and high command transfer economy from then modern GPUs to increase performance on level-set propagation. The main issue with the level-set approach comes down to the extremely high computational cost when processing large images. A set of numerical simulations must be performed on every voxel of an image, so the limited bandwidth and limited number of execution cores on a CPU are not ideal. Research done by Hong and Wang [26] in 2004 designed a GPU-based level-set algorithm to process large-sized biomedical images and reported an average of 12–13x increased processing speed.

6.3.4 ACTIVE CONTOURS

Kass et al. introduced active contours, sometimes known as snakes [21]. Figure 6.4 illustrates this by showing how the contours move inside a picture in an attempt to reduce their energy. Active contour segmentation is very similar to that of the level set approach. In reality, the contour over here is something that may flow along the numerous perspectives on the image itself, and then it comes down to a convergence point. You create a circle around an object that you wish to segment out and then modify along its outlines step by step. When it tries to conform and move along the different kinds of shapes, it looks a little Wiggly like a snake, and hence the name "the snake algorithm". If you wish to segment in an iterative manner, you can use the snake method. A number of dots are placed around the object, and then

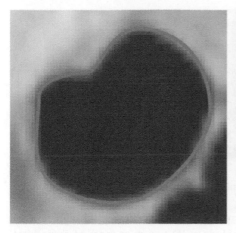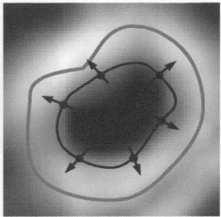

FIGURE 6.4 The active contour approach where the left image is the input, and the right image shows the gradient magnitude.

lines are drawn to comply inside those spots. You want them to be smooth, but also precise around their contour. As a result, the method has a tough time verifying both smoothness and exactness. In light of this, you may be wondering what numerically is truly converging and how it does so. On the curve, we have two functions with parameters that move from zero to one constantly. So, when we visualize two different curves, the lines are far from ideal at first, but as we can see, they converge and grow better and better as we go along. This approach is called active contours since it is converging and improving repeatedly along the shape of the object. There are two distinct, yet data-parallel, processes that may be performed using this approach. We must compute the external energy as a starting point. It is mathematically connected to the tension and stiffness of a contour that its energy is proportionate to its form. In the second phase, the contour is further developed.

Many of the various formulations of the external force field ∇Eext can become trapped in local minima due to boundary concavities, as Xu and Prince have demonstrated [27]. Working with large images (15–150 megapixels) is important because large images have always had a hard time being segmented efficiently. This research focused on a region-based active contour technique, otherwise known as snakes. This algorithm is not well suited for running on multicore CPUs, so they proposed an especially efficient snake algorithm, exploiting massive multi-threaded execution capabilities. This can result in an average speedup factor of 7.

6.4 GPU SEGMENTATION DEMONSTRATION: NVIDIA AIAA

Despite having many tools developed for image segmentation in the medical field, we adopt a popular and free extension called "NVIDIA AI-Assisted Annotation (AIAA) for 3D Slicer" to demonstrate the capabilities of image segmentation based on the GPU. This extension uses artificial intelligence to train models based on human clinical data sets. Once a scan is initiated, the input scans are sent to a server

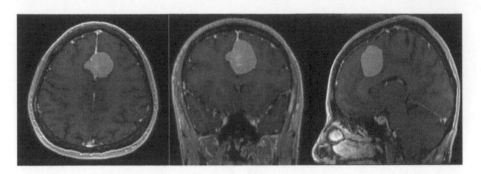

FIGURE 6.5   Three views from a contrast-enhanced brain MRI.

running Linux with an NVIDIA GPU for processing and return a 3D segmentation result to Slicer. For example, this may include a 3D tumor or mass of some kind.

3D Slicer is an open-source software platform for medical image informatics, image processing, and three-dimensional visualization. Mainly written in C++ and based on the NA-MIC kit, 3D Slicer relies on a variety of libraries: VTK, ITK, CTK, CMake, Qt, and Python. 3D Slicer consists of both an application core, as well as having modules that offer specific functionality. The core implements the UI, data I/O, and visualization while exposing developer interfaces for the use of extensions with new modules.

Using this extension, we will walk through an example of segmenting a brain tumor. We are provided a pre-trained AI model for segmenting tumors on contrast-enhanced brain MRI scans, we will be using this for our segmentation.

Step 1. The first step is to load the dataset into 3D Slicer, and once that is completed, we end up having three views from a contrast-enhanced brain MRI as shown in Figure 6.5.

This importing process gives the user a scrollable three-panel window displaying the scans. Each of these three views is fully interactable. If you are familiar with MRI scans, we can scroll through them to see all the layers through the scan. This means you can scroll from the very edge of the skull, all the way into the head to get to the meat of the mass we are trying to segment. This is our region of interest.

Step 2. Once this process is complete, we need to go to what Slicer has coined the segment editor. The segment editor is where the user adds segmentations to the imaging scans. Since we are using the NVIDIA AIAA extension, we need to configure the segmentation accordingly. Once inside the segment editor, we add a new segment using the add button in Slicer's UI and add the NVIDIA AIAA effect. Once the effect is added to the segmentation,

we get more options in the Slicer UI (see Figure 6.6). We want to configure a segment from boundary points that uses the model "annotation_mri_-brain_tumors_t1ce_tc". This model is trained to segment tumors on contrast-enhanced brain MRIs.

Step 3. In each image, we set two boundary points on the left and right sides of the ROI, so the algorithm has a base of where to start segmenting, shown in Figure 6.7 as pink squares when placed.

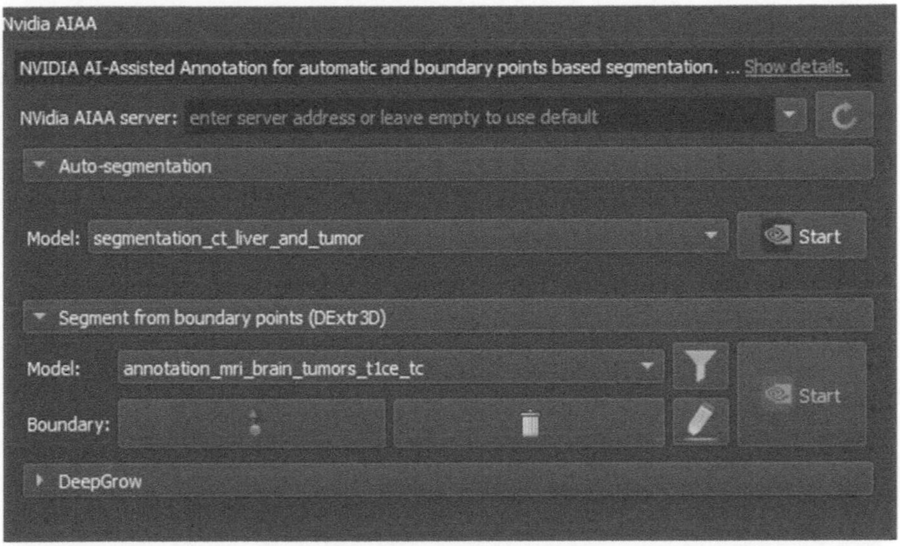

Nvidia AIAA

NVIDIA AI-Assisted Annotation for automatic and boundary points based segmentation. ... Show details.

NVidia AIAA server: enter server address or leave empty to use default

▼ Auto-segmentation

Model: segmentation_ct_liver_and_tumor   ▼   Start

▼ Segment from boundary points (DExtr3D)

Model: annotation_mri_brain_tumors_t1ce_tc   ▼

Boundary: Start

▶ DeepGrow

FIGURE 6.6 NVIDIA AIAA Slicer's UI.

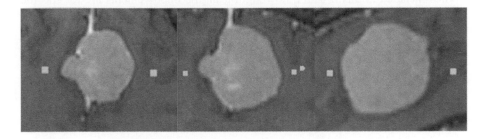

FIGURE 6.7 Setting two boundary points on the left and right sides of the ROI.

Step 4. After the boundary points have been set on each view of the scan, we are then ready to hit the now ungrayed out NVIDIA start button (when compared with Figure 6.7) to send our data to their server for processing on their NVIDIA GPU powered server. After a few seconds, thanks to the power and capabilities of GPU computing, we get returned to Slicer a fully manipulatable 3D representation of the tumor, as shown in Figure 6.8.

6.5 CONCLUSION

We have shown how beneficial it is to adopt GPU-based computation with respect to medical imaging. There are applications where algorithms fail to deliver substantial improvements when optimized for GPUs, and this is to be expected when the algorithms were developed with CPU architecture in mind. This, however, is a fairly small portion of algorithms, with vast majority being parallel by nature, thus thriving on a GPU-based computing framework. We have seen through all of the

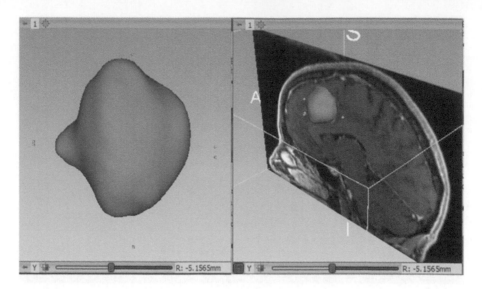

FIGURE 6.8 A fully manipulatable 3D representation of the tumor.

studies included in this research how significant the improvements are for specific algorithms optimized for use on the GPU and the results have spoken for themselves. With anywhere from 2–13x speedup advantages, we can draw the conclusion that GPU-based computing in image segmentation is the way to go at the point of time we are in now and also into the future. Since GPU hardware has gotten significantly better over the past decade alone, we are seeing lots of new implementation of image segmentation arise, leaving nothing but better results that will continue to grow and advance.

REFERENCES

[1] Owens, J. D., Houston, M., Luebke, D., Green, S., Stone, J. E., Phillips, J. C. "GPU computing". In: *Proceedings of the IEEE* 96.5 (2008): 879–899.
[2] Lee, C., Kim, S.-W., Yoo, C. "VADI: GPU virtualization for an automotive plat form". In: *IEEE Transactions on Industrial Informatics* 12.1 (2015): 277–290.
[3] Talukder, S., Sakib, M. I. I., Talukder, Z. R., Das, U., Saha, A., Bayev, N. S. N. "Usensewer: Ultrasonic sensor and gsm-arduino based automated sewerage management". In: 2017 International Conference on Current Trends in Computer, Electrical, Electronics and Communication (CTCEEC). IEEE. 2017, pages 12–17.
[4] Baji, T. "Evolution of the GPU Device widely used in AI and massive parallel processing". In: 2018 IEEE 2nd Electron Devices Technology and Manufacturing Conference (EDTM). IEEE. 2018, pages 7–9.
[5] Bhattacharya, S., Maddikunta, P. K. R., Kaluri, R., Singh, S., Gadekallu, T. R., Alazab, M., Tariq, U., et al. "A novel PCA-firefly based XGBoost classification model for intrusion detection in networks using GPU". In: *Electronics* 9.2 (2020): 219.
[6] Talukder, S., Sakib, I. I., Hossen, F., Talukder, Z. R., Hossain, S. "Attacks and defenses in mobile IP: Modeling with stochastic game petri net". In: *2017 International Conference on Current Trends in Computer, Electrical, Electronics and Communication (CTCEEC)* (2017): 18–23.

[7] Talukder, S., Talukder, Z. "A survey on malware detection and analysis tools". In: *International Journal of Network Security & Its Applications* 12.2 (2020).

[8] Smistad, E., Falch, T. L., Bozorgi, M., Elster, A. C., Lindseth, F. "Medical image segmentation on GPUs–A comprehensive review". In: *Medical Image Analysis* 20.1 (2015): 1–18.

[9] Chen, H., Lu, M., Ma, Z., Zhang, X., Xu, Y., Shen, Q., Zhang, W. "Learned resolution scaling powered gaming-as-a-service at scale". *IEEE Transactions on Multimedia* 23 (2020): 584–596.

[10] Shapiro, L. G., Stockman, G. "Computer vision", Prentice Hall (2001).

[11] Talukder, S., Carbunar, B. "AbuSniff: Automatic detection and defenses against abusive Facebook friends". In: Twelfth International AAAI Conference on Web and Social Media. 2018.

[12] NVIDIA AI-Assisted Annotation (AIAA). https://docs.nvidia.com/clara/tltmi/aiaa/index.html. Accessed: 2021-01-06.

[13] 3D Slicer. https://www.slicer.org/. Accessed: 2021-01-06.

[14] Sharma, N., Aggarwal, L. M. "Automated medical image segmentation techniques". In: *Journal of Medical Physics/Association of Medical Physicists of India* 35.1 (2010): 3.

[15] Taha, A. A., Hanbury, A. "Metrics for evaluating 3D medical image segmentation: Analysis, selection, and tool". In: *BMC Medical Imaging* 15.1 (2015): 1–28.

[16] Di Salvo, R., Pino, C. "Image and video processing on CUDA: State of the art and future directions". In: *MACMESE* 11 (2011): 60–66.

[17] Eklund, A., Dufort, P., Forsberg, D., LaConte, S. M. "Medical image processing on the GPU–Past, present and future". In: *Medical Image Analysis* 17.8 (2013): 1073–1094.

[18] Shi, L., Liu, W., Zhang, H., Xie, Y., Wang, D. "A survey of GPU-based medical image computing techniques". In: *Quantitative Imaging in Medicine and Surgery* 2.3 (2012): 188.

[19] Bankman, I. N. "Introduction to segmentation", Handbook of Medical Imaging, 2000.

[20] Kafieh, R., Rabbani, H., Kermani, S. "A review of algorithms for segmentation of optical coherence tomography from retina". In: *Journal of Medical Signals and Sensors* 3.1 (2013): 45.

[21] Kass, M., Witkin, A., Terzopoulos, D. "Snakes: Active contour models". In: *International Journal of Computer Vision* 1.4 (1988): 321–331.

[22] Sherbondy, A., Houston, M., Napel, S. "Fast volume segmentation with simultaneous visualization using programmable graphics hardware". In: *IEEE Visualization, 2003* (2003): 171–176.

[23] Kauffmann, C., Piche, N. "Cellular automaton for ultra-fast watershed transform on GPU". In: 2008 19th International Conference on Pattern Recognition. IEEE. 2008, pages 1–4.

[24] Wagner, B., Müller, P., Haase, G. "A parallel watershed-transformation algorithm for the GPU". In: *Workshop on Applications of Discrete Geometry and Mathematical Morphology* (2010): 111–115.

[25] Rumpf, M., Strzodka, R. "Level set segmentation in graphics hardware". In: Proceedings International Conference on Image Processing, IEEE. 2001, pages 1103–1106.

[26] Hong, J. J. Y., Wang, M. D. M. "High speed processing of biomedical images using programmable GPU". In: International Conference on Image Processing, 2004, pages 2455–2458.

[27] Xu, C., Prince, J. L. "Snakes, shapes, and gradient vector flow". In: *IEEE Transactions on Image Processing* 7.3 (1998): 359–369.

7 Preliminary Study of Retinal Lesions Classification on Retinal Fundus Images for the Diagnosis of Retinal Diseases

Jaskirat Kaur and Ramanpreet Kaur
Chandigarh Group of Colleges Jhanjeri Mohali Chandigarh, Chandigarh, India

Deepti Mittal
Thapar Institute of Engineering and Technology, Patiala, Punjab, India

CONTENTS

DOI: 10.1201/9781003241409-7

7.1   INTRODUCTION

Retinal diseases pose significant health-related issues having major incidence in developing countries. Retinal diseases mainly comprise systemic and non-systemic diseases. Systemic retinal diseases are those that spread in whole body and affect more than one organ at a time, whereas systemic retinal diseases are those that reside only in retina. The present work is centred on the detailed study of various retinal lesions related to systemic retinal abnormalities. Systemic retinal abnormalities have adverse effects on various parts of body, such as eyes, liver, kidneys, heart, neural system, but the first to be affected is retina, hence the vision impairment [1]. Additionally, prolonged cases of retinal diseases are the significant cause of severe vision loss or total blindness [2]. Vision loss due to systemic retinal diseases accounts for almost 15% of blindness cases worldwide [1]. According to WHO, globally at least 2.2 billion have vision impairment, of whom at least 1 billion have a vision impairment that could have prevented [2]. According to a survey conducted by International Diabetes Federation, the increase in prevalence of retinal diseases affects half a billion only due to diabetes and is projected to affect a billion people by 2045 [3]. Rapid increase in the rate of obesity, inactive lifestyle and lack of physical movement is the main aspect of increased prevalence of systemic retinal diseases. Systemic retinal diseases are the seventh leading cause of deaths worldwide and India tops the list by contributing 49% (72 million) of worlds retinal diseases cases and this figure is expected to almost double by 2025 [4].

Retinal diseases are chronic in nature and are mainly depicted by the incidence of one or more retinal lesions like dark and bright retinal lesions. Bright lesions are mainly categorized into exudates and cotton wool spots and dark lesions into microaneurysms and haemorrhages. Systemic retinal diseases are broadly categorized into non-proliferative retinal diseases and proliferative retinal diseases. Non-proliferative retinal diseases advance from mild to moderate and then severe stage [5]. Mild non-proliferative retinal diseases are depicted by the presence of one retinal lesion, whereas moderate stage is depicted by the incidence of two to four retinal lesions present in not more than two quadrants of retinal fundus image. However, the severe stage of retinal disease is identified by the presence of multiple types of retinal lesions in more than two quadrants of retinal fundus image. Proliferative stage of retinal diseases is an advanced stage depicted by the growth of new retinal blood vasculature in different regions of retinal fundus image, and it may lead to total blindness. Also, no treatment is effective at this stage of retinal disease. Patients depicting non-proliferative stage of retinal diseases generally exhibit no characteristic symptoms and, in most cases, vision is unaffected until a proliferative stage of retinal disease is attained. In brief, vision loss due to systemic retinal diseases is stage dependent and which further is depicted by the presence of retinal lesions in retinal fundus image. It is therefore significant to detect the stage of retinal diseases. One of the key challenges in the process of diagnosing retinal diseases is the accurate detection and segmentation of retinal lesions. Thus, the current study is focused on the preliminary study of the retinal lesions' classification on retinal fundus images for the diagnosis of retinal diseases.

7.2   RETINAL IMAGING MODALITIES

Retinal imaging modalities, such as retinal fundus imaging (FI), fundus fluorescein angiography (FFA) and optical coherence tomography (OCT) are the commonly used diagnostic techniques by expert ophthalmologists to detect non-proliferative retinal diseases and progressive retinal disease cases. There is no perfect retinal imaging modality for all ophthalmological applications and needs. In addition, each imaging modality is limited by its mechanism and type of image being produced. Medical imaging modalities that do not enter the skin are termed as non-invasive. The non-invasive medical imaging modalities like retinal fundus imaging and OCT play a significant role in diagnosis and treatment of retinal abnormalities by identifying the type of retinal lesion, its size, shape and number. The challenges with imaging modalities in extraction of clinically important information related to healthy structures and retinal lesions have received enormous attention. Fundus fluorescein angiography has been the gold standard to understand, confirm diagnosis and treat retinal abnormalities [6]. However, being an invasive procedure, it is quite difficult to be accepted by the patients because of associated side effects such as vomiting and the risk of developing different allergies [7]. Due to this non-invasive retinal imaging methods, such as FI and OCT, are highly used for retinal disease diagnosis during mass screening and to gather information about the particular abnormality.

The diagnostic clarification related to retinal abnormalities is a frequent problem in clinical routine. For imaging the retina, most hospitals use fundus imaging, FFA, or OCT. Presently, there is no consensus concerning the optimal strategy for imaging retina. All modalities have its advantages and limitations. The choice of which modality to use is identified based on the expert ophthalmologist, the availability of the equipment, the condition of the patient, and the experience of the ophthalmologist. To ensure the best treatment of the patient, preferably all lesions related to particular abnormality should be detected. Therefore, choosing the modality with the most benefits and least limitations is essential. With the brief introduction of FFA, OCT and fundus imaging modalities in the following paragraphs, some comparative statements are made to get the better understanding of the preferences among imaging modalities in order to detect non-proliferative and progressive diabetic retinopathy.

Fundus fluorescein angiography (FFA) is a procedure to image retina using a fundus camera by injecting a fluorescent dye. Sodium fluorescein dye is injected into the systemic circulation following which the retina is lit with blue light at a wavelength of 490 nm. Final FFA image is obtained by snapping the fluorescent green light that is emitted by the dye. FFA produces high contrast images of retina and is mainly used to analyse pathologies related to choroid and blood circulation that reside in retina. However, FFA being an invasive technique has a wide range of complications. The most common reactions are transient nausea, vomiting, pain and redness in eyes after the procedure.

Optical coherence tomography (OCT) is a procedure that uses coherent light to capture 2-D and 3-D retinal images from optical scattering media. It is based on the concept of interferometry to generate a cross-sectional view of the retina. Optical coherence tomography is useful in diagnosing retinal conditions related to macula. Lesions present in macula are easier to capture using OCT than in the other parts of retina. It is primarily helpful in identifying diabetic macular oedema, macular hole and age-related macular degeneration. OCT is non-invasive and easy to interpret, but OCT does not identify the changes in blood vessels. Therefore, this imaging modality is unable to document a disease with bleeding in the retina such as diabetic retinopathy.

Fundus imaging is a very popular and primarily used imaging modality. Almost all the ophthalmologists in the world have fundus cameras that provide high re-solution colour fundus photographs. Fundus imaging is done by using digital fundus camera to capture image of the true retinal fundus. Fundus cameras are non-invasive, easy to use, widely available, cost-effective and good at documenting the front view of retina where all the retinal lesions and anatomical structures are clearly visible. The images produced by fundus photography are the 2-D re-presentation of 3-D semi-transparent retinal tissues. They capture 30° to 50° views of the retina.

In summary, FFA, OCT and fundus photography imaging modalities of retinal imaging have its own advantages and disadvantages. Fundus photography is an attractive medical imaging technique in general because of unique set of virtues including (i) low cost making it feasible for a patient from low socio-economic status, (ii) versatility and widespread availability making its clinical relevance high worldwide, (iii) initial imaging modality due to its relative simplicity in comparison to other imaging modalities, (iv) risk-free system making it the first preference among other imaging modalities for screening of retinal abnormalities and (v) fast and portable making it convenient to use. In continuation, the fundus images are easy to study once the observer is trained. As a result, fundus imaging is an ex-tremely useful means of diagnostic imaging and the most widely employed imaging method for screening purposes and detection of retinal lesions related to systemic retinal diseases. Therefore, retinal fundus images are utilized in the present work to design computer-aided methods to diagnose non-proliferative retinal diseases and proliferative retinal diseases.

7.3   FUNDUS IMAGING

Fundus imaging is a procedure in which a 2-D representation of the 3-D retinal semi-transparent tissues of the back portion of the eye, i.e., fundus is projected onto

(a) (b)

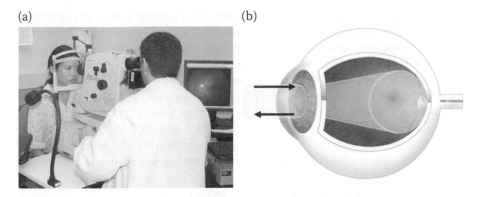

FIGURE 7.1 (a) Retinal imaging with fundus camera; (b) path of transmitted and reflected light from fundus camera [8].

the imaging plane. This projection is attained on the screen of a fundus machine by the image intensities that depict the expanse of light reflected from retina. Fundus photographs thus obtained record the details of the retina, which converts the optical visuals/images in front of our eyes into electrical signals for the brain to interpret. Fundus photography, a highly useful means of diagnostic imaging, has a wide array of clinical applications. The basis of its operation, as shown in Figure 7.1, is the projection of light into the eye through cornea followed by the reflection, processing, and display of image intensities reflected from retinal structures within the eye [8]. Ophthalmologists with the aid of these retinal fundus images take the follow-up, diagnose, and treat various retinal diseases such as diabetic retinopathy, age-related macular degeneration, hypertensive retinopathy etc. In order to construe a fundus image of the retina, it is essential to understand how a fundus imaging system works and how reflected light is converted into an image.

7.3.1 FUNDUS IMAGE FORMATION

The fundus cameras comprise of a complex microscope connected to a flash enabled camera. The design of the fundus camera is based on the working of an indirect ophthalmoscope. The observation illumination produced from either the observing lamp or the automated flash is projected on a circular mirror using a set of filters. This set of mirrors replicates the illumination into a sequence of lenses that focus the illumination. A cover on the topmost lens forms the doughnut shaped illumination. The doughnut shaped illumination is replicated onto a circular mirror with a central aperture to form a ring shape before exiting the camera through the objective lens, and proceeds into the eye through the cornea. The resulting retinal image formed from the reflected light exits the cornea through the central, unilluminated hole of the doughnut formed by the illumination system. As the paths of the projection of light into the retina and reception of light from the retina are not dependent, there are negligible reflections of the illuminating source that are captured in the image. This resulting image formed is directed towards the telescopic eyepiece attached to the fundus machine. Afterwards, when a switch is pushed to capture an image, the mirror intersects the path of the lighting system and light from the bulb is allowed to enter the eye. Concurrently, a mirror is directed opposite the observing telescope, which then sends the light onto the acquisition medium, i.e., film or a digital CD. The produced image on the film is a straight, magnified interpretation of the fundus described by an angle of view termed as field of view (FOV). Generally, an angle of 30° to 50° of retinal area (FOV) is used to create the retinal fundus image 2.5 times bigger than original retinal fundus image. Wideangle fundus cameras capture images between 45° and 145° that offer comparatively low magnification of retinal area and minimizes the image to half of the original size. Whereas, narrow angle fundus cameras capture images at FOV of 20° or less providing five times magnification.

Fundus photography has three modes of examination:

i. Colour fundus photography: In this mode, retina is illumined by white light and observed in full colour. Generally, this mode is the primary mode to capture retinal fundus images during first round of diagnosis.
ii. Red free fundus photography: The illuminating light is filtered to improve the contrast of retinal lesion structures with respect to the background. The filtering process removes red colours from the coloured retinal fundus images.
iii. Stereo fundus photography: Retinal fundus image intensities in this mode depict the amount of mirrored light from more than two angles of view to create a 3-D picture. The 3-D image generated by this process is used to obtain better surface characteristics than the above-mentioned photography modes.

7.4   EYE ANATOMY AND RETINAL DISEASES

The anatomical view of human eye is demonstrated in Figure 7.2 [8]. The retina is a multilayered sensory tissue that lines the back of the eye, senses light and produces electrical impulses. Such electrical impulses transmit to the brain from the optic nerve which are subsequently converted into images through photoreceptors. Photoreceptors are composed of two types: rods and cones. Rods can sense variations in contrast even at low illumination but cannot sense any variation in colour. Whereas cones are very sensitive to changes in colour. Rods and cones reside mainly in the macula, the region which is accountable for day vision. The central region of macula is termed as fovea, where the human eye is able to differentiate visual details with high precision. All these photoreceptors are attached to the brain via bundle of optic nerves. The circular region where the optic nerve exits the pupil is called as blind spot due to the absence of photoreceptors, also termed as optic disk. Retinal blood vasculature having tree-like structure supplies nutrients to the retina. Blood vessels have lesser reflectance as compared to other retinal structures; thus, they appear darker with respect to the background of fundus images. The retinal measures approximately 72% of a sphere about 22 mm in diameter, 0.56 mm thick near the optic disk, and thinnest at the centre of fovea in adult humans.

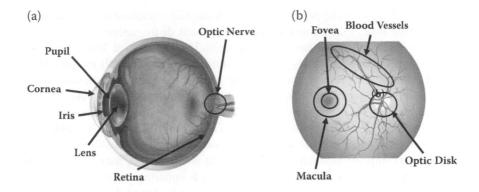

FIGURE 7.2 (a) Cross sectional view of right human eye (b) Photographic view of retina [8].

The retinal image serves as window to assess many systemic abnormalities and brain related abnormalities. The structures that can be visualized on a retinal fundus image are optic disk, peripheral retina, blood vessels and retinal lesions if present. Visually extractable features on retinal fundus images to detect diabetic retinopathy are based on the presence of type, size, shape and number of lesions. Thus, retinal fundus images are used to investigate and monitor the progression of abnormalities that affect the eye. Experienced ophthalmologists visualize these features in retinal fundus images to characterize various stages of retinal diseases and normal retina.

7.4.1 NORMAL RETINA

On retinal fundus images, the appearance of normal retina is homogeneous and clear providing the clean view of the fundus as shown in Figure 7.3 of the right eye. This image has no signs of any abnormality or pathology. There are no lesions, scars, or pigmentary changes in the retinal fundus. The normal retina has uniform

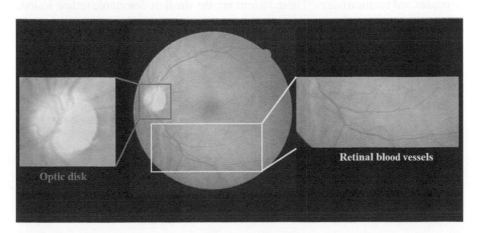

FIGURE 7.3 Appearance of normal retina on fundus image.

appearance along with the presence of main distinguishing structures such as blood vessels, optic disk, macula and fovea. These main distinguishing structures are termed as landmarks or anatomical structures. The network of blood vessels is the collection of dark red, finely elongated structures. Blood vessels merge into the highest light circular region known as the optic disk. The blood vessels in this fundus image are normal in course and calibre. Approximately two and half disk diameters to the right of the optic disk, a dark circular region, the fovea, which is at the centre of the area, is known as macula. These retinal structures like optic disk and blood vessels, can provide valuable information about the health of the retina. Such retinal components, such as optic disk and blood vessels, may provide useful details on retinas health. This is the reason that it is important to analyse and detect changes in their morphology. However, the prime indicator of the occurrence of a particular retinal abnormality or diseases is the appearance of lesions.

7.4.2 Retinal Lesions Associated with Various Retinal Diseases

Retinal lesions are recognized visually as alterations of the normal appearance of the retinal fundus image. Lesions appear with various attributes such as intensities, shape, colour, size etc. in retinal fundus images. They can be divided mainly into bright and dark (red) retinal lesions. Brief descriptions about these retinal lesions are given as below:

7.4.2.1 Dark Lesions

Dark lesions are mainly categorized into microaneurysms and haemorrhages.

7.4.2.2 Microaneurysms

Microaneurysms are the first sign of systemic retinal disease. They are dilated, aneurismal retinal vessels that look as small red dots detached from blood vessels in coloured retinal fundus images as shown in Figure 7.4. These lesions may pump fluid and blood through the eye, resulting in vision-threatening lesions such as exudates and haemorrhages. These lesions are the smallest detectable retinal lesions

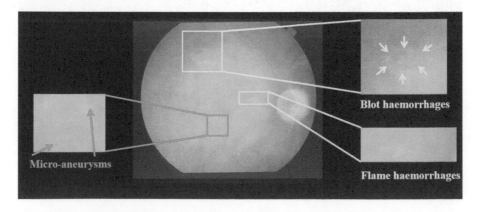

FIGURE 7.4   A fundus image having typical appearance of dark lesions.

and the local expansions of the weakened retinal capillaries. Microaneurysms are of variable size ranging from 10 to 100 micrometres. Some type of blood vessel-related abnormality or high blood pressure can lead to a retinal microaneurysm but the most common cause is diabetes mellitus. Microaneurysms alone are unlikely to cause external symptoms and need no treatment. Most microaneurysms are reversible if preventive measures such as healthy lifestyle, management of diabetes, etc. are taken timely.

7.4.2.3   Haemorrhages

These are distinguished by dark red colour and are of many forms such as: "dot", "blot" and "flame" haemorrhages. Dot haemorrhages are tiny red objects and are usually referred tomicroaneuysms. Haemorrhages of blots and fires lead to blood loss in deeper layers of retina. These manifest as large and dark retinal lesions with abnormal contours on the fundus images [9]. Figure 7.4 shows an example image highlighting different types of haemorrhages inside the marked bound regions of rectangular shape. A retinal haemorrhage can be caused by diabetes, hypertension or blockages in retinal vein. They are more serious retinal disease because they are associated with the onset of chronic diabetic retinopathy. Some of the common symptoms of haemorrhages are (i) visual disturbances producing unclear vision, (ii) presence of blind spots in vision, (ii) pain in the eye.

The detection and differentiation of microaneurysms and haemorrhages can be complex for the expert ophthalmologist as they are characterized by their weak contrast with the background. Also, these lesions have similar attributes in terms of colour and texture with anatomical structures like blood vessels.

7.4.2.4   Bright Lesions

Bright lesions are mainly categorized as exudates and cotton wool spots.

7.4.2.5   Exudates

Retinal exudates are masses of fatty matter moulded in the retina from lipids and protein leakage from microaneurysms [10,11]. The leakage of lipids and protein is due to increased pressure in the walls of microaneurysms that are thinner than normal capillaries. In retinal fundus images, these lesions seem as bright yellow crystalline granules having sharper definition as shown in Figure 7.5. Exudates can have varying shapes, sizes and locations and are the hallmark of the progressive diabetic retinopathy. Their scale may range from a few pixels to as wide as an input image, appearing as a circle. Increasing the exudate scale and positions means increasing the frequency degree of the abnormality. The presence of hard exudates results in various degrees of reduced vision depending on the location of exudates. Exudates may cause rapid vision impairment if not treated on time. In order to cease the further development of exudates, retinal area comprising of exudates are exposed to laser for photocoagulation by physicians.

7.4.2.6   Cotton Wool Spots

Cotton wool spots (or soft exudates) are small, swollen micro infarcts that appear because of obstructed blood vessels resulting in the impaired blood supply to that

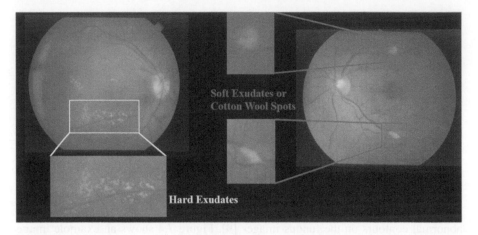

FIGURE 7.5 A fundus image having typical appearance of bright lesions.

area. Furthermore, the decreased blood flow injures the nerve fibres in that location resulting in blood circulation in local capillaries. They appear on fundus images as yellowish or white fluffy patches with blurred edges as depicted in Figure 7.5. Usually, their local spread is less than 1/3 optic disk areas in diameter and they are generally found throughout the retina. Cotton wool spots alone do not induce vision problems but are strongly associated with disorders influencing the development off the eye, as in the case of systemic retinal diseases. They also typically appear with other retinal abnormalities that cause significant symptoms and have long-term implications. Cotton wool spots sometimes vanish alone although any scattered lack of vision can be irreversible.

The designing of computer-aided retinal disease diagnostic method is done by extracting diagnostic information related to systemic retinal diseases from retinal fundus images by collectively identifying the presence of dark lesions such as microaneurysms and haemorrhages, bright lesions such as exudates and cotton wool spots and healthy structures such as blood vessels and optic disk. The computer-aided method is generally developed by using following steps: (i) Retinal image enhancement, (ii) characterization of healthy structures and retinal lesions, and (iii) computer-aided classification and grading method. The following sections highlight the need of these steps in detail.

7.5   NEED AND CHALLENGES IN COMPUTER AIDED RETINAL DISEASES DETECTION METHOD

Retinal fundus imaging is one of the valuable and non-invasive tools for imaging retina. However, due to its qualitative, subjective and experience-based nature, fundus images can be affected by imaging conditions such as illumination, machine settings. The visualization criteria for distinguishing various retinal lesions are slightly confusing and extremely based on upon the ophthalmologist's experience. This frequently results in ambiguity in the diagnostic procedure and reduces its objectivity and reproducibility. The visualization of retinal lesions is a tedious task with retinal fundus images because of their varying sizes, shapes, contrast with respect to the background etc. Moreover, overlapping characteristics of anatomical structures and retinal lesions confuses the ophthalmologists to differentiate them. In practice, an ophthalmologist analysing a huge number of retinal fundus images can have visual tiredness, resulting in the likelihood of spurious responses. It is therefore important to develop a computer-aided system for the identification of retinal diseases that ophthalmologists may use as a non-invasive diagnostic tool to support their findings on the basis of the characteristic visual appearance of retinal lesions on fundus images. Retinal disease diagnosis with the assistance of an efficient and reliable computer-aided detection method may reduce the frequency of further examinations.

7.6 NEED AND CHALLENGES IN RETINAL IMAGE ENHANCEMENT

It is extremely necessary to specifically distinguish all the typical signs of an abnormality found in retinal fundus images to achieve good diagnostic precision. Although artifacts and blur arise during retinal fundus image capture, the interpretation and analysis of retinal fundus images is severely hampered. Artifacts and blur are the prime factors that degrade the contrast resolution and obstruct the meaningful information present in retinal fundus image. Such objects are added due to lightning variations which are often responsible for differences in the non-uniform strength. Additionally, the blur, camera-dependent variables reduce the contrast resolution more and give the picture a noticeable fuzziness. An experienced ophthalmologist's detection of retinal abnormality is dependent on the conception of different structures in a retinal fundus image. Subsequently, the blurred contours of different retinal structures are extremely unwanted when accurately detecting lesions. Therefore, there is need to develop a methodology to enhance the visual quality of retinal fundus images to enhance the representation of the concept of retinal structures; the identification of lesions present in the retinal fundus picture must be effective. Therefore, enhancement methods are primarily designed with the intention to improve visualization of details available in retinal fundus images in order to provide accurate detection of anatomical structures and retinal lesions.

7.7 NEED AND CHALLENGES IN CHARACTERIZATION OF ANATOMICAL STRUCTURES AND LESIONS

Fundus images can be influenced by qualitative and subjective variations that may result in vague investigation and detection of different retinal lesions. Furthermore, the visual criteria for differentiating retinal lesions and anatomical structures are rather subjective and highly dependent upon the ophthalmologist's experience. This often affects the diagnostic procedure by limiting its objectivity. Additionally, the visualization of retinal lesions and anatomical structures with retinal fundus images is not an easy task because of their varying sizes and limited contrast with respect to the background. Therefore, there is a need to characterize anatomical structures and retinal lesions quantitatively in order to develop a computer-aided diagnostic method to support ophthalmologists in their decision-making.

7.7.1 SEGMENTATION OF RETINAL BLOOD VASCULATURE

Precise segmentation of blood vasculature is the first step in extracting diagnostic information for initial identification of diabetic retinopathy. However, challenges faced during blood vessels segmentation from various types of pathological retinal fundus images (i) the occurrence of artefacts due to poor background lightning during image acquisition; (ii) fuzzy appearance due to inappropriate focus; (iii) large variety of thicknesses and tortuosity; (iv) overlying of blood vasculature and lesions due to same intensities; and (iv) possibility of lost evidence due to tiredness and due to the large amounts of data being analyzed. Therefore, there is a need to develop an efficient blood vasculature segmentation method to precisely segment and then remove blood vessels from retinal fundus images. Therefore, blood vasculature segmentation methods for the detection of retinal diseases are designed to eliminate efficiently the blood vasculature from retinal fundus images.

7.7.2 DETECTION OF OPTIC DISK

The accurate detection of optic disk centre and approximate removal of optic disk region can help in reducing the spurious responses during diabetic retinopathy diagnosis and screening. Challenges faced in the automated detection of optic disk are: (i) same features of optic disk and bright lesions in a retinal fundus image in terms of colour, strength and contrast, (ii) partial acquisition of optic disk, (iii) hidden by major blood vessels crossings over the optic disk boundary, and (iv) ambiguous contour of optic disk. Therefore, there is a need to precisely locate and segment optic disk to avoid spurious responses during diagnosis of non-proliferative and progressive retinal diseases.

7.7.3 SEGMENTATION OF RETINAL LESIONS

Retinal lesions are primary visual indicators of various stages and types of retinal diseases. Therefore, retinal lesion identification and segmentation is an important step in diagnosing various retinal diseases. However, the obstacles encountered in the identification and precise segmentation of retinal lesions are (i) the existence of artefacts due to inappropriate lighting, (ii) blurry presence of lesions due to inappropriate concentration, (iii) ambiguity in definition of the class, extent, magnitude and precise contour of the lesions due to related geometry and diversity in structures; (iv) resemblance in the characteristics of healthy parts of retina comprising of optic disk and blood vasculature to those of bright and dark lesions respectively, and (v) likelihood of missing evidence due to human tiredness, while analysing a huge number of retinal images. Therefore, there is a need to reduce the significances of these restrictions in the precise computer-aided segmentation of retinal lesions. Thus, for the detection of retinal diseases, a generalized lesions segmentation method is designed by introducing a novel adaptive image quantization and dynamic decision thresholding-based method. Additionally, for the detection of non-proliferative retinal diseases several dark and bright lesions are segmented regardless of related heterogeneity, bright and faint edges in different retinal fundus images.

7.8 NEED AND CHALLENGES IN COMPUTER AIDED CLASSIFICATION AND GRADING METHOD

Experienced ophthalmologists with retinal photographs envision numerous shape, size and texture-based features to distinguish retinal lesions and then determine the frequency degree of a retinal disease. The grading of the level of non-proliferative retinal disease needs the comprehensive and quantitative authentication of all types of retinal lesions existing in the fundus image. Nevertheless, the skill and expertise of the ophthalmologist greatly depends on the manual labelling and segmentation, accuracy of valuation of lesions and relevant parameters. Therefore, the confusion resides in (i) reading correct contours owing to their varying forms and strengths leading to contradictions, and (ii) missing the probability of retinal lesions with limited number of pixels. In fact, each patient's evaluation is wearisome manually, and is a repetitive operation. In fact, the high risk of tests and the lack of specialists discourage many people receiving proper and timely treatment. This is also important to develop a computer-aided tool for the diagnosis of severity rates to support ophthalmologists, which will reduce the costs related with specialist graders and remove the uncertainty related to manual evaluation. Furthermore, the detection and classification of various retinal lesions is useful not only for detection for particular disease but also for preparation for treatment. The specialists assess the exact location of laser-exposed lesions for diagnosis. Thus, an efficient retinal lesions classification and non-proliferative retinal disease grading method is required for fast and accurate detection of non-proliferative retinal diseases.

The studies reported so far, in the computer-aided detection and grading of systemic retinal diseases, focuses mainly on either segmentation of anatomical structures or the segmentation of particular retinal lesions related to systemic retinal disease such as diabetic retinopathy [12–16]. Most of the methods use particular type of bright or dark lesions or combinations of them to diagnose retinal disease [17–19]. In practice, expert ophthalmologists consider the information related to various combinations of lesions such as their shape, size and location to draw conclusions. Hence, there is a need to develop a more practical, accurate and precise computer-aided diagnostic method by blending information related to retinal lesions and anatomical structures present in retinal fundus images. Thus, a solution is needed in terms of computer aided diagnostic method by introducing objectivity in segmentation of retinal lesions and anatomical structures regardless of associated heterogeneity, bright and faint edges in different retinal fundus images. The computer-aided non-proliferative retinal disease detection method is desirable with an extensive set of geometrical, colour and texture-based features for mathematically interpreting the visualization details of ophthalmologists. Further, the classification methods designed till date reveal that there have been limited numbers of trials to design a computer-aided method that can provide classification among five retinal lesion classes, i.e., No DR, EXU, CWS, MA and HEM followed by grading of a particular retinal disease. Therefore, a significant computer-aided detection method is required to classify these retinal lesion classes and determine the severity level of non-proliferative retinal disease effectively. Retinal lesions with proper and clear boundaries are easily identified by the ophthalmologists. However, the overlapping retinal lesions with anatomical structures or among themselves may result in ambiguous diagnosis and confliction even for the expert ophthalmologists. Thus, the techniques designed must include retinal images of varying attributes to provide a generalized computer-aided detection method for retinal disease diagnosis.

Further, the literature review also revealed that the neural network (NN) classifier had been used in various state-of-the-art-methods [20–22] for the classification of retinal lesions, whereas the multi-step classifiers have never been used to develop computer aided detection methods for retinal lesions despite that multi-step classifiers had been favoured in many other medical applications such as liver disease detection [23], brain tumour detection [24], breast cancer detection [25], retinal image database [26], etc. Therefore, the computer aided detection and grading of non-proliferative diabetic retinopathy in the present study are designed using two-step NN classifiers.

Literature review also reveals that most of the computer-aided diagnostic methods have utilized open-source benchmark databases and the limitation in using a particular open-source benchmark database is that it remains specific to only one type of retinal lesion. Therefore, few researchers have used various benchmark databases available publicly to provide an efficient computer-aided diagnostic solution. Furthermore, images in open-source benchmark databases are of superior quality than the images encountered by ophthalmologists in their clinical practice. Therefore, there is also a need to provide a practical solution that should work well with clinical retinal images. Thus, it is prerequisite to develop a composite database by combining publicly available retinal images dataset and clinically acquired images to provide a generalized computer-aided method for the diagnosis of retinal abnormality.

7.9 CONCLUSION

The present study is conducted to provide a general background to design a computer-aided retinal disease diagnostic method. Detailed understanding of various retinal lesions related to systemic retinal diseases and their characteristic visual appearance is also provided in this chapter. This preliminary research study is designed to understand the mathematical interpretation of various retinal anatomical structures (landmarks) and lesions to detect various retinal diseases and grade severity level of non-proliferative and proliferative retinal diseases from retinal fundus images. Finally, the need of (i) computer-aided retinal disease detection, (ii) retinal image enhancement, (iii) characterization of landmark (healthy) structures, (iv) characterization of retinal lesions and (v) computer-aided retinal disease classification and grading method have also been discussed.

REFERENCES

[1] Sarah, W., Gojka, R., Anders, G., Richard, S., Hilary, K. "Global prevalence of diabetes: Estimates for the year 2000 and projection for 2030," *Diabetes Care* 27.5 (2004): 1047–1053.

[2] WHO: Blindness and vision impairment, Available: https://www.who.int/news-room/fact-sheets/detail/blindness-and-visual-impairment. [Accessed: Jun. 11, 2020].

[3] International Diabetes Federation. "Diabetes complications," [Online]. Available: https://www.idf.org/aboutdiabetes/what-is-diabetes/complications.html. [Accessed: Jun. 11, 2020].

[4] Firstpost: Diabetes is indias fastest growing disease, Available: https://www.firstpost.com/india/diabetes-is-indias-fastest-growing-disease-72-million-cases-recorded-in-2017-figure-expected-to-nearly-double-by-2025–4435203.html.   [Accessed: Dec. 3, 2017].

[5] Chu, J., Ali, Y. "Diabetic retinopathy: A review," *Drug Development Research* 2.4 (1989): 226–237.

[6] Salz, D. A., Witkin, A. J. "Identifying and monitoring diabetic retinopathy," [Online]. Available: http://retinatoday.com/2016/03/identifying-and-monitoring-diabetic-retinopathy/. [Accessed: Dec. 5, 2017].

[7] "RxList-Fluorescite side effects center," [Online]. Available: https://www.rxlist.com/fluorescite-side-effects-drug-center.htm. [Accessed: Jan. 3, 2015].

[8] The university of british columbia, Department of Ophthalmology & Visual Sciences, Available: https://ophthalmology.med.ubc.ca/. [Accessed: June. 21, 2020].

[9] Sjølie, A., Stephenson, J., Aldington, S., Kohner, E., Janka, H., Stevens, L., Fuller, J. "Retinopathy and vision loss in insulin-dependent diabetes in Europe. The EURODIAB IDDM Complications Study," *Ophthalmology* 2 (1997): 252–260.

[10] Frith, P., Gray, R., MacLennan, S., Ambler, P. The Eye in Clinical Practice, 2nd ed., Blackwell Science Ltd., London (2001).

[11] Hollyfield, J. G., Anderson, R. E., LaVail, M. M. (Eds.). "Retinal degenerative diseases, Springer," *Laser Photocoagulation: Ocular Research and Therapy in Diabetic Retinopathy* 572 (2006): 195–200.

[12] Rokade, P. M., Manza, R. R. "Automatic detection of hard exudates in retinal images using Haar wavelet transform," *International Journal of Application or Innovation Engineering and Management* 4.5 (2015): 402–410.

[13] Zhang, B., Zhang, L., Zhang, L., Karray, F. "Retinal vessel extraction by matched filter with first-order derivative of Gaussian," *Computers in Biology and Medicine* 40.4 (2010): 438–445.

[14] Welfer, D., Scharcanski, J., Marinho, D. R. "A coarse-to-fine strategy for automatically detecting exudates in color eye fundus images," *Computerized Medical Imaging and Graphics* 34.3 (2010): 228–235.

[15] Zhang, X. et al. "Exudate detection in color retinal images for mass screening of diabetic retinopathy," *Medical Image Analysis* 18.7 (2014): 1026–1043.

[16] Liu, Q. et al. "A location-to-segmentation strategy for automatic exudate segmentation in colour retinal fundus images," *Computerized Medical Imaging Graphics* 55 (2017): 78–86.

[17] Habib et al. "Incorporating spatial information for microaneurysm detection in retinal images,"*Advances in Science, Technology and Engineering Systems Journal* 2.3 (2017): 642–649.

[18] Usman Akram, M., Khalid, S., Tariq, A., Khan, S. A., Azam, F. "Detection and classification of retinal lesions for grading of diabetic retinopathy," *Computers in Biology and Medicine* 45.1 (2014): 161–171.

[19] Figueiredo, I. N., Kumar, S., Oliveira, C. M., Ramos, J. D., Engquist, B. "Automated lesion detectors in retinal fundus images," *Computers in Biology and Medicine* 66 (2015): 47–65.

[20] Santhi, D., Manimegalai, D., Parvathi, S., Karkuzhali, S. "Segmentation and classification of bright lesions to diagnose diabetic retinopathy in retinal images," *Biomedical Engineering* 61.4 (2016): 443–453.

[21] Salem, N. M., Nandi, A. K. "Segmentation of retinal blood vessels using scale-space features and K-nearest neighbour classifier," *International Conference on Acoustics, Speech, Signal Processing* (2006): 1001–1004.

[22] Garcia, M., Valverde, C., Lopez, M. I., Poza, J., Hornero, R. "Comparison of logistic regression and neural network classifiers in the detection of hard exudates in retinal images," *35th Annual International Conference of the IEEE Engineering in Medicine and Biology Society (EMBC)* (2013): 5891–5894.

[23] Mittal, D., Kumar, V., Saxena, S. C., Khandelwal, N., Kalra, N. "Neural network based focal liver lesion diagnosis using ultrasound images,"*Computerized Medical Imaging and Graphics* 35.4 (2011): 315–323.

[24] Kharat, K., Kulkarni, P., Nagori, M. "Brain tumor classification using neural network based methods," *International Journal of Computer Science and Informatics* 1.4 (2012): 85–90.

[25] Esener, I. I., Ergin, S., Yuksel, T. "A new feature ensemble with a multistage classification scheme for breast cancer diagnosis," *Journal of Healthcare Engineering* 2017 (2017).

[26] Kaur, J., Mittal, D. "Construction of benchmark retinal image database for diabetic retinopathy analysis." *Part H: Journal of Engineering in Medicine, SAGE* 234.9 (2020).

8 Automatic Screening of COVID-19 Based on CT Scan Images Through Extreme Gradient Boosting

G. Madhu and G. Nagachandrika
VNR Vignana Jyothi Institute of Engineering and
Technology, Hyderabad, India

A. Govardhan
JNTUH College of Engineering, Hyderabad, India

K. Lakshman Srikanth
Legato Health Technologies LLP, Bangalore, India, and
GAR Infoban, Kokapet SEZ, Rangareddy, Telangana, India

CONTENTS

DOI: 10.1201/9781003241409-8

8.1   INTRODUCTION

COVID-19 is a deadly infection that led to a pandemic. It is caused by the Coronavirus of Severe Acute Respiratory Syndrome (SARS-CoV-2). The World Health Organization (WHO) declared COVID-19 as a global pandemic disease that led to global health crisis having a major impact on our day-to-day life [1]. The COVID-19 disease rapidly affected the world, and until now the global confirmed COVID-19 cases are 41,759,688, comprising 1,138,181 deaths and total recovered cases are 28,370,985 [2]. The SARS-CoV2 virus detection tests are classified into two types [3,4]: a) RT-PCR: Reverse Transcription-Polymerase Chain Reaction [3] and b) RAT-Rapid Antigen Tests. Since RT-PCR takes many hours, it is a time-consuming method with low sensitivity that may not be widely available in certain geographic areas [5][6]. Due to this reason, RT-PCR is not suggested as primary diagnostic tool for COVID-19 detection. The RAT recognizes antigenic fragments of the virus and can produce results in as little as 30 minutes [4]. The limitation of the RAT procedure is varied between laboratory conditions, missing half the infected cases, and less reliable for negative tests than RT-PCR, less effective later in the disease. Deep investigations for COVID-19 identification have been conducted that include testing chest X-rays (CXRs) and computed tomography (CT) scan images, but there are numerous challenges, including the enrolment of clinicians as well as patients in such studies [7]. Few studies stated that there have been instances where RT-PCR tests were found to be negative, but patients were declared positive through CT scan images. As a result, automated diagnostic tools are desperately required to deal with this situation, which can aid clinicians and radiologists in implementing COVID-19 screening protocols while also increasing sensitivity. Thus, spatial details and labelling complexity of contaminated areas continue to pose a significant challenge to COVID-19 automated screening procedures [8]. Thus, CT scans, which fuse a sequence of X-ray images, provide an opportunity for RT-PCR procedures; thereby providing huge assistance to radiologists [9]. The study is motivated by the facts versus CT scans built on false-positive rates, rapid identification, improved quarantining, scanner contagion, and poverty of change in public health management [9]. Recently, several studies [10,11] have used convolutional neural networks (CNN) to identify and classify COVID-19 using X-rays and CT scan images. These studies showed high performance only on large datasets and high computational power. Recent advances in AI, on the other hand, motivated us to create an automated diagnostic method for detecting COVID-19 through CT scan images. This would improve automation in the screening stage of the pandemic, which is vital in avoiding further spread of the infection. To overcome these challenges, this research uses SARS-CoV2 CT scan pictures to establish a machine learning (ML)-based diagnosis for COVID-19 screening. The study's primary contributions are as follows:

a. Creates a COVID-19 classification algorithm based on ML with the attributes of local and global features
b. HOG, LBP, SIFT, and SURF were utilized as descriptors for feature extraction in the COVID-19 CT scan images
c. Using incremental PCA for dimensionality reduction on the COVID-19 dataset, a low-rank approximation for the local and global feature set is created
d. Extreme Gradient Boosting (XGBoost) is employed for COVID-19 classification
e. Tested the efficacy of the suggested technique using the COVID-19 dataset
f. Analyzed the experimental effects using cutting-edge approaches

8.2 METHODOLOGY

8.2.1 TRADITIONAL METHODS

COVID-19 research is currently being conducted efficiently in various disciplines. Recently, several authors successfully developed ML-based computer-aided diagnostic tools and achieved significant results on lung disease identification and classification using CT scans and X-ray images [12,13].

The application of COVID-19 shows an unpredictable dispersion and concealing inside the X-ray or CT scan image [14]. However, automatic diagnosis systems for COVID-19 have gathered a lot of consideration in the literature [15]. They have published several research articles signifying computer-aided diagnostic tools in COVID-19 recognition by X-ray and CT scan images [16,17]. Yaghobzadeh et al. [18] presented a study of deep learning (DL) and ML papers in the diagnosis of COVID-19. A summary of seven important uses of artificial intelligence for COVID-19 research was proposed by Vaishya et al. [19].

The efficacy of ML techniques for COVID-19 identification, prognosis, and new problems with novel challenges of COVID-19 disease was posed by Zimmerman and Dinesh [20]. Fang Zhu et al. [21] published a paper on using ML to forecast COVID-19 patient severity progression based on chest CT scan images and lab measurements. Nayarisseri et al. [22] presented a study on COVID-19 protease inhibitors through an ML methodology. This method is used to create shape-based molecules and helped in the identification of molecular landing and molecular dynamics models.

Randhawa et al. [23] suggested a COVID-19 virus genome classification system based on ML and alignment-free. This methodology consolidated supervised learning algorithms with a digital signal processing system for genome analysis. Öztürk et al. [24] provided a shrunken features-based ML approach for COVID-19 classification through chest X-rays and CT scan images. The experimentation is carried out on smaller datasets with inter-class imbalance, which is handled through the over-sampling and augmentation methods.

Using chest CT scan images, Liu et al. [25] suggested an improved ML procedure for distinguishing COVID-19 from standard pneumonia. This method used a combination of bagged tree algorithms and features of statistical texture to discriminate COVID-19 pneumonia from normal pneumonia, with a classifier accuracy of 94.16%. Tamal et al. [26] presented the ML technique to identify COVID-19, which is based on a set of radionics features of COVID-19 and attained overall sensitivity and specificity of 99.6% and 85%, respectively, by support vector machine and 87.8% and 97%, respectively, by ensemble bagging algorithm. Using chest X-rays, Elaziz et al. [27] established a new ML approach to categorize COVID-19 as positive or negative. Features collected with multi-channel fractional exponent moments and increased optimization of the manta-ray feed have been used for the selection of features, and both data set1 and data set2, respectively, have achieved an overall accuracy of 96.0% and 98.09%, respectively.

For categorization of CT scan images, Sun et al. [28] developed an adaptive, deep forest selection feature for COVID-19. The 1,495 COVID-19 impacted records and 1,027 community-acquired people with community-acquired pneumonia were evaluated with accuracy, sensitivity, and an F1 score of 91.79%, 93.05%, and 93.07%, respectively. Through CT scan, Yu et al. [29] developed a quick diagnostic approach for deep characterization of COVID-19. Pretrained deep neural network models utilize COVID-19 CT scan image deep function extraction to categorize cases of COVID-19 severity. The experimental results show that Dense-Net-201 with the SVM paradigm outperformed the competition in COVID-19 severity classification. Goel et al. [30] proposed an automatic screening method for the classification of COVID-19 applying improved Generative Adversarial Network (GAN) on the SARS-CoV2 CT scan datasets. The model had a 99.22% overall accuracy, with a 97.82% PPV and a 99.77% NPV. DL algorithms for identifying COVID-19 in lung CT scan images were presented by Vinay Arora et al. [31]. Super-residual dense neural networks were utilized in this model to detect COVID-19 on SARS-COV-2 CT Scan images and COVID-CT scan images. Transfer learning prototypes were used to classify CT scan pictures as positive or negative for COVID-19. When compared to other models, the MobileNet model achieved substantial results.

The comparative study of computer-assisted tests employed with chest CT scans and X-ray pictures was presented by SethyPrabira Kumar et al. [32]. The assessment is conducted with 65 COVID-19 categorization ML models. All of the previous classifiers were found to be good with chest X-rays. Ibrahim et al. [33] suggested a DL-based computer-aided framework for classifying the severity of COVID-19 infection in 3D chest X-rays. There are two stages to this model: a) feature study and b) classification. In the first stage, preprocessing is utilized to extract features, which are then used to segment the lung area using VGG16 and fuzzy c-means clustering, then norm-VGG16 is used to feature the generation of segmented images. This study develops an automatic diagnostic model based on the challenges of SARS-CoV2 CT scan images.

8.2.2 PROPOSED METHOD

In this research, we develop *M-Cov*, which helps radiologists in the diagnosis of COVID detection. The *M-Cov* framework is divided into four stages: i) feature extraction, ii) normalization, iii) feature selection, and iv) classification of COVID-19 using SARS-CoV-2 CT scan images. Figure 8.1 depicts the suggested implementation of the ML system. In stage 1, we adapted Histogram of Oriented Gradients (HOG), Local Binary Pattern (LBP), Scale-Invariant Feature Transform (SIFT), and Speeded Up Robust Features (SURF) descriptors for feature extraction of COVID-19 CT scan images with a focus on COVID-19 detection.

Second, we performed normalization on the COVID-19 CT scan image dataset using the z-score method. Third, a dimensionality reduction was conducted on COVID-19 CT scan images using incremental PCA, and a low-rank approximation for the local and global CT scan feature set was constructed. Finally, Extreme Gradient Boosting (XGBoost) was employed for COVID-19 detection and classification.

8.2.2.1 Histogram of Oriented Gradients (HOG) Features

The HOG was created by Dalal and Triggs [34] and is a function descriptor for human detection that includes gradient orientation in a particular portion of an image or region of interest. Except for object orientation, it uses neighborhood cells and is invariant to geometric and photometric shifts. These progressions will occur in broader spatial regions. It counts the number of times an image's edge orientation takes place. Figure 8.2 depicts the model for implementing the HOG descriptor on the CT scan image.

Let *Gx* and *Gy* be the horizontal and vertical gradients of the input image that can be computed for each pixel (x, y) using a one-dimensional mask using the following equations:

$$G_x = I(x + 1, y) - I(x - 1, y) \qquad (8.1)$$

$$G_y = I(x, y + 1) - I(x, y - 1) \qquad (8.2)$$

Then, calculate the magnitude and gradient direction or orientation of the gradient as follows:

$$\text{Magnitude}(M(x, y)) = \sqrt{G_x^2 + G_y^2} \qquad (8.3)$$

$$\text{Gradient direction}(\theta) = arctan\left(\frac{G_x}{G_y}\right) \qquad (8.4)$$

The HOG descriptor has great invariance in little disfigured features, but it has inadequate competence to illustrate local features which are very sensitive to noise.

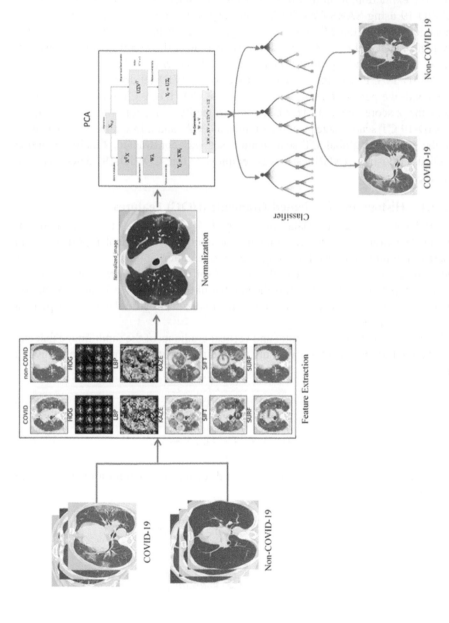

FIGURE 8.1 Proposed (*M-Cov*) COVID-19 detection and classification framework overview.

HOG

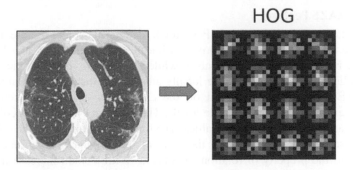

FIGURE 8.2 Histogram of oriented gradients of COVID-19 CT scan image.

8.2.2.2 Local Binary Pattern (LBP) Features

LBP [35,36] is a textural operator for defining the local neighborhood in grayscale images that thresholds the center pixel's assessment with each pixel's neighborhood and treats the results as a binary number [37]. It labels pixels in an image by each pixel's neighborhood thresholding with a binary number assessment of the center pixel. It defines the image's local features and has the advantages of low computation and reliable classification. The local textual feature of the CT scan image I(x, y) is characterized as follows:

$$L_T = T(G_c, G_n) \tag{8.5}$$

where g_c is the center pixel's grey value, and circular points "n" are converted to binary patterns, and $G_n = g_0, g_1, \dots g_{n-1}$. As a result, the LBP of the center pixel measure can be described as follows:

$$LBP_{PR} = \sum_{n=0}^{n-1} F(G_n - G_c) * 2^n \tag{8.6}$$

$$\text{where } F(x) = \begin{cases} 1, & \text{if } x \geq 0; \\ 0, & \text{otherwise} \end{cases} \tag{8.7a}$$

The model for the implementation of the LBP features on the COVID-19 CT scan image is shown in Figure 8.3.

LBP

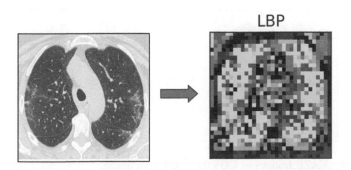

FIGURE 8.3 Local binary pattern features of COVID-19 CT scan image.

8.2.2.3 KAZE Features

KAZE features, proposed by Pablo Fernandez Alcantarilla et al. [38], are multiscale 2D feature detectors that can employ non-linear scale-space using non-linear diffusion filter techniques. Lowering noise while keeping the image's object borders leads to blurring of images that are locally adaptive to incorporate feature values. The KAZE detector is established on the calculation of a normalized Hessian Matrix determinant at multiple scale levels. The shifting window protocol uses the detector reaction limit as function values. The function definition, on the other hand, discovers significant orientation in the form of the circular neighborhood, which gives rise to the property of rotation invariance. With a small increase in computational complexity, the KAZE feature sets are invariant to ration, size, and minimal affine, and have additional uniqueness at diverging scales. The classic non-linear diffusion formulation [34] is seen in the following calculation:

$$\frac{\partial L}{\partial t} = div(c(x, y, t) * \nabla L) \tag{8.7b}$$

where $\boldsymbol{div}$ is the divergence, ∇ is the gradient operators, $\boldsymbol{c}$ is conductivity function, and L is the image luminance. The time t is the scale parameter.

The model for the implementation of the LBP features on the COVID-19 CT scan image is shown in Figure 8.4.

8.2.2.4 SIFT Features

D.G. Lowe [39,40] proposed a scale-invariant feature transform (SIFT) feature detector for finding unique local features in the image. SIFT detector is classified into two phases [41]: i) feature extraction and ii) description; first extract the key points of objects from a collection of reference images and store the results into the database. As a result, object identification in a new image is accomplished by assessing each function of the new image to the input database one by one. Low-level features are concerned with the descriptor process in object matching to locate candidate identical features based on Euclidean distance. The Difference-of-Gaussians (DOG) operator is at the heart of this detector shown in Equation (8.9), which is used to find possible image features of interest and approximates the Laplacian-of-Gaussian (LOG)

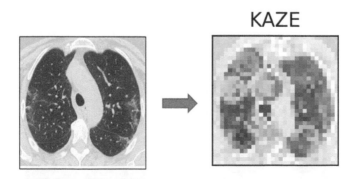

FIGURE 8.4 KAZE features of COVID-19 CT scan image.

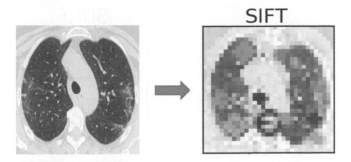

FIGURE 8.5   SIFT features of COVID-19 CT scan image.

operator. The normalized scale Equation (8.8) shows how the Laplacian is normalized about the scale stage, which is described as follows [42]:

$$\nabla^2_{norm} L(x, y; s) = s(L_{xx} + L_{yy}) = \left(\frac{\partial^2 L}{\partial x^2} + \frac{\partial^2 L}{\partial y^2} \right) \qquad (8.8)$$

$$DOG(x, y; s) = L(x, y; s + \Delta s) - L(x, y; s) \qquad (8.9)$$

Before the orientation is determined by the local gradient direction, the features are examined to determine the object's position and size. Finally, the feature set is transformed into a representation that can cope with lighting changes and local shape distortion. Some features detected for a CT scan COVID-19 image are shown in Figure 8.5; here, major features detected by descriptors are shown.

8.2.2.5   Speeded Up Robust Features (SURF)

Herbert Bay et al. (2006) [43] presented the technique as a SURF feature descriptor that computes small portions of the allocated image and is based on feature detectors and multiscale space theory. This is determined by the Hessian Matrix factor, and the basic concept of SURF is to generate a scale-invariant local feature descriptor from input image data using any feature extraction method. The SURF algorithm [44] is like SIFT in that it has two major parts, the first of which uses squared cut streams and the Hessian matrix to find the image's focal points. Also, by obtaining constrained features about this stage, feature descriptors can be created. These are often generated by examining localized feature squared images and the region surrounding a point of interest (POI), and hence Haarwavelet responses within a specific neighborhood, as well as their answers at specific interval-based sampling points. SURF characteristics are pivot and scale-invariant but only have a small affine invariance. The mahotas SURF Python library is used in this study to compute local regions of blood images using feature extraction. The POI is calculated using the entire image as well as image regions that are very similar to the interest points that are being viewed for further study. Feature detection for a CT scan COVID-19 image is showed in Figure 8.6; major features are detected using the SURF technique, as shown in Figure 8.6.

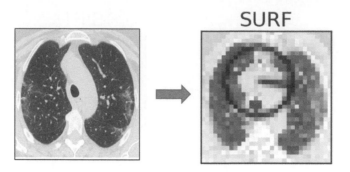

FIGURE 8.6   SURF features of COVID-19 CT scan image.

8.2.2.6   Normalization

This involves transforming feature dataset into a generic format using the standardization technique before implementing feature selection with principal component analysis (PCA). This is done to ensure that all variables, regardless of form, are internally compatible with one another. The procedure of the *z-score* consists of the subtraction and division by the appropriate standard deviation of the mean intensity of the whole CT scan image or region of interest. The COVID-19 CT scan dataset's local and global features were standardized using the *z-score* normalization method [45], which rescales feature set values to give them the qualities of a typical normal distribution with mean–average feature values and a standard deviation from the mean of one. Figure 8.7 shows a normalized image of a COVID-19.

$$\text{CT scan}.z - \text{score(featureset)} = \frac{x - \mu}{\sigma} \tag{8.10}$$

8.2.2.7   Principal Component Analysis (PCA)

In ML applications, PCA [46] is one of the most widely utilized techniques for reducing dimensions. It is a linear transformation process that transforms data into a new coordinate system, resulting in the generation of a new collection of features known as principal components of the original features. In this case, similarity

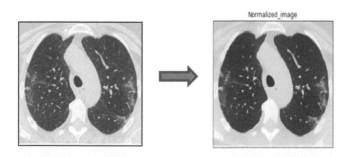

FIGURE 8.7   Normalized COVID-19 CT scan image.

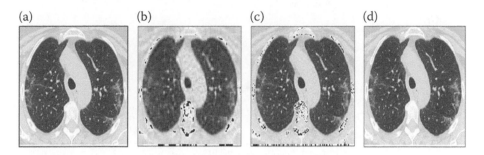

FIGURE 8.8   (a) Input COVID-19 image, (b) compressed image with first 20 principal components, (c) compressed image with first 50 principal components, (d) compressed image with first 200 principal components.

indicates that there is information continuity, which can be minimized and compressed. Figure 8.8 shows the compressed images of the first 20, 50, and 200 principal components. Build a sharp picture like the original using the first 200 principal components.

8.2.3   DATASETS USED

To guide clinical decisions, access to first-hand CT images and clinical information is essential for providing information to a deeper understanding of the patterns of virus infections and providing systemic models for prompt diagnosis and timely medical interferences, as the COVID-19 pandemic spreads globally. An important way to help combat COVID-19 globally is to build a thorough database available to CT images and accompanying clinical symptoms. As stated in the traditional methods, some datasets were established and are available for COVID-19-related researchers, doctors, and data scientists. This study used SARS-CoV2 datasets [47], which includes a total of 1,252 CT scan images for COVID-19 positive cases and 1,230 negative images, which have been made publicly accessible [47]. The datasets were gathered from real-time patients in hospitals in Sao Paulo, Brazil. Figure 8.9 illustrates some examples of COVID-19 positive and negative CT scan images.

8.2.4   EXPERIMENTS PERFORMED

We examined seven different ML algorithms in this study to discover which one would perform best in an automated COVID-19 screening using SARS-CoV-2 CT scan images for coronavirus prediction. In this vein, we used Adaboost [48], Bagging [49], k-Nearest Neighbour (k-NN) [50], Nave Bayesian [51], Random Forest [52], Support Vector Machine (SVM) [53], and Extreme Gradient Boosting (XGBoost) [54] as ML algorithms in our experiments. All these ML algorithms were run with their default hyperparameter settings, as described in the Python library packages.

(a)

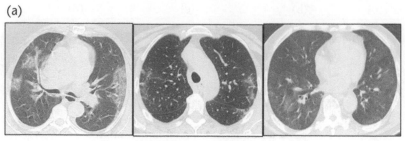

CT Scan Images Positive cases

(b)

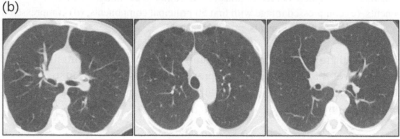

CT Scan Images Negative cases

FIGURE 8.9 Illustrate the tests of CT scan images: (a) COVID-19 positive, (b) COVID-19 negative.

8.2.4.1 Adaboost

Adaptive Boosting (AdaBoost) invented by Yoav Freund and Robert Schapire [48] is a well-known ML boosting technique. The aim is to combine various weak classifiers to build a strong classifier. Consider the dataset $\{(x_1, y_1), (x_2, y_2)...(x_n, y_n)\}$ where each instance $x_i \in \mathbb{R}^n$ has an associated class $y_i \in \{-1, 1\}$; where n is the dimension of the dataset, x is the set of data values, y is the target variable that is either positive class or negative class. A set of weak classifiers $\{k_1, k_2, ... k_n\} \in \{-1, 1\}$ for every instance. Later, the $(n-1)^{th}$ iteration in this enhanced classifier forms a linear combination of the weak classifiers showed in the following equation:

$$A_{(n-1)}(x_i) = \varphi_1 k_1(x_i) + \varphi_2 k_2(x_i) + ...+ \varphi_{n-1} k_{n-1}(x_i) \qquad (8.11)$$

Where the class will be the sign of $A_{(n-1)}(x_i)$. At the nth iteration, we need to extend a better-boosted classifier by combining a new week classifier k_n with another weight φ_n, shown in Equation (8.12).

$$A_{(n)}(x_i) = \varphi_1 k_1(x_i) + \varphi_2 k_2(x_i) + ...+ \varphi_{n-1} k_{n-1}(x_i) + \varphi_n k_n(x_i) \qquad (8.12)$$

This will determine which weak classifier is the best choice for k_n, its weights φ_n. In our experiments, we used the Python package *AdaBoostClassifier* [55] for COVID-19 classification using SARS-CoV-2 CT scan images.

8.2.4.2   Bagging

Leo Breiman [55] developed Bootstrap aggregating (Bagging), which aims to increase the model's stability and accuracy while also removing the difficulties of overfitting. It takes a few weak models and aggregating the predictions to choose the best prediction. Let X be the training sample, and generate samples of X_1, X_2, X_3 ... X_N using bootstrapping. Now for each sample to train its classifier $v_i(x)$ the final classifier will be an average of the outputs from all these individual classifiers. In the process of classification, this technique corresponds to the following voting:

$$V(x) = \frac{1}{N} \sum_{i=1}^{N} v_i(x) \qquad (8.13)$$

However, bagging reduces the variance of the classifier by declining the discrepancy in error when we train the model on various datasets. We used the Python program BaggingClassifier [56] to classify COVID-19 using SARS-CoV-2 CT scan images in our experiments.

8.2.4.3   *k*-Nearest Neighbor

In 1951, Evelyn Fix and Joseph Hodges [50] developed the *k*-nearest neighbor's algorithm, a non-parametric technique. Later extended by Thomas Cover and commonly used in the area of pattern recognition problems for classification and regression. This classifier depends on learning by relationship, i.e., by contrasting offered test samples with training samples that are similar to it. The *k*-NN classifier pursuits in a metric space (X, d) given a point $y \in X$, and for the k training examples that are nearest to the anonymous sample. Here, nearest or proximity is described in terms of distance measure like Euclidean distance, defined as follows:

$$d(X_1, X_2) = \sqrt{\sum_{i=1}^{n} (x_{1i} - x_{2i})^2} \qquad (8.14)$$

Where $X_1 = (x_{11}, x_{12}, \ldots x_{1n})$ and $X_2 = (x_{21}, x_{22}, \ldots x_{2n})$ are the two data samples. In the *k*-NN classification, the anonymous attribute is designated among its k neighbors, the most prevalent class. In our experiments, we used the Python package *KNeighborsClassifier* [57] in the COVID-19 classification by applying SARS-CoV-2 CT Scan Images.

8.2.4.4   Naïve Bayesian Classification

The Naïve Bayesian algorithm is a classification strategy based on the Bayesian theorem and conditional independence assumptions [51], which implies that the given qualities $X1$, $X2$, ... Xn is conditionally independent of one another when it comes to Y. First, the common probability distribution $P(X, Y)$ is found and a conditional probability distribution is generated based onan assumption of conditional independence [58].

$$P(X = x|Y = C_j) = \prod_{l=1}^{n} P(X^{(l)} = x^{(l)}) \text{ for } j = 1, 2, \dots K \tag{8.15}$$

By the learning model, the output label y is calculated with Bayes' theorem, i.e.,

$$P(Y = C_j|X = x) = \frac{P(X = x|Y = C_j)P(Y = C_j)}{\sum_{j=1}^{K} P(X = x|Y = C_j)P(Y = C_j)} \tag{8.16}$$

and

$$y = arg_{C_j}^{max} P(Y = C_j) \prod_l P(X^{(l)} = x^{(l)}|Y = C_j) \tag{8.17}$$

We used the Python package sklearn.naiveBayes [59] to classify COVID-19 using SARS-CoV-2 CT scan images in our experiments.

8.2.4.5 Random Forest

Tin Kam Ho [52] was invented in 1995 employing a random subspace approach to random decision-making forests. An extension of these decision forests was developed by Leo Breiman [60] who disclosed *"Random Forests"* as a brand. Used for regression and classification, the forest develops an ensemble of decision trees by training with the bagging strategy. The basic concept of the bagging strategy is that a mixture of learning methods increases the model performance. These forests are trained on the given data of the equivalent size as the training set, known as bootstraps, which are formed from the random sampling on the training data set to this one. Previously, a forest is created with a set of bootstraps that are not already enclosed from the given dataset [also called out of the bag (OOB)] that is utilized as the testing dataset [61]. In our experiments, we used the Python package *RandomForestClassifier* [62] in the COVID-19 classification using SARS-CoV-2 CT scan images.

8.2.4.6 Support Vector Machine (SVM)

In 1963, Vladimir N. Vapnik et al. [53] created the SVM, which is based on kernel functions and may be used for both linear and non-linear classification. The data is mapped into the feature space of a higher-dimensional using these kernel functions, and the groups are separated by a hyperplane. Allow for an n-dimensional feature vector for each class $X = (x_1, x_2, x_3 \dots x_n)$ and its class label Y is assigned into two class, i.e., $\{-1, +1\}$. The boundary hyperplane has the following properties:

$$W^T X + b = 0 \tag{8.18}$$

Where W stands for weight vector, and b stands for the bias value. The idea behind this strategy is to reduce the cost function $C(W)$, which is characterized as follows:

$$C(W) = \frac{1}{W^T * W} \qquad (8.19)$$

In data points of the linearly non-separable case, Equation (8.18) can be composed as follows:

$$W^T \varphi(X) + b = 0 \qquad (8.20)$$

Where φ is the kernel function applied to transform the data into higher-dimensional space. In our experiments, we used the Python package libsvm [63] in the COVID-19 classification by applying SARS-CoV-2 CT scan images.

8.2.4.7   Extreme Gradient Boosting (XGB)

XGBoost stands for "Extreme Gradient Boosting", which was coined by Friedman [54]. Chen and Guestrin [64] developed an integrated distributed gradient boosting library in 2016, which is scalable throughout multiple languages. It is commonly used to solve classification and regression problems. Let D be a dataset with m features and n samples, as described in Equation (8.21).

$$D = \{(x_1, y_1)((x_2, y_2)...((x_n, y_n)\} \text{ where}(x_i, y_i) \in \mathbb{R}^m \qquad (8.21)$$

Let $\hat{y}_i$ be the predicted value of an ensemble tree model that is generated from the below Equation (8.22):

$$\hat{y}_i = \sum_j \theta_j x_{ij} \qquad (8.22)$$

Where θ denotes the parameter, and Equation (8.22) is a linear combination of weighted features. The forecast value can have various interpretations based on the given task that is regression or classification. In our experiments, XGBoost was used to generate the gradient boosted decision trees for the classification of SARS-CoV-2 CT scan images. This research develops an additive model in a forwarding fashion by using *GradientBoostingClassifier* [64] python library for COVID-19 classification.

8.3   RESULTS

This research develops a ML-based approach called XGBoost classifier for screening and COVID-19 classification using SARS-CoV2 CT scan images, and the scheme showed in Figure 8.1. In the initial step, features are extracted by global feature descriptors, such as HOG, LBP, and local feature descriptors such as SIFT, SURF, and the generated features are used in the quantification of CT scan images feature extraction by in-depth analysis to detect coronavirus.

The next step is to utilize PCA to determine which feature subset is appropriate for COVID-19 classification.

After the first 50 variables, the proportion of each eigenvector contributes very little, but they collectively contribute more than 50% of the data variance, so we should have at least 200 variables for the prediction shown in Figure 8.10. The proposed model could be simplified by employing PCA and using the altered CT scan data based on 150 components (instead of 300 features), and 148 features would explain >98% of the variance. To visualize the data in Figure 8.11, we project original COVID-19 data onto the new feature space and map the first two components. Similarly, z-score normalization retained some components in PCA over feature variance, as presented in Figure 8.12. Over variance of PCA projected data, the number of components kept using the Elbow approach, as shown in Figure 8.12.

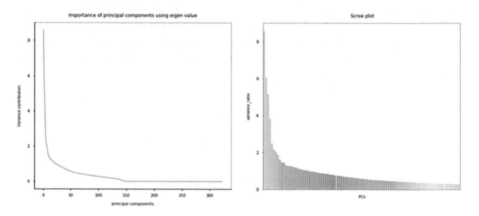

FIGURE 8.10   The importance of principal components and their bar plot.

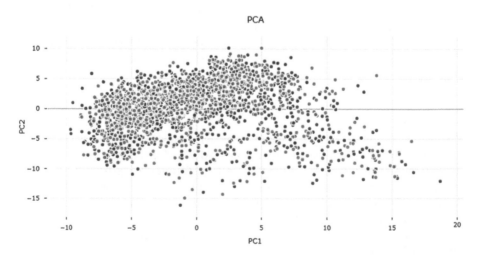

FIGURE 8.11   The first two principal components for visualizing the data.

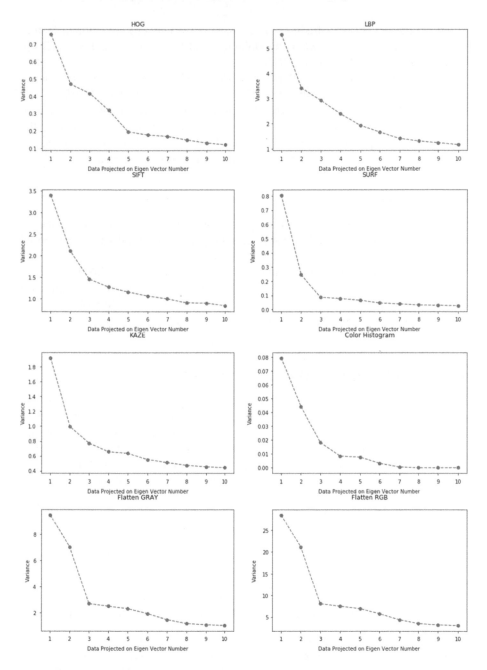

FIGURE 8.12   PCA feature variance comparison PCA ($n = 10$) Z-Score normalization on COVID-19 data.

The suggested model's findings were obtained by selecting the optimal feature set, comparing it to other ML methodologies, and testing it on SARS-CoV2 CT scan pictures, as briefly given in Table 8.1.

Results show in Table 8.1 that the *M-Cov* model improves the performance concerning COVID-19 classification. This model exhibits better COVID-19 detection results in CT scan images that were tested and attained training accuracy of 98.78% and test accuracy of 93.96%, respectively. It has been found that the proposed model produces more reliable COVID-19 classification outcomes, assisting in better COVID-19 diagnosis and preventing disease spread.

8.3.1 COMPARATIVE STUDY

The performance significance of the suggested model is compared to state-of-the-art techniques. As demonstrated in Table 8.2, the performance measure of proposed ML methodology outclasses that of the other models.

The ROC curve for global and local features of SARS-CoV2 CT scan COVID-19 images is shown in Figure 8.13 for different classifiers. Finally, we conclude that the XGBoost technique performed well on COVID-19 classification, assisting in enhanced COVID-19 diagnosis, and preventing disease dissemination.

8.4 CONCLUSION AND FUTURE WORKS

In this research, the authors develop an *M-Cov* methodology for screening and revelation of COVID-19 from SARS-CoV2 CT scan images. We looked at a more in-depth study of a variety of features that are intriguing because of their superior performance in COVID-19 image classification. Furthermore, it is used to extract feature descriptors from CT scan images using global and local feature descriptors. Researchers used principal component analysis to find the best function

TABLE 8.1

The Contrast of Various Classifiers Metrics with Different Feature Sets

Models	COVID-19 CT Scan Image Feature Dataset + PCA (n = 10)			
	Metrics			
	Test Accuracy	Precision	Recall	F1-Score
Adaboost	85.64	87.55	85.51	86.52
Bagging	84.38	86.19	84.57	85.37
k-NN	77.93	82.14	75.23	78.53
Naïve Bayes	76.07	84.00	68.69	75.57
Random Forest	88.66	92.89	85.51	89.05
SVM	83.12	89.30	78.03	83.29
Proposed (*M-Cov*)	**93.96**	**95.20**	**92.96**	**94.07**

TABLE 8.2

Comparison of the Proposed Model's Performance with the Existing Advanced Pretrained Models

Method	Accuracy (%)	Sensitivity (%)	Specificity (%)	F1-score (%)
AlexNet	96.44	97.56	95.34	96.70
CGAN	82.93	96.51	89.57	80.00
Ensemble CNN	86.09	93.46	87.44	87.52
GoogleNet	95.54	97.19	93.89	95.71
VGG19	95.12	92.58	98.25	95.67
Proposed	98.78	99.12	97.95	98.48

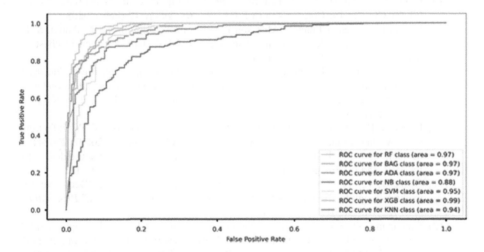

FIGURE 8.13 ROC curves for classifiers trained over feature projections of global feature and local features of COVID-19 data.

subset for COVID-19 classification. When evaluated using SARS-CoV2 CT scan images, the suggested screening model outperformed existing ML algorithms, according to the findings of the studies. Finally, our findings indicate significant performance on COVID-19 classification, assisting in improved COVID-19 diagnosis and preventing disease spread. Furthermore, via telemedicine, it may be ideal to deliver rapid diagnosis in isolated areas where COVID centers are not readily available. It can also be used in telemedicine to provide rapid diagnosis in remote areas where radiologists are not always available. DL techniques that perform better in combining clinical reports with imaging data should be investigated in future works.

REFERENCES

[1] World Health Organization. "World Health Organization coronavirus update." (2020). [Online]. Retrieved May 5, 2020. https://www.who.int/emergencies/diseases/novel-coronavirus-2019.

[2] World Meter. "Coronavirus cases." https://www.worldometers.info/coronavirus/ [Accessed, June 2021].

[3] Xie, X., Zhong, Z., Zhao, W., Zheng, C., Wang, F., Liu, J. "Chest CT for typical 2019-nCoV pneumonia: Relationship to negative RT-PCR testing." *Radiology* 12 (Feb. 2020).

[4] "Key Challenges Faced by Covid-19 Tests: Opinion." Hindustan Times, 5 Oct. 2020, http://www.hindustantimes.com/india-news/key-challenges-faced-by-covid-19-tests/story-GxvVfnEVFhpWvvcqKYfItM.html, 5 Oct. 2020,

[5] Ai, T., Yang, Z., Hou, H., Zhan, C., Chen,C., Lv, W., et al. "Correlation of chest CT and RT-PCR testing in coronavirus disease 2019 (COVID-19) in China: A report of 1014 cases." *Radiology* 26 (Feb. 2020).

[6] Fang, Y., Zhang, H., Xie, J., Lin, M., Ying, L., Pang, P., et al. "Sensitivity of chest CT for COVID-19: Comparison to RT-PCR." *Radiology* 19 (Feb. 2020).

[7] Rajaraman, S., Siegelman J., Alderson P. O., Folio L. S., Folio L. R., Antani S. K. "Iteratively pruned deep learning ensembles for COVID-19 detection in chest X-rays." *arXiv preprint arXiv* 2004.08379 (2020).

[8] Han, Zhongyi, Wei, Benzheng, Hong, Yanfei, Li, Tianyang, Cong, Jinyu, Zhu, Xue, Wei, Haifeng, Zhang, Wei. "Accurate screening of COVID-19 using attention based deep 3D multiple instance learning." *IEEE Transactions on Medical Imaging* 39 (2020):2584–2594.

[9] Kanne, J. P. "Chest CT findings in 2019 novel coronavirus (2019-nCoV) infections from Wuhan, China: Key points for the radiologist." *Radiology* (2020): 200241.

[10] Murala, S., Wu Q. J. "Local ternary co-occurrence patterns: a new feature descriptor for MRI and CT image retrieval." *Neurocomputing* 119 (2013): 399–412.

[11] Gjesteby, L., Yang, Q., Xi, Y., Zhou, Y., Zhang, J., Wang, G. "Deep learning methods to guide CT image reconstruction and reduce metal artifacts." *Proceedings of SPIE* 10132 (2017): 101322W.

[12] American College of Radiology. "Recommendations for Chest Radiography and CT for Suspected COVID19 Infection." https://www.acr.org/Advocacy-and-Economics/ACR-Position-Statements/Recommendations-for-Chest-Radiography-and-CT-for-Suspected-COVID19-Infection, Updated March 22 (2020).

[13] Castellano, G., Bonilha, L., Li, L., Cendes, F. "Texture analysis of medical images." *Clinical Radiology* 59.12 (2004): 1061–1069.

[14] Wang, D., Hu, B., Hu, C., Zhu, F., Liu, X., Zhang, J., Wang, B., Xiang, H., Cheng, Z., Xiong, Y., Zhao, Y., Li, Y., Wang, X., Peng, Z. "Clinical characteristics of 138 hospitalized patients with 2019 novel Coronavirus-infected pneumonia in Wuhan, China." *JAMA* 323.11 (2020 Mar 17): 1061–1069. DOI: 10.1001/jama.2020.1585. PMID: 32031570; PMCID: PMC7042881.

[15] Doi, K. "Computer-aided diagnosis in medical imaging: Historical review, current status, and future potential." *Computerized Medical Imaging and Graphics* 31.4–5 (2007): 198–211.

[16] Shi, F., Wang, J., Shi, J., Wu, Z., Wang, Q., Tang, Z., He, K., Shi, Y., Shen, D. "Review of artificial intelligence techniques in imaging data acquisition, segmentation and diagnosis for covid-19." *IEEE Reviews in Biomedical Engineering* 14 (2020):4–15.

[17] Dong, D., Tang, Z., Wang, S., Hui, H., Gong, L., Lu, Y., Xue, Z., Liao, H., Chen, F., Yang, F., et al. "The role of imaging in the detection and management of covid-19: A review." *IEEE Reviews in Biomedical Engineering* 14 (2020):16–29.

[18] Yaghobzadeh, R., Kamel, S. R., Shirazi, K. "A review of COVID-19 diagnostic methods." *Journal of Archives in Military Medicine* 7.4 (2019): e106802. DOI: 10.5 812/jamm.106802.

[19] Vaishya, R., Javaid, M., Khan, I. H., Haleem, A. "Artificial intelligence (AI) applications for COVID-19 pandemic." *Diabetology & Metabolic Syndrome* 14.4 (2020 Jul–Aug): 337–339. DOI: 10.1016/j.dsx.2020.04.012. Epub 2020 Apr 14. PMID: 32305024; PMCID: PMC7195043.

[20] Zimmerman, A., Kalra, D. "Usefulness of machine learning in COVID-19 for the detection and prognosis of cardiovascular complications." *Reviews in Cardiovascular Medicine* 21.3 (2020 Sep 30): 345–352. DOI: 10.31083/j.rcm.202 0.03.120. PMID: 33070540.

[21] Zhu, F., Li, D., Zhang, Q., Tan, Y., Yue, Y., Bai, Y., Li, J., Li, J., Feng, X., Chen, S., Xu, Y., Xiao, S. Y., Sun, M., Li X. "Prediction of COVID-19 severity from chest CT and laboratory measurements: Evaluation of a machine learning approach." *JMIR Medical Informatics* (2020 Sep 21). DOI: 10.2196/21604. Epub ahead of print. PMID: 33038076.

[22] Nayarisseri, A., Khandelwal, R., Madhavi, M., Selvaraj, C., Panwar, U., Sharma, K., Hussain, T., Singh, S. K. "Shape-based machine learning models for the potential novel COVID-19 protease inhibitors assisted by molecular dynamics simulation." *Current Topics in Medicinal Chemistry* (2020 Jul 4). DOI: 10.2174/156802 6620666200704135327. Epub ahead of print. PMID: 32621718.

[23] Randhawa, G. S., Soltysiak, M. P. M., El Roz, H., de Souza, C. P. E., Hill, K. A., Kari, L. "Machine learning using intrinsic genomic signatures for rapid classification of novel pathogens: COVID-19 case study." *PLoS One* 15.4 (2020 Apr 24): e0232391. DOI: 10.1371/journal.pone.0232391. PMID: 32330208; PMCID: PMC7182198.

[24] Öztürk, Ş., Özkaya, U., Barstuğan, M. "Classification of coronavirus (COVID-19) from X-ray and CT images using shrunken features." *International Journal of Imaging Systems and Technology* (2020 Aug 18). DOI: 10.1002/ima.22469. Epub ahead of print. PMID: 32904960; PMCID: PMC7461473.

[25] Liu, C., Wang, X., Liu, C., Sun, Q., Peng, W. "Differentiating novel coronavirus pneumonia from general pneumonia based on machine learning." *BioMedical Engineering OnLine* 19.1 (2020 Aug 19): 66. DOI: 10.1186/s12938 020 00809 9. PMID: 32814568; PMCID: PMC7436068.

[26] Tamal, M., Alshammari, M., Alabdullah, M., Hourani, R., Alola, H. A., Hegazi, T. M. "An integrated framework with machine learning and radiomics for accurate and rapid early diagnosis of COVID-19 from chest X-ray." *Expert Systems with Applications* 180 (2021): 115152–11560.

[27] Elaziz, M. A., Hosny, K. M., Salah, A., Darwish, M. M., Lu, S., Sahlol, A. T. "New machine learning method for image-based diagnosis of COVID-19." *PLoS One* 15.6 (2020): e0235187.

[28] Sun, L., Mo, Z., Yan, F., Xia, L., Shan, F., Ding, Z., Song, B., Gao, W., Shao, W., Shi, F., Yuan, H., Jiang, H., Wu, D., Wei, Y., Gao, Y., Sui, H., Zhang, D., Shen, D. "Adaptive feature selection guided deep forest for COVID-19 classification with chest CT." *IEEE Journal of Biomedical and Health Informatics* 24.10 (2020 Oct): 2798–2805. DOI: 10.1109/JBHI.2020.3019505. Epub 2020 Aug 26. PMID: 32845849.

[29] Yu, Z., Li, X., Sun, H., Wang, J., Zhao, T., Chen, H., Ma, Y., Zhu, S., Xie, Z. "Rapid identification of COVID-19 severity in CT scans through classification of

deep features." *BioMedical Engineering OnLine* 19.1 (2020 Aug 12): 63. DOI: 10.1186/s12938-020-00807-x. PMID: 32787937; PMCID: PMC7422684.

[30] Goel, T., Murugan, R., Mirjalili, S., Chakrabartty, D. K. "Automatic screening of covid-19 using an optimized generative adversarial network." *Cognitive Computation* (2021): 1–16.

[31] Arora, V., Ng, E. Y. K., Leekha, R. S., Darshan, M., Singh, A. "Transfer learning-based approach for detecting COVID-19 ailment in lung CT scan." *Computers in Biology and Medicine* 104575 (2021).

[32] Sethy, P. K., Behera, S. K., Anitha, K., Pandey, C., Khan, M. R. "Computer aid screening of COVID-19 using X-ray and CT scan images: An inner comparison." *Journal of X-Ray Science and Technology Preprint* (2021): 1–14.

[33] Ibrahim, M. R., Youssef, S. M., Fathalla, K. M. "Abnormality detection and intelligent severity assessment of human chest computed tomography scans using deep learning: A case study on SARS-COV-2 assessment." *Journal of Ambient Intelligence and Humanized Computing* (2021): 1–24.

[34] Dalal, N., Triggs, B. "Histograms of oriented gradients for human detection." In 2005 IEEE Computer Society Conference on Computer Vision and Pattern Recognition (CVPR'05). IEEE 1 (2005): 886–893.

[35] Ojala, T., Pietikainen, M., Maenpaa, T. "Multiresolution grayscale and rotation invariant texture classification with local binary patterns." *IEEE Transactions on Pattern Analysis and Machine Intelligence* 24.7 (2002 Aug 7): 971–987.

[36] Krishnan, M. M., Shah, P., Choudhary, A., Chakraborty, C., Paul, R. R., Ray, A. K. "Textural characterization of histopathological images for oral sub-mucous fibrosis detection." *Tissue and Cell* 43.5 (2011 Oct 1): 318–330.

[37] Ojala, T., Pietikäinen, M., Harwood, D. A. "Comparative study of texture measures with classification based on featured distributions." *Pattern Recognition* 29 (1996): 51–59.

[38] Alcantarilla, P. F., Bartoli, A., Davison, A. J. "KAZE features." In European Conference on Computer Vision. Springer (2012 Oct 7): 214–227.

[39] Lowe, D. G. "Object recognition from local scale-invariant features." In Proceedings of the International Conference on Computer Vision. (1999): 1150–1157. DOI: 10.1109/ICCV.1999.790410.

[40] Lowe, D. G. "Distinctive image features from scale-invariant keypoints." *International Journal of Computer Vision* 60.2 (2004): 91–110.

[41] Nixon, M., Aguado, A. "Feature extraction and image processing for computer vision." Academic Press (2019 Nov 17).

[42] Lindeberg, Tony. "Scale Invariant Feature Transform." Scholarpedia, http://www.scholarpedia.org/article/Scale_Invariant_Feature_Transform [Accessed, June 2021].

[43] Bay, H., Tuytelaars, T., Gool, L. V. "Surf: Speeded up robust features." In European Conference on Computer Vision 2006. Springer (2006): 404417.

[44] Bay, H., Ess, A., Tuytelaars, T., Gool, L. V. "Speeded up robust features (SURF)." *Computer Vision and Image Understanding* 110.3 (2008): 346359.

[45] Reinhold, J. C., Dewey, B. E., Carass, A., Prince, J. L. "Evaluating the impact of intensity normalization on MR image synthesis." *SPIE Conference Proceedings* 10949 (2019 Mar): 109493H. DOI: 10.1117/12.2513089. PMID: 31551645; PMCID: PMC6758567.

[46] Jolliffe, I. T. "Principal component analysis." 2nd edition, Springer-Verlag New York, New York (2002).

[47] Soares, E., Angelov, P., Biaso, S., Higa, F. M., Kanda, A. D. "SARS-CoV-2 CT-scan dataset: A large dataset of real patients CT scans for SARS-CoV-2 identification." *medRxiv* (2020). 10.1101/2020.04.24.20078584. [online]. www.kaggle.com/plameneduardo/sarscov2-ctscan-dataset.

[48] Freund, Y., Schapire, R. E. "Experiments with a new boosting algorithm." *ICML* 96 (1996): 148–156.

[49] Breiman, L. "Bagging predictors". *Department of Statistics, University of California Berkeley* (September 1994). Technical Report No. 421. Retrieved 2019-07-28.

[50] Hodges, J. L., Fix, E. "Nonparametric discrimination: consistency properties." Report for the USAF School of Aviation Medicine, Randolph Field (1951).

[51] Murphy, K. P. "Naive Bayes classifiers." *University of British Columbia* 18.60 (2006).

[52] Ho, T. K. "Random Decision Forests." In Proceedings of the 3rd International Conference on Document Analysis and Recognition, Montreal, QC (1995): 278–282.

[53] Cortes, C., Vapnik Vladimir, N. "Support-vector networks." *Machine Learning* 20.3 (1995): 273–297.

[54] Friedman, J. H. "Greedy function approximation: A gradient boosting machine." *Annals of Statistics* (2001): 1189–1232.

[55] Freund, Y., Schapire, R. "A decision-theoretic generalization of on-line learning and an application to boosting." (1995). [Online]. https://scikit-learn.org/stable/modules/generated/sklearn.ensemble.AdaBoostClassifier.html.

[56] Scikit-learn: Machine Learning in Python, Pedregosa, et al., JMLR 12, pp. 2825-2830, 2011. [online: https://scikit-learn.org/stable/modules/generated/sklearn.ensemble.BaggingClassifier.html] [Access date: April 2021].

[57] Scikit-learn: Machine Learning in Python, Pedregosa, et al., JMLR 12, pp. 2825-2830, 2011. [online: https://scikit-learn.org/stable/modules/generated/sklearn.neighbors.KNeighborsClassifier.html] [Access date: May 2021].

[58] Liu, R., Boyuan, Y., Enrico, Zio, Xuefeng, C. "Artificial intelligence for fault diagnosis of rotating machinery: A review." *Mechanical Systems and Signal Processing* 108 (2018): 33–47.

[59] Scikit-learn: Machine Learning in Python, Pedregosa, et al., JMLR 12, pp. 2825-2830, 2011. [online: https://scikit-learn.org/stable/modules/naive_bayes.html] [Access date: April 2021].

[60] Breiman, L. "Random forests". *Machine Learning* 45.1 (2001): 5–32. DOI: 10.1 023/A:1010933404324.

[61] Sarica, A., Cerasa, A., Aldo, Q. "Random forest algorithm for the classification of neuroimaging data in Alzheimer's disease: A systematic review." *Frontiers in Aging Neuroscience* 9 (2017): 329.

[62] Scikit-learn: Machine Learning in Python, Pedregosa, et al., JMLR 12, pp. 2825 2830, 2011. [online: https://scikit-learn.org/stable/modules/generated/sklearn.ensemble.RandomForestClassifier.html] [Access date: May 2021].

[63] Scikit-learn: Machine Learning in Python, Pedregosa, et al., JMLR 12, pp. 2825-2830, 2011. [online: https://scikit-learn.org/stable/modules/generated/sklearn.svm.SVC.html] [Access date: April 2021].

[64] Chen, T., Guestrin, C. "XGBoost: A scalable tree boosting system." In Proceedings of the 22nd AcmSigkdd International Conference on Knowledge Discovery and Data Mining. (2006): 785–794. https://doi.org/10.1145/2939672.2939785.

9 Investigations on Convolutional Neural Network in Classification of the Chest X-Ray Images for COVID-19 and Pneumonia

Ganesh Laveti
Gayatri Vidya Parishad College of Engineering for Women, Visakhapatnam, Andhra Pradesh, India

P. Chaya Devi and R. Goswami
Anil Neerukonda Institute of Technology & Sciences, Visakhapatnam, Andhra Pradesh, India

CONTENTS

9.1 INTRODUCTION

In December 2019, a type of Human-to-Human transmittable pneumonia with an unknown cause emerged in the city of Wuhan, China [1]. The virus was later identified as Severe Acute Respiratory Syndrome Coronavirus 2 (SARS-CoV-2) and the disease it caused was termed COVID-19 [2]. Since its inception, the infection has spread to more than 130 countries and has created an unsafe situation around the world [3].

DOI: 10.1201/9781003241409-9

Effective diagnosis, timely treatment, and isolation of infected patients are the primary steps in the fight against mitigating the spread of COVID-19 [4]. The high resemblance in the clinical features of regular pneumonia and the deadly COVID-19 pneumonia makes it difficult to differentiate them in their early stage [5]. The uncertainty in diagnosis causes delay in proper medication and isolation procedures of COVID-19 positive patients and accelerates the spread of the pandemic.

The tests that support medical practitioner for diagnosis of regular pneumonia include chest X-ray (CXr-radiation), ultrasound, computed tomography (CT), and magnetic resonance imaging (MRI) of lungs [6]. Currently, CXr-radiation has wide clinical availability and minimal processing time, hence preferred over other diagnosis methods. There are numerous schemes available from researchers all over the world for CXr-radiation imaging-based pneumonia detection. In his paper, Praveen et al. suggested unsupervised fuzzy classification method [7] and Rachna Jain et al. considered various CNN models and studied the performance [8]. So-Mi Cha et al. in his article discussed customization of pretrained CNNs to achieve high performance in CXr-radiation-based pneumonia classification [9].

In contrast to regular pneumonia diagnosis methods, as of today, the effective method used for screening COVID-19 infected patients is through reverse transcriptase-polymerase chain reaction (RT-PCR) test [10]. The test is conducted on nasopharyngeal or oropharyngeal swabs, sputum, lower respiratory tract aspirates, and bronchoalveolar washings of suspected patient [11–13]. Though RT-PCR tests show high specificity and rapid detection in diagnosing early infection of some viruses, there have been some positive COVID-19 cases reported false and is therefore not to be considered as the only method of screening suspected patients [14,15].

COVID-19 affected patient show signs of infection that include shortness of breathing, cough, rise in temperature, and dyspnea. The condition may worsen in some cases that cause SARS, and eventually death [16]. Hence, some studies suggest radiography imaging such as chest CT and CXr-radiation as an alternative method of examination for COVID-19 [17,18]. CT imaging of chest proves to be one of the best COVID-19 pneumonia diagnosis methods. Studies also suggest its effectiveness in identifying respiratory infections caused by other viruses. To assist radiologists in chest CT imaging-based COVID-19 disease detection, quantification, and diagnosis, in his paper, Gozes et al. proposed an automated CT imaging analysis tool based on Artificial Intelligence [19]. Wang et al. developed a deep learning method that extracts features of COVID-19 graphically, based on radiographic changes of CT images [20]. A deep learning system for infection quantification in COVID-19 chest CT images was proposed by Shan et al. [21].

Studies show that CXr-radiation imaging is also effective for lung infection detection due to viruses. Hamimi et al., in their paper, presented the role of radiology in diagnosing MERS-CoV. It states that CXr-radiation and CT images both show features of pneumonia [22]. CXr-radiation imaging with data mining tools distinguish SARS and pneumonia, which are the findings of Xie et al. [23]. Also, there are various studies that reveal the advantages of using CXr-radiation imaging over CT for the identification of COVID-19 [18,24].

Ali Narin et al. propose in his work a pre-trained CNN, ResNet 50, as the efficient deep learning algorithm for COVID-19 detection using CXr-radiation images. In this work, they evaluated the performance of ResNet50, InceptionV3, and InceptionResNetV2. The image data set comprises 50 COVID-19 and 50 non-infected CXr-radiation images, used for training and testing of ResNet50 [25]. In an intensive study, Linda Wang et al. developed a deep learning CNN design, COVID-Net for detection of COVID-19 cases from CXr-radiation images. A huge CXr-radiation image data set, COVIDx comprised images collected from 13,725 patient cases which are being used in their work [26].

In this chapter, the findings of Ali Narin et al. on detection of COVID-19 cases through CXr-radiation imaging with ResNet50 are being re-evaluated [25]. Also, for training and testing of ResNet50, this work uses a new dataset from the works of Linda Wang et al. In addition, this chapter investigates the performance of the various optimization algorithms for use with ResNet50. To test for the feasibility of CNN-based solutions to the classification problem, this work considers three output image classes: non-infected, pneumonia, and COVID-19 instead of the two classes: COVID-19 and non-infected [25]. In contrast to the works of Ali Narin et al., we consider three output classes and large dataset size, so they could help analyse the actual learning behaviour of CNN towards the features of regular pneumonia and COVID-19 CXr-radiation images [27].

This entire chapter is organized into four sections with Section 9.1 focuses on Literature Survey. Section 9.2 of this chapter discusses the used Dataset and processing of Dataset images. While Section 9.3 presents the methodology followed in the investigation of CNN application for COVID-19 and pneumonia classification, and Section 9.4 discusses the obtained preliminary results and conclusions.

9.2 DATASET AND PROCESSING

The dataset considered in this work has 13,800 CXr-radiation images, collected from 13,725 patient cases [26]. The dataset was further reduced to 13,476 CXr-radiation images after processing for high degree capture angle errors. This set of CXr-radiation images comprises 7,966 images of non-infected cases collected from 8,066 patients, 5,434 images of pneumonia or non-COVID-19 pneumonia cases from 5,538 patients, and 76 images of COVID-19 cases from 121 patients.

The images in the dataset are collected from well-known publicly available data repositories: RSNA Pneumonia Detection Challenge dataset [28], COVID-19 Image Data Collection [29], and COVID19 Chest X-radiation Dataset Initiative [26]. As the images are from different data repositories, they are available in variable sizes and in different image formats that include Digital Imaging and Communications in Medicine (DCM), Portable Network Graphics (PNG), and Joint Photographic Expert Group (JPG). Figure 9.1 illustrates the sample images of CXr-radiation images from the database that represent the three special cases. It is clear from the figure that unless specified, even for a practitioner, it is complex in categorizing non-COVID-19 pneumonia and COVID-19 pneumonia based on CXr-radiation images. Hence, training a deep CNN to perform this complex classification requires a huge and clear image dataset and computation power.

9.3 METHODOLOGY

The work has been carried out in two stages and investigates the practicability in deep learning CNNs for the classification of COVID-19 from regular pneumonia cases. It is

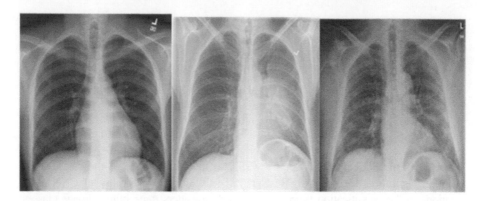

FIGURE 9.1 CXr-radiation images from the database COVIDx, from left to right: non-infected, regular pneumonia, and COVID-19.

because of the entire learning pattern of CNN that it shows an improvement in accuracy, influences the optimization algorithm [30], and stage 1 implements an arbitrary CNN architecture and evaluates its performance with three different optimization algorithms. The optimization algorithms are SGDM [31], RMSProp [32], and ADAM [33].

Stage 2 focuses on training and performance evaluation of pre-trained CNN ResNet50, with the new image dataset. To fit the learnable parameters in the best way, the ResNet50 in this stage uses the identified best optimization algorithm in stage 1. In both the stages, the metrics: conf-mat, percentage validation accuracy (PAV-1), and PAV-2 are used in the performance evaluation. Here, the PAV-1 and PAV-2 metrics can be defined as in Equations (9.1) and (9.2), respectively and the methodology followed is depicted in Figure 9.2.

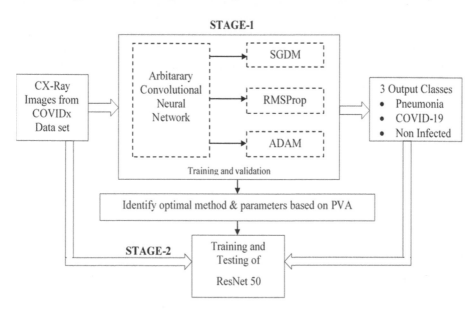

FIGURE 9.2 Methodology followed to solve the detection problem.

$$\text{Percentage validation Accuracy (PAV}-1)$$
$$= \frac{\text{Number of Image classes correctly identified}}{\text{Total number of Images}} \qquad (9.1)$$

$$\text{Percentage validation Accuracy (PVA}-2)$$
$$= \frac{\text{Number of abnormal Images identified correctly}}{\text{Total number of abnormal Images}} \qquad (9.2)$$

For the training of CNN, we use 75% of the image dataset and the rest of 25% for testing. Three classes non-infected, pneumonia, and COVID-19 form the output classes of CNN. Hence, the entire training set comprises 5,975 images of non-infected, 4,076 images of pneumonia, and 57 images of COVID-19 cases and testing set comprises 1,991 images of non-infected, 1,358 images of pneumonia, and 19 images of COVID-19 cases. The experiments conducted in this work use an Intel Core i5–8250U Processor, with 8GB RAM and Windows 10 operating system.

9.4   RESULTS

The feasibility of CNN to classify COVID-19 and pneumonia cases is examined with MATLAB 2019. The general CNN architecture comprises the basic layers of input, convolution, and fully connected layer. To make CNN recognize the complex features of the considered CXr-radiation image dataset, various intermediate neural layers have been embedded in its basic architecture.

As discussed earlier, this work implements a CNN with arbitrary architecture in its stage 1, whose details are given in Table 9.1.

There are in total 22 layers which include 05 Convolutional structured layers made of Batchnormalization, Relu, and Maxpooling layers. The Input layer has a size of 380 × 380 × 1, hence all the images collected from the database have been re-sized into 380 × 380 × 1 pixels. In addition, 03 Fullyconnected layers with Softmax and the Crossentropyex Classification layer have been used at the Output layer.

The learning rate, cross-validation, optimization technique, and kind of image dataset all affect CNN classification performance [34]. As a result, the CNN architecture in Table 9.1 is trained in three phases to find the best algorithm for COVIDx. In the first phase, the SGDM method with a momentum of $\zeta = 0.9$ is used as an optimizer. For the second phase training, the RMSProp optimization method is used with a Squared Gradient Decay factor of $\beta ii = 0.999$ and $\varepsilon = 10e\text{-}8$. In the third phase of the training, the ADAM optimization method is used with a Gradient Decay factor of $\beta i = 0.9$, $_{Squared}$ Gradient Decay factor of $\beta ii = 0.999$, and $\varepsilon = 10e\text{-}8$. In all the phases, the CNN has been trained over 06 epochs with 78 iterations in every epoch. To avoid data overfitting, we use a learning rate of 0.01 and a network validation frequency of 30 [35]. The input images have been transformed into different forms, whose sizes at the output of each layer are shown in Figure 9.3.

Figures 9.4, 9.5, and 9.6 depict the performance of SDGM, RMSProp, and ADAM CNN, respectively in terms of its Loss and Percentage validation

TABLE 9.1

Layers and Initialized Parameters of CNN with Arbitrary Architecture

S.No	Name of the Layer	Parameters
1.	Input Layer	380 by 380 by 1 and 'zero-center' normalization
2.	Convolution Layer_1	Eight 3 by 3 by 1, stride 1 by 1 with 'same' padding convents
3.	Batchnormalization Layer_1	Eight channel Batchnormalization
4.	Relu-Layer_1	Rectified Linear Unit
5.	Maxpooling Layer_1	2 by 2 maxpooling with stride,2 by 2 and [0 0 0 0] padding
6.	Convolution Layer_2	Sixteen 3 by 3 by 8, stride 1 by 1 with 'same' padding convents
7.	Batchnormalization Layer_2	Sixteen channel Batchnormalization
8.	Relu-Layer_2	Rectified Linear Unit
9.	Maxpooling Layer_2	2 by 2 maxpooling with stride [2 2] and [0 0 0 0] padding
10.	Convolution Layer_3	Thirty-two 3 by 3 by 16, stride 1 by 1 with 'same' padding convents
11.	Batchnormalization Layer_3	Thirty-two channel Batchnormalization
12.	Relu-Layer_3	Rectified Linear Unit
13.	Maxpooling Layer_3	2 by 2 maxpooling with stride [2 2] and [0 0 0 0] padding
14.	Convolution Layer_4	Sixty-Four 3 by 3 by 32, stride 1 by 1 with 'same' padding convents
15.	Batchnormalization Layer_4	Sixty-Four channel Batchnormalization
16.	Relu-Layer_4	Rectified Linear Unit
17.	Maxpooling Layer_4	2 × 2 maxpooling with stride [2 2] and [0 0 0 0] padding
18.	Convolution Layer_5	One Twenty-Eight 3 by 3 by 64, stride 1 by 1 with 'same' padding convents
19.	Batchnormalization Layer_5	One Twenty-Eight channel Batchnormalization
20.	Relu-Layer_5	Rectified Linear Unit
21.	Fully connected Layer	03 Fully connected Layers
22.	softmax	Softmax
23.	Classification Layer:	Crossentropyex with COVID-19, normal, and pneumonia classes

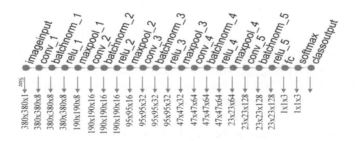

FIGURE 9.3   CNN layer graph with the image size at the output of each layer.

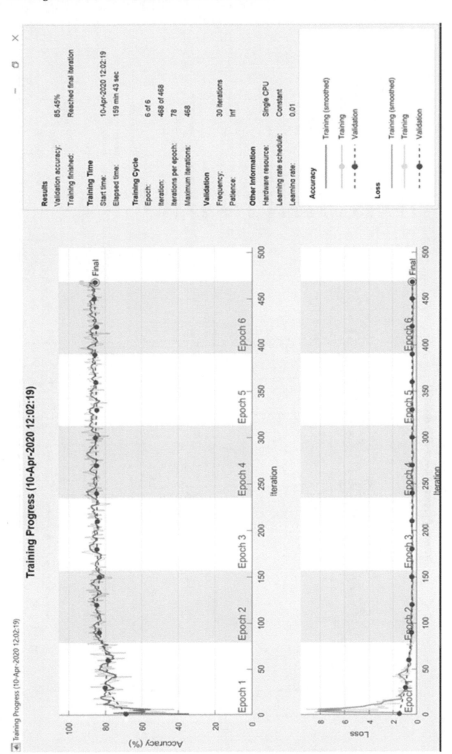

FIGURE 9.4 Training phase of SGDM optimizer-based CNN (stage 1).

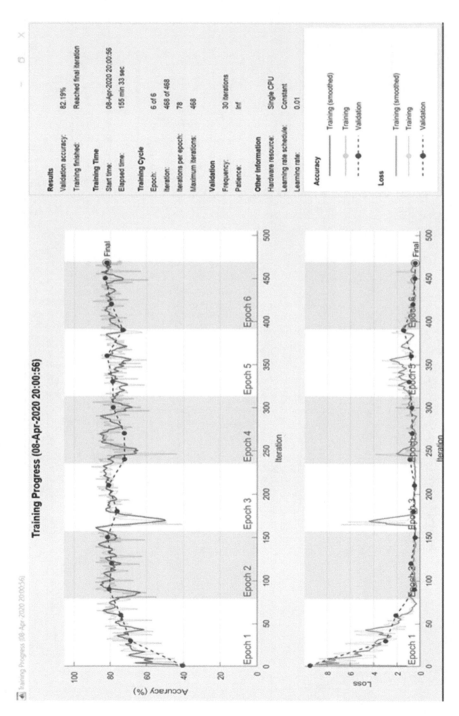

FIGURE 9.5 Training phase of RMSP propoptimizer-based CNN (stage 1).

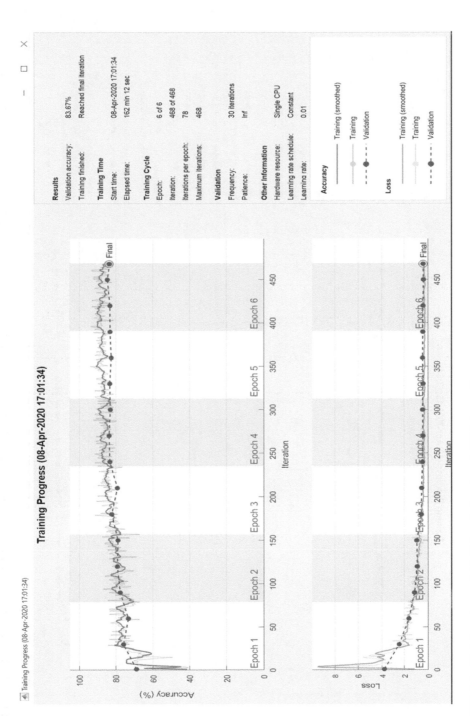

FIGURE 9.6 Training phase of ADAM optimizer based CNN (stage 1).

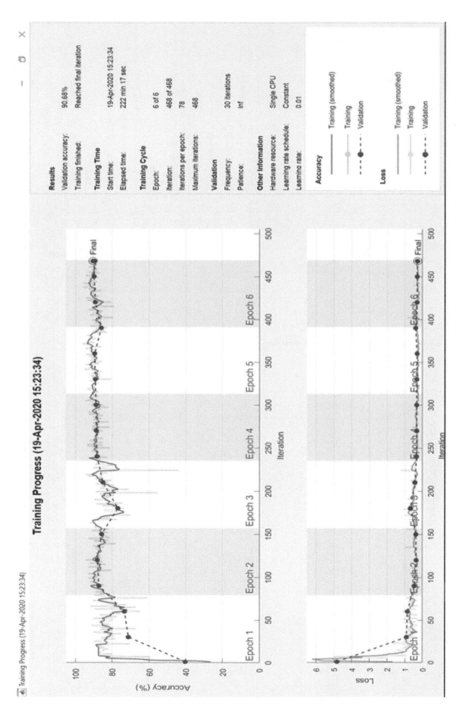

FIGURE 9.7 Training phase of SGDM optimizer-based ResNet50 CNN (stage 2).

Accuracy (PVA-1). This percentage accuracy gives a first level performance metric and is calculated as in Equation (9.1). The validation accuracy obtained is 85.45% for CNN with an SGDM optimizer, which is found to be the best value than the other two optimizers. However, SGDM observes to be optimal, this deviation in validation accuracy with respect to RMSProp and ADAM optimizers is less. Hence, to identify the optimal optimization algorithm requires a detailed analysis of other factors (Figure 9.7).

In practice, similar to the considered classification problem with unequal image samples in each class, relying on the classification performance of CNN based on the validation accuracy alone is misleading. Because it is highly unpredictable to decide whether the model has been trained equally for all classes or one or two classes are being neglected by the model. In such circumstances, the conf-mat of CNN provides detailed classification accuracy.

Figures 9.8, 9.9, and 9.10 describe the conf-mat of CNN in three different phases. Considering the special classes COVID-19 and pneumonia as abnormal cases, there has been a total of 1,377 images out of a total of 3,368 CXr-radiation images that test the performance of CNN. The 1,377 images comprise both COVID-19 and pneumonia CXr-radiation images. Table 9.2 provides the complete details of identified and missed abnormal cases. Detailed performance analysis of CNN's

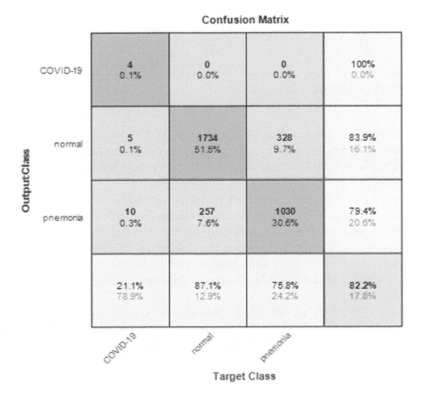

FIGURE 9.8 Conf-mat of RMSProp-CNN.

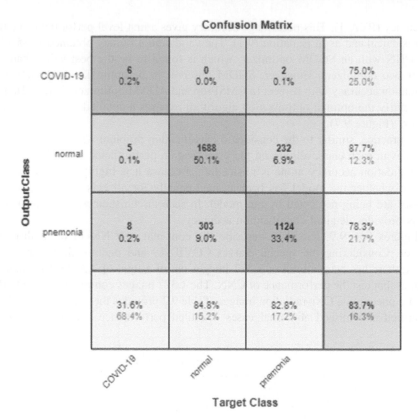

FIGURE 9.9   Conf-mat of ADAM-CNN.

based on conf-mat presents that CNN with an SGDM optimizer has a second level Percentage Validation Accuracy (PVA-2) of 93, calculated from Equation (9.2). While CNN with RMSProp and ADAM has a percentage accuracy 74.8 and 81.6, respectively.

In the context of the considered problem, second-level PVA defines how confident a CNN is in identifying abnormal classes, while first level accuracy of a CNN defines how confident it is in identifying the classes correctly. It needs to be noted that network with best second level accuracy considers being the ideal network for medical imaging and signal diagnosis. Hence, results show that the proposed CNN with an SDGM optimizer architecture is superior over the other two algorithms.

Stage 2 implements a CNN, which resembles the architecture of ResNet50. The deep transfer learning in MATLAB provides flexibility to train pre-trained CNN with any new image dataset. To test ResNet50 performance to detect COVID-19 cases with CXr-radiation imaging, we use the same training, and test image sets

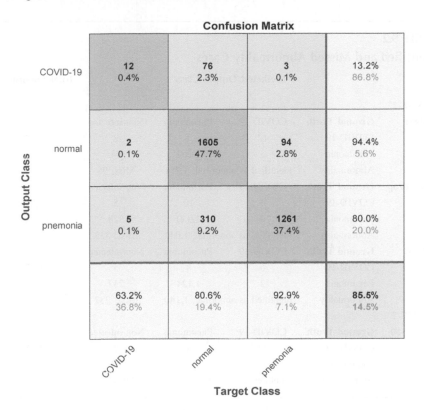

FIGURE 9.10   Conf-mat of SGDM-CNN.

defined in stage 1. ResNet50 has been trained over 06 epochs with 78 iterations in every epoch. The training process considers SGDM optimization with a learning rate of 0.01 and a network validation frequency of 30 iterations. The input image size considered is $224 \times 224 \times 3$. Figure 9.6 shows the training progress parameters of ResNet50. From Figure 9.6, it observes that PVA-1 of ResNet50 is 90.6. The value is found to be good compared to CNN-SDGM of stage-1. The conf-mat of ResNet50 is given in Figure 9.11, while Table 9.2 provides information about the miss and identified abnormal cases, used in the calculation of PVA-2 of ResNet50. Table 9.3 shows the performance accuracy comparison of the considered four methods. This shows that the deep-learning algorithms are suboptimal in classification of COVID-19 and regular pneumonia.

9.5 CONCLUSION

Currently, there is a lot of work progressing in the fields of virology, biomedicine, the Internet of Things (IoT), and machine learning to find solutions to fight

TABLE 9.2

Identified and Missed Abnormality Cases

		Predicted/Output Class			Total Abnormality
STAGE-1					
SGDM	**Ground Truth**	COVID-19	Pneumonia	Non-infected	
	COVID-19	12	5	2	1,377
	Pneumonia	3	1,261	94	
	Abnormality	Identified as abnormal: 1,281		Miss: 96	
RMS Prop	**Ground Truth**	COVID-19	Pneumonia	Non-infected	
	COVID-19	4	10	5	1,377
	Pneumonia	0	1,030	328	
	Abnormality	Identified as abnormal: 1,044		Miss: 333	
ADAM	**Ground Truth**	COVID-19	Pneumonia	Non-infected	
	COVID-19	6	8	5	1,377
	Pneumonia	2	1,124	232	
	Abnormality	Identified as abnormal: 1,140		Miss: 237	
STAGE-2					
ResNet-50	**Ground Truth**	COVID-19	Pneumonia	Non-infected	
	COVID-19	13	4	2	1,377
	Pneumonia	0	1,296	62	
	Abnormality	Identified as abnormal: 1,313		Miss: 64	

against the COVID-19 pandemic. As a result, the number of new diagnosis methods and databases like COVIDx is growing at a rapid rate. This work comes up with one solution to detect COVID-19 cases from CXr-radiation images. The initial focus is to identify the practicability of CNN. Hence we evaluated the performance of arbitrary architecture CNN with SGDM, RMSProp, and ADAM optimizers. The results obtained show that the SGDM optimizer is best as it fails to identify 96 abnormal cases. While the RMSProp and ADAM optimizers fail to identify 333 and 237 abnormal cases. It is also observed that percentage accuracy, PVA-1 (85.5%) and PVA-2 (93%), of SGDM is less, and needs improvement with betterment in network architecture. So, we train and test pre-trained CNN ResNet50 with SDGM optimizer with the COVIDx image dataset. The performance measures of ResNet50 show promising results (PVA-1 (90.7%) and PVA-2 (95.3%)) to confirm that CNNs can effectively detect pneumonia and are sub-optimal in detecting COVID-19 cases. Additionally, increasing the amount of COVID-19 CXr-radiation patient samples and using K-fold-cross validation during the training phase increases the learning pattern of CNNs, potentially resulting in near-90% accuracy.

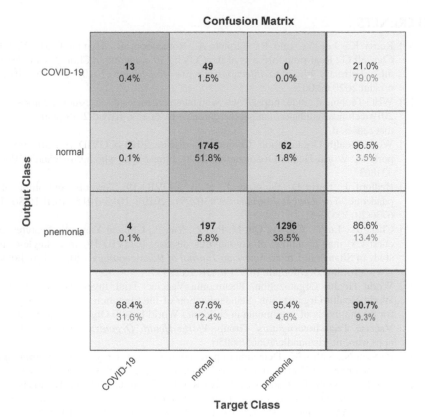

FIGURE 9.11 Conf-mat of CNN-SGDM-ResNet50.

TABLE 9.3
Performance Metrics of Evaluated CNNs

	Percentage Accuracy in Classification of Basic Classes		Percentage Accuracy in the Classification of Sub-classes Relative to Infected Cases	
Total Cases Used in Testing	Non-infected 1,991	Infected 1,377	COVID-19 19	Pneumonia 1,358
CNN-SGDM	80.61	93.02	63.15	92.85
CNN-RMSProp	87.09	75.81	21.05	75.84
CNN-ADAM	84.78	82.26	31.57	82.76
CNN-ResNet-50	87.64	95.35	68.42	95.43

REFERENCES

[1] Roosa K., Lee Y., Luo R., Kirpich A., Rothenberg R., Hyman J. M., Yan P., Chowell G., Real-time forecasts of the COVID-19 epidemic in China from February 5th to February 4th, 2020. *Infectious Disease Modelling* 5 (2020): 256–263. 10.101 6/j.idm.2020.02.002.

[2] WHO Technical guide, https://www.who.int/emergencies/diseases/novel-coronavirus-2019/technical-guidance/naming-the-coronavirus-disease-(covid-2019)-and-the-virus-that-causes-it.

[3] World Health Organization, Coronavirus disease 2019 (COVID-19): Situation report, 92. World Health Organization, 2020. https://apps.who.int/iris/handle/10665/331863.

[4] Bedford J., Enria D., Giesecke J., et al., COVID-19: Towards controlling of a pandemic. *The Lancet Journals* 395(10229) (2020): 1015–1018. 10.1016/S0140-6736(20)30673-5.

[5] Cheng Z., Lu Y., Cao Q., Qin L., Pan Z., Yan F., Clinical Yang W., Features and chest CT manifestations of coronavirus disease, (COVID-19) in a single-centre study in Shanghai, China. *American Journal of Roentgenology* (2020): 1–6. https://www.ajronline.org/doi/pdf/10.2214/AJR.20.22959.

[6] World Health Organization, Pneumonia Vaccine Trial Investigators' Group & World Health Organization. Standardization of interpretation of chest radiographs for the diagnosis of pneumonia in children / World Health Organization Pneumonia Vaccine Trial Investigators' Group. *World Health Organization* (2001). https://apps.who.int/iris/handle/10665/66956.

[7] Parveen N., Sathik M., Detection of pneumonia in chest X-ray images. *Journal of X-Ray Science and Technology* 19(4) (2011): 423–428. 10.3233/XST-2011-0304.

[8] Jain R., Nagrath P., Kataria G., Sirish Kaushik V., Jude Hemanth D., Pneumonia detection in chest X-ray images using convolutional neural networks and transfer learning. *Measurement* 165 (2020). 10.1016/j.measurement.2020.108046.

[9] Cha S., Lee S., Ko B., Attention-based transfer learning for efficient pneumonia detection in chest X-ray images. *Applied Sciences* (2021). 10.3390/app11031242.

[10] Wang W., Xu Y., Gao R., Lu R., Han K., Wu G., Tan W., Detection of SARS-CoV-2 in different types of clinical specimens. *Journal of American Medical Association* E1–E2 (2020). 10.1001/jama.2020.3786.

[11] Noh J., Yoon S., Kim D., et al., Simultaneous detection of severe acute respiratory syndrome, Middle East respiratory syndrome, and related bat coronaviruses by real-time reverse transcription PC. *Archives of Virology* 162(6) (2017): 1617–1623. 10.1 007/s00705-017-3281-9.

[12] Shen M., Zhou Y., Ye J., Maskri A., Kang Y., Zeng S., Recent advances and perspectives of nucleic acid detection for coronavirus. *Journal of Pharmaceutical Analysis* (2020). 10.1016/j.jpha.2020.02.010.

[13] Wan Z., Zhang Y., He K., Liu J., Lan K., Hu Y., Zhang C., A melting curve-based multiplex RT-qPCR assay for simultaneous detection of four human coronaviruses. *International Journal of Molecular Sciences* (2016): 2–10. https://doi.org/17.1880. 10.3390/ijms17111880.

[14] Tahamtan A., Ardebili A., 'Real-time RT-PCR in COVID-19 detection: issues affecting the results'. *Journal Expert Review of Molecular Diagnostics*, (2020). 10.1 080/14737159.2020.1757437

[15] Wang Y., Kang H., Liu X., et al., Combination of RT-qPCR testing and clinical features for diagnosis of COVID-19 facilitates management of SARS-CoV-2 Outbreak. *Journal of Medical Virology* (2020): 538–539. 10.1002/jmv.25721.

[16] Mahase E., Coronavirus: covid-19 has killed more people than SARS and MERS combined, despite lower case fatality rate. *The BMJ* 368 (2020). 10.1136/bmj.m641.

[17] Ng M., Lee E., Yang J., Yang F., Li X., Wang H., Lui M., Lo C., Leung B., Siu T., Khong P., Hui C., Yuen K., Kuo M., Imaging profile of the COVID-19 infection: Radiologic findings and literature review. *Radiology: Cardiothoracic Imaging* 2 (2020): e200034. 10.1148/ryct.2020200034.

[18] Tao A., Yang Z., Correlation of chest CT and RT-PCR testing in coronavirus disease 2019 (COVID-19) in china: A report of 1014 cases. *Radiology* (2020). 10.114 8/radiol.2020200642.

[19] Gozes, O., Frid-Adar, M., Greenspan, H., Browning, P., Zhang, H., Ji, W., Bernheim, A., Rapid AI development cycle for the Coronavirus (COVID-19) pandemic: Initial results for automated detection & patient monitoring using deep learning CT image analysis. arXiv preprint arXiv:2003.05037 (2020).

[20] Wang S., Kang B., Ma J., Zeng X., Xiao M., Guo J., Cai M., Yang J., Li Y., Meng X., Xu B., A deep learning algorithm using CT images to screen for Corona Virus Disease (COVID-19). *European Radiology* 31(8) (2021): 6096–6104. 10.1007/s00330-021-07715-1.

[21] Shan F., Gao Y., Wang J., Shi W., Shi N., Han M., Xue Z., Shi Y., Abnormal lung quantification in chest CT images of COVID-19 patients with deep learning and its application to severity prediction. *Medical Physics* 48(4) (2021): 1633–1645. 10.1 002/mp.14609.

[22] Hamimi A., MERS-CoV: Middle East respiratory syndrome corona virus: Can radiology be of help? Initial single center experience. *The Egyptian Journal of Radiology and Nuclear Medicine* (2015). 10.1016/j.ejrnm.2015.11.004.

[23] Xie X., Li X., Wan S., Gong Y., Mining X-ray images of SARS patients. *Data Mining: Theory, Methodology, Techniques, and Applications* (2006): 282–294. https://link.springer.com/chapter/10.1007/11677437_22.

[24] Rubin G., Ryerson C., Haramati L., et al., The role of chest imaging in patient management during the covid-19 pandemic: A multinational consensus statement from the Fleischner society. *Radiology* 296(1) (2020): 172–180. 10.1148/radiol.202 0201365.

[25] Ali N., Ceren K., Ziynet P., Automatic detection of Coronavirus Disease (COVID-19) using X-ray images and deep convolutional neural networks. *Pattern Analysis and Applications* 24 (2020): 1207–1220. 10.1007/s10044-021-00984-y.

[26] Linda W., Zhong Q. L., Alexander W., COVID-Net: A tailored deep convolutional neural network design for detection of COVID-19 cases from chest X-ray images. *Scientific Reports* 10(1) (2020): 19549. 10.1038/s41598-020-76550-z.

[27] Tawfiq L., Hu Y. H., Hwang J., Handbook of neural network signal processing, CRC Press, Boca Raton (2002). 10.1121/1.1480419.

[28] Radiological Society of North America, Pneumonia detection challenge. (2019). https://www.kaggle.com/c/rsnaPneumonia-detection-challenge/data.

[29] Joseph P. C., Paul M., Lan D., COVID-19 image data collection. 2020.arXiv 2003.11597 (2020). https://github.com/ieee8023/covid-chestxray-dataset.

[30] Huan L., Yibo Y., Dongmin C., Zhouchen L., Optimization algorithm inspired deep neural network structure design. In Proceedings of the 10th Asian Conference on Machine Learning Research, PMLR95 (2018): 614–629.

[31] Ning Q., On the momentum term in gradient descent learning algorithms, neural networks. *The Official Journal of the International Neural Network Society* 12(1) (1999): 145–151. 10.1016/S0893-6080(98)00116-6.

[32] Duchi J., Hazan E., Singer Y., Adaptive subgradient methods for online learning and stochastic optimization. *Journal of Machine Learning Research* 12 (2011): 2121–2159.

[33] Kingma D., Ba Jimmy A., A method for stochastic optimization. *International Conference on Learning Representations* (2014). https://arxiv.org/pdf/1412.6980.pdf.

[34] Dogo E., Afolabi, O., Nwulu N., Twala, B., Aigbavboa C., A comparative analysis of gradient descent-based optimization algorithms on convolutional neural networks (2018): 92–99. 10.1109/CTEMS.2018.8769211.

[35] MatLab Help: [https://in.mathworks.com/help/deeplearning/ug/setting-up-parameters-and-training-of-a-convnet.html] (Accessed: Jan 2021).

10 Improving the Detection of Abdominal and Mediastinal Lymph Nodes in CT Images Using Attention U-Net Based Deep Learning Model

Hitesh Tekchandani and Shrish Verma
National Institute of Technology, Raipur, India

Narendra D. Londhe
Psoriasis Clinic and Research Centre, Psoriatreat, Pune, Maharashtra, India

National Institute of Technology, Raipur, India

CONTENTS

10.1   INTRODUCTION

Lymph nodes (LNs) segmentation plays a vital role in the staging of diseases [1], evaluating treatment reactions and responses [2], surgical planning [3], and deciding

DOI: 10.1201/9781003241409-10

resection areas [3]. Computed tomography (CT) is a ubiquitous radiological modality for the detection and evaluation of LNs. Manual detection and segmentation of LNs in CT images is a challenging, complex, and time-consuming task due to their sparsely distributed location, clutter, varying size, cluster formation, unclear boundaries, and low contrast from surrounding organs like muscles and vessels [1,2,4,5]. Moreover, tissues that have similar attenuation constants to the LNs are usually located near the LNs [4]. This further makes the detection and segmentation of LNs challenging and observer-dependent. Irrespective of the clinical importance of marking individual LN, it is generally not conducted or partially done as it consumes a large time and attention of the radiologists [6].

In view of the above points, many researchers have applied machine learning and deep learning (DL)-based algorithms to automate the detection of abdominal LNs (ALNs) and mediastinal LNs (MLNs) in CT images. In general, machine learning methods assume LNs as the blob-like structure to detect and segment them. Kitasaka et al. [3] applied a 3-D minimum directional difference filter to enhance blob structure-like regions and then applied a region growing technique for segmentation of ALNs. They achieved a very low sensitivity of 57% at 58 false positive (FP) per volume (57%@58 FP/vol). Oda et al. [4] used multi-scale and multi-shape ellipsoidal structured detection filters for detecting both spherical and ellipsoidal-shaped ALNs. They could achieve less sensitivity at very high FP was 56.8%@262.3 FP/vol. Nakamura et al. [7] implemented local intensity structure analysis-based multi-scale blob structure enhancement filter followed by support vector machine (SVM) to improve the detection of ALNs, bettering the performance to sensitivity 70.5%@13 FP/vol. Cherry et al. [8] use manually defined search regions and random forest method for ALNs candidate lesion extraction. Then from these lesions, statistical features were calculated and fed to for the intended task of ALNs segmentation. With this method, they achieve a low sensitivity of 79.8%@15 FP/vol. This method requires expert anatomical knowledge of the abdominal region.

Seff et al. [9] adapted the output of semantic LNs contour detection as input for calculation of histogram of oriented gradients (HOG) for obtaining semantic objectness cues. Linear SVM is used for candidate level classification and achieved a sensitivity of 78%@3 FP/vol for both abdominal and mediastinal regions. Seff et al. [2] in their other attempt used multi-resolution HOG descriptors for LNs detection. The achieved sensitivity was 73.1%@6 FP/vol and 78%@6 FP/vol for ALNs and MLNs, respectively. Beichel et al. [10] proposed an optimal surface finding approach for LNs detection. Their approach requires more manual interaction and hyperparameter selection. They achieved a Dice score (DS) of 84.7%. Tan et al. [11] proposed dynamic programming and active contours-based approach for LNs segmentation. This proposed method only detects compact and homogeneous LNs. The achieved DS was 83.2%.

Barbu et al. [12] applied Haar and self-aligning features for the detection of ALNs enhancing the performance to sensitivity = 80@3.2 FP/vol. Nakamura et al. [13] used thresholding and region growing techniques for the detection of ALNs. Further, they used texture and shape features for FP reduction. Furthermore, to optimize the set of feature values, sequential selection methods were implemented. The achieved sensitivity was 74.7@11.8 FP/vol. Nimura et al. [14] proposed radial structure tensor analysis (RST) and SVM-based ALN candidate localization and segmentation. The achieved sensitivity was 82@21.6 FP/vol. Nogues et al. [15] proposed a holistically neural network (HNN)-based method for the segmentation of LNs present in the thoracoabdominal (TA) region which includes both ALNs and MLNs. The predictions from HNN's were formulated into the conditional random field (CRF) which were solved by different structured optimization (SO) methods. They achieved a DS of 82.1%.

In DL-based attempts, Roth et al. [1] applied convolution neural network (CNN) along with augmentation methods for ALNs detection and improved the performance to 83%@3 FP/vol for ALNs and 70%@3 FP/vol for MLNs. Further, Roth et al. [16] designed a two-stage coarse to fine method for ALNs detection. In the first stage, the candidate generation process is completed with a sensitivity of ~100% at very high FP levels. The second stage is similar to [1] and attained the sensitivity of 77%@3 FP/vol. Sengupta [17] proposed a V-Net based DL model for ALNs segmentation. Their proposed approach requires many complex pre-processing steps like fixation of image orientation, modality-based voxel intensity normalization, and patch selection algorithms for reducing memory constraints. Shin et al. [18] proposed a deep convolutional neural network (DCNN) and transfer learning (TL)-based computer-aided detection system (CAD) for the detection of LNs in the TA region. Weights from ImageNet [19] were used for TL. Their proposed system could achieve a sensitivity of 70@3 FP/vol and 86@3 FP/vol for ALNs, and MLNs respectively. Li et al. [20] proposed a reinforcement learning-based DL model. Their proposed method requires Response Evaluation Criteria in Solid Tumors (RECIST) [21] criteria-based annotation. Further, this method suffers from low DS of 77.17%. Cai et al. [22] proposed Graph-Cut and CNN-based weakly supervised slice-propagated segmentation (WSSS) approach. Their method requires many pre-processing steps like, RECIST-based initial lesion segmentation, adaption of data distribution from RECIST slices, and extrapolation. They achieved a DS of 84.4%. Hoogi et al. [23] proposed an active contour and CNN-based segmentation method for ALNs. This proposed approach attained a very low sensitivity of 51% and DS of 76.8% only.

Feulner et al. [6] proposed spatial prior and discriminative learning-based segmentation approach for MLNs segmentation from chest CT images. The limitation of their 4 stage complex method is that it heavily relies on anatomical knowledge. Furthermore, they achieved a very low sensitivity of 52%@3.1 FP/vol. Feuerstein et al. [24] use hessian eigenvalues and anatomical knowledge for MLNs detection and segmentation. The shortcoming of their proposed approach was the requirement of rigorous anatomical knowledge of organs like bronchial tree, upper aortic arch, vessels, and bone. They have achieved a sensitivity of 82.1%@113.4 FP/vol. Oda et al. [25] proposed intensity targeted radial structure tensor (ITRST) filter for MLNs detection. Their proposed method was able to detect MLNs whose short axis measurement was ≥ 10 mm only. The achieved sensitivity was 84.2%@9.1 FP/vol. Liu et al. [26] have used random forest and SVM classifiers for MLNs segmentation. The limitation of their method was an annotation of segmented 11 surrounding organs to identify the ROI before the segmentation of LNs. They achieved a sensitivity of 88%@8 FP/vol for the MLNs segmentation task. In other similar attempts, Zhao et al. [27] and Allen et al. [28] applied the random forest method for MLNs segmentation where they used 500 features for the intended task.

In another DL approach, Oda et al. [29] applied 3D U-Net [30] for MLNs segmentation from chest CT images. Due to data imbalance between LNs and other organs in CT images, they trained their model to segment 4 extra other organs like lungs, airways, aortic arches, and pulmonary arteries. The achieved sensitivity was 95.5%@16.3 FP/vol with a very low DS of 52.3 ± 23.1%. Bouget et al. [31] also proposed U-Net based segmentation approach and Mask R-CNN based bounding box instance detection method for MLNs segmentation. The achieved sensitivity and DS were 75%@9 FP/vol and 76% respectively. Tang et al. [32] proposed a generative adversarial network (GAN)-based augmentation and U-Net based segmentation approach. With this proposed methodology they achieved a DS of 82.5%.

The limitation of most of the abovementioned approaches is that they could detect large LNs only (≥ 10 mm) neglecting small LNs having clinical importance. Moreover, these approaches assume a blob-like structure in all LNs, but in fact, the shape and size of LNs vary with the patient to patient and also depends upon the location of LNs. Furthermore, most of the existing methods require many pre-processing steps like ROI segmentation which itself is a complex task in the case of medical image segmentation. Additionally, if any of the ROI segmentation approaches fails, then this will negatively affects overall systems performance. Furthermore, these approaches require a lot of feature selection and their calculation which can introduce the bias and errors in detection. Additionally, high numbers of FPs disqualify these methods for clinical adaptation. Very few of the above, conducted studies jointly for both ALNs and MLNs and many could not use them interchangeably. These limitations of the previous work kept this area open for more advanced research. CNN-based DL architectures are highly reliable for the solution of the above mention problems.

Hence, in this chapter, the attention mechanism and TL-based U-Net architecture for ALNs and MLNs segmentation in CT images is proposed. This is the first time that due to structural similarity between ALNs and MLNs, the full and partial TL of attention U-Net for ALNs is used for the detection of MLNs and vice-versa. Further, a comparative study between the proposed methodology and the state-of-the-art methods like SegNet, U-Net, and ResUNet has been also presented. The chapter is organized as follows: Section 10.2 covers methodology, which includes Section 10.2.1 for dataset details, and Section 10.2.2 presents the proposed model architecture. Section 10.3 explains the training configurations for the proposed methodology and experimental setup. Section 10.4 and 10.5 contain results and discussion, respectively. Finally, Section 10.6 concludes the chapter.

10.2   METHODOLOGY

U-Net model is specially designed for medical imaging tasks, as this model is also able to perform well with limited training samples [30]. U-Net model consists of two paths, namely contracting path and expanding path for capturing context and localization, respectively. U-Net is a fully convolution network (FCN) [33] based architecture having no dense layers, i.e., it mainly contains convolutional layers for the classification task. Skip connection in U-Net architecture collects information from multiple contracting feature extraction levels and connects these to different expanding levels. This enhances the predicting capabilities of U-Net architectures.

This also limits U-Net extracting similar low level features repeatedly which leads to excess network parameters and consequently to network overfitting.

Very recently introduced attention mechanism [34] for DL architectures provides a solution for the abovementioned problem by providing a focus on target structures with the help of trainable parameters. In the very recent past, attention-based DL approaches have been popularly used in various medical image-processing tasks like abdominal organ segmentation [35], prostate segmentation [36], atrial segmentation [37], pancreas segmentation [38], liver tumor segmentation [39], and bladder segmentation [40].

Generally, in CNN-based DL architectures, the last few layers are dense, i.e., fully connected layers. These layers contain features and don't have any location-specific information to focus on segmentation tasks. Wherever the U-Net model is fully made up of convolution layers, these layers contain desired localizer information and trainable parameters. Hence, there is a possibility of integration of attention mechanism with U-Net architecture. The attention approach contains trainable weighted parameters that guide U-Net to focus on target structures. The simplicity of this approach is that these trainable weighted parameters can be trained using the backpropagation approach, which is already in use for optimization of base U-Net architecture. These weighted coefficients downgrade the gradients of the background and activate the gradients of the foreground during backpropagation. This kind of attention mechanism is called soft attention [41].

As skip connections enhance the performance of U-Net based models [30], therefore, in this chapter we integrate skip connection with an attention mechanism. In the attention mechanism, linear transformation followed by non-linear transformation is applied. In this chapter, we use a (1 x 1 x 1) convolution filter as a linear transformation and a sigmoid as a non-linear transformation. Attention mechanism can be represented using the following equation:

$$\alpha = \sigma(f_{att}(x, g; \theta_{att})) \tag{10.1}$$

where α represents attention coefficients, σ represents sigmoid transformation (non-linear transformation), θ_att is characterized by features x and g, obtained after linear transformation like (1 x 1 x 1) convolution. (1 x 1 x 1) convolution not only provides linear transformation with reduced complexity but also provides lower-level feature space for the application of attention mechanisms.

Moreover, we have also utilized TL for reducing the trainable parameter count for the intended task. TL can be defined as the use of knowledge learned from the source domain/task to a novel task [42]. In terms of CNN-based DL models, TL is the transfer (copy) of weights of a previously trained model to a similar new model for solving a new problem with a minimum training of the new model. The advantage of TL approaches is that they not only reduce the computation complexity by eliminating the need of training from scratch, but also enhances the performance of DL architectures by reducing overfitting problems. TL is a very effective approach where training dataset size is very small, which is many times a case in the medical imaging domain. TL is successfully applied in many medical imaging tasks like polyp detection [43], diabetic retinopathy [44], and kidney localization [45].

For the proposed work of detection of ALNs and MLNs, the online dataset CT Lymph Node [46] is being used. These both types of LNs have anatomical structural similarities. Hence, with the aim of providing fast and robust LN detection, the use of TL of one type of LN (abdominal/mediastinal) for the detection of another type of LN (mediastinal/abdominal) is also being explored in the proposed study in this chapter. Hence, in this chapter, we have applied TL approaches with the attention U-Net model for ALNs and MLNs segmentation. Weights and architecture from the trained model of ALNs segmentation are used in MLNs segmentation and vice-versa.

Instead of transferring the weights from a natural image dataset like ImageNet [19], it will more beneficial to transfer weights from networks trained for LNs. Moreover, the ImageNet is a fully connected network designed for classification work while the aimed study here is segmentation of LNs and the proposed DL architecture is fully convolutional. Also if the source and target model architectures are the same, then TL approaches are more effective with minimum fine-tuning [47].

In any CNN based DL model, initial layers extract general features hence called general layers, and last layers extract task-specific features hence called specific layers [47]. Hence, to ensure the best performance of the proposed DL architecture, the experiments with zero, partial and full adaptation of weights from the source model has been conducted in this chapter.

Figure 10.1 shows the workflow of the proposed approach. Firstly, CT windowing is applied to input images. The windowing technique [48] is generally used to highlight the particular organ in CT scans. By adjusting Hounsfield units (HU), the appearance of the target organ can be highlighted. As the DL models are data-driven approaches, hence we have also used data augmentation to populate the training dataset size. Data augmentation is some type of geometrical or statistical transformation method used to increase data set size without actually collecting data. Further, the dataset has been divided into training and testing sets. Once, the training is completed with the proposed attention U-Net and TL approaches, the trained model is evaluated on testing data.

In this section, the architecture details of implemented U-Net, ResUNet, and attention U-Net models are presented. For representation simplicity, we make blocks of similar and repeated layer operations. Moreover, the output dimensions of the last layer of each block are also shown in respective blocks. Figure 10.2 shows the implemented U-Net architecture for LNs segmentation. Figure 10.2A shows the main architecture. Where _CP represents operation in the contraction path, and _EP represents operation in the expansion path. Figure 10.2B provides details of the convolution block (CB). Figure 10.2C represents the center block.

Figure 10.3 shows architecture details of the implemented ResUNet model for the intended task. ResUNet [49,50] model is the integration of residual concept [51] into the U-Net model. Figure 10.3A shows the main architecture of ResUNet which is similar to the main architecture of U-Net (Figure 10.2A). Residual connections are shown in CB and center block in Figure 10.3B and Figure 10.3C, respectively.

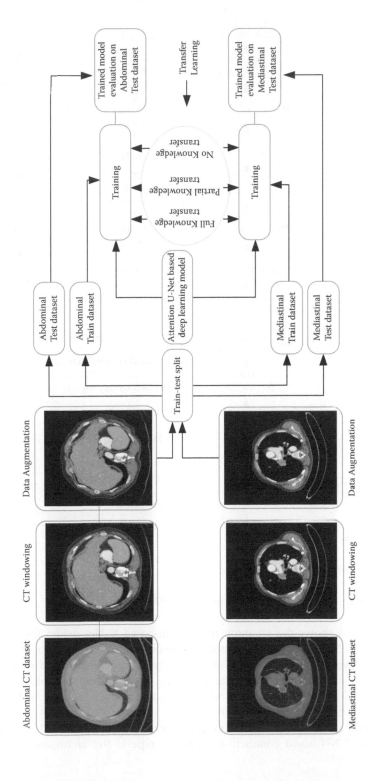

FIGURE 10.1 Workflow of the proposed approach.

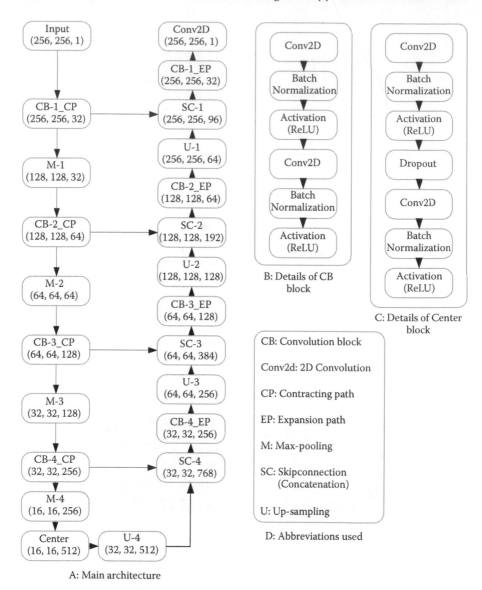

A: Main architecture

FIGURE 10.2 Architecture details of implemented U-Net based model.

Figure 10.4 shows the attention mechanism-based U-Net model for the same intended task. Here Figure 10.4A shows the main architecture. The attention block (AB) is shown in Figure 10.4D. For simplicity of representation of main architecture, we included the concatenation layer into the attention block module (Figure 10.4D) which concatenates skip connections. The attention mechanism is shown in the black box in Figure 10.4D.

The basic similarity among architectures presented in Figures 10.2, 10.3, and 10.4, is the CNN-based contraction-expansion type U-Net architecture. The CB

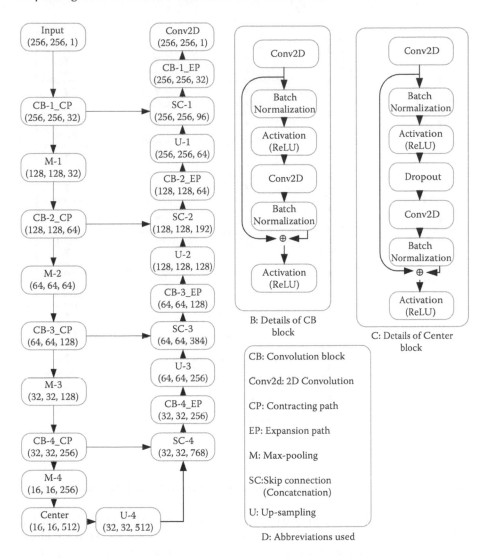

FIGURE 10.3 Architecture details of implemented ResUNet-based model.

block of Figure 10.3 i.e., ResUNet is different from the other two, i.e., Figures 10.2 and 10.4. The addition operation in the CB block of Figure 10.3 is used to implement residual operation [51], which is used for simple implementation of identity mapping. Identity mapping is used for reducing the complexity of the optimization process. The notable and significant difference between Figures 10.4, 10.2, and 10.3 is the presence of AB block. AB block is the implementation of the attention mechanism in Figure 10.4. It can be observed from Figure 10.4 that, AB block is inserted in the expansion path of the main architecture of Figure 10.4. This AB block basically contains blocks for the implementation of Equation (10.1). Conv2d (1 x 1 x 1), is used for implementing linear operation, and the Activation (Sigmoid)

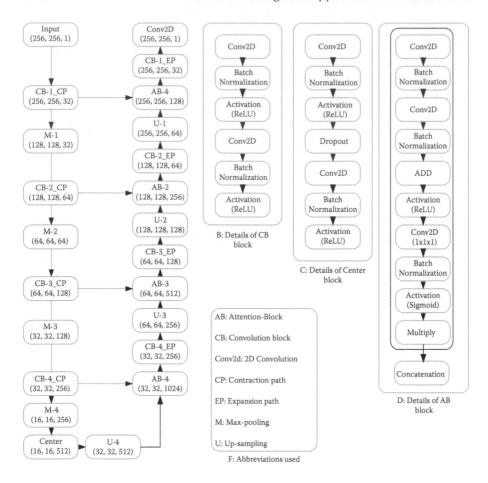

FIGURE 10.4   Architecture details of implemented attention-based U-Net based model.

block is used for implementing the non-linear operation. ADD block is used for collecting information from both down and up sampling operations. Multiply block is used to generate trainable parameters. Finally, the concatenation block is used for the integration of skip connections.

10.2.1 DATASET DETAILS

CT Lymph Node dataset from [46] has been adapted here for ALNs and MLNs segmentation in CT images. The original dataset consists of 595 and 388, ALNs and MLNs CT images from 86 and 90 patients, respectively. In this work, we use CT windowing as a pre-processing step. Window width (WW) and window level (WL) are two important parameters for windowing in CT. WW refers to the range of CT numbers contained by CT slice, and WL refers to the window center. Manipulations in WL and WW provides adjustments in brightness and contrast, respectively. WL and WW were set to 60 and 400, and 40 and 400 for ALNs and MLNs, respectively.

The effect of CT windowing on the appearance of ALNs and MLNs can be observed from Figure 10.1.

To collect medical images is a difficult task because of patient privacy and ethical issues. Data augmentation is the state-of-art strategy for populating the original dataset [52]. Elastic deformation [53] is used as an augmentation approach in this work. Elastic deformation not only improves the performance of the proposed approach, but also makes the proposed model more generalize by adding transformation invariance property to the network. Elastic deformation incorporates the variation in the dataset by corresponding to LNs CT appearance taken while patient movement or pose variation. After the augmentation, the size of the dataset is increased from 595 to 5,595 and 388 to 5,388 for ALNs and MLNs, respectively.

10.3 TRAINING CONFIGURATION AND EXPERIMENTAL SETUP

All the experiments were performed on the HP Z6 workstation using Keras [54] DL library. Epoch and batch size was set to 80 and 10, respectively. Rectified linear unit (ReLU) and Adam [55] were used as activation function and optimizer. Size of convolutional kernel and stride were set to (2, 2) and (1, 1) respectively. Glorot uniform [56] is used as a kernel initializer. For loss function, the summation of binary cross-entropy and Dice loss [57] is used with class weights. Class weights are used because of class imbalance, as LNs are very small in size compared to other organs. Class weights are set to 0.95 for one class (i.e., target class) and 0.05 for zero class (i.e., background pixels). Following Equations (10.2) and (10.3) represents binary cross-entropy and Dice loss:

$$bce = -(b log\,(p)) + (1 - b)\log(1 - p) \tag{10.2}$$

$$DS = \frac{2(|G \cap P|)}{|G| + |P|} \tag{10.3}$$

$$DL = 1 - DS \tag{10.4}$$

where bce is binary cross-entropy, DS is the Dice score, DL is Dice loss, b indicates binary (0 or 1), p is predicted probability, G is ground truth, and P is prediction.

10.4 RESULTS

To evaluate the performance of proposed approaches, sensitivity, Dice score (DS), and Hausdorff distance (HD) [58] are selected as evaluation parameters. The numerical representation of DS is given in Equation (10.3). HD measures the degree of resemblance of two images and it is the largest minimal distance between two boundaries [58]. Low HD signifies higher resemblance or better segmentation. For any given two-point sets P = {p1,...,pn} and Q = {q1,...,qm}, the HD can be defined as:

$$HD\,(P,\ Q) = max\,(h\,(P,\ Q),\ h\,(Q,\ P)) \tag{10.5}$$

TABLE 10.1

Sensitivity, Dice Scores, and Hausdorff Distance of Proposed Approaches

	ALNs				MLNs			
	SegNet	U-Net	ResUNet	Attention U-Net	SegNet	U-Net	ResUNet	Attention U-Net
SEN	80%	87%	90.31%	93.08%	94.8%	95.38%	97.38%	99%
DS	78.59%	89.18%	90.88%	91.69%	90.70%	92.14%	93.92%	97%
HD	5.7	2.25	2.12	1.36	1.87	1.65	1.57	0.96

where h can be defined using the following Equation (10.6):

$$h(P, Q) = \max_{p \in P} \min_{q \in Q} \|p - q\| \tag{10.6}$$

The evaluation of the above-mentioned performance parameters for the proposed work of LNs detection is given in Table 10.1 using 5-fold cross-validation. This includes the detection of ALNs and MLNs using SegNet [59], U-Net, ResUNet, and Attention U-Net.

Attention U-Net achieves DS and sensitivity of 91.69% and 93.08%, respectively for ALNs segmentation, and 97% and 99% for MLNs segmentation. It is observable from Table 10.1 that the proposed attention U-Net model provides 13.1% and 13.08% improvement for ALNs segmentation, and, 6.3% and 4.2% improvement for MLNs segmentation in DS and sensitivity, respectively over the SegNet model. Further, the proposed model provides 2.51% and 6.08% improvement for ALNs segmentation, and, 4.86% and 3.62% improvement for MLNs segmentation in DS and sensitivity, respectively compared to the U-Net model.

In comparison with the ResUNet model, the proposed approach achieves an improvement of 0.81% and 2.77% improvement for ALNs segmentation and 3.08% and 1.62% improvement for MLNs segmentation in DS and sensitivity, respectively.

Table 10.2 presents sensitivity, Dice scores, and Hausdorff distance of full, partial, and zero TL approaches. Descriptions of the used acronyms are as follows:

TABLE 10.2

Sensitivity, Dice Scores, and Hausdorff Distance of TL Approaches

	ALNs			MLNs		
	MfTrANet	MpTrANet	MzTrANet	AfTrMNet	ApTrMNet	AzTrMNet
SEN	10%	84.5%	93.08%	11%	89.18%	99%
DS	6%	87.4%	91.69%	5.7%	90.30%	97%
HD	323.25	3.2	1.36	334.12	2.02	0.96

AfTrMNet – full adaptation of weights from attention U-Net model trained for ALNs dataset to attention U-Net for segmentation of MLNs.

ApTrMNet – partial adaptation of weights from attention U-Net model trained for ALNs dataset to attention U-Net for segmentation of MLNs.

AzTrMNet – zero adaptation of weights from attention U-Net model trained for ALNs dataset to attention U-Net for segmentation of MLNs (i.e., model is trained using MLNs dataset).

MfTrANet – full adaptation of weights from attention U-Net model trained for MLNs dataset to attention U-Net for segmentation of ALNs.

MpTrANet – partial adaptation of weights from attention U-Net model trained for MLNs dataset to attention U-Net for segmentation of ALNs.

MzTrANet – zero adaptation of weights from attention U-Net model trained for MLNs dataset to attention U-Net for segmentation of ALNs (i.e., model is trained using ALNs dataset).

In the partial TL approach first 14 layers of the model are freezed, i.e., these are non-trainable and they contains the same transferred weights. The rest of the model layers are trainable. It's observable from Table 10.3 that the full transfer approach suffers from very poor performance parameters for both ALNs and MLNs segmentation, because there is no training. Moreover, the last few layers of any DL models are task-specific, and hence full adaption will not work efficiently for different tasks of ALNs, and MLNs segmentation. However partial adaption approach shows significant performance both in ALNs and MLNs segmentation with the reduction of 29,376 number of the trainable parameter (observable from Table 10.6).

Further, we have also explored training of proposed approach with combine data set, i.e., ALNs and MLNs training data were mixed during the training phase and then testing of the trained model were performed on individual ALNs and MLNs test dataset. From this, we have achieved a DS of 66.64%.

Tables 10.3 and 10.4 show some samples with ground truth, predicted masks, and DS of ALNs and MLNs, respectively using the proposed approach. Ground truths and predicted masks are overlaid in original images with red and green colors, respectively. It's observable from Tables 10.3 and 10.4 that, proposed approach properly segments varying and small sizes LNs located in different locations. Further, it's also noticeable that, proposed approach properly segments multiple and cluttered LNs.

10.5   DISCUSSIONS

In this section, we will present the model parameters, statistical analysis to validate the significant contribution of the proposed model over existing approaches. Lastly, we will present a comparative study of performances mentioned in various literature and the proposed approach.

Table 10.5 shows the total number of trainable parameters for proposed and implemented approaches. It's observable from Table 10.5 that, attention U-Net only having a 7% additional training parameter compare to U-Net and ResUNet but gives significant performance enhancement over other implemented approaches.

TABLE 10.3
Some Segmented Samples with Ground Truth and Predicted Masks of ALNs.
Red Color for Ground Truth Masking and Green Color for Predicted Masking.
DS Shows Dice Score

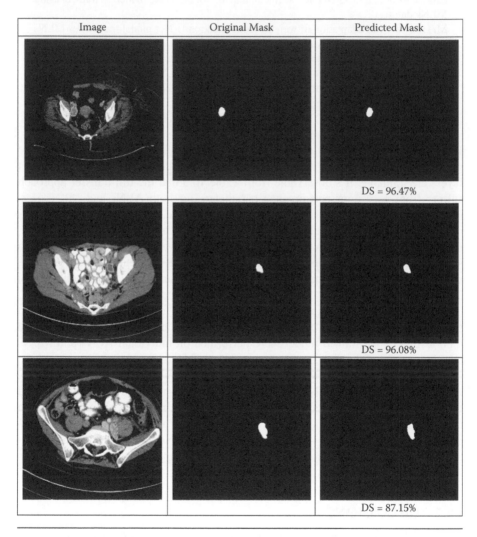

Table 10.6 shows total parameters, trainable parameters, and non-trainable parameters of attention U-Net for different TL approaches. It's observable from Table 10.6 that, Partial adaption approach significantly reduces trainable parameter count and gives satisfactory results (Table 10.2). This gives a scope for exploring TL approaches with different levels of adaptions for reducing trainable parameter count and hence, reduction in overfitting and getting fast results.

TABLE 10.4
Some Segmented Samples of Ground Truth and Predicted Masks of MLNs. Red Color for Ground Truth Masking and Green Color for Predicted Masking. DS Shows Dice Score

Image	Original Mask	Predicted Mask
		DS = 93%
		DS = 92.67%
		DS = 95.47%

In this chapter, we have also performed the Paired t-test [60] with significant value of 0.05, for validating significant contribution of the proposed attention U-Net approach compared to other experimented approaches (SegNet, U-Net, and ResUnet). We decided on the null hypothesis that, attention U-Net doesn't provide any significant improvement over other experimented approaches, and vice-versa for the alternative hypothesis. Table 10.7 shows the results of the Paired t-test in terms of t-stat and p-value. The p-value < 0.01 indicates that we can reject the null

TABLE 10.5

Number of Model Parameters of Proposed and Implemented Approaches

	SegNet	U-Net	ResUNet	Attention U-Net
Total parameters	1,369,089	3,500,577	3,500,577	3,766,997
Trainable parameters	1,367,169	3,494,689	3,494,689	3,759,181
Non-trainable parameters	1,920	5,888	7,816	7,816

TABLE 10.6

Number of Model Parameters of Attention U-Net for Different TL Approaches

	Attention U-Net		
	Full Adaption	Partial Adaption	Zero Adaption
Total parameters	3,766,997	3,766,997	3,766,997
Trainable parameters	0	3,729,805	3,759,181
Non-trainable parameters	3,766,997	37,192	7,816

TABLE 10.7

Results of Paired of Paired t-test

Attention U-Net Paired With	ALNs Detection		MLNs Detection	
	t-stat	p-Value	t-stat	p-Value
SegNet	26.30288	<0.01	12.90890	<0.01
U-Net	13.24271	<0.01	14.19356	<0.01
ResUNet	−1.4711	0.072	11.22738	<0.01

hypothesis and this validates that attention U-Net provides a significant improvement over other experimented models. In the case of ResUNet for ALNs detection, though we can't reject the null hypothesis, it is observable from Table 10.1 that proposed attention U-Net provides 2.77% improvement in sensitivity compared to ResUNet for ALNs detection, which shows significant improvement.

Tables 10.8 and 10.9 show a comparative study of performances mentioned in various literature and the proposed method for ALNs, and MLNs segmentation, respectively. From Table 10.8, it is observable that the proposed attention-based U-Net approach achieves 10.08% and 10.45% improvement in sensitivity and DS, respectively, compared to existing approaches for ALNs segmentation task. Further,

TABLE 10.8
Comparative Study of Performances Mentioned in Various Literature and the Proposed Method for ALNs Segmentation

Authors	Dataset		Methodology	Sensitivity	Dice Score
	No. of Patients	No. of ALNs			
Kitasaka et al. [3]	5	220	3-D minimum directional difference filter	57%	–
Wang et al. [61]	35	111	Graph-based segmentation	–	81.24%
Barbu et al. [12]	54	569	Haar features, non-maximal suppression	80%	79.7%
Oda et al. [4]	16	88	Ellipsoidal structure detection filter	56.8%	–
Nakamura et al. [7]	28	NA	Local intensity structure analysis	70.5%	–
Cherry et al. [8]	301	119	Random Forest	79.8%	–
Nimura et al. [14]	23	61	Radial structure tensor analysis	82%	–
Nakamura et al. [13]	28	NA	Sequential feature selection method	74.7%	–
Roth et al. [1]	86	595	Convolutional neural network	83%	–
Seff et al. [2]	86	595	Shallow hierarchy of linear classifiers	73.1%	–
Seff et al. [9]	86	595	Semantic Boundary Cues	78%	–
Shin et al. [18]	86	595	Deep convolutional neural network	70%	–
Nogues et al. [15]	171	(ALNs + MLNs) – 411	Holistically-Nested Neural Networks	–	82.1%± 9.6%
Li et al. [17]	176	(ALNs + MLNs) – 984	Reinforcement learning	–	77.17%
Cai et al. [22]	176	(ALNs + MLNs) – 984	Graph Cut, CNN	–	84.4%
Beichel et al. [10]	–	(ALNs + MLNs + head/neck +axillary) – 111	optimal surface finding	–	84.7%
Tan et al. [11]	48	(ALNs + MLNs + Pelvis)- 54	Dynamic programming	–	83.2%
Hoogi et al. [23]	86	595	Active contour, CNN	51%	76.8%
Proposed approach	**86**	**595**	**Attention-based U-Net model**	**93.08%**	**91.69%**

TABLE 10.9

Comparative Study of Performances Mentioned in Various Literature and the Proposed Method for MLNs Segmentation

Authors	Dataset		Methodology	Sensitivity	Dice score
	No. of Patients	No. of MLNs			
Roth et al. [1]	90	388	Convolutional neural network	70%	–
Seff et al. [2]	90	388	Shallow hierarchy of linear classifiers	78%	–
Seff et al. [9]	90	388	Semantic Boundary Cues	78%	–
Shin et al. [18]	90	388	Deep convolutional neural network	86%	–
Feuerstein et al. [24]	5	NA	Hessian analysis	82.1%	–
Feulner et al. [6]	54	1,086	Discriminative learning and spatial prior	52	–
Allen et al. [28]	10	NA	Random forests	95%	–
Liu et al. [26]	70	316	Spatial prior	88%	–
Oda et al. [25]	47	548	Intensity targeted radial structure tensor analysis	84.2%	–
Oda et al. [29]	45	NA	Fully convolutional networks	95.5%	52.3 ± 23.1%
Bouget et al. [31]	15	148	Semantic Segmentation	75%	76%
Tang et al. [32]	–	–	GAN, U-Net	–	82.5%
Proposed approach	**90**	**388**	**Attention-based U-Net model**	**99%**	**97%**

it's observable from Table 10.9 that the proposed attention U-Net model achieves 15% and 3.5% improvement in DS and sensitivity, respectively, compared to existing approaches for MLNs segmentation task.

10.6 CONCLUSION AND FUTURE WORK

In this chapter, the detection of lymph nodes (mediastinal and abdominal) in CT images has been implemented using the attention-based U-Net approach. To overcome the problem of the limited dataset, elastic deformation is used as a data augmentation approach for increasing the training dataset. Furthermore, based on the structural similarity between MLNs and ALNs, transfer learning has been attempted. The transfer learning approach has been evaluated by considering zero, partial, and full adaptations of weights for the detection of both MLNs and ALNs simultaneously. The applicability of attention U-Net for detection of LNs has also been justified by comparing the results with state of art DL approaches like SegNet, U-Net, and ResU-Net. From the results, it can easily be implied that attention U-Net performance is better than other state of art DL approaches by 3% to 13% (approx) sensitivity in the detection of ALNs while by 2% to 5% (approx) sensitivity in the detection of MLNs. Further, the achieved p-Values from paired t-test also justify the significant contribution of the proposed approach. The attention U-Net has also attended the highest performance compared to other works from the literature for the detection of both ALNs and MLNs.

10.7 FUTURE WORK

Very recently our group had also explored the application of generative adversarial networks (GANs) for MLNs severity detection [62]. GANs [63] are CNN-based DL models and used for synthesizing images from learning of original data distribution. Their ability to better modeling of data distribution along with transfer learning may be further explored for the intended task. Similarly, a hybrid network based on attention mechanism and capsule networks [64] can be further studied for the segmentation of LNs.

REFERENCES

[1] Roth H. R., Lu L., Seff A., Cherry K. M., Hoffman J., Wang S., et al. A new 2.5 D representation for lymph node detection using random sets of deep convolutional neural network observations. *Int. Conf. Med. image Comput. Comput. Interv.* (2014): 520–527.

[2] Seff A., Lu L., Cherry K. M., Roth H. R., Liu J., Wang S., et al. 2D view aggregation for lymph node detection using a shallow hierarchy of linear classifiers. *Int. Conf. Med. Image Comput. Comput. Interv.* (2014): 544–552.

[3] Kitasaka T., Tsujimura Y., Nakamura Y., Mori K., Suenaga Y., Ito M., et al. Automated extraction of lymph nodes from 3-D abdominal CT images using 3-D minimum directional difference filter. *Int. Conf. Med. Image Comput. Comput. Interv.* (2007): 336–343.

[4] Oda M., Kitasaka T., Fujiwara M., Misawa K., Mori K. Method for detecting enlarged lymph nodes from 3d abdominal CT images with a multi-shape and multi-scale ellipsoidal structure detection filter. *Int. MICCAI Work Comput. Clin. Challenges Abdom. Imaging.* (2012): 238–245.

[5] Gomolka R., Klonowski W., Korzynska A., Siemion K. Automatic segmentation of morphological structures in microscopic images of lymphatic nodes-preliminary results. *Int. J. Med. Physiol.* 2 (2017).

[6] Feulner J., Zhou S. K., Hammon M., Hornegger J., Comaniciu D. Lymph node detection and segmentation in chest CT data using discriminative learning and a spatial prior. *Med. Image Anal.* 17 (2013): 254–270.

[7] Nakamura Y., Nimura Y., Kitasaka T., Mizuno S., Furukawa K., Goto H., et al. Automatic abdominal lymph node detection method based on local intensity structure analysis from 3D x-ray CT images. *Med. Imaging 2013 Comput. Diagnosis* 8670 (2013): 86701K.

[8] Cherry K. M., Wang S., Turkbey E. B., Summers R. M. Abdominal lymphadenopathy detection using random forest. . *Med. Imaging 2014 Comput. Diagnosis* 9035 (2014): 90351G.

[9] Seff A., Lu L., Barbu A., Roth H., Shin H.-C., Summers R. M. Leveraging mid-level semantic boundary cues for automated lymph node detection. *Int. Conf. Med. Image Comput. Comput. Interv.* (2015): 53–61.

[10] Beichel R. R., Wang Y. Computer-aided lymph node segmentation in volumetric CT data. *Med. Phys.* 39 (2012): 5419–5428.

[11] Tan Y., Lu L., Bonde A., Wang D., Qi J., Schwartz L. H., et al. Lymph node segmentation by dynamic programming and active contours. *Med. Phys.* 45 (2018): 2054–2062. 10.1002/mp.12844.

[12] Barbu A., Suehling M., Xu X., Liu D., Zhou S. K., Comaniciu D. Automatic detection and segmentation of lymph nodes from CT data. *IEEE Trans. Med. Imaging* 31 (2011): 240–250.

[13] Nakamura Y., Nimura Y., Kitasaka T., Mizuno S., Furukawa K., Goto H., et al. Investigation of optimal feature value set in false positive reduction process for automated abdominal lymph node detection method. *Med. Imaging 2015 Comput. Diagnosis* 9414 (2015): 94143N.

[14] Nimura Y., Hayashi Y., Kitasaka T., Furukawa K., Misawa K., Mori K. Automated abdominal lymph node segmentation based on RST analysis and SVM. In: Aylward S., Hadjiiski L. M., editors. *Prog. Biomed. Opt. Imaging - Proc. SPIE*, 9035 (2014): 90352U. 10.1117/12.2043349.

[15] Nogues I., Lu L., Wang X., Roth H., Bertasius G., Lay N., et al. Automatic lymph node cluster segmentation using holistically-nested neural networks and structured optimization in CT images. *Int. Conf. Med. Image Comput. Comput. Interv.* (2016): 388–397.

[16] Roth H. R., Lu L., Liu J., Yao J., Seff A., Cherry K., et al. Improving computer-aided detection using convolutional neural networks and random view aggregation. *IEEE Trans. Med. Imaging* 35 (2015): 1170–1181.

[17] Sengupta D. Deep learning architectures for automated image segmentation. University of California (2019).

[18] Shin H.-C., Roth H. R., Gao M., Lu L., Xu Z., Nogues I., et al. Deep convolutional neural networks for computer-aided detection: CNN architectures, dataset characteristics and transfer learning. *IEEE Trans. Med. Imaging* 35 (2016): 1285–1298.

[19] Deng J., Dong W., Socher R., Li L.-J., Li K., Fei-Fei L. Imagenet: A large-scale hierarchical image database. *2009 IEEE Conf. Comput. Vis. Pattern Recognit.* (2009): 248–255.

[20] Li Z., Xia Y. Deep reinforcement learning for weakly-supervised lymph node segmentation in CT images. *IEEE J. Biomed. Heal. Informatics* 1 (2020). 10.1109/JBHI.2020.3008759.

[21] Nishino M., Jagannathan J. P., Ramaiya N. H., den Abbeele A. D. Revised RECIST guideline version 1.1: What oncologists want to know and what radiologists need to know. *Am. J. Roentgenol.* 195 (2010): 281–289.

[22] Cai J., Tang Y., Lu L., Harrison A. P., Yan K., Xiao J., et al. Accurate weakly-supervised deep lesion segmentation using large-scale clinical annotations: Slice-propagated 3d mask generation from 2d recist. *Int. Conf. Med. Image Comput. Comput. Interv.* (2018): 396–404.

[23] Hoogi A., Lambert J. W., Zheng Y., Comaniciu D., Rubin D. L. A fully-automated pipeline for detection and segmentation of liver lesions and pathological lymph nodes. ArXiv Prepr ArXiv170306418 (2017).

[24] Feuerstein M., Deguchi D., Kitasaka T., Iwano S., Imaizumi K., Hasegawa Y., et al. Automatic mediastinal lymph node detection in chest CT. *Med. Imaging 2009 Comput. Diagnosis* 7260 (2009): 72600V.

[25] Oda H., Bhatia K. K., Oda M., Kitasaka T., Iwano S., Homma H., et al. Automated mediastinal lymph node detection from CT volumes based on intensity targeted radial structure tensor analysis. *J. Med. Imaging* 4 (2017): 44502.

[26] Liu J., Hoffman J., Zhao J., Yao J., Lu L., Kim L., et al. Mediastinal lymph node detection and station mapping on chest CT using spatial priors and random forest. *Med. Phys.* 43 (2016): 4362–4374.

[27] Zhao W., Shi F. A method for lymph node segmentation with scaling features in a random forest model. *Curr. Proteomics* 15 (2018): 128–134.

[28] Allen D., Lu L., Yao J., Liu J., Turkbey E., Summers R. M. Robust automated lymph node segmentation with random forests. *Med. Imaging 2014 Image Process.* 9034 (2014): 90343X.

[29] Oda H., Bhatia K. K., Roth H. R., Oda M., Kitasaka T., Iwano S., et al. Dense volumetric detection and segmentation of mediastinal lymph nodes in chest CT images. In: Mori K., Petrick N., editors. *Med. Imaging 2018 Comput. Diagnosis, SPIE* 1 (2018). 10.1117/12.2287066.

[30] Ronneberger O., Fischer P., Brox T. U-net: Convolutional networks for biomedical image segmentation. *Int. Conf. Med. Image Comput. Comput. Interv.* (2015): 234–241.

[31] Bouget D., Jørgensen A., Kiss G., Leira H. O., Langø T. Semantic segmentation and detection of mediastinal lymph nodes and anatomical structures in CT data for lung cancer staging. *Int. J. Comput. Assist. Radiol. Surg.* (2019): 1–10.

[32] Tang Y., Oh S., Xiao J., Summers R., Tang Y. CT-realistic data augmentation using generative adversarial network for robust lymph node segmentation. *Med. Imaging 2019 Comput. Diagnosis, San Diego, California, United States* 139 (2019). 10.111 7/12.2512004.

[33] Long J., Shelhamer E., Darrell T. Fully convolutional networks for semantic segmentation. *Proc. IEEE Conf. Comput. Vis. Pattern Recognit.* (2015): 3431–3440.

[34] Bahdanau D., Cho K., Bengio Y. Neural machine translation by jointly learning to align and translate. ArXiv Prepr ArXiv14090473 (2014).

[35] Sinha A., Dolz J. Multi-scale self-guided attention for medical image segmentation. *IEEE. J. Biomed. Heal. Informatics* (2020).

[36] Wang Y., Deng Z., Hu X., Zhu L., Yang X., Xu X., et al. Deep attentional features for prostate segmentation in ultrasound. *Int. Conf. Med. Image Comput. Comput. Interv.* (2018): 523–530.

[37] Li C., Tong Q., Liao X., Si W., Sun Y., Wang Q., et al. Attention based hierarchical aggregation network for 3D left atrial segmentation. *Int. Work. Stat. Atlases Comput. Model. Hear.* (2018): 255–264.

[38] Schlemper J., Oktay O., Schaap M., Heinrich M., Kainz B., Glocker B., et al. Attention gated networks: Learning to leverage salient regions in medical images. *Med. Image Anal.* 53 (2019): 197–207.

[39] Li C., Tan Y., Chen W., Luo X., He Y., Gao Y., et al. ANU-Net: Attention-based nested U-Net to exploit full resolution features for medical image segmentation. *Comput. Graph.* 90 (2020): 11–20. 10.1016/j.cag.2020.05.003.

[40] Nie D., Gao Y., Wang L., Shen D. ASDNet: Attention based semi-supervised deep networks for medical image segmentation. *Int. Conf. Med. Image Comput. Comput. Interv.* (2018): 370–378.

[41] Xu K., Ba J., Kiros R., Cho K., Courville A., Salakhudinov R., et al. Show, attend and tell: Neural image caption generation with visual attention. *Int. Conf. Mach. Learn.* (2015): 2048–2057.

[42] Hesamian M. H., Jia W., He X., Kennedy P. Deep learning techniques for medical image segmentation: Achievements and challenges. *J. Digit. Imaging* (2019): 1–15.

[43] Tajbakhsh N., Shin J. Y., Gurudu S. R., Hurst R. T., Kendall C. B., Gotway M. B., et al. Convolutional neural networks for medical image analysis: Full training or fine tuning? *IEEE Trans. Med. Imaging* 35 (2016): 1299–1312.

[44] Raghu M., Zhang C., Kleinberg J., Bengio S. Transfusion: Understanding transfer learning for medical imaging. *Adv. Neural Inf. Process. Syst.* (2019): 3342–3352.

[45] Ravishankar H., Sudhakar P., Venkataramani R., Thiruvenkadam S., Annangi P., Babu N., et al. Understanding the mechanisms of deep transfer learning for medical images. *Deep Learn. Data Labeling Med. Appl.* (2016): 188–196.

[46] National Institute of Health. CT lymph nodes. *Cancer Imaging Arch.* (2015). https:// wiki.cancerimagingarchive.net/display/Public/CT+Lymph+Nodes.

[47] Yosinski J., Clune J., Bengio Y., Lipson H. How transferable are features in deep neural networks? *Adv. Neural Inf. Process. Syst.* (2014): 3320–3328.

[48] Knipe H., Murphy A. Radiology reference. (n.d.). https://radiopaedia.org/articles/ windowing-ct.

[49] Diakogiannis F. I., Waldner F., Caccetta P., Wu C. Resunet-a: A deep learning framework for semantic segmentation of remotely sensed data. *ISPRS J. Photogramm. Remote Sens.* 162 (2020): 94–114.

[50] Sambyal N., Saini P., Syal R., Gupta V. Modified U-Net architecture for semantic segmentation of diabetic retinopathy images. *Biocybern. Biomed. Eng.* 40 (2020): 1094–1109. 10.1016/j.bbe.2020.05.006.

[51] He K., Zhang X., Ren S., Sun J. Deep residual learning for image recognition. *2016 IEEE Conf. Comput. Vis. Pattern Recognit.* (2016): 770–778. 10.1109/CVPR.2 016.90.

[52] Tekchandani H., Verma S., Londhe N. D. Mediastinal lymph node malignancy detection in computed tomography images using fully convolutional network. *Biocybern. Biomed. Eng.* 40 (2020): 187–199. 10.1016/j.bbe.2019.05.002.

[53] Simard P. Y., Steinkraus D., Platt J. C. Best practices for convolutional neural networks applied to visual document analysis. *Icdar* 3 (2003).

[54] Chollet F. Keras: The python deep learning library (2015).

[55] Kingma D. P., Ba J. Adam: A method for stochastic optimization. *ArXiv Prepr ArXiv14126980* (2014).

[56] Glorot X., Bengio Y. Understanding the difficulty of training deep feedforward neural networks. *Proc. Thirteen. Int. Conf. Artif. Intell. Stat.* (2010): 249–256.

[57] Dash M., Londhe N. D., Ghosh S., Semwal A., Sonawane R. S. PsLSNet: Automated psoriasis skin lesion segmentation using modified U-Net-based fully convolutional network. *Biomed. Signal. Process Control.* 52 (2019): 226–237. 10.1 016/j.bspc.2019.04.002.

[58] Huttenlocher D. P., Klanderman G. A., Rucklidge W. J. Comparing images using the Hausdorff distance. *IEEE Trans. Pattern Anal. Mach. Intell.* 15 (1993): 850–863. 10.1109/34.232073.

[59] Badrinarayanan V., Kendall A., Cipolla R. Segnet: A deep convolutional encoder-decoder architecture for image segmentation. *IEEE Trans. Pattern Anal. Mach. Intell.* 39 (2017): 2481–2495.

[60] Hsu H., Lachenbruch P. Paired t test. *Wiley Encycl. Clin. Trials* (2008). 10.1002/ 9780471462422.eoct969.

[61] Wang Y., Beichel R. Graph-based segmentation of lymph nodes in ct data. *Int. Symp. Vis. Comput.* (2010): 312–321.

[62] Tekchandani H., Verma S., Londhe N. Performance improvement of mediastinal lymph node severity detection using GAN and Inception network. *Comput. Methods Programs Biomed.* 194 (2020): 105478. 10.1016/j.cmpb.2020.105478.

[63] Goodfellow I., Pouget-Abadie J., Mirza M., Xu B., Warde-Farley D., Ozair S., et al. Generative adversarial nets. *Adv. Neural Inf. Process. Syst.* (2014): 2672–2680.

[64] Sabour S., Frosst N., Hinton G. E. Dynamic routing between capsules. *Adv. Neural Inf. Process. Syst.* (2017): 3856–3866.

11 Swarm Optimized Hybrid Layer Decomposition and Reconstruction Model for Multi-Modal Neurological Image Fusion

Manisha Das and Deep Gupta
National Institute of Technology, Nagpur, Maharashtra, India

Petia Radeva
Universitat de Barcelona, & Computer Vision Center, Barcelona, Spain

Ashwini M. Bakde
All India Institute of Medical Sciences, Nagpur, Maharashtra, India

CONTENTS

DOI: 10.1201/9781003241409-11

11.1   INTRODUCTION

Diagnostic radiology plays a decisive role in assessing and treating critical ailments. Anatomical and functional imaging modalities help in visualizing the structural details of tissue, organs, etc. Prevalent anatomical imaging modalities used in neuroimaging are computed tomography (CT), magnetic resonance T1/T2/proton density weighted (MR-T1/T2/PD), etc. CT is good at imaging the dense tissues structures like bones and intracranial calcifications while MR images give clear visualization of textural details of soft tissues, tumors, cysts, etc. Fusing the complementary diagnostic information of CT and MR images eases the visualization and analysis of the underlying anatomical anomalies and helps radiologists in more accurate and faster diagnosis [1,2]. Modalities like Single-Photon Emission Computed Tomography (SPECT-Tc, SPECT-T1) and Positron Emission Tomography (PET) fall under functional imaging. These modalities highlight various metabolic activities of tissues and are used extensively to detect malignant tumors. Both PET and SPECT images have a lower resolution which can pose a bottleneck in drawing accurate medical interpretations. Fusing low-resolution PET/SPECT images and high-resolution CT/MR images result in more realistic and concise images of a variety of bodily structures and further helps the radiologists to reach to more factual and precise diagnosis [1,2].

Both spatial and transform domains implementation of image fusion methods have been presented in the literature [3]. Spatial domain methods process individual pixels or regional activities while in the transform domain approaches, initially, the input images undergo a multi-level transform to give low and high-frequency sub-bands. The activity levels of the transform coefficients are then calculated and fused followed by reconstruction. The transformed coefficients localize the spatial structures well and give better performance to their spatial domain counterparts. Exploiting the fact that Multi-Scale Decomposition (MSD) extract both spectral and spatial information from images, a variety of these approaches are presented in the literature [4,5] for image fusion. Fusion methods based on pyramid decomposition provide improved localization of textural features but lack directional selectivity [6]. Wavelet family transforms such as Non-Subsampled Contourlet Transform (NSCT) [7], Stationary Wavelet Transforms (SWT) [8] and Non-Subsampled Shearlet Transform (NSST) [9–14] effectively captures singularities and gives improved fusion performance. These approaches are still widely used in medical image fusion as they provide an excellent representation of various spatial and spectral structures. The performance of MSD based methods hugely depends on the decomposition method, basis function, and decomposition levels. Balancing the trade-off between the fusion performance and the computational complexity is a challenging task that is usually done using the hit and trial approach.

The main motivation of medical image fusion is to derive perceptually enhanced fused images as they are finally analyzed by radiologists. As Human visual perception is extremely sensitive to spatial textures, it is of prime concern to retain the diagnostic edges of the source images. Recently Liang et al. [15] presented a novel decomposition model for image tone mapping using Hybrid Layer Decomposition (HLD) model. The HLD model effectively preserves the structures of the detail layer by imposing a ℓ_0 sparsity on detail layers. Further, a ℓ_1 sparsity on base layers preserves edges by performing an edge-aware smoothing. However, the model uses three regularization parameters namely λ_1, λ_2, and λ_3 for controlling the smoothness degree of textural and structural parts of the input image. These parameters are usually fixed using the hit and trial approach [15–18]. In the case of fusion, using the same set of values for these parameters for images coming from different modalities does not work well in terms of edge preservation. Further, while reconstruction equal weights are given to both textural and structural parts which in the case of image fusion can limit the edge information carried by fused images [16,17].

To address the challenges discussed above, we present a unified multi-modal neurological image fusion framework for both anatomical-anatomical and anatomical-functional fusion using an optimized two-scale HLD model. The optimized HLD model is obtained by optimizing the regularization parameters during decomposition and weights during reconstruction using whale optimization algorithm. Firstly, source images are decomposed using an optimized two-scale HLD model to yield a base layer (B_2) and a detail layer (D_2) at scale-2 and a detail layer (D_1) at scale-1, having local brightness, textural and structural information, respectively. D_1 and D_2 layers are fused considering their local novel sum modified spatial frequency and weighted local energy to capture and preserve local structural and textural details. Choose-max rule is used to fuse B_2 to highlighting background brightness for better visualization. The whale optimization algorithm optimizes HLD model parameters to strengthen the edge preservation and mutual information of fused images to yield perceptually enhanced fusion results.

The rest of the chapter is arranged as follows: a brief introduction to various building blocks of the proposed fusion framework, implementation steps, and the experimental settings is presented in Section 11.2. Section 11.3 presents subjective and objective fusion results and detailed performance comparisons among the proposed and state-of-the-art fusion methods. Finally, Section 11.4 presents the conclusion.

11.2 METHODOLOGY

11.2.1 HYBRID LAYER DECOMPOSITION

The HLD model shown in Figure 11.1 imposes hybrid ℓ_0 and ℓ_1 gradient sparsity on the detail and base layers, respectively [15]. The piece-wise smoothness property of ℓ_1 sparsity term preserves edges and piece-wise constant property ℓ_0 conserve structural details of the image being decomposed. At scale-1 decomposition level, $\ell_0 - \ell_1$ priors are imposed on the input image (I) to get a scale-1 base layer B_1 and a scale-1 detail layer D_1 using Equations (11.1) and (11.2). Here, p and K denote the pixel index and number, respectively. The partial derivative operator is represented

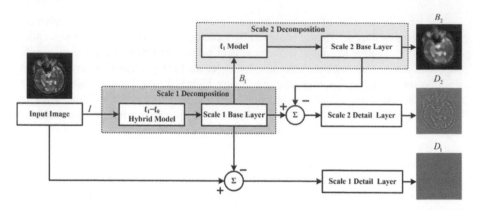

FIGURE 11.1   Block diagram of two-scale HLD model.

by ∂_i along x and y directions. The gradient regularization terms λ_1 and λ_2 control the smoothness degree of the base and detail layers, respectively. The first term of Equation (11.1) minimizes the difference between the original input image and the base layer. Edge-preserving prior depicted by the second term of Equation (11.1) imposes ℓ_1 gradient sparsity on the base layer. Finally, the third term of Equation (11.1) models a structural prior on detail layer using ℓ_0 gradient sparsity using function $(x) = \begin{cases} 1, x \neq 0 \\ 0, x = 0 \end{cases}$. At scale-2 decomposition, B_1 is subjected to a simplified model shown in Equations (11.3) and (11.4) for capturing the textural information to generate a scale-2 base layer B_2 and scale-2 detail layer D_2. The smoothness degree of the B_2 is controlled by. As shown in Figure 11.1 the two-scale HLD model decomposes the input image into B_2, D_1, D_2 containing local brightness, structural and textural information, respectively. During the reconstruction, the original image can be obtained by simply adding the three layers, i.e., $I = D_1 + D_2 + B_2$. A weighted average reconstruction, i.e., $w_1 D_1 + w_2 D_2 + w_3 B_2$ can also be performed by processing each decomposition layer separately to get the desired results depending upon the image processing application [15].

$$B_1 = \min_B \sum_{p=1}^{K} \left\{ (I_p - B_p)^2 + \lambda_1 \sum_{i=\{x,y\}} \left| \partial_i B_p \right| + \lambda_2 \sum_{i=\{x,y\}} H\left(\partial_i (I_p - B_p) \right) \right\} \quad (11.1)$$

$$D_1 = I - B_1 \quad\quad\quad\quad\quad (11.2)$$

$$B_2 = \min_B \sum_{p=1}^{K} \left\{ (B_{1,p} - B_p)^2 + \lambda_3 \sum_{i=\{x,y\}} \left| \partial_i B_p \right| \right\} \quad\quad (11.3)$$

$$D_2 = B_1 - B_2 \quad\quad\quad\quad\quad (11.4)$$

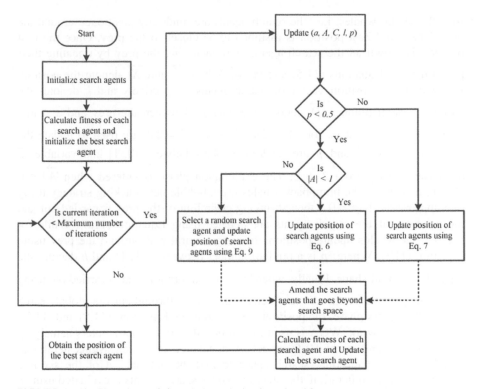

FIGURE 11.2 Flowchart of the whale optimization algorithm.

11.2.2 WHALE OPTIMIZATION ALGORITHM

Inspired by the foraging behavior of humpback whales, the whale optimization algorithm (WOA) comes under swarm-based meta-heuristics [19]. The flowchart of WOA is depicted in Figure 11.2 and its mathematical model is given as follows;

$$\vec{D} = \left| \vec{C}. \ \overrightarrow{X^*}(k) - \vec{X}(k) \right| \tag{11.5}$$

$$\vec{X}(k+1) = \overrightarrow{X^*}(k) - \vec{A}. \vec{D} \quad if \ p < 0.5 \tag{11.6}$$

$$\vec{X}(k+1) = \vec{D}. \ e^{bl}. \ \cos(2\pi l) - \overrightarrow{X^*}(k) \quad if \ p \geq 0.5 \tag{11.7}$$

$$\overrightarrow{D^r} = \left| \vec{C}. \ \overrightarrow{X^r}(k) - \vec{X}(k) \right| \tag{11.8}$$

$$\vec{X}(k+1) = \overrightarrow{X^r}(k) - \vec{A}. \ \overrightarrow{D^r} \tag{11.9}$$

Initially, all the whales, i.e., the search agents are randomly positioned around the prey. The initial best position is assumed to be closer to the prey. Once the best position is known all the search agents start encircling the prey by updating their position using Equations (11.5) and (11.6). Where $\vec{X}$ and $\vec{X^*}$ denote the position vector and best position vector of search agents, respectively and k denotes the current iteration number. $\vec{D}$ denotes the distance between the prey and a search agent. The coefficient vectors $\vec{A} = 2\vec{a} \cdot \vec{r} - \vec{a}$, $\vec{C} = 2\vec{r}$ are used to update the position vectors. $\vec{r}$ and p are random numbers between [0, 1] and variable $\vec{a}$ decreases linearly from 2 to 0. The exploitation phase is entered when $|\vec{A}| < 1$. During this phase, the humpback whales use a bubble net attacking strategy using two approaches. If $p < 0.5$ then shrinking encircling of the prey is carried out and the positions of the search agents are updated using Equation (11.6). While for $p \geq 0.5$, the whales update positions forming a spiral path around the prey using Equation (11.7). Where, p is a random number between $[-1, 1]$ and b decides the logarithmic spiral shape. Finally, when $|\vec{A}| \geq 1$ exploration is also carried out using a random position vector $\vec{X^r}$ to diversify the search throughout the global search space. During this phase, the position is updated using Equations (11.8) and (11.9). In the proposed work, WOA is used to optimize the six free parameters namely λ_1, λ_2, λ_3, w_1, w_2, and w_3 of HLD model. A population of search agents iteratively searches a six-dimensional search space to find the optimal set of the six free parameters. At each iteration, the fitness of all the search agents is evaluated using a fitness function. The main motivation to tune the HLD model's free parameters is to obtain perceptually appealing images and hence fitness function is framed accordingly using the edge index $Q_{RS/F}$ [20] and the mutual information $MI_{RS/F}$ [21] of the fused images. $Q_{RS/F}$ measures the extent to which micro diagnostic edges of the input modalities are conserved while the $MI_{RS/F}$ gives the extent of transfer of complementary information from input modalities to the fused image. In this way, at each iteration, the WOA seeks to elevate the visualization and information content of fused images by searching the set of six free parameters of the HLD model and finally converges to give the optimized HLD model.

11.2.3 Proposed Method

In this section, detailed implementation steps of the proposed Optimized Hybrid Layer Decomposition and Reconstruction model-based Image Fusion Framework (OHLDR-IFF) for multi-modal neurological image fusion are given. The flow diagram of the proposed fusion method for anatomical-anatomical fusion and anatomical-functional fusion is illustrated in Figures 11.3 and 11.4, respectively.

Implementation steps:
Step 1: Take two source images as $R = R_{i,j}$ and $= S_{i,j}$. Here the row and column pixel indices are represented by I and j, respectively. For anatomical-

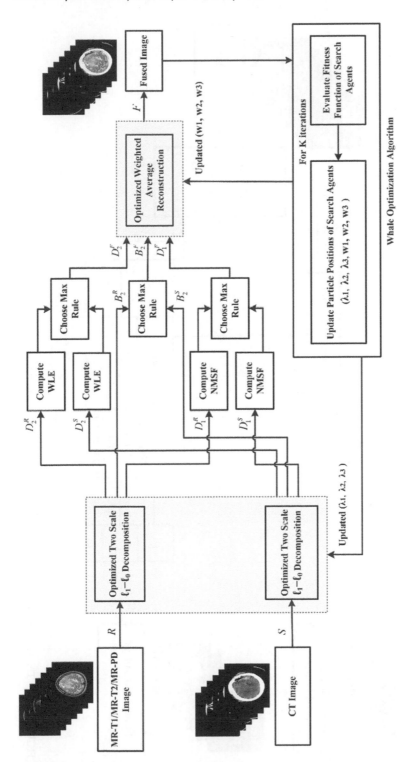

FIGURE 11.3 The proposed OHLDR-IFF for anatomical-anatomical image fusion.

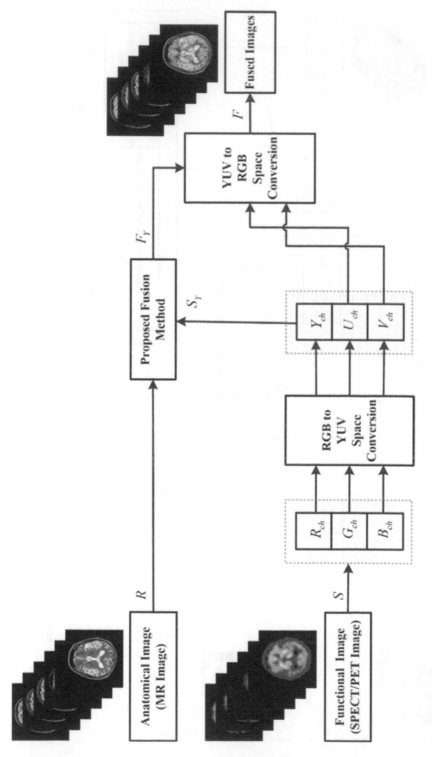

FIGURE 11.4 The proposed OHLDR-IFF for anatomical-functional image fusion.

functional image fusion, convert the functional image RGB to YUV color space follows [14];

$$\begin{bmatrix} Y_{ch} \\ U_{ch} \\ V_{ch} \end{bmatrix} = \begin{bmatrix} 0.299 & 0.587 & 0.114 \\ -0.169 & -0.331 & 0.5 \\ 0.5 & -0.419 & -0.081 \end{bmatrix} \begin{bmatrix} R_{ch} \\ G_{ch} \\ B_{ch} \end{bmatrix} \tag{11.10}$$

Where R_{ch}, G_{ch}, B_{ch}, Y_{ch}, U_{ch}, and V_{ch} refer to red, green, blue, luminance, and two chrominance components of an image, respectively. Now represent the anatomical image by $R = R_{i,j}$ and the luminance component of the functional image by $S = S_{i,j}$.

Subject the source images to a two-scale optimized HLD model as follows;

$$\left[D^X_{1_{i,j}}, D^X_{2_{i,j}}, B^X_{2_{i,j}} \right] = HLD(X_{i,j}) \tag{11.11}$$

Where, $D_{1_{i,j}}$ and $D_{2_{i,j}}$ refers scale-1 and scale-2 detail layers, while $B_{2_{i,j}}$ represents the base layer at scale-2, respectively and $X \in (R, S)$

Step 2: Initialize WOA with $P = 30$ search agents and $K = 12$ number of iterations. The search space is 6-Dimensional, i.e., . $N_D = 6$ and the upper and lower bound of all the search variables are set to 0 and 1, respectively. Also, initialize the position vector $\overrightarrow{X} p$ of all the search agents.

Step 3: $D^X_{1_{i,j}}$ layers contain the majority of the structural information and hence to preserve spatial textures of the source images, estimate the novel sum modified spatial frequency (*NMSF*) [22] of $D^X_{1_{i,j}}$ layers.

$$NMSF^{D_1^X}_{i,j} = \sqrt{ \left(RF^{D_1^X}_{i,j} \right)^2 + \left(CF^{D_1^X}_{i,j} \right)^2 + \delta } \tag{11.12}$$

$$RF^{D_1^X}_{i,j} = \sqrt{ \frac{1}{M(N-1)} \sum_{i=1}^{M} \sum_{j=2}^{N} (D_1^X(i, j-1) - D_1^X(i, j))^2 } \tag{11.13}$$

$$CF^{D_1^X}_{i,j} = \sqrt{ \frac{1}{(M-1)N} \sum_{i=2}^{M} \sum_{j=1}^{N} (D_1^X(i, j) - D_1^X(i-1, j))^2 } \tag{11.14}$$

$$\delta = \begin{bmatrix} \frac{1}{(M-1)(N-1)} \sum_{i=2}^{M} \sum_{j=2}^{N} (D_1^X(i, j) - D_1^X(i-1, j-1))^2 + \\ \frac{1}{(M-1)(N-1)} \sum_{i=1}^{2} \sum_{j=2}^{N} (D_1^X(i-1, j) - D_1^X(i, j-1))^2 \end{bmatrix} \tag{11.15}$$

Where, $RF^{D_1^X}_{i,j}$, $CF^{D_1^X}_{i,j}$ and δ refer to the row, column, and diagonal frequency of the neighborhood pixels of D_1^X, respectively. Now fuse the coefficients of $D_{1_{i,j}}^X$ layers and obtain the fused $D_{1_{i,j}}^F$ using the choose-max scheme as follows;

$$D_{1_{i,j}}^F = \begin{cases} D_{1_{i,j}}^R, & \text{if } NMSF_{i,j}^{D_1^R} \geq NMSF_{i,j}^{D_1^S} \\ D_{1_{i,j}}^S, & \text{otherwise} \end{cases} \tag{11.16}$$

Step 4: $D_{2_{i,j}}^X$ contains mostly the textural information and hence to preserve the local contrast and textures, for fusing these layers the concept of weighted local energy$WLE_{i,j}^{D_2^X}$ [9,22]. Estimate $WLE_{i,j}^{D_2^X}$ of layers as follows;

$$WLE_{i,j}^{D_2^X} = \sum_{i=1}^{x} \sum_{j=1}^{y} (D_2^X(x + i, y + j))^2 w_{i,j} \tag{11.17}$$

Here, the template $w = \frac{1}{16}[1\ 2\ 1;\ 2\ 4\ 2;\ 1\ 2\ 1]$ is used for normalization. Now fuse the $D_{2_{i,j}}^X$ coefficients using the choose-max rule and get the fused $D_{2_{i,j}}^F$ layer as follows;

$$D_{2_{i,j}}^F = \begin{cases} D_{2_{i,j}}^R, & \text{if } WLE_{i,j}^{D_2^R} \geq WLE_{i,j}^{D_2^S} \\ D_{2_{i,j}}^S, & \text{otherwise} \end{cases} \tag{11.18}$$

Step 5: B_2^X contains the local mean background brightness of the source images, so to retain perceptual contrast these layers are fused by the choose-max scheme. The fused base layer $B_{2_{i,j}}^F$ is obtained as follows;

$$B_{2_{i,j}}^F = \begin{cases} B_{2_{i,j}}^R, & \text{if } B_{2_{i,j}}^R \geq B_{2_{i,j}}^S \\ B_{2_{i,j}}^S, & \text{otherwise} \end{cases} \tag{11.19}$$

Step 6: Obtain the fused image $F_{i,j}$ using weighted average reconstruction as follows;

$$F_{i,j} = w_1 D_{1_{i,j}}^F + w_2 D_{2_{i,j}}^F + w_3 B_{2_{i,j}}^F \tag{11.20}$$

For anatomical-functional fusion case, the image obtained after reconstruction represent only the luminance component (F_Y) and hence the colored fused image ($F_{i,j}$) is obtained by performing RGB to YUV color space conversion as follows;

$$\begin{bmatrix} R_{ch} \\ G_{ch} \\ B_{ch} \end{bmatrix} = \begin{bmatrix} 1 & 0 & 0.114 \\ 1 & -0.39 & 0.58 \\ 1 & 2.03 & 0 \end{bmatrix} \begin{bmatrix} F_Y \\ U_{ch} \\ V_{ch} \end{bmatrix} \tag{11.21}$$

Step 7: Define the fitness function ($Fitness(F_{i,j})$) of WOA aiming to maximize the visual perception of fused images $F_{i,j}$ as a product edge index $Q_{RS/F}$ [20] and the mutual information $MI_{RS/F}$ [21].

$$Fitness\,(F_{i,j}) = Q_{RS/F} \times MI_{RS/F} \qquad (11.22)$$

$$Q_{RS/F} = \frac{\sum_{i=1}^{M} \sum_{j=1}^{N} Q_{RF}(i,j) w_R(i,j) + Q_{SF}(i,j) w_S(i,j)}{\sum_{i=1}^{M} \sum_{j=1}^{N} w_R(i,j) + w_S(i,j)} \qquad (11.23)$$

$$MI_{RS/F} = I\,(x_R;\, x_F) + I\,(x_S;\, x_F) \qquad (11.24)$$

Where, Q_{RF} and Q_{SF} denote the edge preservation metric [20] weighted by w_R and w_S, respectively. $I\,(x_R;\, x_F)$ and $I\,(x_S;\, x_F)$ denotes the mutual information of the fused concerning images R and S, respectively.

Step 8: Use WOA to optimize the free parameters of the HLD model by executing the following steps for K times.

1. Find the fitness value of each search agent using step 7.
2. Update a, l, p values, and coefficient vectors $\vec{A}$ and $\vec{C}$.
3. Update the positions of all the search agents.

11.2.4 DATASET

The source of the experimental dataset contains pre-registered multi-modal neurological image pairs (publicly available at http://www.med.harvard.edu/AANLIB/home.html). For carrying out experiments and validation, 75 pairs of anatomical-anatomical images are considered which includes 50 CT-MR-T2 image pairs, 10 CT-MR-T1 image pairs, and 15 CT-MR-PD image pairs. Further, 51 image pairs which include 29 MR-SPECT and 22 MR-PET image pairs are used for anatomical-functional fusion assessment.

11.2.5 EXPERIMENTS PERFORMED

To validate the performance of the proposed fusion framework the performance is compared with five state-of-the-art image fusion approaches namely NSCT domain fuzzy logic-based fusion method (NSCT-FL) [7], NSST domain parameter adaptive pulse coupled neural network-based (NSST-PAPCNN) method [9], NSST domain morphological gradient and PCNN based (NSST-MG-PCNN) method [10], SWT domain method based on Laws texture energy features (SWT-TEF) [8], domain bounded measure PCNN method in NSST domain (NSST-BMPCNN) [13]. Furthermore, for anatomical-functional image fusion recently proposed image fusion methods such as NSST domain coupled neural P system based (NSST-CNPS) method [12], parameter adaptive dual-channel PCNN method proposed in NSST-domain (NSST-PADCPCNN) [11] and Laplacian re-decomposition (LRD) [6] scheme based fusion approach are also considered.

11.2.6 Performance Metrics

Eight state-of-the-art quantitative metrics namely entropy (EN) [14], standard deviation (SD) [14], spatial frequency (SF) [14], mutual information $(MI_{RS/F})$ [21], edge index $(Q_{RS/F})$ [20], similarity index $(Q_C^{RS/F})$ [23], structural similarity index $(Q_Y^{RS/F})$ [24] and fractional order differentiation based edge index $(Q_P^{RS/F})$ [25] are used to evaluate fusion performance. EN and SD measure the information content and overall contrast of the fused images, respectively. Higher values of SF indicate higher clarity of spatial textures. $Q_P^{RS/F}$ gives the edge information content of the fused images. $Q_C^{RS/F}$ and $Q_Y^{RS/F}$ give the measure of correlation among the input and fused images. The mathematical expressions of the metrics are tabulated in Table 11.1.

11.3 RESULTS AND DISCUSSIONS

11.3.1 Performance Comparison of Source and Fused Images

This experiment demonstrates the ability of the proposed OHLDR-IFF to integrate the complementary information present in the source images and generate more detailed and visually enhanced fused images. Six pairs of various anatomical-anatomical and anatomical-functional images and the corresponding fused images are presented in Figure 11.5. It is visualized clearly that the fused images provide excellent demarcation between the hard and soft tissues of the brain. It also depicts the detailed anatomy of various soft tissue structures, grey and white matters. In the

---

TABLE 11.1

Metrics Used for Quantitative Fusion Performance

Sr. No.	Evaluation metric	Mathematical Formulations
1.	EN [14]	$-\sum_{i=0}^{L-1} p(i)\log_2 p(i)$
2.	SD [14]	$\sqrt{\sum_{i=1}^{M}\sum_{j=1}^{N} \frac{[F(i,j)-(1/M\times N)\sum_{i=1}^{M}\sum_{j=1}^{N}F(i,j)]^2}{M\times N}}$
3.	SF [14]	$SF = \sqrt{RF^2 + CF^2}$
		$RF = \sqrt{\frac{1}{M(N-1)}\sum_{i=1}^{M}\sum_{j=2}^{N}(F(i,j-1)-F(i,j))^2}$
		$CF = \sqrt{\frac{1}{(M-1)N}\sum_{i=2}^{M}\sum_{j=1}^{N}(F(i,j)-F(i-1,j))^2}$
4.	$MI_{RS/F}$ [21]	$I(x_R; x_F) + I(x_S; x_F)$
5.	$Q_{RS/F}$ [20]	$\frac{\sum_{i=1}^{M}\sum_{j=1}^{N} Q^{RF}(i,j)w_R(i,j) + Q^{SF}(i,j)w_S(i,j)}{\sum_{i=1}^{M}\sum_{j=1}^{N} w_R(i,j) + w_S(i,j)}$
6.	$Q_C^{RS/F}$ [23]	$\sum_{w\in W} sim(R,S,F|w)(Q(R,F|w) + (1-sim(R,S,F|w))(Q(S,F|w))$
7.	$Q_Y^{RS/F}$ [24]	$\frac{1}{|W|}\sum_{w\in W} Q(R,S,F|w)$
8.	$Q_P^{RS/F}$ [25]	$\frac{\sum_{i=1}^{M}\sum_{j=1}^{N} R^{FR}(i,j)W^R(i,j) + R^{FS}(i,j)W^S(i,j)}{\sum_{i=1}^{M}\sum_{j=1}^{N} W^R(i,j) + W^S(i,j)}$

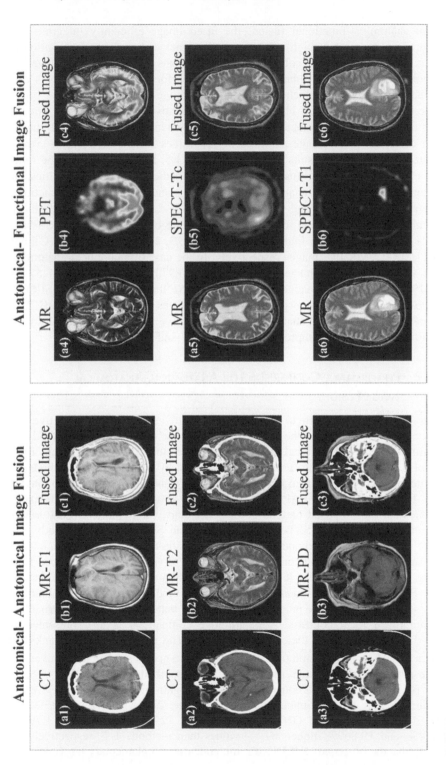

FIGURE 11.5 Subjective comparison of source and fused images (a) source image 1 (b) source image 2 (c) Fused image obtained by the proposed OHLDR-IFF.

case of anatomical-functional fusion, the fused image efficiently integrates the structures and textures of high-resolution MR images and explicit visualization of various color maps of low-resolution functional images indicating various levels of metabolic activities. To validate the subjective performance a bar graph is also presented in Figure 11.6 which presents a quantitative comparison.

The bar graphs in Figure 11.6 present a comparative view of *EN*, *SD*, and *SF* values of the six image pairs and fused images shown in Figure 11.5. For all the six fusion cases the fused image achieves higher values of *EN*, *SD*, and *SF* which validates the subjective results shown in Figure 11.5. Further to justify the reliability of our approach for fusing a variety of medical imaging modalities, an average of 75 anatomical-anatomical image pairs and 51 anatomical-functional image pairs are calculated and presented in Table 11.2. In the case of anatomical-anatomical image fusion, the fused images have 24.844%, 0.710%, 19.216%, and 9.901%, 44.461%, 0.950% higher values of *EN*, *SD*, and *SF* than source CT and MR-T1/MR-T2/MR-PD images respectively. In the case of anatomical-anatomical image fusion, the fused images have 5.591%, 25.970%, 0.065%, and 28.574%, 24.221%, 59.399% higher values of *EN*, *SD*, and *SF* than source MR and SPECT-T1/SPECT-Tc/PET images, respectively. This indicates that the proposed OHLDR-IFF method yields images that are more informative than the individual source modalities and also offer improved textural clarity and contrast.

11.3.2 PERFORMANCE COMPARISON FOR ANATOMICAL-ANATOMICAL IMAGE FUSION

In this experiment, we aim to highlight the improvement in the subjective and quantitative performance of the OHLDR-IFF over the state-of-the-art methods for anatomical-anatomical medical image fusion. For subjective comparison, there pairs of CT-MR images and fused images obtained by various fusion methods are presented in Figure 11.7. From Figures 11.7 (c), (d), and (h), it can be seen that the NSCT-FL [7] and NSST-PAPCNN [9] method good representation of spatial structures but the proposed method gives better clarity and contrast to textures of the source images. The NSST-MG-PCNN [10] and SWT-TEF [8] methods give precise demarcation of hard and soft tissues alongside the skull boundaries but fail to preserve the anatomical details of the MR images which can be observed from Figures 11.7 (e), (f), and (h). It can be seen from Figures 11.7 (g) and (h) that the NSST-BMPCNN [13] method and the proposed method give good representation to soft tissue structures but the proposed OHLDR-IFF better preserves the sharp edges with improved local contrast. A quantitative comparison is also presented in Table 11.3 for supporting the subjective results. The proposed method ranks top most in EN, $MI_{RS/F}$, $Q_{RS/F}$ and $Q_C^{RS/F}$ metrics. It also gives significant improvement for the remaining metrics than most of the fusion methods.

To present a precise and concise picture of the gain in performance an average comparison for 75 anatomical-anatomical image pairs is also presented in Table 11.4. The proposed OHLDR-IFF achieves 12.846%, 19.689%, 11.799%, 19.874%, and 19.869% higher $MI_{RS/F}$ values than methods 1–5, respectively indicating that the proposed OHLDR-IFF integrate the complementary information of

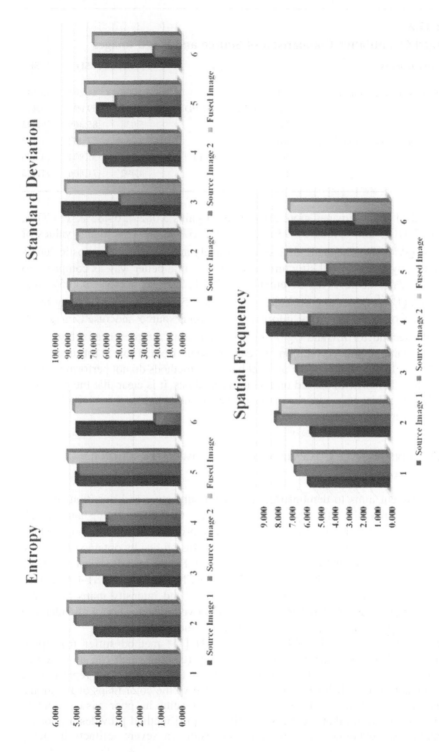

FIGURE 11.6 Bar graphs for quantitative comparison of source and fused images.

TABLE 11.2

Averaged Quantitative Comparison of Source and Fused Images

Source Image Pairs	Images	EN	SD	SF
Anatomical-Anatomical Image Pairs	CT	4.036	84.763	5.789
	MR-T1/MR-T2/MR-PD	4.585	59.092	6.837
	Fused Images	**5.038**	**85.365**	**6.902**
Anatomical-Functional Image Pairs	MR-T2	4.254	57.002	7.417
	PET/SPECT TC/SPECT-T1	3.494	57.804	4.656
	Fused Images	**4.492**	**71.806**	**7.422**

the individual source images more effectively. It gains 3.082%, 6.482%, 11.071%, 9.283%, 7.410% and 0.460%, 0.936%, 5.301%,2.373%, 2.942% higher values of $Q_{RS/F}$ and $Q_P^{RS/F}$ than the methods 1–5, respectively and preserves diagnostic details represented by sharp spatial structures and textures in a better way as compared to other methods. It achieves an increment of 0.509%, 9.058%, 5.246%, 9.495%, and 9.788% for $Q_Y^{RS/F}$ values as compared to methods 1–5, respectively indicating better preservation of complementary information between source and fused images. It also ranks second for EN and $Q_C^{RS/F}$ metrics indicating the presence of higher information content and correlation. It can be seen from Table 11.4 that some methods give higher values of SF and SD but these methods do not perform well for most of the other metrics. Based on the above analysis, it is clear that the proposed OHLDR-IFF achieves a superior and consistent subjective and quantitative performance over other fusion methods.

11.3.3 PERFORMANCE COMPARISON FOR ANATOMICAL-FUNCTIONAL IMAGE FUSION

This experiment aims to demonstrate a detailed subjective and quantitative comparison to justify the efficacy of the proposed OHLDR-IFF for anatomical-functional image fusion as compared to recently proposed fusion methods. Three pairs of anatomical-functional images along with fusion results obtained from five existing and proposed OHLDR-IFF are presented in Figure 11.8. It is observed from Figures 11.8 (c), (d), and (h) that the NSST-PAPCNN [9] and NSST-CNPS [12] methods effectively fuse the anatomical structures and intensity maps of source images but the proposed OHLDR-IFF gives improved visualization with enhanced clarity and contrast as compared to the other two methods.

The fusion results of the NSST-PADCPCNN [11] method suffer from poor contrast and also lack color consistency in many regions which can be observed from Figure 11.8 (e). Figure 11.8 (f) shows that the LRD method can represent the soft tissue details of MR images but cease to preserve the color maps of functional images in case of MR-SPECT fusion which results in poor visual fidelity. Figure 11.8 (g) shows that the NSST-BMPCNN [13] method provides a poor representation of anatomical details and also results in severe artifacts in many

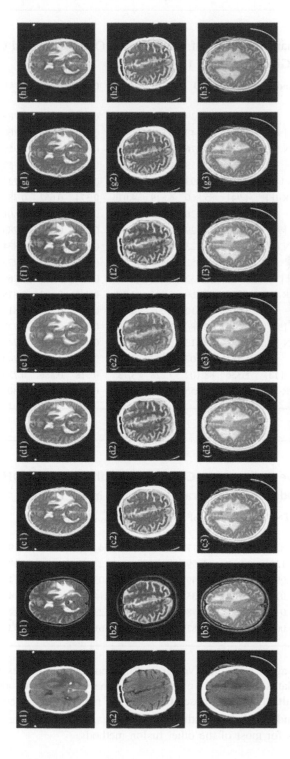

FIGURE 11.7 (a) CT image, (b) MR image and subjective comparison of fusion results obtained by (c) NSCT-FL [7], (d) NSST-PAPCNN [9], (e) NSST-MG-PCNN [10], (f) SWT-TEF [8], (g)NSST-BMPCNN [13], (h) proposed OHLDR-IFF.

TABLE 11.3

Quantitative Performance Analysis of the Proposed OHLDR-IFF and Other Methods for Images Given in Figure 11.7

Pair No.	Fusion Method	EN	SD	SF	$MI_{RS/F}$	$Q_{RS/F}$	$Q_C^{RS/F}$	$Q_Y^{RS/F}$	$Q_P^{RS/F}$
Pair 1	NSCT-FL [7]	4.463	88.339	7.062	3.524	0.550	0.543	**0.789**	0.329
	NSST-PAPCNN [9]	4.593	87.348	6.886	3.449	0.527	0.580	0.760	0.326
	NSST-MG-PCNN [10]	4.373	**88.876**	6.392	3.520	0.461	**0.666**	0.759	0.313
	SWT-TEF [8]	4.560	87.458	**7.262**	3.420	0.507	0.575	0.752	0.322
	NSST-BMPCNN [13]	4.680	84.993	6.730	3.375	0.542	0.537	0.735	0.328
	Proposed OHLDR-IFF	**4.941**	85.860	6.819	**4.010**	**0.574**	0.662	0.781	**0.339**
Pair 2	NSCT-FL [7]	4.368	86.026	6.399	3.459	0.540	0.531	0.801	**0.351**
	NSST-PAPCNN [9]	4.579	85.329	6.356	3.413	0.535	0.557	0.786	0.349
	NSST-MG-PCNN [10]	4.301	**86.523**	5.663	3.614	0.505	0.629	**0.834**	0.328
	SWT-TEF [8]	4.550	84.452	**6.602**	3.412	0.529	0.534	0.770	0.348
	NSST-BMPCNN [13]	4.600	81.532	6.187	3.344	0.537	0.527	0.769	0.341
	Proposed OHLDR-IFF	**4.795**	82.260	5.996	**3.859**	**0.545**	**0.692**	0.818	0.348
Pair 3	NSCT-FL [7]	5.106	92.512	7.505	4.111	0.559	0.538	**0.815**	0.349
	NSST-PAPCNN [9]	5.240	92.580	7.394	3.662	0.526	0.576	0.770	0.345
	NSST-MG-PCNN [10]	5.141	**94.213**	6.631	3.712	0.465	0.599	0.744	0.323
	SWT-TEF [8]	5.251	92.102	**7.637**	3.625	0.512	0.559	0.749	0.341
	NSST-BMPCNN [13]	5.336	88.102	7.228	3.735	0.518	0.486	0.736	0.338
	Proposed OHLDR-IFF	**5.408**	81.955	7.254	**4.511**	**0.587**	**0.741**	0.802	**0.353**

TABLE 11.4

Averaged Quantitative Performance Comparison of the Proposed OHLDR-IFF and Other Methods for Anatomical–Anatomical Image Fusion

Fusion Method	EN	SD	SF	$MI_{RS/F}$	$Q_{RS/F}$	$Q_C^{RS/F}$	$Q_Y^{RS/F}$	$Q_P^{RS/F}$
NSCT-FL [7]	4.828	86.376	7.172	3.455	0.544	0.617	0.789	0.344
NSST-PAPCNN [9]	**5.130**	86.025	6.998	3.257	0.527	0.615	0.727	0.342
NSST-MG-PCNN [10]	4.995	**87.596**	6.498	3.487	0.505	**0.678**	0.754	0.328
SWT-TEF [8]	5.010	85.148	**7.358**	3.252	0.514	0.606	0.724	0.338
NSST-BMPCNN [13]	5.011	82.535	6.786	3.252	0.523	0.600	0.722	0.336
Proposed OHLDR-IFF	5.066	82.378	6.870	**3.899**	**0.561**	0.660	**0.793**	**0.346**

regions of the fused images. The objective performance comparison is presented in Table 11.5 which validates the subjective performance analysis discussed above. It is evident from the results that the proposed OHLDR-IFF ranks first for metrics SD, $Q_{RS/F}$, $Q_C^{RS/F}$, $Q_Y^{RS/F}$ and $Q_P^{RS/F}$ for all three fusion cases. It also achieves higher values of other metrics for most of the other fusion methods.

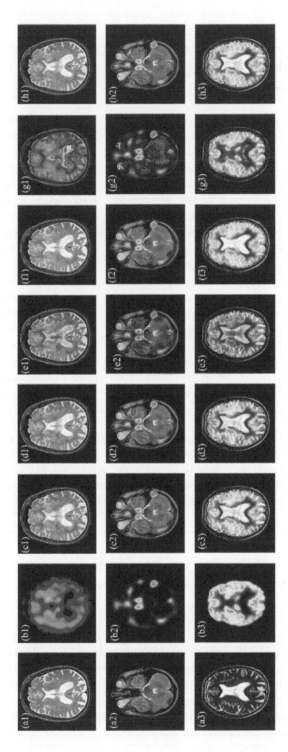

FIGURE 11.8 (a) MR image (b) SPECT-Tc/SPECT-T1/PET image and subjective comparison of fusion results obtained by (c) NSST-PAPCNN [9] (d) NSST-CNPS [12] (e) NSST-PADCPCNN [11] (f) LRD [6] (g) NSST-BMPCNN [13] (h) Proposed OHLDR-IFF.

TABLE 11.5

Quantitative Performance Analysis of the Proposed OHLDR-IFF and Other Methods for Images Given in Figure 11.8

Pair No.	Fusion Method	EN	SD	SF	$MI_{RS/F}$	$Q_{RS/F}$	$Q_C^{RS/F}$	$Q_Y^{RS/F}$	$Q_P^{RS/F}$
Pair 1	NSST-PAPCNN [9]	5.489	85.207	8.332	0.524	0.714	0.704	0.687	0.275
	NSST-CNPS [12]	5.349	85.671	8.368	0.577	0.749	0.787	0.772	0.294
	NSST-PADCPCNN [11]	5.356	76.649	8.441	0.419	0.721	0.596	0.605	0.237
	LRD [6]	**5.630**	81.564	**8.465**	0.500	0.666	0.592	0.598	0.193
	NSST-BMPCNN [13]	5.238	63.646	7.694	**0.657**	0.688	0.618	0.650	0.192
	Proposed OHLDR-IFF	5.417	**85.893**	8.237	0.644	**0.764**	**0.913**	**0.947**	**0.379**
Pair 2	NSST-PAPCNN [9]	4.639	87.032	7.780	0.556	0.590	0.673	0.686	0.221
	NSST-CNPS [12]	4.621	84.641	7.842	0.498	0.581	0.646	0.656	0.242
	NSST-PADCPCNN [11]	4.057	70.366	7.561	0.294	0.578	0.364	0.434	0.190
	LRD [6]	**4.842**	88.132	**8.110**	0.579	0.502	0.667	0.698	0.205
	NSST-BMPCNN [13]	4.164	76.648	7.054	**0.671**	0.567	0.672	0.693	0.177
	Proposed OHLDR-IFF	4.314	**88.744**	7.830	0.636	**0.615**	**0.764**	**0.815**	**0.350**
Pair 3	NSST-PAPCNN [9]	4.350	61.415	6.829	0.239	0.723	0.685	0.697	0.281
	NSST-CNPS [12]	4.429	61.209	**6.830**	0.237	0.715	0.689	0.709	0.280
	NSST-PADCPCNN [11]	4.281	53.412	6.709	0.160	0.679	0.487	0.659	0.182
	LRD [6]	**4.609**	59.279	6.824	0.262	0.652	0.777	0.790	0.294
	NSST-BMPCNN [13]	3.586	46.579	5.777	**0.333**	0.528	0.416	0.534	0.182
	Proposed OHLDR-IFF	4.241	**62.194**	6.810	0.302	**0.738**	**0.895**	**0.939**	**0.379**

Next, to justify and infer the gain in quantitative performance a concise averaged analysis for 51 pairs of anatomical-functional images is presented in Table 11.6. The OHLDR-IFF gives the highest overall contrast and achieves 1.311%, 4.269%, 13.238%, 2.517%, and 21.845% higher SD values than methods 1–5, respectively. In addition to achieving higher color contrast, the proposed OHLDR-IFF also offers

TABLE 11.6

Averaged Quantitative Performance Comparison of the Proposed OHLDR-IFF and Other Methods for Anatomical–Functional Image Fusion

Fusion Method	EN	SD	SF	$MI_{RS/F}$	$Q_{RS/F}$	$Q_C^{RS/F}$	$Q_Y^{RS/F}$	$Q_P^{RS/F}$
NSST-PAPCNN [9]	4.610	70.876	7.473	0.416	0.681	0.683	0.680	0.268
NSST-CNPS [12]	4.558	68.866	**7.515**	0.400	0.687	0.738	0.744	0.283
NSST-PADCPCNN [11]	4.319	63.411	7.385	0.304	0.673	0.550	0.591	0.238
LRD [6]	**4.833**	70.042	7.484	0.423	0.575	0,593	0.610	0.199
NSST-BMPCNN [13]	4.253	58.932	6.698	**0.564**	0.614	0.574	0.616	0.185
Proposed OHLDR-IFF	4.492	**71.806**	7.422	0.474	**0.694**	**0.857**	**0.896**	**0.367**

excellent edge preservation and by gaining 2.042%, 1.117%, 3.242%, 20.733%, 13.143% and 36.575%, 29.629%, 53.868%, 84.068%, 97.735% higher values of $Q_{RS/F}$ and $Q_P^{RS/F}$ metric values compared to fusion methods 1–5, respectively. The proposed OHLDR-IFF also gives 25.546%, 16.202%, 55.887%, 44.573%, 49.311% and 31.722%, 20.373%, 51.506%, 46.916%, 45.367%, higher values of $Q_C^{RS/F}$ and $Q_Y^{RS/F}$ metrics of fusion methods 1–5, respectively, which show that the proposed OHLDR-IFF surpasses other methods in terms of preservation of complimentary information and correlation with respect to source images.

The LRD [6] method gives the highest EN values but its subjective results lack color fidelity leading to poor visualization of metabolic intensity maps for MR-SPECT fusion. The NSST-BMPCNN [13] method yields a slightly higher value of $MI_{RS/F}$ than the proposed OHLDR-IFF but results in poor contrast and artifacts in many regions. It can be inferred from the above discussion that the proposed OHLDR-IFF gains significant improvement in both subjective and quantitative performance for fusing anatomical-functional images as well.

11.4 CONCLUSION

An optimized HLD decomposition and reconstruction model-based framework for multi-modal neurological image fusion is presented. The edge-preserving two-scale HLD model effectually represents various structures, textures, and brightness components of source images. Fusion rules are crafted by considering the inherent characteristics of the three decomposed layers to merge the diagnostic information of the source modalities. Further, optimizing the regularization parameters and reconstruction weights using a whale optimization algorithm leads to further enhancement of perceptual quality of fused images. The optimization process also overcomes the shortcomings of the conventional hit and trial approach for free parameter setting. The detailed subjective and quantitative performance analysis demonstrates the utility and efficacy of the proposed OHLDR-IFF to fuse the complementary diagnostic information. The proposed OHLDR-IFF successfully fuses a variety of multi-modal neurological image pairs and can be used as an assistance tool by radiologists for visualizing more detailed, factual, and comprehensive representations of various bodily structures and their physiology.

REFERENCES

[1] Dasarathy, B. V. "Information fusion in the realm of a medical applications-a bibliographic glimpse at its growing appeal," *Information Fusion*, 13, 1 (2012): 1–9.
[2] James, A. P. and Dasarathy, B. V. "Medical image fusion: A survey of the state of the art," *Information Fusion*, 19 (2014): 4–19.
[3] Hermessi, H., Mourali, O., and Zagrouba, E. "Multimodal medical image fusion review: Theoretical background and recent advances," *Signal Processing*, 108036 (2021).
[4] Du, J., Li, W., Lu, K., and Xiao, B. "An overview of multi-modal medical image fusion," *Neurocomputing*, 215 (2016): 3–20.
[5] Dogra, A., Goyal, B., and Agrawal, S. "From multi-scale decomposition to non-multiscale decomposition methods: A comprehensive survey of image fusion techniques and its applications," *IEEE Access*, 5 (2017): 16040–16067.

[6] Li, X., Guo, X., Han, P., Wang, X., Li, H., and Luo, T. "Laplacian re-decomposition for multimodal medical image fusion," *IEEE Transactions on Instrumentation and Measurement* (2020).

[7] Yang, Y., Que, Y., Huang, S., and Lin, P. "Multimodal sensor medical image fusion based on type-2 fuzzy logic in nsct domain," *IEEE Sensors Journal*, 16, 10 (2016): 3735–3745.

[8] Ganasala, P. and Prasad, A. D. "Medical image fusion based on laws of texture energy measures in stationary wavelet transform domain," *International Journal of Imaging Systems and Technology* (2019).

[9] Yin, M., Liu, X., Liu, Y., and Chen, X. "Medical image fusion with parameter-adaptive pulse coupled neural network in nonsubsampled shearlet transform domain," *IEEE Transactions on Instrumentation and Measurement*, 68, 1 (2018): 49–64.

[10] Ramlal, S. D., Sachdeva, J., Ahuja, C. K., and Khandelwal, N. "Multimodal medical image fusion using non-subsampled shearlet transform and pulse coupled neural network incorporated with morphological gradient," *Signal, Image and Video Processing*, 12, 8 (2018): 1479–1487.

[11] Panigrahy, C., Seal, A., and Mahato, N. K., "MRI and SPECT image fusion using a weighted parameter adaptive dual channel PCNN," *IEEE Signal Processing Letters*, 27 (2020): 690–694.

[12] Li, B., Peng, H., Luo, X., Wang, J., Song, X., Pérez-Jiménez, M. J., and RiscosNúñez, A. "Medical image fusion method based on coupled neural p systems in nonsubsampled shearlet transform domain," *International Journal of Neural Systems* (2020): 2050050–2050050.

[13] Tan, W., Tiwari, P., Pandey, H. M., Moreira, C., and Jaiswal, A. K. "Multimodal medical image fusion algorithm in the era of big data," *Neural Computing and Applications* (2020): 1–21.

[14] Das, M., Gupta, D., Radeva, P., and Bakde, A. M. "Nsst domain CT–MR neurological image fusion using optimised biologically inspired neural network," *IET Image Processing*, 14, 16 (2020): 4291–4305.

[15] Liang, Z., Xu, J., Zhang, D., Cao, Z., and Zhang, L. "A hybrid l1-l0 layer decomposition model for tone mapping," in *Proceedings of the IEEE Conference on Computer Vision and Pattern Recognition* (2018): 4758–4766.

[16] Liu, D., Zhou, D., Nie, R., and Hou, R. "Infrared and visible image fusion based on convolutional neural network model and saliency detection via hybrid l0-l1 layer decomposition," *Journal of Electronic Imaging*, 27, 6 (2018): 063036.

[17] Singh, S. and Anand, R. "Multimodal medical image fusion using hybrid layer decomposition with CNN-based feature mapping and structural clustering," *IEEE Transactions on Instrumentation and Measurement*, 69, 6 (2020): 3855–3865.

[18] Das, M., Gupta, D., Radeva, P., and Bakde, A. M. "Optimized CT-MR neurological image fusion framework using biologically inspired spiking neural model in hybrid $\ell_1 - \ell_0$ layer decomposition domain," *Biomedical Signal Processing and Control*, 68 (2021): 102535.

[19] Mirjalili, S. and Lewis, A. "The whale optimization algorithm," *Advances in Engineering Software*, 95 (2016): 51–67.

[20] Xydeas, C. and Petrovic, V. "Objective image fusion performance measure," *Electronics Letters*, 36, 4 (2000): 308–309.

[21] Qu, G., Zhang, D., and Yan, P. "Information measure for performance of image fusion," *Electronics Letters*, 38, 7 (2002): 313–315.

[22] Gupta, D. "Nonsubsampled shearlet domain fusion techniques for CT–MR neurological images using improved biological inspired neural model," *Biocybernetics and Biomedical Engineering*, 38, 2 (2018): 262–274.

[23] Cvejic, N., Loza, A., Bull, D., and Canagarajah, N. "A similarity metric for assessment of image fusion algorithms," *International Journal of Signal Processing*, 2, 3 (2005): 178–182.

[24] Yang, C., Zhang, J.-Q., Wang, X.-R., and Liu, X. "A novel similarity based quality metric for image fusion," *Information Fusion*, 9, 2 (2008): 156–160.

[25] Sengupta, A., Seal, A., Panigrahy, C., Krejcar, O., and Yazidi, A. "Edge information based image fusion metrics using fractional order differentiation and sigmoidal functions," *IEEE Access*, 8 (2020): 88385–88398.

12 Hybrid Seeker Optimization Algorithm-based Accurate Image Clustering for Automatic Psoriasis Lesion Detection

Manoranjan Dash and Rajendra Sonawane
National Institute of Technology, Raipur, India

Narendra D. Londhe
Psoriasis Clinic and Research Centre, Psoriatreat, Pune, Maharashtra, India

National Institute of Technology, Raipur, India

Subhojit Ghosh
Psoriasis Clinic and Research Centre, Psoriatreat, Pune, Maharashtra, India

CONTENTS

DOI: 10.1201/9781003241409-12

12.1 INTRODUCTION

Psoriasis is a chronic skin disease that can affect people of every age group. Recent times have witnessed the spread of psoriasis across the world; about 125 million people worldwide are living with psoriasis [1–4]. In psoriasis patients, the skin cells grow faster in about 4–5 days compared to 25–30 days in healthy person and form thick patches of reddish, dry, and itchy skin [5]. Researchers have majorly evidenced genetic fault as the cause of psoriasis. The body parts, such as scalp, joints, and nails, are severely affected by psoriasis. However, it may occur anywhere in the body [6,7]. Moreover, the disease brings social embarrassment and poor quality of life to the patients [8,9].

Psoriasis requires prolonged and attentive treatment. The present methods of therapy adopted by dermatologists are not very effective, which involves visual inspection and sense of touch. The quantification of severity of psoriasis disease by subjective analysis is inefficient and time-consuming due to the labor-intensive examination procedure [10]. Hence a quantitative investigation becomes mandatory for automatic, precise, and fast diagnosis. Objective assessment of any skin image for diagnosis is initiated with lesion segmentation. As compared to standard skin images, lesion segmentation in psoriasis image is challenging task because of the vague boundary in psoriasis lesion, noise effects present in the image, and color diversity of the lesion [11].

With the aim of developing an effective computer-aided diagnosis system, Shrivastava et al. [5,12–16] have conducted a large volume of work on psoriasis severity detection using manually segmented psoriasis lesion images. Few attempts have been made towards lesion segmentation in psoriasis images using the classifier-based [17,18], contour-based [19], clustering-based [20,21], and model-based [9,22] approaches. However, a common limitation with majority of the reported works is validated on small data size. Lesion detection based on clustering techniques [20,21,23] provide the local optimum clusters by updating the cluster centroids with the rearrangement of the data points. A major limitation of the clustering-based techniques is that it often converges to local rather than global optimal centroids [24] due to random initialization of centroids. This results in inaccurate lesion detection. One of the possible ways to avoid convergence to local optima is to employ an evolutionary optimization algorithm that has a greater chance of getting global optimum solution.

In the recent past, many works have proven the effectiveness of swarm intelligence-based evolutionary approaches for image segmentation owing to their effectiveness in solving high dimensional segmentation problems for complex database. A dynamic clustering approach to achieve an optimum number of centroids, based on particle swarm optimization (PSO) for image segmentation was employed in Omran et al. [25]. Ramos and Almeida [26] proposed an ant colony model with a region growing technique for segmenting digital images, which were further implemented for medical images by Huang et al. [27]. Another image segmentation model was proposed by Ma et al. [28] using artificial bee colony (ABC) to find out thresholds in a continuous grayscale window. Cinsdikici and Aydin [29] proposed a blood vessels segmentation technique for ophthalmoscope images using a combination of matched filter and ant colony optimization (ACO) algorithm. In another similar attempt by Aydin and Ugur [30], a color-based clustering scheme using ACO was presented for recognition of flower boundaries. The search capabilities of PSO and ABC algorithm on multilevel thresholding were discussed by Akay [31]. A clustering algorithm based on the ABC model was implemented by Sag and Cunkas [32] for image segmentation. However, quite often for complex problems evolutionary techniques during the iterative process gets trapped to the sub-optimal local minima, especially approaches demanding faster executions. Hybridizing an evolutionary technique with a local search technique overcomes the limitation pertaining to slower execution and possibility of local convergence [33].

In this context, a Hybrid Seeker Optimization Algorithm (HSOA) using the combination of SOA and the classical K-means clustering has been proposed for psoriasis lesion detection using image clustering. Combining both global and local search procedures will compensate for their individual disadvantages, i.e., high computational cost and local convergence, respectively. The proposed approach solves the detection problem by mapping the input image into a set of clusters, which isolates the psoriasis lesion from the normal skin. The centroids obtained from SOA are further fine-tuned by using the K-means clustering technique to obtain the globally optimal centroids.

12.2   METHODOLOGY

12.2.1   DATABASE

The psoriasis images of distinct severity level from 65 patients irrespective of gender and age were acquired from Psoriasis Clinic and Research Centre, Psoriatreat, Pune, India. A Sony NEX-5 camera having 22 mm lens and 350 dpi was used to capture the images from Indian patients. This digital photographing is carried out with the proper direction and observation of dermatologist. Further, these photographs were processed in JPEG format with the color depth of 24 bits per pixel. The ground truth used for the different experiments is prepared manually and verified by dermatologists.

12.2.2   SEEKER OPTIMIZATION ALGORITHM

The recent evolutionary optimization method that mimics the behavior of human search population based on memory, experience, and ambiguity cognitive is known as Seeker Optimization Algorithm (SOA) [34]. Seeker is an individual human of this population. The entire population of this algorithm is distributed into three different subpopulations with regards to the indexes of the seeker [34].

The subsequent attributes are framed for individual seeker i: the current position $S_i = (S_{i1}, S_{i2}, \ldots\ldots S_{iD})$, the dimension of the problem D, the iteration number n, the personal best position P_i accomplished, and the neighborhood best position g. The seekers' positions have been updated employing step length and search direction. The step length has been calculated by uncertainty reasoning behavior and search direction is achieved based on the seeker's behavior. Search direction β_{ij} and step length l_{ij} are separately computed for each individual i on each dimension j at each iteration n, where $\beta_{ij} \geq 0$ and $l_{ij} \in \{-1; 0; 1\}$. The position of each seeker is updated at each iteration as given in Equation (12.1).

$$S_{ij}(n+1) = S_{ij}(n) + \beta_{ij} \cdot l_{ij} \qquad (12.1)$$

where $i = 1, 2, 3, \ldots\ldots$ SN; $j = 1, 2, \ldots..$, D (SN is the number of seekers). Furthermore, an inter subpopulation learning process takes place for every iteration. In case of SOA, the present location of the best ones in each of the other two subpopulations are swapped with the worst two individuals of each subpopulation [35,36].

The total updating process is continued until the convergence of objective function or number of iterations is accomplished.

12.2.3 HYBRID SEEKER OPTIMIZATION ALGORITHM (HSOA)

As per the objective of the present work, the task of psoriasis image segmentation has been expressed in terms of clustering-based optimization problem. The objective function framed for the same is given as

$$F(Cen) = \sum_{q=1}^{K} \sum_{p=1}^{N} \|x_{p,q} - Cen_q\|^2 \qquad (12.2)$$

where N and K are search space size and cluster numbers, respectively; $x_{p,q}$ = pixel position at p, q. Starting with a random cluster centers Cen, the segmentation task includes iterative updating of Cen so as to increase the similarity among the pixels in a specified cluster. With similar pixels, the Euclidean distance between the cluster center and the pixels in the corresponding cluster reduces, thus reducing $F(Cen)$.

Majority of the clustering based segmentation techniques have bank on the classical K-means clustering for segmentation because of its simple execution procedure and minimal computational burden. However, a common limitation of K-means clustering for different applications pertains to its premature convergence to the sub-optimal local minima. Further the final outcome in K-means clustering is heavily dependent on the initialized cluster center [37]. Hence, the classical K-means algorithm has been hybridized with a global search-based SOA to lower its dependence on the initial parameterization and also increase the probability of global convergence. Like other evolutionary technique, SOA is initialized with a population of possible solution spread across the entire search space. For the present problem, every solution corresponds to a set of cluster centers. During the execution of SOA, the solutions are grouped into sub-populations. Each solution is iteratively updated based on the suitability of its earlier values and the overall best solution in the population. In each iteration the intra-homogeneous attributes are maximized with the updated cluster centers, the Euclidean distances and hence the objective function (Equation (12.2)) is evaluated. Further to which the best solution (cluster center with the least value of Equation (12.2)) for the sub-populations and the overall population is updated.

In the initial iterations, the solutions are randomly spread in the search space. Based on the space covered by the individual solutions during the updation, in the

TABLE 12.1

Parameters Setting for Seeker Optimization

Parameters	Value
Population size	100
Scaling parameter	0.95
Number of iterations	10

later iterations all the solutions move in a common direction. In the second stage of the proposed scheme, with reduced variability among the solutions, the classical K-means algorithm is executed by considering the final solution obtained by SOA as the initial solution. With the initial solution not chosen randomly but obtained from the convergence, the principal limitation of the K-means algorithm with regard to dependence on the initial solution is avoided. Also, with the hybridization, the probability of global convergence is also enhanced. The technique initiates with a conversion of the original RGB image into CIE LAB coordinates. The conversion facilitates application of SOA to color image considering only A and B coordinates. Improved accuracy with greater processing speed has been achieved using CIE Lab color space [38,39].

Initial clusters obtained from the seeker optimization are used to increase the probability of global convergence. It also reduces the computational time of the task, as compared to execution by using SOA only. The parameters considered for the execution of seeker optimization are detailed in Table 12.1. The population size, scaling parameter, and the number of iterations are chosen by executing a number of pilot runs to attain the best solution. For the two-class problem (psoriasis lesion and healthy skin), the SOA is executed with a population of optimal centroids {(x1, y1), (x2, y2)}. As mentioned above, with the final solution obtained after the execution of SOA, the same is considered as the initial seed solution for K-means algorithm, which further refines the solution in terms of similarity among the population of same cluster and variability among the population of different clusters.

The step-wise implementation process of HSOA is given as:

The pseudo-code for the hybrid optimization technique is:

Step-I: Read the RGB input psoriasis images
Step-II: Convert RGB to CIE Lab coordinates
Step-III: //Implementation of SO algorithm//
for n = 0;
Create SN arbitrary positions homogenously in search space
*   Find and capture the best position by calculating for all the searchers*
Repeat

> *Compute search direction and step length for each seeker;*
> *Update each seeker's position using Equation (12.1);*
> *Evaluate all the seekers and save the historical best position*
> *Implement the inter-subpopulation learning operation*
> $n = n + 1;$
> *till* $n = N_{\mathrm{max}}$
> *Step-IV: Apply K-means clustering techniques to optimum cluster centroids*

12.2.4 POST PROCESSING

Post-processing techniques are employed here to shape boundaries and remove glitches in psoriasis lesion segmentation. Opening and closing are the two morphological operations adopted [40]. Both opening and closing operations are performed assuming the structural element of the same size and shape. From Figure 12.1 it can be observed that with morphological post-processing, uniformity and clarity are achieved in the boundary of the segmented psoriasis image.

12.3 RESULTS

The hybrid optimization-based clustering for effective psoriasis lesion segmentation methodology is executed on psoriasis dataset and the outcomes are detailed in the subsequent sections.

12.3.1 EXPERIMENTAL RESULTS

The proposed algorithm has been executed on MATLAB and processed on Intel Core processor with clock frequency = 1.9 GHz and RAM = 4 GB. For objective assessment and to quantify the extent of segmentation accomplished post convergence of the proposed algorithm, four different indices have been calculated and matched with the ground truth. The indices computed are the Jaccard Index (*JI*), sensitivity (*Sn*), specificity (*Sp*), and accuracy (*A*) as detailed in Table 12.2.

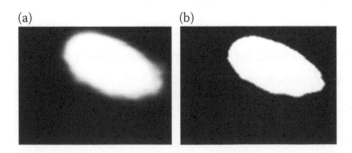

(a)   (b)

FIGURE 12.1   Post-processing result: (a) Segmented psoriasis image and (b) result of morphological processing.

TABLE 12.2

Performance Indices

S. No.	Indices	Formula
1	Jaccard index	$\frac{S \cap G}{S \cup G}$
2	Accuracy	$\frac{T^+ + T^-}{T^+ + T^- + F^+ + F^-}$
3	Sensitivity	$\frac{T^+}{T^+ + F^-}$
4	Specificity	$\frac{T^-}{T^- + F^+}$

S-Segmented image, G-Ground truth, T^+ = True Positive, T^- = True Negative, F^-= False Negative, and F^+ = False Positive.

Accuracy explains the capability to segregate the lesion and skin appropriately. The capacity to define the lesions properly and the skins properly are well-defined by sensitivity and specificity correspondingly.

The segmentation of psoriasis lesion has been tested on 522 images collected from 65 patients irrespective of age, gender, and religion. The sample lesion segmentation for eight test images with the distinct class of severity along with JI value by means of both SOA and HSOA is illustrated in Figure 12.2. The ground truth is also depicted in Figure 12.2 to analyze the segmentation results of the HSOA method visually. The closeness of the HSOA-based segmentation technique to the ground truth as compared with SOA approach is reproduced in the test images. To quantify the performance obtained using SOA and proposed HSOA method, the performance indices (JI, A, Sp, Sn) are estimated for the segmented images. The percentage of mean accuracy over the set of 522 images using PSO, ABC, SOA, PSO + K-means, ABC + K-means, and HSOA are presented in Table 12.3.

The proposed HSOA method produced A = 91.4%, a quite superior performance compared to PSO (A = 83.2%), ABC (A = 83.6%), SOA (A = 85.1%), ABC + K-means (A = 87.8%), and PSO+K-means (A = 86.9%) has been achieved. The comparative analysis of the proposed HSOA and SOA approach has been shown in Table 12.4 on the entire set of images in terms of the other three indices (JI, Sn, and Sp). It can be witnessed that proposed HSOA method (JI = 87.3%, Sn = 93.1%, and Sp = 92.0%) has better performance over SOA (JI = 78.4%, Sn = 87.6%, and Sp = 88.8%).

12.4   DISCUSSIONS

The effectiveness of the proposed scheme has been highlighted comparing the detected psoriasis lesions with the ground truths in terms of peak signal to noise ratio (PSNR).

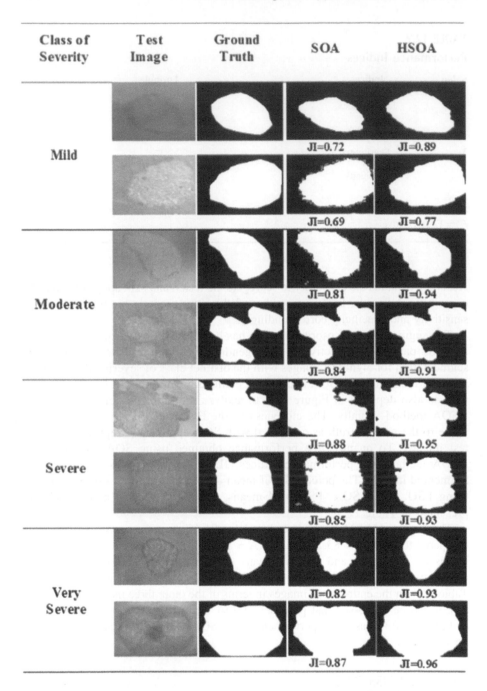

FIGURE 12.2 Lesion segmentation on 8 test images considering the class of severity using SOA and HSOA.

TABLE 12.3

Calculation of Mean Accuracy (in Percentage)

Class of Severity	No. of Images	Segmentation Methods					
		PSO	ABC	SOA	PSO + K-means	ABC + K-means	Proposed HSOA
Mild	67	73.4	73.8	75.7	79.1	80.4	84.9
Moderate	155	81.6	82.1	83.2	84.0	84.7	89.3
Severe	172	84.9	85.2	86.5	89.2	90.3	93.7
Very Severe	128	87.8	88.5	90.3	91.3	92.0	94.2
Total	**522**	**83.2**	**83.6**	**85.1**	**86.9**	**87.8**	**91.4**

TABLE 12.4

Calculation of Mean Jaccard Index, Sensitivity, and Specificity (in Percentage)

Class of Severity	No.of Images	SOA			Proposed HSOA		
		Mean JI	Mean Sn	Mean Sp	Mean JI	Mean Sn	Mean Sp
Mild	67	66.4	78.4	80.3	78.5	88.2	86.8
Moderate	155	71.8	86.6	88.7	84.9	91.7	90.2
Severe	172	83.3	88.2	89.3	89.8	94.4	93.5
Very Severe	128	86.1	93.0	92.5	91.4	95.6	94.8

The objective of this chapter is to attain a high value of PSNR. The formula to calculate the PSNR is given by Equation (12.3)

$$PSNR = 20 \log_{10}\left(\frac{255}{R}\right) in \ dB \tag{12.3}$$

where R = Root Mean Square Error (MSE) among reference image (ground truth) and segmented image. PSNR is always expressed in decibel (dB) and is computed between ground truth and grayscale detected or segmented image [41]. An image can be categorized into low quality if the PSNR value is below 30 dB, whereas PSNR of 40 dB and above for an image indicates better quality [42]. The value of PSNR is calculated for 522 psoriasis images and the corresponding best, worst, and Mean±SD are depicted in Table 12.5. For the hybrid methods, the average value of PSNR is more than 40 dB showing the high quality of image segmentation and stability. Out of six different methods, the HSOA has the high mean (42.07 dB) and low standard deviation (4.13 dB) PSNR values, which signify the superior performance of HSOA.

TABLE 12.5
Estimated PSNR (in dB) for 522 Psoriasis Images

Method	PSNR (dB)		
	Best	Worst	Mean±SD
PSO	41.84	30.03	36.87 ± 11.09
ABC	41.96	30.87	36.92 ± 10.72
SOA	42.94	31.19	37.14 ± 10.27
PSO+ K-means	43.51	36.26	40.23 ± 7.34
ABC+ K-means	43.88	37.15	40.68 ± 6.81
Proposed HSOA	45.52	38.39	42.07 ± 4.13

Further, to analyze the effectiveness of the proposed optimization technique in minimizing the objective function, the iterative variation of the objective function (F (Cen)) is analyzed for a set of images. The variation of F (Cen) with the corresponding metric value for three prototypical images (best, average, and worst) is depicted in Figure 12.3. The metric values reported corresponding to the segmented image after the 10th iteration. For all the cases a significant reduction is observed in the objective function during the initial iterations. Also, the appropriateness of the objective function ineffectively quantifying all the four metrics is well exhibited.

Further, the outcome of HSOA is being related to other existing techniques namely Otsu's thresholding [43], K-means clustering and SOA. The comparisons have been performed using four indices as presented in Table 12.6. From Table 12.6, it can be found that HSOA delivers enhanced performance as compared to other methods. However, convolutional neural network based U-Net clustering technique [44] provides better accuracy as compared to the proposed method but is lagging in other three parameters. Also, U-Net is a supervised learning technique which requires more number of images for better generalization.

12.5 CONCLUSION

In this chapter, an automated approach for psoriasis lesion segmentation in photographic color images is proposed. The two-stage method involves the generation of initial cluster centroids using SO algorithm, which are further refined to improve segmentation using K-means algorithm in the second stage. The lesion segmentation is followed by post-processing using morphological operations. The experiments are performed on 522 psoriasis images from 65 patients using both isolated SOA and the proposed HSO algorithm. The effectiveness of HSOA-based segmentation technique is judged by five quantitative parameters, i.e., Jaccard Index (JI), sensitivity (Sn), specificity (Sp), accuracy (A), and PSNR. A compressive analysis was carried out on the entire image data set, which confirmed the superiority of the proposed HSO algorithm. The proposed algorithm outperforms the widely used standard evolutionary techniques, i.e., PSO, ABC, and SO algorithms. The work provides a platform for the dermatologist to use

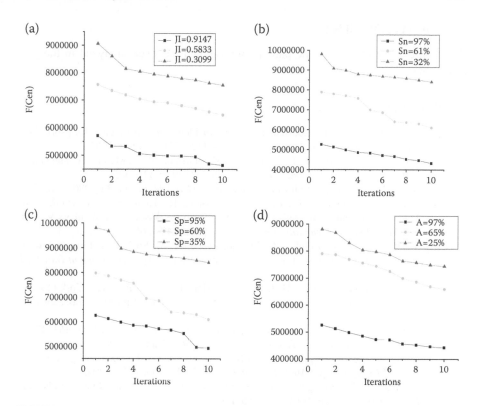

FIGURE 12.3 Comparative study of the objective function with iterations considering the best as black, worst as blue, and average as the red color value of (A) Jaccard Index, (B) sensitivity, (C) specificity, and (D) accuracy.

TABLE 12.6

Performance Comparison of HSOA with Other Existing Segmentation Methods

Methods	Technique	Parameters (in %)			
		Jaccard Index	Accuracy	Sensitivity	Specificity
Otsu's	Thresholding	66.3	70.7	74.9	76.1
K-means	Clustering	69.8	73.6	78.2	77.5
SOA	Optimization	78.4	85.1	87.6	88.8
U-Net	Convolutional network	86.6	92.3	91.8	89.7
HSOA	**Hybrid Optimization**	**87.3**	**91.4**	**93.1**	**92.0**

photographic image for evaluating the psoriasis lesion effectively and provide necessary treatment with better outcome over subjective assessment. Further, the algorithm can be designed to operate on more diversified data and for full body images, so that the impact of psoriasis and the proposed treatment by dermatologists may be evaluated.

ACKNOWLEDGMENT

We would like to thank all the patients whose data has been analyzed in the present work.

REFERENCES

[1] Huerta, C., Rivero, E., Rodriguez, L. A. G. Incidence and risk factors for psoriasis in the general population. *Arch Dermatol.* 143(12) (2007): 1559–1565.

[2] Sander, H. M., Morris, L. F., Phillips, C. M., Harrison, P. E., Menter, A. The annual cost of psoriasis. *J Am Acad Dermatol.* 28(3) (1993): 422–425.

[3] Adam, B. A. Psoriasis in hospital population. *Med J Malaysia.* 34(1980): 370–374.

[4] Yee, K. C., Choon, S. E., Khaw, G. E., Baba, R., Hussein, S. H., Ratti, S. K. Malaysian patients' knowledge of psoriasis: Psoriasis Association Members Vs non-members. *Persat Dermatologi Malaysia.* (1999): 840–848.

[5] Shrivastava, V. K., Londhe, N. D., Sonawane, R. S., Suri, J. S. First review on psoriasis severity risk stratification: An engineering perspective. *Comput Biol Med.* 63(2015): 52–63.

[6] Roenigk, H. H., Maibach, H. I. Psoriasis. Marcel Dekker Inc., New York (1985).

[7] Camisa, C. Handbook of psoriasis. Wiley Online Library, Massachusetts, USA (2008).

[8] Henseler, T. Genetics of psoriasis. *Arch Dermatol Res.* 290(9) (1998): 463–476.

[9] Taur, J. S., Lee, G.-H., Tao, C.-W., Chen, C.-C., Yang, C.-W. Segmentation of psoriasis vulgaris images using multiresolution-based orthogonal subspace techniques. *IEEE Trans Syst Man, Cybern Part B.* 36(2) (2006): 390–402.

[10] Feldman, S. R., Krueger, G. G. Psoriasis assessment tools in clinical trials. *Ann Rheum Dis.* 64(suppl 2) (2005): ii65–ii68.

[11] Xie, F., Bovik, A. C. Automatic segmentation of dermoscopy images using self-generating neural networks seeded by genetic algorithm. *Pattern Recognit.* 46(3) (2013): 1012–1019.

[12] Shrivastava, V. K., Londhe, N. D., Sonawane, R. S., Suri, J. S. Reliable and accurate psoriasis disease classification in dermatology images using comprehensive feature space in machine learning paradigm. *Expert Syst Appl.* 42(15–16) (2015): 6184–6195.

[13] Shrivastava, V. K., Londhe, N. D., Sonawane, R. S., Suri, J. S. Exploring the color feature power for psoriasis risk stratification and classification: A data mining paradigm. *Comput Biol Med.* 65(2015): 54–68.

[14] Shrivastava, V. K., Londhe, N. D., Sonawane, R. S., Suri, J. S. Computer-aided diagnosis of psoriasis skin images with HOS, texture and color features: A first comparative study of its kind. *Comput Methods Programs Biomed.* 126(2016): 98–109.

[15] Shrivastava, V. K., Londhe, N. D., Sonawane, R. S., Suri, J. S. A novel approach to multiclass psoriasis disease risk stratification: Machine learning paradigm. *Biomed Signal Process Control.* 28(2016): 27–40.

[16] Shrivastava, V. K., Londhe, N. D., Sonawane, R. S., Suri, J. S. Reliability analysis of psoriasis decision support system in principal component analysis framework. *Data Knowl Eng.* 106(2016): 1–17.

[17] Nidhal, K. A., Nizar, S. D., Muhsin, A. A., Hind, R. Psoriasis detection using color and texture features. *J Comput Sci.* 6(6) (2010): 648–652.

[18] Taur, J.-S. Neuro-fuzzy approach to the segmentation of psoriasis images. *J VLSI Signal Process Syst Signal, Image Video Technol.* 35(1) (2003): 19–27.

[19] Bogo, F., Samory, M., Fortina, A. B., Piaserico, S., Peserico, E. Psoriasis segmentation through chromatic regions and geometric active contours. In: 2012 Annual International Conference of the IEEE Engineering in Medicine and Biology Society (2012): 5388–5391.

[20] Juang, L.-H., Wu, M.-N. Psoriasis image identification using k-means clustering with morphological processing. *Measurement.* 44(5) (2011): 895–905.

[21] Shrivastava, V. K., Londhe, N. D. Measurement of psoriasis area and severity index area score of Indian psoriasis patients. *J Med Imaging Heal Informatics.* 5(4) (2015): 675–682.

[22] Ma, G., He, B., Yang, W., Shu, C. Easy-interactive and quick psoriasis lesion segmentation. In: 2013 International Conference on Optical Instruments and Technology: Optoelectronic Imaging and Processing Technology (2013): 90450T.

[23] Su, M.-C., Chou, C.-H. A modified version of the K-means algorithm with a distance based on cluster symmetry. *IEEE Trans Pattern Anal Mach Intell.* (6)(2001): 674–680.

[24] Kalyani, S., Swarup, K. S. Particle swarm optimization based K-means clustering approach for security assessment in power systems. *Expert Syst Appl.* 38(9) (2011): 10839–10846.

[25] Omran, M. G. H., Salman, A., Engelbrecht, A. P. Dynamic clustering using particle swarm optimization with application in image segmentation. *Pattern Anal Appl.* 8(4) (2006): 332.

[26] Ramos, V., Almeida, F. Artificial ant colonies in digital image habitats-a mass behaviour effect study on pattern recognition. arXivPreprcs/0412086. (2004)

[27] Huang, P., Cao, H., Luo, S. An artificial ant colonies approach to medical image segmentation. *Comput Methods Programs Biomed.* 92(3) (2008): 267–273.

[28] Ma, M., Liang, J., Guo, M., Fan, Y., Yin, Y., SAR image segmentation based on artificial bee colony algorithm. *Appl Soft Comput.* 11(8) (2011): 5205–5214.

[29] Cinsdikici, M. G., Aydin, D. Detection of blood vessels in ophthalmoscope images using MF/ant (matched filter/ant colony) algorithm. *Comput Methods Programs Biomed.* 96(2) (2009): 85–95.

[30] Aydin, D., Ugur, A. Extraction of flower regions in color images using ant colony optimization. *Procedia Comput Sci.* 3 (2011): 530–536.

[31] Akay, B. A study on particle swarm optimization and artificial bee colony algorithms for multilevel thresholding. *Appl Soft Comput.* 13(6) (2013): 3066–3091.

[32] Sag, T., Cunkas, M. Development of image segmentation techniques using swarm intelligence (ABC-based clustering algorithm for image segmentation). In: International Conference on Computing and Information Technology Al-Madinah Al-Munawwarah, Saudi Arabia (2012): 95–100.

[33] Puri, P., Ghosh, S. A hybrid optimization approach for PI controller tuning based on gain and phase margin specifications. *Swarm Evol Comput.* 8 (2013): 69–78.

[34] Dai, C., Zhu, Y., Chen, W. Seeker optimization algorithm. *Lect Notes Comput Sci.* 4456 (2007): 167–176.

[35] Tuba, M., Brajevic, I., Jovanovic, R. Hybrid seeker optimization algorithm for global optimization. *Appl Math Inf Sci.* 7(3) (2013): 867.

[36] Kumar, M. R., Ghosh, S., Das, S. Identification of fractional order circuits from frequency response data using seeker optimization algorithm. In: 2015 International Conference on Industrial Instrumentation and Control (ICIC) (2015): 197–202.

[37] Selim, S. Z., Ismail, M. A. K-means-type algorithms: A generalized convergence theorem and characterization of local optimality. *IEEE Trans Pattern Anal Mach Intell.* 1 (1984): 81–87.

[38] Bansal, S., Aggarwal, D. Color image segmentation using CIELab color space using ant colony optimization. *Int J Comput Appl.* 29(9) (2011): 28–34.

[39] Connolly, C., Fleiss, T. A study of efficiency and accuracy in the transformation from RGB to CIELAB color space. *IEEE Trans Image Process.* 6(7) (1997): 1046–1048.

[40] Jailani, R., Hashim, H., Taib, M. N., Sulaiman, S. Border segmentation on digitized psoriasis skin lesion images. In: 2004 IEEE Region 10 Conference TENCON 2004 (2004): 596–599.

[41] Huang, L., Xia, T., Zhang, Y., Lin, S. Human skin detection in images by MSER analysis. In: 2011 18th IEEE International Conference on Image Processing (2011): 1257–1260.

[42] Cheddad, A., Condell, J., Curran, K., Mc Kevitt, P. Skin tone based steganography in video files exploiting the YCbCr colour space. In: 2008 IEEE International Conference on Multimedia and Expo (2008): 905–908.

[43] Moghaddam, R. F., Cheriet, M. AdOtsu: An adaptive and parameterless generalization of Otsu's method for document image binarization. *Pattern Recognit.* 45(6) (2012): 2419–2431.

[44] Dash, M., Londhe, N. D., Ghosh, S., Semwal, A., Sonawane, R. S. PsLSNet: Automated psoriasis skin lesion segmentation using modified U-Net-based fully convolutional network. *Biomed Signal Process Control.* 52 (2019): 226–237.

13 A COVID-19 Tracker for Medical Front-Liners

*Akshansh Jaiswal, Aman Shinde, Avani Pathak,
Chaithra Bhat, Manali Kaswa, Rajeev Ramesh,
Siddhant Singh, Vikramjit Banerjee, and
Prashant Gadakh*
International Institute of Information Technology, Pune, India

Sandeep Patil
National Institute of Technology, Silchar, India

CONTENTS

DOI: 10.1201/9781003241409-13

13.1 INTRODUCTION

Since the beginning of the COVID-19 outbreak, healthcare professionals have truly been selfless warriors, giving everything to uphold their job responsibilities. The COVID-19 pandemic has added to the stress of an already overburdened healthcare workforce. India has one medical doctor for every 1,404 people and 1.7 nurses per 1,000 people, according to the Ministry of Health and Family Welfare (MoHFW). The existing healthcare system for managing patients is distributed, less efficient and slow. It is not capable of handling 90,000 patients daily and the 130 crores population including urban and rural [1]. The public health care system requires a reboot. It should be more centralized, data-driven and rapid. Field workers find it harder to attend to all patients directly. Even though the addresses of people in quarantine are given, their exact locations are not known. There is a need to develop a cross-platform application [2], which helps government organizations, medical officers and field workers to digitalize and automate the entire process and analyze and derive insights based on geographical clusters and locations. Hence, the aim of the chapter is to develop an integrated digital platform for medical front-liners, which will help in assisting the governing bodies from the time a patient is detected positive till they are discharged [3]. It will also provide daily, weekly and monthly insights.

13.2 METHODOLOGY

13.2.1 Background

We initially surveyed all the existing systems. We found them usable; however, they weren't customized for the medical front-liners. Features like ambulance tracking, analysis dashboard, bed availability and hospital availability were already present as individual applications, but a one-stop solution was found to be missing.

Some of them were Aarogya Setu [4], Corona Warrior [5], CoBuddy-Covid19, COVID-19 Care Tamil Nadu [6], etc. We then thoroughly analyzed the pros and cons of each of them. It helped us form the objectives of this framework. Some of the lacunae were technical glitches, privacy and use of native applications, which have high release lag and requires respective expertise [7]. Also, there was very little use of the latest technologies.

Aarogya Setu uses Bluetooth, GPS, AI and data analytics and the prime goal is contact tracing. The salient features are self-assessment, user status, national news, E-pass registration and information dissemination. Corona Warrior had dedicated knowledge sections for different stakeholders and educational quizzes and games. The main aim was information sharing. CoBuddy-Covid19 had a location-tracking module mainly for quarantined patients. It also included a face recognition module, but was abandoned due to privacy issues. COVID-19 Care Tamil Nadu consisted of a visual map, district-wise reports, containment zone indicator and government orders.

The major advantage of the above apps over our system was support of local languages and voice-assisted app operation. Our team visited the Thane Municipal

Corporation war room to understand the problem and requirements better. We also checked the entire manual process currently being carried out for the Coronavirus patient tracking. There were many features that we also liked from the existing systems, one of them being automated discharge report generation [8,9].

We intend to apply data science and machine learning in the smart prediction of new hotspots or patients. Also, the existing system is decentralized and makes it cumbersome for doctors and field-workers to attend to all patients directly.

Our app can help the system in using the digital way to fill up forms, thus also reducing paper documentation. The application can be customized as per the use case and location.

13.2.2 PROPOSED SYSTEM

Our system aims at automating the process of all the stakeholders involved in the treatment of a COVID-19 patient. It is a standalone multi-user app and a website for the stakeholders, which is cross platform and dynamic.

The proposed system consists of the following components: Android/iOS application, website, maintenance and support, initial orientation and training, routine changes and updates, and database.

The system should be able to:

- Tag the geographical location and assign health center (HC)
- Record the current condition of the patient and take relevant decisions on whether the patient needs to be hospitalized or not
- Check the availability of the required medical facility and allocation of the patient
- Monitor the process flow until the patient is given proper treatment [10]
- Perform analysis on geospatial data of the patients [7,11]

There are six stakeholders involved in this framework. Following are the roles and responsibilities of each.

- War Room – Master User
- Medical Officer – Doctors who can prescribe bed type and assign field workers
- Field Worker – Go to the patient's place and fill the medical form
- Ambulance driver – Transport the patients
- Hospital – Admit and discharge the patients
- Police Officers – Take legal action on the non-contactable patients

The complete process can be viewed in Figure 13.1.

The process starts by getting patient's data from the ICMR website. It includes patient details who were tested COVID-19 positive the previous day. From the address field, we extract the latitude and longitude of the patient [12]. Using these coordinates, we mark the precise location of the patient on the map with a dot whose color is initially red, which indicates that the patient is a new patient. The

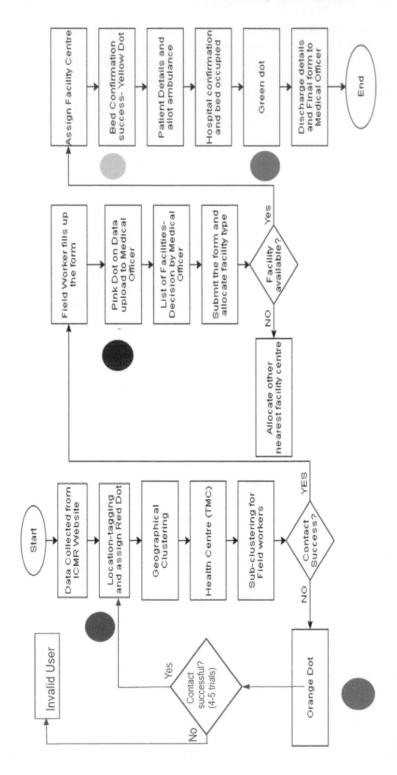

FIGURE 13.1 Flowchart of the entire system.

governing body has certain groups of HCs each with their own area of jurisdiction. All the patients are assigned to a particular HC according to clustering algorithms.

After this, each field worker under an HC will be assigned a patient. The field worker then calls each patient assigned to them and confirms whether the address given by the patient is accurate and if the patient will be available at the given address at a specific time or not. If the patient does not answer or the address seems false, the particular patient details will be sent to the police who will help the HC in tracking down the patient. The patient's dot will then turn orange, which signifies that the HC is unable to contact the patient and requires police assistance. If the patient has successfully confirmed their location, the field worker assigned to them will go to the particular patient's address. Upon reaching, the field worker will note down the patient's symptoms like SPO2, pulse and temperature, fill and upload the patient's form on the webapp. The patient's dot will now change to pink, which signifies that the patient's form has been filled and uploaded for the medical officer to be reviewed.

After reviewing it, the medical officer will assign a facility type according to the patient's condition. The particular patient's facility request will be sent to the hospital assigned and they can either accept or reject a patient. If rejected, the medical officer will assign another nearest facility for the patient's treatment. If accepted, the patient will be assigned that hospital and the governing body will assign a particular ambulance according to the patient's condition. The patient's dot will now turn yellow, which signifies confirmation of a bed for the patient. The ambulance driver will receive patient information and the hospital information so that they can transport the patient to the concerned hospital quickly. The patient will also receive an SMS regarding the ambulance driver's details. When the patient reaches the assigned hospital, the patient's dot will change to green, which signifies that the patient has been successfully admitted. The patient's treatment will now start and upon recovering, they will be discharged from the hospital.

13.2.3 SYSTEM REQUIREMENTS

The functions of the application are user-specific and hence we have listed them below:

1. Governing Body (war room)
   * The war room needs to access the whole system and will be the master user of the application
   * Will be able to see the health workers available, HCs allocated, patients involved in the system each day
   * Allocate ambulance for COVID-19 positive patients' pick-up
   * Generate reports for individuals as well as grouped patient data
   * Continuous monitoring through map and live tracking of ambulance
2. Medical Officer
   * Study the form filled by the field worker and allocate the facility type to be given to the patient

- See the availability of beds in the respective hospital and assign them to the patient
3. Field Worker
   - Field worker will receive the patient's details and contact them
   - She/he needs to contact the patient, go to their address and fill a form containing fields like basic information, temperature, pulse, health issues, oxygen level, etc.
   - The field worker will submit the filled form to the medical officer for further review
4. Police
   - If the HC or field worker is unable to contact the patient, the patient's details are sent to the police
   - The police will then take the necessary action and investigate to trace the patient and update the details if the patient is found or else mark the status as not found
5. Ambulance Driver
   - Ambulance driver gets the patient's address and contact details as well as hospital's address and contact details
   - Ambulance type is selected by the governing body for patient's pick-up to the hospital
   - Live ambulance tracking dashboard is available, which is used for monitoring the patient's location
   - The ambulance driver has an option to keep their duty status as On/Off as per their availability
6. Hospital
   - The hospital needs to continuously update the bed availability status on the webapp
   - Based on the bed availability, the hospital has to accept/reject the patient
   - Provide the required treatment to positive patient
   - Also, they need to manage patient's data till they recover

The class diagram Figure 13.2 gives a detailed description of the stakeholders involved and their attributes.

13.2.4 TECHNICAL DETAILS

- Mobile App: Android 4.1+ and iOS 8+
- Browser Support: Chrome 72–79, Firefox 65–71, Microsoft Edge, Opera 58–65, Pale Moon 28.3–28.8, Safari 13, Sea Monkey, Vivaldi 2.3-2.10 and Yandex browser
- Geolocation Tracking: Smartphone GPS
- Front-end software: HTML5, CSS3 and JavaScript
- Back-end software: PHP and MySQL
- SMS API: D7 NETWORK API
- Geolocation API: Google Maps API
- Google Charts API

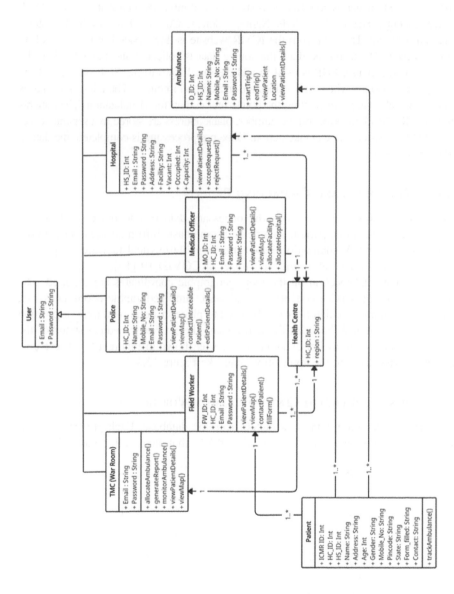

FIGURE 13.2 Class diagram of the framework.

13.3 MODULES

13.3.1 DATA COLLECTION AND PRE-PROCESSING

The source of Data Collection is the ICMR (Indian Council for Medical Research) website. The data which is collected consists of critical information about the COVID-19 positive patients. The fields include Name, Address, Contact, Past Medical History, Travel History, etc. The data from the ICMR website is downloaded in the form of an excel document. Based on the data, the source data is collected and tabulated into the database for further use. PHP is used to add the excel rows to the SQL database. Data cleaning process starts where null values are treated and imputed. The address format is corrected, which is used for plotting the points on the map for visualization. The patients with blank ICMR id, incorrect phone number, blank address are stored in a separate excel file so that the master user can take action. Once pre-processing is completed, the data is ready for further use.

13.3.2 GEOCODING AND GEOTAGGING PATIENTS

Google Maps helps us to visualize the necessary data in one place, such as the patient's precise location, patient's name and some basic information along with the status of the patient. Visualization-based maps enable medical facilities to prepare in advance and can severely limit the impact of COVID-19 [13].

To mark patients' location on the map, geographic coordinates are required. The Google's geocoding service converts text addresses into geographic coordinates, i.e., latitude and longitude, which later can be used to place markers on a map or position the map. To distinguish between the current and the previous medical status of the patient, there is need to assign dynamic markers as shown in Figure 13.3. These dots can then be visualized in the application map like Figure 13.4.

13.3.3 ASSIGNING HEALTH CENTER AND FIELD WORKER

The patient geolocation data is extracted from the database. Each government has divided their governing area into wards or HC that take full responsibility of

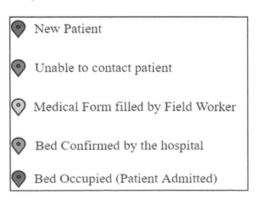

FIGURE 13.3 Dot color specification.

FIGURE 13.4 Different markers and information window.

managing the patients under them. The HC data is taken from the government in the form of .kmz files. The files are then converted to JavaScript arrays. Every patients' geographic coordinates were checked against every HC coordinate to allot an HC. The containsLocation() function of the Google Maps API was used for this purpose. The field workers are manually assigned by the medical officer using the webapp.

13.3.4 HOSPITAL MANAGEMENT SYSTEM

The hospital management system is controlled by every hospital by their respective admins. Hospitals can manage their bed counts and patient's acceptance/rejection along with patient discharge events [2]. There are different hospital facility types: CCC (Covid-19 Care Centre), DCHC (Dedicated Covid-19 HC), DCH (Dedicated Covid-19 Hospital), HC (Home quarantine), ICU, Oxygen and Ventilator.

Hospitals can accept and reject new patients using their dashboard. This makes the entire process hassle-free. Upon accepting a patient the bed count in the hospital will be automatically updated. For the existing patients, the application will provide hospitals with the feature to discharge the patients. This will also update the bed count again. Once a patient has been discharged their entry will move to discharged patients for generating reports and further analysis [14].

13.3.5 AMBULANCE MANAGEMENT SYSTEM

The ambulance management system is controlled by the Master User/Admin. As soon as the medical officer assigns a hospital to a patient, the Master User/Admin receives request to allocate an ambulance to the patient. According to the needs of the patient, the Master User/Admin decides which type of ambulance should be

(a)   (b)

FIGURE 13.5   (a) and 13.5 (b) Ambulance driver dashboard and routing.

allocated. The types of ambulances can be cardiac, ventilator, oxygen, and normal ambulance. After selecting the type of ambulance, the Master User/Admin then selects the ambulance driver allocated to a particular patient.

For allocating the nearest ambulance from the patient's address our proposed system uses Google Maps' Distance Matrix API. The nearest ambulance ID gets automatically mapped with the patient details using this API. The ambulance driver has its dashboard as shown in Figure 13.5(a). Using this dashboard the ambulance driver can set this duty as ON/OFF. According to the duty preference of the ambulance driver the system helps the Master User/Admin in allocating an ambulance to the patient. After an ambulance is allocated to the patient, it is expected that the ambulance driver keeps himself online in the mobile app. This will help the Master User/Admin and the medical officer to get live tracking of the ambulance. Google Maps Direction API is used to find the fastest and most convenient route between the ambulance's location and the patient's address. A route with least congestion is selected and displayed on the dashboard as shown in Figure 13.5(b).

For sending SMS to all the patients and ambulance drivers, our web app uses the D7 SMS API, which accepts the contact details of the sender and sends a text message including the details, respectively. All the information about the ambulance, such as ambulance number, driver's contact number, ambulance current location and estimated time to reach patient's location is sent to the patient and the medical officer via text message. Also, all the details of the patient, such as the patient's contact number, patient's address and the hospital allocated to the patient, are sent to the ambulance driver via text message.

Patient Discharge Report

ICMR ID	*7571*
Patients Name	*Mr. Tanmay Bhat*
Age	*35*
Gender	*M*
Address	*301, Diamond WIng, Lodha Belmonte, Laxmi Nagar Balkum Pada Thane, Thane, Maharashtra, 400607*
Mobile No.	*9876543210*
Covid-19 Test	*Positive*
Date	*13-11-2020*
Health Center Name	*Manpada*
Field Worker	*Mr. Akash Shukla*
Form Filled Date	*03-11-2020*
Temperature	*102 F*
Pulse Rate	*90*
Facility Type	*DCHC*
Medical Officer	*Dr. Naveed Kasturia*
Hospital	*Ruby Hospital*

FIGURE 13.6   Actual generated discharge report.

13.3.6   REPORT GENERATION

There were two types of automated reports generated for administration.

13.3.6.1   Patient Discharge Report

After a patient is discharged, a discharge report in the form of pdf is generated. One such report can be checked in Figure 13.6. The PDFMake API is used to generate the report.

The framework produces the PDF record on the fly from the MySQL database in this web application. A download interface will be given on the front-end or UI on which the end user will tap and will get an alternative to spare the created PDF record as per their chosen location. The system utilizes the PDFMake API for producing PDF reports. As we are not saving this PDF report anywhere within the physical area of the server, we are going to send the information within the Response object as an attachment.

Reports are generally created in PDF format since a PDF file could be a "read-only" document that cannot be modified without taking off an electronic impression while other designs like image, word, excel, etc. can effectively be modified without taking off an electronic impression [8].

FIGURE 13.7 Generating reports based on custom conditions.

13.3.6.2 Custom Data Reports

The data can be downloaded in the form of excel using custom attributes according to the requirements from the webapp as shown in Figure 13.7. Every HC needs to send an audit report to the higher authorities. The excel format is used to digitally send the documents. First the database rows are converted to octet stream binary file in RFC 2046 and then to excel. Content-disposition with excel content-types to indicate we want to save rather than display.

The report can be generated for a patient in a certain timeframe by selecting start date and end date. The categories like HC allotted, hospital allotted, and ambulance allotted can be selected for filtering the rows of excel.

13.3.7 ANALYTICS

The analytics dashboard was uniquely curated for all users. Different metrics like age-wise patient distribution, gender-wise distribution are used. Patient's age is an important attribute in determining the type of treatment. The comprehensive role-wise metrics can be seen in Table 13.1.

The analysis data has the least access. For example, an HC can visualize data confining to only that HC.

Also, daily, weekly and monthly patient rate is displayed in the form of graphs. Google Charts library was used in JavaScript. The data was extracted from the SQL database in the form of an array. Then, different functions were applied to generate charts as shown in Figure 13.8(a) and (b). The graphs give a nice view to the government to be ready for the future outbreak. The graphs were also displayed HC-wise so that the center with the highest number of patients can be focused on.

TABLE 13.1

Metrics List

Master User	Health Center	Hospital
Gender-wise distribution	Contact status count	Bed availability
Patient dot color-wise distribution	Form filled status	Insurance-wise distribution
Allocation of hospital and health center status	Patient dot color-wise distribution	Senior Citizen, Discharged Patients, Currently Admitted, Critical Patients count
Health center-wise patient frequency	Gender-wise distribution	Ambulance Allocation status
Age-wise patient distribution	Hospital-wise patient frequency	Age-wise patient distribution
Daily, weekly and monthly line charts for patient count	Age-wise patient distribution	Symptom severity distribution

FIGURE 13.8 (a) and 13.8 (b) Analysis and graphs displayed to the master-user.

The co-morbidity aspect was also visualized to get an idea of which patients succumbed more to COVID-19.

After significant amount of data is collected, machine learning can be applied to predict the growth of COVID-19. Based on the symptoms recorded by the field worker, the severity of the disease can be predicted beforehand so that facilities can be arranged. Mortality and recovery can also be predicted. This becomes impactful in cases of breathing equipment scarcity. Also, early diagnosis using machine learning classification can be done [15].

13.4 MATHEMATICAL MODEL

i. Let HC be the health center array, P be the patient array, N_p be the total patients.
Then,
P_j = HC_i where P_j (lat, lng) in Polygon (HC_i) ∀ P where $1 \leq i \leq 28, 0 \leq j \leq N_p$
State (P_j) = Red where $0 \leq j \leq N_p$

ii. Let N_f be the total field workers in an HC_i, FW be the field worker array.
Then,
For each FW assign N_p/N_f number of patients where FW ∈ HC_i&& P_j∈ HC_i

iii. Contact () is the function which determines if the patient's contact is successful or not. FillForm is the function for filling forms.
State (P_j) = Contact (P_j)? Fillform(P_j): Orange where $0 \leq j \leq N_p$

iv. Form = {HC_i, FW_k,P_j, Sysdate, Insurance, Pulse, Temperature, Comorbidity, SPO2, Symptoms, H_x}

v. FillForm () is the function which returns True after the patient's form is filled by the Field worker.
State (P_j) = Fillform(P_j)? Pink: pass where State (P_j) = Red where $0 \leq j \leq N_p$

vi. Let F Type= {Oxygen, Ventilator, ICU, HQ}, Htype = {CCC, DCHC, DCH}, H be the hospital structure {Name, Ftype, Htype}, N_{hosp} be the total hospitals
Then,
Medical Officer MO of the HC where patient belongs assigns H_x to P_j where $0 \leq j \leq N_p$&& MO ∈ HC_i && P_j∈ HC_i&& $0 \leq x \leq N_{hosp}$&& FType ∈ H_x&& State(P_j) = Pink

vii. FacilityConfirmed() is the function through which a hospital confirms that the patient can be admitted and given the chosen facility
State (P_j) = FacilityConfirmed(P_j)? Yellow: go to step 6 where $0 \leq j \leq N_p$

viii. Let A be the ambulance array, N_a be the total ambulances
Then, AssignAmbulance () is the function through which a MO assigns closest ambulance to a patient and Available () is the function that returns True if ambulance is available.
AssignAmbulance(P_j, A_y) where MO ∈ HC_i && P_j∈ HC_i&& $0 \leq y \leq N_a$&&Available(A_y)=True

ix. BedOccupied() is the function through which a hospital confirms that the patient has been successfully admitted
State (P_j) = BedOccupied(P_j)? Green: go to step 6 where $0 \leq j \leq N_p$

x. Discharge is the function a hospital carries out to discharge the patient
Discharge (P_j) by H_x where $0 \leq j \leq N_{pi}$&& P_j∈ H_x && $0 \leq x \leq N_{hosp}$

13.5 RESULTS

The outcome of our framework is improved patient tracking as with the help of the above system; it will be easier and more accessible to track patients across various stages of the events. It will also lead to efficient hospital management as the complete process will be automated. One more advantage is faster patient allotment; a digital solution will help patients get a comprehensive view of the type of beds available. This will help eliminate the major concern of getting a bed for positive patients. Human resources will be managed effectively, as our system will help in efficiently assigning resources like police, field worker, etc. and make sure everyone is occupied. The data stored in the database can serve as a central data pool. This data can then be mapped to any data warehouse for data mining and pattern prediction. The app can help in emergency allocation of ambulances in case a patient is critical with optimal routing and tracking.

13.6 APPLICATIONS

There are humongous real-world problems where this system can be used with little modification.

- Coronavirus vaccine dissemination
- Apart from pandemics like COVID-19, communicable diseases such as dengue can be efficiently managed
- Vaccination drives for kids (e.g., polio)
- Annual medical check-up of senior citizens
- Emergency accident patients
- National screening of diseases like TB

13.7 CONCLUSION

Thus, we created an efficient, robust, fully automated, data-driven and centralized digital and integrated platform for the medical front-liners. The powerful backend design and implementation along with smooth and easy-to-use GUI of our application will help its stakeholders to control any situation effectively. Our framework aims at integrating all the entities involved in controlling the spread of coronavirus.

In the future application of this system, we can couple it with interesting and informative visualization and analysis on historical data, thus enabling us to predict and provide better services and overcome more real-world applications. This application can also be scaled to a national level and help people across India to control any kind of a pandemic situation. Patient interaction can be included in the system so that it reaches every type of stakeholder. Integration of a contact transmission module will serve more purpose to the existing system.

13.8 FUTURE WORK

Future work constitutes:

- Pre-hospitalization diagnosis
- Appointment booking

- Adding telemedicine facility
- Adding diagnostics for easier clinical tests
- Better visualization on historical data
- Patient interaction in the system
- Contact transmission module
- Mobile push notifications to the mobile app
- Multi-factor authentication for login
- Hashing the passwords using SHA for better security
- Local language support and voice user interface

REFERENCES

[1] Kumar, A., Nayar, K. and FazaludeenKoya, S., "COVID-19: Challenges and its consequences for rural health care in India," *Public Health in Practice*, 1, 22 (2020): 12.

[2] Mallik, R., Hazarika, A., Ghosh, S., Sing, D. and Bandyopadhyay, R., "Development of an Android application for viewing Covid-19 containment zones and monitoring violators who are trespassing into it using Firebase and Geofencing." Transactions of the Indian National Academy of Engineering 5.2 (2020): 163–179.

[3] Emmanuel, G., Hungilo, G. G. and Emanuel, A. W. R., "A mobile application system for community health workers-A review," in Proceedings of the 2019 5th International Conference on Computing and Artificial Intelligence - ICCAI 19 (2019).

[4] "Aarogya Setu," [Online]. Available: https://play.google.com/store/apps/details?id= nic.goi.aarogyasetu&hl=en.

[5] "Corona Warrior," [Online]. Available: https://play.google.com/store/apps/details? id=com.intutrack.covidtrack&hl=en.

[6] "COVID-19 Care Tamil Nadu," [Online]. Available: https://play.google.com/store/ apps/details?id=com.rvmatrix.corona&hl=en.

[7] Amirkhanyan, A., Cheng, F. and Meinel, C., "Real-time clustering of massive geodata for online maps to improve visual analysis," in Proceedings of the 2015 11th International Conference on Innovations in Information Technology (IIT) (2015).

[8] "Flash Report," [Online]. Available: https://echalliance.com/wp-content/uploads/ 2020/04/covid-flash-report-final.pdf.

[9] "Covid Thane," [Online]. Available: https://covidthane.org/covid-19.html.

[10] Soppin, S., Nagaraj, C. B. and Iyer, M., "Tracking the crowd and Covid-19 patients for the prevention and spread of disease," *Community Medicine*, 27, 03 (2020).

[11] Franch-Pardo, I., Napoletano, B., Rosete-Verges, F. and Billa, L., "Spatial analysis and GIS in the study of COVID-19. A review," *Science of the Total Environment*, 08, 06 (2020).

[12] Gupta, R., Bedi, M., Goyal, P., Wadhera, S. and Verma, V., "Analysis of COVID-19 tracking tool in India," *Digital Government: Research and Practice*, 1, 04 (2020): 1–8.

[13] Shi, G. and Barker, K., "Extraction of geospatial information on the Web for GIS applications," in Proceedings of the IEEE 10th International Conference on Cognitive Informatics and Cognitive Computing (ICCI-CC11) (2011).

[14] Balaraman, P. and Kosalram, K., "E –Hospital Management & Hospital Information Systems – Changing trends," *International Journal of Information Engineering and Electronic Business*, 5, 1 (2013): 50–58.

[15] Mittal, S., "An exploratory data analysis of COVID-19 in India," *International Journal of Engineering Research & Technology*, 9 (2020).

14 Implementation of One Dimensional Convolutional Neural Network for ECG Classification on Python Platform

Mitul Kumar Ahirwal and Ravi Singh
Maulana Azad National Institute of Technology, Bhopal,
India

Nikhil Agrawal
Indian Institute of Information Technology, Nagpur, India
vel

CONTENTS

14.1 INTRODUCTION

An ECG is typically used to diagnose and monitor different conditions of the human heart. It is used for diagnosis and to understand symptoms of heart abnormalities,

DOI: 10.1201/9781003241409-14

for example, chest pain, heart palpitations (sensations of fast-beating and fluttering), shortness of breath, and dizziness [1]. The ECG is very helpful in detection of the following conditions:

- Arrhythmias: A condition where the heart starts beating either too quickly, too slowly, or irregularly
- Cardiomyopathy: A condition where the walls of the heart get thick or enlarged
- Heart attacks: A condition where the blood supply to the heart is suddenly blocked
- Coronary heart disease: A condition in which the blood supply to the heart is essentially blocked by a plaque formation

A series of ECGs tests are to be conducted over a period of time to essentially monitor a person who has been previously diagnosed with abovementioned heart conditions. Mainly, ECG is used for arrhythmia classification [1–3]. It is a condition that involves irregular beating of the heart; it can be improper, too slow, or too fast. It occurs whenever electrical impulses of the heart do not function properly; these changes are detected in ECG. Depending upon severity, treatments include anti-arrhythmic medicines, implantable devices, and eventually surgery may be suggested to patients. Following are the types of arrhythmia:

- Supraventricular ectopic beats: It is a condition when the heart either adds an extra beat or skips a beat hence also known as premature heartbeat.
- Ventricular ectopic beats: It is a condition when the electric signals in the heart start in a different place and travel a different way through the heart.
- Fusion beats: It is a condition when a ventricular impulse and a supra-ventricular impulse coincide to effectively produce a hybrid complex.
- Unknown beats: All the other abnormal beats that do not fall in the above categories are considered unknown.

In Figure 14.1, a general representation of ECG signal is given, in which peaks represent the beats of the heart. Further, different parts of the peak in ECG signal are shown, these parts or components are called PQRST wave. Details of PQRST waves are available in [4–6].

The abnormality in heart is reflected in ECG and observing the changes in PQTSR wave, such as length of PR interval, length of QRS interval, etc., will be helpful in detection of different types of arrhythmia and other heart diseases. Despite several computer-aided methods being developed for early prediction of the risk of any possible cardiovascular disease in the past few years, still it is a very challenging dilemma [7–10]. Hence there is need for developing more fully automatic techniques with high applicability, high accuracy, and low complexity. Therefore, in this chapter, a detailed description of implementation of One Dimensional Convolutional Neural Network (1D-CNN) for ECG classification has been provided over Python platform.

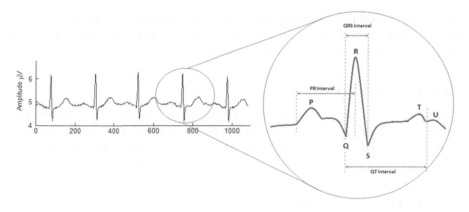

FIGURE 14.1   Visualization of ECG signal and PQRST wave.

14.2   OVERVIEW OF 1D-CNN

Over the past decade, because of the self-learning capability of artificial neural network algorithms, convolutional neural networks have become very popular for signal and image classification purposis not balancedes. The convolutional layers perform the work of feature extraction in an automatic manner; therefore, they do not require a handcrafted feature extraction step. CNNs have mainly two types of blocks, convolutional blocks and output blocks [11,12].

14.2.1   CONVOLUTIONAL BLOCK

This block generally consists of one 1D-convolutional layer, one batch normal-ization layer, followed by one 1D-max-pooling layer with a rectified linear unit (ReLU) layer. The ReLU activation can be replaced by other type of activation functions. The function of the 1D convolutional layer is to create a convolution kernel that is convolved with the input-layer over a single dimension to produce convoluted signals or called features. The batch normalization essentially standar-dizes the input values and therefore it is applied after the 1D-convolutional layer and before the max-pooling layer for improving the performance and to stabilize the learning process of the neural network. The 1D max-pooling is used to resize; basically reduce the input by picking the maximum value on the window defined by the pool size. In general it is also called as pooling layer, because in this, operations other than max can also be used. The stride is used to specify the value by which the kernel or pooling window should be moved over input [11,12].

14.2.2   OUTPUT BLOCK

This block contains one flatten layer, one dense layer with ReLu layer (may also be replaced by other activation functions), and one dense layer with a softmax layer. Multi-dimensional input vectors obtained from previous CNN layers are trans-formed into a single dimension by a flatten layer. Then the output of the flatten layer is given as the input to dense/fully connected layers. The output from the first dense layer is given as the input to the second dense layer. Finally, the output of the last dense layer is the result of the entire model [12].

14.2.3 TRAINING OF MODEL

The training and learning is done by adaptation of weights of the model, this adaptation is done with the help of Adam optimizer, and many other optimizers are also available. The optimizers also take help of different loss functions, generally for classification categorical cross entropy function is used.

14.2.4 PYTHON PLATFORM

Nowadays, python language is gaining popularity among researchers. One of the reasons behind its popularity is the support of many data science and machine learning libraries. It is open source and many online compilers/interpreters are available for python, Google Colab is an online interpreter for python [13–15]. In this chapter, the CNN model is developed in Google Colab and ECG data is accessed through CSV files stored in Google Drive. Along with the theoretical description of model and data code is also provided in this chapter in sequential steps. First step is to import required libraries as provided in below step 1.

STEP 1   IMPORT REQUIRED LIBRARIES

```
from google.colab import drive
import numpy as np
import pandas as pd
import tensorflow as tf
import seaborn as sns
import matplotlib.pyplot as plt
import keras
from tensorflow.keras.utils import to_categorical
from sklearn.utils import resample
import itertools
from sklearn.metrics import classification_report, confusion_
matrix
```

In this chapter two databases have been used, first one is binary class database and the second is multi-class database.

14.3   DATABASE 01

Binary class database (Data set 01): This database contains 549 samples of recordings from 290 subjects/patients. Physikalisch-Technische Bundesanstalt

(PTB) [16–19], which is also called the National Metrology Institute of Germany, has furnished this collection of digitized ECG recordings for research and algorithmic benchmarking purposes. Following are the key specifications of this database.

- Sampling Frequency: 125 Hz
- Number of Classes: 02 [0: Normal (NOR), 1: Abnormal (ABNOR)]
- Number of Samples in (0) NOR class: 4047
- Number of Samples in (1) ABNOR class: 10505
- Total Number of Samples: 14552

This data set is stored in two CSV files, these files are first saved in Google Drive and with the help of the below step loaded into Google Colab file as shown in below step 2. Step 2 consists of 4 substeps – mount Google Drive, import CSV files, check for null values in data, and data balancing (if not having equal numbers of samples in both classes).

STEP 2   LOAD DATA AND PREPROCESSING

Mount Google Drive
```
drive.mount('/content/drive/')
```

For mounting Google Drive, there is need for logging in your Gmail account and one link/code will be provided that will be pasted in a text box in the running cell of Google Colab.

Read.csv files
```
ABNOR  =  pd.read_csv("/content/drive/MyDrive/ECG  Data/
ptbdb_abnormal.csv")
NOR  =  pd.read_csv("/content/drive/MyDrive/ECG  Data/
ptbdb_normal.csv")
```

In the above, data is loaded from two CSV files into two variables named ABNOR and NOR for abnormal ECG samples and normal ECG samples, respectively. After this "ABNOR.shape" and "NOR.shape" commands can be executed to check the dimension of these variables.

Give Index to columns of variables

```
column_name = ['C0']
for num in range(NOR.shape[1]-1):
  tem = 'C'+str(num+1)
  column_name.append(tem)
NOR.columns = column_name

new_column_name = ['C0']
for num in range(ABNOR.shape[1]-1):
  tem = 'C'+str(num+1)
  new_column_name.append(tem)
ABNOR.columns = new_column_name
```

In Figures 14.2 and 14.3, normal and abnormal ECG beats are visualized, respectively.

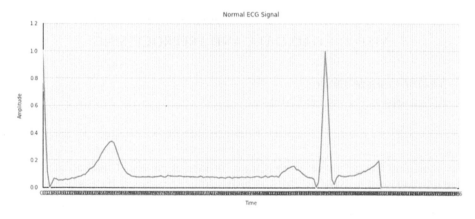

FIGURE 14.2 Normal ECG beat from PTB database.

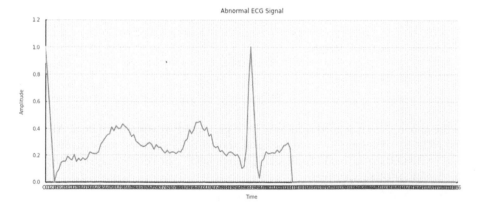

FIGURE 14.3 Abnormal ECG beat from PTB database.

Checking null values

```
NOR.isnull().sum()
ABNOR.isnull().sum()
```

Plot abnormal ECG samples

```
sns.set_style('whitegrid')
plt.figure(figsize = (15,6))
plt.plot(ABNOR.iloc[5, 0:187], color = 'red')
plt.title("Abnormal ECG Signal")
plt.ylabel('Amplitude')
plt.xlabel('Time')
plt.axis([0, 187, 0, 1.2])
plt.show()
```

Plot normal ECG samples

```
sns.set_style('whitegrid')
plt.figure(figsize = (15,6))
plt.plot(NOR.iloc[5, 0:187], color = 'red')
plt.title("Normal ECG Signal")
plt.ylabel('Amplitude')
plt.xlabel('Time')
plt.axis([0, 187, 0, 1.2])
plt.show()
```

Here, the data set is not balanced; therefore, a data augmentation technique must be employed. For data augmentation, a simple re-sampling method is used by which 4,045 normal ECG beats are used to generate 10,505 normal ECG beats that are equal in number of abnormal ECG beats.

Data Balancing

```
NOR = resample(NOR, n_samples = 10505, replace = True, ran-
dom_state = 123)
NOR.shape
```

Now, total samples are 21,010, which are then divided into training and testing samples in ratio of approx 70:30. Further implementation details are given in later sections.

Make labels/target output

```
ytrain = train.iloc[:, 187]
ytrain.shape

ytest = test.iloc[:, 187]
ytest.shape

# Remove last column from data
train = train.iloc[:,:-1]
test = test.iloc[:,:-1]

# Employing One Hot Encoding Technique
ytrain=keras.utils.np_utils.to_categorical(ytrain)
ytest=keras.utils.np_utils.to_categorical(ytest)

# converting into numpy array
train=np.asarray(train)
train=train.reshape(14000, 187, 1)

test=np.asarray(test)
test=test.reshape(7010, 187, 1)
```

STEP 3   PREPARE DATA FOR TRAINING AND TESTING

Split data in training and testing set

```
train_NOR=NOR.iloc[0:7000]
test_NOR=NOR.iloc[7000:10505]
train_ABNOR=ABNOR.iloc[0:7000]
test_ABNOR=ABNOR.iloc[7000:10505]
train=[train_NOR,train_ABNOR]
train=pd.concat(train,sort=False)
test=[test_NOR,test_ABNOR]
test=pd.concat(test,sort=False)
train.shape
test.shape
```

14.4   IMPLEMENTATION OF 1D-CNN MODEL 1 FOR BINARY CLASSIFICATION

Two CNN models are developed, one for binary classification and another for multi-class classification. Before training and testing, labels for both the datasets are processed through One Hot encoding.

For PTB database labels are:

- Class 0 (Normal Beats): [1,0]
- Class 1 (Abnormal Beats): [0,1]

This model consists of three convolutional blocks followed by an output block. Out of the three convolutional blocks, first and second contain a convolution layer with 80 and 40 filters, respectively. The kernel size is 4 and ReLu has its activation function. It is then followed by a batch normalization layer and a max-pooling layer having a pool size of 3. For the third convolution layer 20 filters with a kernel size of 4 are used. After convolution blocks, output blocks contain a flatten layer, 2 dense layers with 50 units, and ReLu as activation function, followed by a dense layer having 2 units with a softmax activation function, which yields final output as predicted class labels. For training Adam optimizer is used with categorical cross entropy loss function. This model architecture is given in Table 14.1. This is the step 4 of implementation, which is given below:

TABLE 14.1

Detailed Parameters of the Proposed 1D-CNN Model 1

Type of Layer	Output Shape	Other Parameters
Conv1D	(184;80)	Filters - 80, Kernel Size - 4, Pool Size – 3, Activation - Relu
Batch Normalization	(184;80)	
Max Pooling 1D	(61;80)	
Activation	(61;80)	
Conv1D	(58;40)	Filters - 40, Kernel Size - 4, Pool Size – 3, Activation - Relu
Batch Normalization	(58;40)	
Max Pooling 1D	(19;40)	
Activation	(19;40)	
Conv1D	(16;20)	Filters - 20, Kernel Size - 4, Pool Size – 3, Activation - Relu
Batch Normalization	(16;20)	
Max Pooling 1D	(5;20)	
Activation	(5;20)	
Flatten	(100)	-
Dense	(50)	Units - 50, Activation – Relu
Dense	(50)	Units - 50, Activation – Relu
Output Layer	(2)	Units - 2, Activation – SoftMax

STEP 4   CREATE AND TRAIN 1D-CNN MODEL

Build Model by adding layers

```
def build_model():
model = tf.keras.models.Sequential()
# Layer 1
model.add(tf.keras.layers.Conv1D(80, 4, activation='relu',
input_shape=(187,1)))
model.add(tf.keras.layers.BatchNormalization())
model.add(tf.keras.layers.MaxPooling1D(3))
# Layer 2
model.add(tf.keras.layers.Conv1D(40, 4, activation='relu'))
model.add(tf.keras.layers.BatchNormalization())
model.add(tf.keras.layers.MaxPooling1D(3))
# Layer 3
model.add(tf.keras.layers.Conv1D(20, 4, activation='relu'))
model.add(tf.keras.layers.BatchNormalization())
model.add(tf.keras.layers.MaxPooling1D(3))
# Flatten Layer
model.add(tf.keras.layers.Flatten())
# Dense Layer 1
model.add(tf.keras.layers.Dense(50, activation='relu'))
# Dense Layer 2
model.add(tf.keras.layers.Dense(50, activation='relu'))
# Output Layer
model.add(tf.keras.layers.Dense(2, activation='softmax'))
model.compile(optimizer='adam',  loss='categorical_crossen-
tropy', metrics=['accuracy'])
    return model
model = build_model()
model.summary()
```

After model development, training is done with the help of below commands.

Train Model

```
history = model.fit(train, ytrain, validation_data=(test,
ytest), epochs=7)

Epoch 7/7
438/438 [==============================] - 5s 12ms/step -
loss: 0.0088 - accuracy: 0.9969 - val_loss: 0.0336 - va-
l_accuracy: 0.9896
```

After training, for plotting of training and validation accuracy and loss below commands are used.

Plot training and validation graphs

```
pd.DataFrame(history.history)
pd.DataFrame(history.history)[['accuracy', 'val_accuracy']]
.plot()
pd.DataFrame(history.history)[['loss', 'val_loss']].plot()
```

Figures 14.4 and 14.5

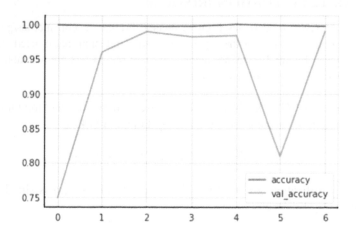

FIGURE 14.4   Training and validation accuracy of Model 1 over PTB database.

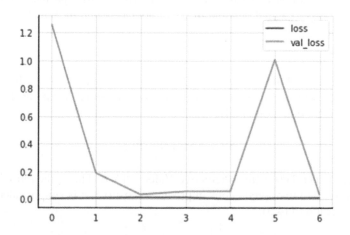

FIGURE 14.5   Training and validation loss of Model 1 over PTB database.

Binary Classification	Predicted Negative	Predicted Positive
Actual Negative	True Negative (TN)	False Positive (FP)
Actual Positive	False Negative (FN)	True Positive (TP)

FIGURE 14.6 Binary confusion matrix.

Now, the next step is to evaluate the developed and trained model with testing samples. For this, few famous fidelity parameters/matrices are used.

14.5 MODEL EVALUATION (RESULTS)

Performance of CNN models has been evaluated through several metrics/parameters listed below. For calculation of these parameters the confusion matrix needs to be defined as shown in Figure 14.6. More details on these parameters are available in [20]. The six parameters used are as follows:

 i. Accuracy (ACC): This is the ratio of correct predictions and total number of predictions; accuracy is obtained by Equation (14.1),

$$ACC = (TP + TN)/(TP + TN + FP + FN), \qquad (14.1)$$

 ii. Mis-Classification (MC): This is just opposite of ACC, it is simply calculated by Equation (14.2),

$$MC = 1 - ACC, \qquad (14.2)$$

 iii. Sensitivity or Recall (RC): This is the ratio of true positive and total predictions in actual positive; it is simply calculated by Equation (14.1),

$$RC = TP/(FN + TP), \qquad (14.3)$$

 iv. Specificity (SP)/(Selectivity or True Negative Rate (TNR)): This is the ratio of true negative and total predictions in actual negative; it is calculated by Equation (14.4),

$$SP = TN/(TN + FP), \qquad (14.4)$$

 v. Precision (PR)/(Positive Predictive Value (PPV)): This is the ratio of true positive and total predictions in predicted positive; it is simply calculated by Equation (14.5),

$$PR = TP/(TP + FP), \qquad (14.5)$$

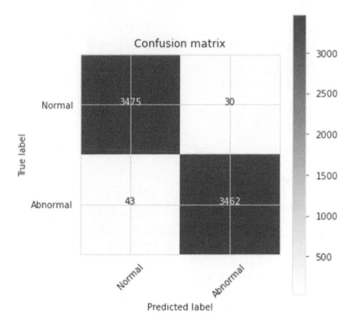

FIGURE 14.7 Confusion matrix of Model 1 over PTB database.

vi. F1 Score: This is parameter based on previous above parameters; it is calculated as Equation (14.6),

$$F1 = 2 * ((PR * RC)/(PR + RC)),$$
(14.6)

In above equations, notations used in Figure 14.7 are used.

STEP 5 CALCULATION OF PARAMETERS FROM CONFUSION MATRIX

```
def binary_class_parameters (conf_matrix):
  TP = conf_matrix[1][1]
  TN = conf_matrix[0][0]
  FP = conf_matrix[0][1]
  FN = conf_matrix[1][0]
  print('True Positives:', TP)
  print('True Negatives:', TN)
  print('False Positives:', FP)
  print('False Negatives:', FN)
  # (1) accuracy
  ACC = (float (TP+TN) / float(TP + TN + FP + FN))

  # (2) mis-classification
  MC = 1- ACC
```

```
    # (3) sensitivity (Recall)
    RC = (TP / float(TP + FN))

    # (4) specificity
    SP = (TN / float(TN + FP))

    # (5) precision
    PR = (TP / float(TP + FP))

    # (6) f_1 score
    F1 = 2 * ((PR * RC) / (PR + RC))
    print('1. Accuracy:', ACC)
    print('2. Mis-Classification:', MC)
    print('3. Sensitivity (Recall):', RC)
    print('4. Specificity:', SP)
    print('5. Precision:', PR)
    print('6. f_1 Score:', F1)

binary_class_parameters(cm)

True Positives: 3462
True Negatives: 3475
False Positives: 30
False Negatives: 43
1. Accuracy: 0.989586305278174
2. Mis-Classification: 0.010413694721825961
3. Sensitivity (Recall): 0.9877318116975748
4. Specificity: 0.9914407988587732
5. Precision: 0.9914089347079038
6. f_1 Score: 0.9895669572674003
```

Plot confusion matrix

```
# change ytest back to original labels with argmax because
above we converted labels via OneHot encoding
ytest= np.argmax(ytest, axis = 1)
print('shape of ytest=', ytest.shape)

shape of ytest= (7010,)

cm = confusion_matrix(ytest, ypred)
np.set_printoptions(precision=2)
print(cm)

[[3475  30]
 [43 3462]]
cm_df = pd.DataFrame(cm,
      columns = ['Predicted Negative', 'Predicted Positive'],
       index = ['Actual Negative', 'Actual Positive'])
# Showing the confusion matrix
cm_df
```

	Predicted Negative	Predicted Positive
Actual Negative	3475	30
Actual Positive	43	3462

Evaluate Model: Test model with testing set

```
loss,accuracy = model.evaluate(test, ytest)
print('Loss=',loss)
print('Accuracy=',accuracy)
220/220  [==============================]  -  1s  5ms/step  -
loss: 0.0336 - accuracy: 0.9896
Loss= 0.03358101472258568
Accuracy= 0.9895862936973572

P = model.predict(test)
print('P=',P)
print('shape of P=',P.shape)
P= [[9.99987721e-01 1.22830306e-05]
   [9.96684968e-01 3.31508578e-03]
   [9.99894500e-01 1.05506406e-04]
   ...
   [2.30675361e-17 1.00000000e+00]
   [1.47991985e-09 1.00000000e+00]
   [3.70952435e-11 1.00000000e+00]]
shape of P= (7010, 2)
# converting predictions to classes/labels
ypred = np.argmax(P, axis = 1)
print('shape of ypred=',ypred.shape)

shape of ypred= (7010,)
```

The entire process is repeated for another dataset of ECG having multiple classes. Here, another model of CNN has been developed.

14.6   DATABASE 02

This is multiple classes' database taken from MIT-BIH Arrhythmia Database, which is a collection of 48 half-hour recordings [16,19,21–23]. ECG recordings collected from 47 subjects who were tested by the Boston Israel Hospital Arrhythmia Laboratory are used in this database. In this dataset, ECG is labeled in three classes of abnormal beats, one normal and one unknown beats. More details about this data set are given below as key points.

- Sampling Frequency: 125 Hz
- Number of Classes: 05 [0: Non-Ecotic Normal Beats (N), 1: Supraventricular Ectopic Beats (S), 2: Ventricular Ectopic Beats (V), 3: Fusion Beats (F), 4: Unknown Beats (U)]
- Number of Samples in (0) N class: 72471
- Number of Samples in (1) S class: 2223
- Number of Samples in (2) V class: 5788
- Number of Samples in (3) F class: 641
- Number of Samples in (4) U class: 6431
- Total Number of Samples: 87554

Up till the data loading step, all commands are same as previous study, separate variables are below created for training and testing data, in which data have been loaded from CSV files.

Importing dataset from drive

```
train_data = pd.read_csv("/content/drive/MyDrive/ECG Data/
mitbih_train.csv", header=None)
test_data = pd.read_csv("/content/drive/MyDrive/ECG Data/
mitbih_test.csv", header=None)
train_data.shape
(87554, 188)
test_data.shape
(21892, 188)
```

The last column (187) of samples is the label of the sample; it needs to be converted into integer.

Converting Labels into integers

```
train_data.iloc[:, 187].unique()

# casting into int
train_data[187] = train_data[187].astype('int')
test_data[187] = test_data[187].astype('int')
```

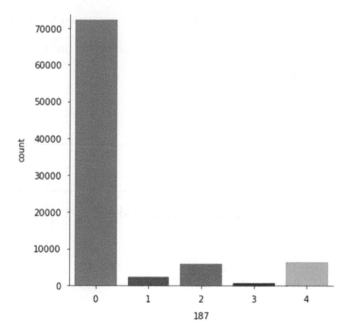

FIGURE 14.8 Bar plots of numbers of samples in each class (187 is the column number for class labels).

This database is also imbalanced as different numbers of samples are present in each class. To balance this database the same re-sampling method is used as in the previous database. After applying the re-sampling method, the number of samples in each class becomes 20,000 and the total number of samples becomes 100,000. These samples are divided into training and testing subsets.

Figure 14.8 shows the imbalance in the database, this is the bar plot of numbers of samples in each class given in column number 187 (last column). To make the number of samples equal in each class, samples are removed from class 0, while repetition of samples has been done in other classes by the re-sampling function of python.

Comparison of All classes of ECG Signal

```
sns.set_style('whitegrid')
plt.figure(figsize = (15,6))
plt.plot(df_0.iloc[2, 0:187], color = 'red', label = 'Normal
ECG signal')
plt.plot(df_1.iloc[2, 0:187], color = 'blue', label =
'Supraventricular ECG signal')
plt.plot(df_2.iloc[2, 0:187], color = 'green', label =
'Ventricular ECG signal')
plt.plot(df_3.iloc[2, 0:187], color = 'pink', label = 'Fusion
ECG signal')
```

```
plt.plot(df_4.iloc[2, 0:187], color = 'black', label =
'Unknown ECG signal')
plt.title("Comparison of All classes of ECG Signal")
plt.ylabel('Amplitude')
plt.xlabel('Time')
plt.axis([0, 187, 0, 1.2])
plt.legend()
plt.show()
```

Plot of normal ECG signal

```
sns.set_style('whitegrid')
plt.figure(figsize = (15,6))
plt.plot(df_0.iloc[2, 0:187], color = 'red')
plt.title("Normal ECG Signal")
plt.ylabel('Amplitude')
plt.xlabel('Time')
plt.axis([0, 187, 0, 1.2])
plt.show()
```

Splitting data into Classes

```
df_0 = train_data[train_data[187] == 0]
df_1 = train_data[train_data[187] == 1]
df_2 = train_data[train_data[187] == 2]
df_3 = train_data[train_data[187] == 3]
df_4 = train_data[train_data[187] == 4]
```

Plotting number of samples in each class

```
sns.catplot(x = 187, kind = 'count', data = train_data)
```

In Figures 14.9 and 14.10, plots of normal ECG beats and plots of abnormal ECG beats are shown, respectively.

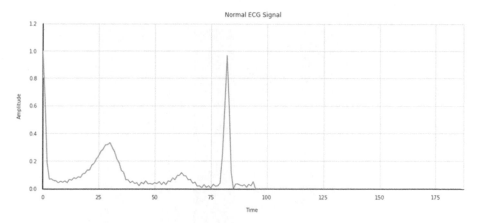

FIGURE 14.9   Normal ECG beat from MIT-BIH database.

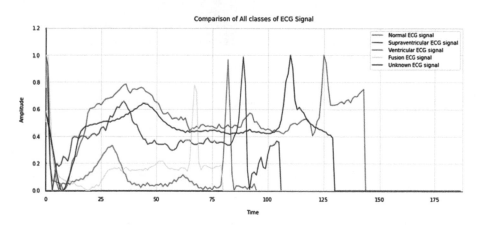

FIGURE 14.10   Comparison of all classes of ECG signal.

Data balancing

```
# Downsampling the high number of dataframes in class-0 by se-
lecting the random 20000 samples from class-0 samples
df_0_train = df_0[df_0[187]==0].sample(n =20000, random_
state=123)

# Upsampling the dataframes of all classes except class-0, upto
20000 samples
df_1_train = resample(df_1, n_samples = 20000, replace = True,
random_state = 123)
df_2_train = resample(df_2, n_samples = 20000, replace = True,
random_state = 123)
df_3_train = resample(df_3, n_samples = 20000, replace = True,
random_state = 123)
```

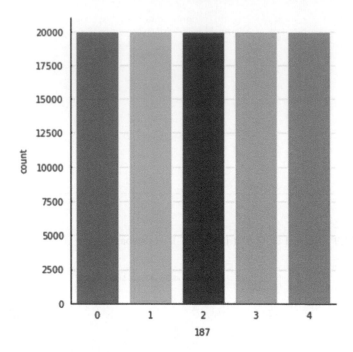

FIGURE 14.11 Bar plots of numbers of samples in each class after re-sampling.

```
df_4_train = resample(df_4, n_samples = 20000, replace = True,
random_state = 123)

# Merging all dataframes to create new train samples
df_train = pd.concat([df_0_train, df_1_train, df_2_train,
df_3_train, df_4_train])
```

Figure 14.11 shows the bar plots of numbers of samples in each class after the process of re-sampling.

Prepare dataset for training and testing

```
# creating labels
target_train = df_train[187]
target_test = test_data[187]

# applying one hot encoding
y_train = to_categorical(target_train)
y_test = to_categorical(target_test)

# Removing Last Column of Training and Testing Data
X_train = df_train.iloc[:,:-1].values
X_test = test_data.iloc[:,:-1].values
```

```
# For conv1D, dimensionality should be 187x1 where 187 is
number of features and 1 = 1D Dimensionality of data.
X_train = X_train.reshape(len(X_train),X_train.shape[1],1)
X_test = X_test.reshape(len(X_test),X_test.shape[1],1)
X_train.shape
X_test.shape
```

Plotting number of samples in each class after data balancing

```
sns.catplot(x = 187, kind = 'count', data = df_train)
```

14.7   IMPLEMENTATION OF 1D-CNN MODEL 2 FOR MULTI CLASS CLASSIFICATION

First, all the class labels are defined for multi-class classification for ECG. For this model in MIT-BIH database labels are defined with the help of One Hot encoding scheme as given below:

- Class 0 (N)= [1,0,0,0,0]
- Class 1 (S)= [0,1,0,0,0]
- Class 2 (V)= [0,0,1,0,0]
- Class 3 (F)= [0,0,0,1,0]
- Class 4 (U)= [0,0,0,0,1]

For dataset 2, a new model is developed in which three convolution blocks are present; each of them containing a convolution layer, a max-pooling layer, and a batch normalization layer. Also, ReLU activation function is used. Then for the output layer, a flatten layer, two dense layers, and a softmax layer is used. In case of convolution blocks, the first block contains a convolution layer that has 64 filters with kernel size 6, max-pooling layer has 2 strides and a pool size of 3. Second block and third block have the same filters but kernel size is 3 and for the max-pooling layer a pool size of 2 with 2 strides was then employed. Also the entire convolution layers contain ReLu as activation function. Then for the output blocks, after a flatten layer the first dense layer is of unit 64 and following that the second dense layer contains 64 units and both of these were having a ReLu as activation function. Now a dense layer containing 5 units with softmax activation function is then used which gives the final predictions using 5 neurons, for a class each. For training Adam optimizer is used with categorical cross entropy loss function. Same model architecture is given in Table 14.2.

TABLE 14.2

Detailed Parameters of the Proposed 1D-CNN Model 2

Type of Layer	Output Shape	Other Parameters
Conv1D	(187;64)	Filters - 64, Padding - Valid, Kernel Size - 6, Pool Size – 3
Batch Normalization	(187;64)	with stride 2, Activation - Relu
Max Pooling 1D	(94;64)	
Activation	(94;64)	
Conv1D	(94;64)	Filters - 64, Padding - Valid, Kernel Size - 6, Pool Size – 3
Batch Normalization	(94;64)	with stride 2, Activation - Relu
Max Pooling 1D	(47;64)	
Activation	(47;64)	
Conv1D	(47;64)	Filters - 64, Padding - Valid, Kernel Size - 6, Pool Size – 3
Batch Normalization	(47;64)	with stride 2, Activation - Relu
Max Pooling 1D	(24;64)	
Activation	(24;64)	
Flatten	(1536)	-
Dense	(64)	Units - 64, Activation – Relu
Dense	(64)	Units - 64, Activation – Relu
Output Layer	(5)	Units - 5, Activation – SoftMax

Plotting accuracy and loss plots of training process (shift this section at last after "Creating Model 2" and "Training of model 2")

```
# converting history to dataframe
pd.DataFrame(history.history)
pd.DataFrame(history.history)[['accuracy','val_accuracy']].
plot()
pd.DataFrame(history.history)[['loss','val_loss']].plot()
```

Training of model 2 (shift this section after "Creating Model 2")

```
history = model.fit(X_train, y_train, epochs = 10, batch_size =
500, validation_data=(X_test, y_test))

Epoch 10/10
200/200 [==============================] - 9s 45ms/step -
loss: 0.0127 - accuracy: 0.9962 - val_loss: 0.1318 - va-
l_accuracy: 0.9740
```

Creating Model 2

```
def build_model():
model = tf.keras.models.Sequential()
# Layer 1
model.add(tf.keras.layers.Conv1D(filters = 64, kernel_size = 6,
activation='relu', padding = 'same', input_shape = (187, 1)))
model.add(tf.keras.layers.BatchNormalization())
model.add(tf.keras.layers.MaxPooling1D(pool_size=(3),
strides = (2), padding = 'same'))
# Layer 2
model.add(tf.keras.layers.Conv1D(filters = 64, kernel_size =
6, activation='relu', padding = 'same'))
model.add(tf.keras.layers.BatchNormalization())
model.add(tf.keras.layers.MaxPooling1D(pool_size=(3),
strides = (2), padding = 'same'))
# Layer 3
model.add(tf.keras.layers.Conv1D(filters = 64, kernel_size =
6, activation='relu', padding = 'same'))
model.add(tf.keras.layers.BatchNormalization())
model.add(tf.keras.layers.MaxPooling1D(pool_size=(3),
strides = (2), padding = 'same'))
# Flatten Layer
model.add(tf.keras.layers.Flatten())
# Dense Layer 1
model.add(tf.keras.layers.Dense(units = 64, activation=
'relu'))
# Dense Layer 2
model.add(tf.keras.layers.Dense(units = 64, activation=
'relu'))
# Output Layer
model.add(tf.keras.layers.Dense(units  =  5,  activation=
'softmax'))
model.compile(optimizer = 'Adam', loss = 'categorical_crossen-
tropy',
 metrics = ['accuracy'])
   return model
model = build_model()
model.summary()
```

Figures 14.12 and 14.13

14.8 MODEL EVALUATION FOR MULTI-CLASS CLASSIFICATION (RESULTS)

In multi-class classification problem there are some changes in calculation and representation of confusion matrix [20]. Multi-class confusion matrix is

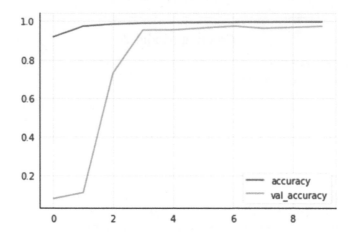

FIGURE 14.12   Training and validation accuracy of Model 2 over MIT-BIH database.

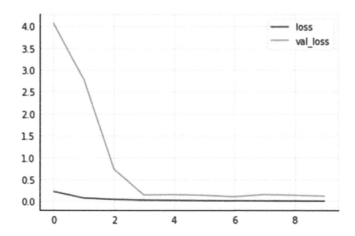

FIGURE 14.13   Training and validation loss of Model 2 over MIT-BIH database.

shown in Figure 14.14, and equations for calculation of parameters are also provided.

In case of multi-class classification problems for calculation of parameters, few modifications are required in the calculation procedure as given in Equations (14.7) to (14.10).

    i. Accuracy (ACC):

$$ACC = \frac{\Sigma_{i=1}^{N} \, TP \, of \, class_i}{Total \, number \, of \, samples \, in \, all \, classes}, \tag{14.7}$$

Where, N is the number of classes.

Multiple Classes		Predicted Class					
		0	1	2	3	4	
Actual Class	0	TP0	FN0 FP1	FN0 FP2	FN0 FP3	FN0 FP4	Total actual samples in class 0 (TP0 + FN0 = 00, 01, 02, 03, 04 cell of CM)
	1	FN1 FP0	TP1	FN1 FP2	FN1 FP3	FN1 FP4	Total actual sample in class 1 (TP1 + FN1 = 10, 11, 12, 13, 14 cell of CM)
	2	FN2 FP0	FN2 FP1	TP2	FN2 FP3	FN2 FP4	Total actual sample in class 2 (TP2 + FN2 = 20, 21, 22, 23, 24 cell of CM)
	3	FN3 FP0	FN3 FP1	FN3 FP2	TP3	FN3 FP4	Total actual sample in class 3 (TP3 + FN3 = 30, 31, 32, 33, 34 cell of CM)
	4	FN4 FP0	FN4 FP1	FN4 FP2	FN4 FP3	TP4	Total actual sample in class 4 (TP4 + FN4 = 40, 41, 42, 43, 44 cell of CM)
		Total predicted sample in class 0 (TP0 + FP0 = 00, 10, 20, 30, 40 cell of CM)	Total predicted sample in class 1 (TP1 + FP1 = 01, 11, 21, 31, 41 cell of CM)	Total predicted sample in class 2 (TP2 + FP2 = 02, 12, 22, 32, 42 cell of CM)	Total predicted sample in class 3 (TP3 + FP3 = 03, 13, 23, 33, 43 cell of CM)	Total predicted sample in class 4 (TP4 + FP4 = 04, 14, 24, 34, 44 cell of CM)	

FIGURE 14.14   Confusion matrix (CM) representation for multiple classes.

ii. Mis-classification (MC): Calculated in a similar way as in binary class classification.

iii. Sensitivity (Recall (RC)):

$$RC = \frac{\sum_{i=1}^{N} \frac{TP_i}{TP_i + FN_i}}{N},$$ (14.8)

iv. Specificity (SP):

$$SP = \frac{\sum_{i=1}^{N} \frac{TN_i}{TN_i + FP_i}}{N},$$ (14.9)

v. Precision (PR):

$$PR = \frac{\sum_{i=1}^{N} \frac{TP_i}{TP_i + FP_i}}{N}, \tag{14.10}$$

vi. F-1 score: Calculated in a similar way as in binary class classification.

Plotting Confusion matrix

```
# change y_test back to original labels with argmax because
above we converted labels via OneHot encoding
y_test= np.argmax(y_test, axis = 1)
print('shape of ytest=', y_test.shape)

cm = confusion_matrix(y_test, y_pred)
np.set_printoptions(precision=2)
print(cm)

[[17695  284   88   48    3]
 [59    487    6    3    1]
 [23     15 1394   13    3]
 [5       1   14  142    0]
 [20      2    7    0 1579]]

cm_df = pd.DataFrame(cm,
       columns = ['Predicted N', 'Predicted S','Predicted V',
'Predicted F', 'Predicted U'],
          index = ['Actual N', 'Actual S','Actual V', 'Actual
F','Actual U'])
# Showing the confusion matrix
cm_df
```

	Predicted N	Predicted S	Predicted V	Predicted F	Predicted U
Actual N	17695	284	88	48	3
Actual S	59	487	6	3	1
Actual V	23	15	1394	13	3
Actual F	5	1	14	142	0
Actual U	20	2	7	0	1579

Testing model with test set

```
loss,accuracy = model.evaluate(X_test, y_test)
print('Loss=',loss)
print('Accuracy=',accuracy)
685/685 [==============================] - 4s 5ms/step -
loss: 0.1224 - accuracy: 0.9728
Loss= 0.12235521525144577
Accuracy= 0.9728211164474487

P = model.predict(X_test)
print('P=',P)
print('shape of P=',P.shape)

P= [[1.0000000e+00 4.0602437e-08 3.4501978e-12 4.8875959e-11
4.4054124e-15]
 [9.9973112e-01  2.6234591e-04  5.9669942e-06  5.6929446e-07
4.0664108e-09]
 [9.9999273e-01  7.1593918e-06  7.9904163e-09  2.2878226e-08
6.1702799e-08]…
 [2.3139862e-08  2.2593814e-13  1.0924292e-07  4.2288839e-08
9.9999988e-01]
 [9.8547299e-13  3.5435247e-14  7.9479289e-13  2.4665398e-16
1.0000000e+00]
 [1.8409403e-09  7.0325521e-12  3.8641987e-09  3.6986190e-17
1.0000000e+00]]

shape of P= (21892, 5)
# converting predictions to classes/labels
y_pred = np.argmax(P, axis = 1)
print('shape of y_pred=',y_pred.shape)
shape of y_pred= (21892,)
```

Figure 14.15

Multi-class parameters calculation from confusion matrix

```
def multi_class_parameters (conf_matrix):
  # (1) accuracy
  ACC = (sum(conf_matrix.diagonal()) / sum(sum(conf_matrix)))

  # (2) mis-classification
  MC = 1- ACC

  [row, col]=conf_matrix.shape
  if (row>2):
    PR=[None] * row
    RC=[None] * row
```

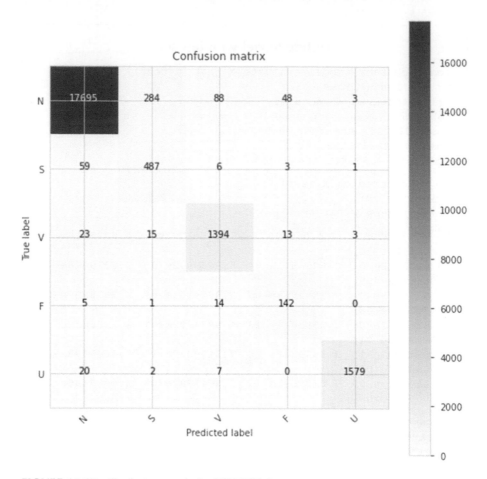

FIGURE 14.15   Confusion matrix for MIT-BIH data set.

```
F1=[None] * row
SP=[None] * row
ind= list(range(0, row))
for cm in range(0, row):
  TN=None
  ind= list(range(0, row))
  PR[cm]=conf_matrix[cm,cm]/(conf_matrix[:,cm]).sum()
  RC[cm]=conf_matrix[cm,cm]/(conf_matrix[cm,:]).sum()
  F1[cm]=(2*(PR[cm])*(RC[cm]))/((PR[cm])+(RC[cm]))
  ind.pop(cm)
  TN=(conf_matrix[np.ix_(ind,ind)]).sum()
  SP[cm]=TN/(conf_matrix[ind,:]).sum()

# (3) Sensitivity (Recall)
Avg_RC = sum(RC)/row

# (4) Specificity
Avg_SP = sum(SP)/row
```

```
    # (5) Precision
    Avg_PR = sum(PR)/row

    # (6) f_1 score
    Avg_F1 = sum(F1)/row

    print('1. Accuracy:', ACC)
    print('2. Mis-Classification:', MC)
    print('3. Sensitivity (Recall):', Avg_RC)
    print('4. Specificity:', Avg_SP)
    print('5. Precision:', Avg_PR)
    print('6. f_1 Score:', Avg_F1)
else:
    TP = conf_matrix[1][1]
    TN = conf_matrix[0][0]
    FP = conf_matrix[0][1]
    FN = conf_matrix[1][0]
    MC = 1- ACC

    # (1) accuracy
    ACC = (float (TP+TN) / float(TP + TN + FP + FN))

    # (2) mis-classification
    # (3) sensitivity (Recall)
    RC = (TP / float(TP + FN))

    # (4) specificity
    SP = (TN / float(TN + FP))

    # (5) precision
    PR = (TP / float(TP + FP))

    # (6) f_1 score
    F1 = 2 * ((PR * RC) / (PR + RC))

    print('1. Accuracy:', ACC)
    print('2. Mis-Classification:', MC)
    print('3. Sensitivity (Recall):', RC)
    print('4. Specificity:', SP)
    print('5. Precision:', PR)
    print('6. f_1 Score:', F1)
multi_class_parameters(cm)

1. Accuracy: 0.9728211218710031
2. Mis-Classification: 0.027178878128996886
3. Sensitivity (Recall): 0.9347535798230293
4. Specificity: 0.9897156358292681
5. Precision: 0.8439847614474371
6. f_1 Score: 0.8825448070503394
```

14.9 CONCLUSION

This chapter demonstrates the stepwise flow for development of classification model for ECG classification. Two famous datasets have been taken, PTB and MIT-BIH, that are publicly available on Physionet website. A simple method for data balancing is also suggested. Several types of fidelity parameters are also used and explained with simple procedure. Confusion matrix of binary and multi-class classification problem are illustrated for easy understating of concepts. After proper training and evaluation, accuracy of 98.58% and 97.28% is achieved in binary and multi-class ECG classification, respectively. Necessary commands and codes required for the development of 1D-CNN model are also provided. One of the main highlights of this chapter is the use of Google Colab platform, which is very easy to use.

REFERENCES

[1] Serhani, M. A., et al. ECG monitoring systems: Review, architecture, processes, and key challenges. *Sensors* 20(6) (2020): 1796.
[2] Chen, X., Wang, Y., Wang, L. Arrhythmia recognition and classification using ECG morphology and segment feature analysis. *IEEE/ACM Transactions on Computational Biology and Bioinformatics* 16(1) (2018): 131–138
[3] Apandi, Z. F. M., Ikeura, R., Hayakawa, S. Arrhythmia detection using MIT-BIH dataset: A review. *2018 International Conference on Computational Approach in Smart Systems Design and Applications (ICASSDA)* (2018): 1–5. 10.1109/ICASSDA.2018.8477620.
[4] Ahirwal, M. K., Kumar, A., Singh, G. K. Biomedical signals. In: *Computational Intelligence and Biomedical Signal Processing. SpringerBriefs in Electrical and Computer Engineering*. Springer, Cham (2021). 10.1007/978-3-030-67098-6_1.
[5] Navin, O., Kumar, G., Kumar, N., Baderia, K., Kumar, R., Kumar, A. R-peaks detection using Shannon energy for HRV analysis. In: *Advances in Signal Processing and Communication, Lecture Notes in Electrical Engineering*, ed. by B. Rawat, A. Trivedi, S. Manhas, V. Karwal, 526, Springer, Singapore (2019). 10.1007/978-981-13-2553-3_39.
[6] Anand, R. S., Kumar, V. Efficient and reliable detection of QRS-segment in ECG signals. In: Proceedings of the First Regional Conference, IEEE Engineering in Medicine and Biology Society and 14th Conference of the Biomedical Engineering Society of India. An International Meet, New Delhi, India (1995): 2/56–2/57. 10.1109/RCEMBS.1995.511734.
[7] Somani, S., Russak, A. J., Richter, F., Zhao, S., Vaid, A., Chaudhry, F., De Freitas, J. K., Naik, N., Miotto, R., Nadkarni, G. N., Narula, J., Argulian, E., Glicksberg, B. S. Deep learning and the electrocardiogram: review of the current state-of-the-art. *Europace* 23(8) (August 2021): 1179–1191.
[8] Xu, S. S., Mak, M.-W., Cheung, C. C. Towards end-to-end ECG classification with raw signal extraction and deep neural networks. *IEEE Journal of Biomedical and Health Informatics* 23(4) (2018): 1574–1584.
[9] Kiranyaz, S., Ince, T., Abdeljaber, O., Avci, O., Gabbouj, M. 1-D convolutional neural networks for signal processing applications. *ICASSP 2019 - 2019 IEEE International Conference on Acoustics, Speech and Signal Processing (ICASSP)* (2019): 8360–8364. 10.1109/ICASSP.2019.8682194.

[10] Murat, F., et al. Application of deep learning techniques for heartbeats detection using ECG signals-analysis and review. *Computers in Biology and Medicine* 120 (2020): 103726.

[11] Manaswi, N. K. Understanding and working with Keras. In: *Deep Learning with Applications Using Python*. Apress, Berkeley, CA (2018). 10.1007/978-1-4842-351 6-4_2.

[12] Nanna Vecchia, A., Girardi, F., Fina, P. R., Scalera, M., Dimauro, G. Personal heart health monitoring based on 1D convolutional neural network. *Journal of Imaging* 7 (2021): 26.

[13] Google Colab Free GPU Tutorial (July 2021), [online]. Available: https://medium. com/deep-learning-turkey/google-colab-free-gpu-tutorial-e113627b9f5d.

[14] Colaboratory: Frequently Asked Questions (June 2021), [online]. Available: https:// research.google.com/colaboratory/faq.html.

[15] Erickson, B. J. Magician's corner: How to start learning about deep learning. *Radiology: Artificial Intelligence* (2019): e190072.

[16] PTB and MIT-BIH datasets on Kaggle: ECG Heartbeat Categorization Dataset | Kaggle. Available: https://www.kaggle.com/shayanfazeli/heartbeat.

[17] PTB Diagnostic ECG Database v1.0.0 (physionet.org). Available: https://www. physionet.org/content/ptbdb/1.0.0/.

[18] Bousseljot, R., Kreiseler, D., Schnabel, A. Nutzung der EKG-Signaldatenbank CARDIODAT der PTB über das Internet. *Biomedizinische Technik, Band 40, Ergänzungsband* 1 (1995): S317.

[19] Kachuee, M., Fazeli, S., Sarrafzadeh, M. ECG heartbeat classification: A deep transferable representation. arXiv preprint arXiv:1805.00794 (2018).

[20] Marina, S., Lapalme, G. A systematic analysis of performance measures for classification tasks. *Information Processing & Management* 45(4) (2009): 427–437.

[21] MIT-BIH Arrhythmia Database v1.0.0 (physionet.org). Available: https://www. physionet.org/content/mitdb/1.0.0/.

[22] Moody, G. B., Mark, R. G. The impact of the MIT-BIH arrhythmia database. *IEEE Engineering in Medicine and Biology* 20(3) (May–June 2001): 45–50. PMID: 11446209.

[23] Goldberger, A., Amaral, L., Glass, L., Hausdorff, J., Ivanov, P. C., Mark, R., ... & Stanley, H. E. PhysioBank, PhysioToolkit, and PhysioNet: Components of a new research resource for complex physiologic signals. *Circulation* 101(23) (2000): e215–e220.

15 Pneumonia Detection from X-Ray Images by Two Dimensional Convolutional Neural Network on Python Platform

Mitul Kumar Ahirwal, Vipul Sharma, and Kuldeep Kumar Gautam
Maulana Azad National Institute of Technology, Bhopal, India

CONTENTS

15.1 INTRODUCTION

Pneumonia is a type of lung infection that affects the small air sacs called alveoli. The physical symptoms of pneumonia range from a combination of productive or dry cough and chest pain to fever and difficulty in breathing. Pneumonia is caused when someone becomes infected with viruses or bacteria in their lungs. The diagnosis of pneumonia is traditionally based on symptoms and physical examination

DOI: 10.1201/9781003241409-15

of the patient. Tests like chest X-ray, blood tests, and culture of the sputum are performed to diagnose pneumonia [1,2].

These tests require expertise and are often unavailable in underdeveloped regions of the world. During times when the medical resources are severely constrained and the volume of patients is high, a need for automated, fast, and accurate diagnosis methods rises. These methods should not consume much time or resources and should have low complexity to be applicable in a multitude of scenarios. The use of deep learning in automated and reliable medical diagnosis offers a much-needed solution in such scenarios. These models can be used with low cost and with less human intervention and can increase the access to diagnosis for people.

Considering all this, the chapter discusses one such use of deep learning model in classification of pneumonia using just the chest X-ray image. The chest X-ray images can be divided into two [1–4]:

- Normal image: Lungs with no visible inflammation
- Pneumonia image: Lungs with visible patches of inflammation

In Figure 15.1, an X-ray image of a normal and healthy pair of lungs is shown. There is no visible inflammation.

In Figure 15.2, an X-ray image of a pair of lungs having pneumonia is shown. We can observe that there are patches of inflammation on the X-ray.

This chapter discusses the detailed description of the implementation of a type of deep learning model, namely two-dimensional convolutional neural network (2DCNN), for X-ray image classification using python, tensorflow, and keras.

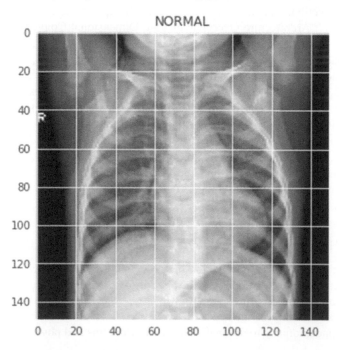

FIGURE 15.1 X-ray of a normal pair of lungs [5].

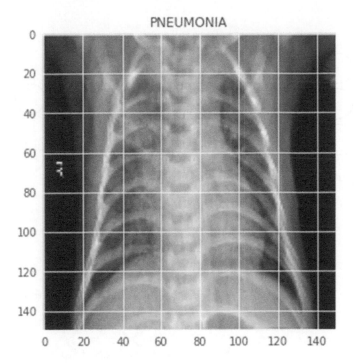

FIGURE 15.2   X-ray of a pair of lungs with pneumonia [5].

15.1.1   ARCHITECTURE OVERVIEW OF TWO-DIMENSIONAL CONVOLUTIONAL NEURAL NETWORK (2DCNN)

Recent years have seen an increase in the compute ability, like GPUs, and the amount of data available, like image and video data. Many complex and deep neural networks have been proposed that exploit these resources effectively to understand high dimensional and complex data [6–8]. One such architecture is convolutional neural network (CNN), it was created specifically for the purpose of handling image data; although it later gained wide adoption in many other fields and forms of data.

CNNs share many similarities with ordinary neural networks in that they also receive an input value, i.e., pixel intensity and perform dot product of that value using some weights and biases which might be passed through some activation function. Normal neural networks are not able to handle the size and dimensions of image data; they are composed entirely of fully connected neurons that increase the network size without being able to efficiently extract information from the image data. CNNs are designed to automatically extract feature from the input space and reduce the size of the input space at each layer to reduce the number of parameters in the network. These features allow them to process image data efficiently.

CNNs are designed with the consideration of color channels in image data. Their neurons handle a 3D volume as an input and output a 3D volume of data, i.e., a third dimension of number of channels is handled by neurons in addition to height and width as shown in Figure 15.3.

(a)

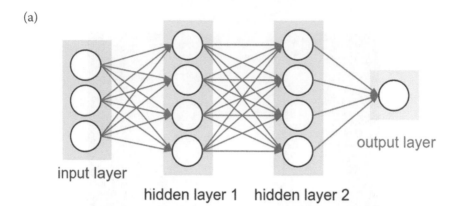

input layer

hidden layer 1   hidden layer 2

(b)

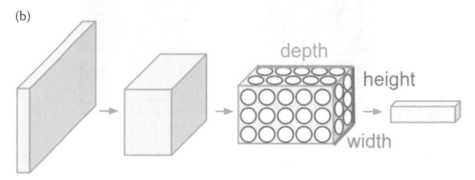

FIGURE 15.3   The comparison of (a) regular neural network and (b) CNN showing the 3D nature of neurons in CNNs [9,10].

In two-dimensional CNNs, the neurons in the next layer are connected to small two-dimensional region of the previous layer; the fully connected structure is avoided in CNN. This method of only focusing on a small region of input by each neuron helps extract local spatial features from the data instead of overloading each neuron with the complete input space resulting in no learning of the neuron. Because of this feature CNNs can detect edges, color distribution, etc. in an image, which makes them very powerful for image classification and in fields where data contains spatial characteristics which need to be extracted.

CNNs are mainly made of the following sequence of layers/blocks:

Convolutional Block: A convolutional layer uses multiple small size learnable windows called kernels or filters. These kernels move or stride along the two dimensions of the image data while extracting local features from small regions of the input space. The movement of these kernels is a configurable hyperparameter for a convolutional layer, the number of steps moved each time, i.e., the stride and the number of pixels skipped over each time, i.e., the dilation rate have to be set by the designer of the neural network [8].

Essentially, the filters slide over the width and height of the image taking the dot products of the input matrix and the value in kernel matrix at that location. This produces a two-dimensional activation or a feature map or a convolved feature. These features are learnt in such a way that they become sensitive to detect image regions like a particular object, an edge, etc.

ReLU (Rectified Linear Unit): This is an activation function which is applied element wise to each entry in the output matrix. It is calculated as *max(0,x)*. ReLU allows us to build deep networks without worrying about vanishing gradient problem during backpropagation [6–8]. There are multiple variants of ReLU, namely Leaky ReLU, bounded ReLU, etc., all of them serve the same purpose of introducing a non-linearity, i.e., allowing complex relationships in the data to be learned.

Pooling: The main function of the pooling layer is to down sample the input matrix along the height and width dimension. It reduces the spatial size of the intermediate representations to reduce number of parameters in the network and prevent overfitting. One common pooling type is "Max Pooling" which simply takes the maximum value of a feature map to pass onto the next layer. It also allows detecting features in different illumination conditions and angles of the image.

Fully Connected Layer: This layer is a normal neural network layer; all the neurons have full connections to previous layer's activations. Before passing activations to fully connected layers, they are first flattened to a one-dimensional vector. There can be multiple fully connected layers in the output block of the neural network which may have ReLU layers in between them. The last layer of the network typically consists of the number of neurons equal to the number of classes in the data and has Softmax activation, although, there can be other ways like, for binary classification we can also have a single neuron with Sigmoid activation.

The networks are trained with backpropagation and loss functions like cross-entropy loss are optimized using many optimizers of which "Adam" is a common one.

Python has become the prevalent language for data science because of its massive collection of ready-made libraries for machine learning. There are many options available to researchers and developers for developing small models using free GPUs and drive storage. One such platform is Kaggle, which provides free and interactive Jupyter notebook and resources like CPU, GPU, TPU, and drive storage [11]. The models discussed in this chapter can be implemented on Kaggle using the data provided in [4,5].

15.2 DATASET

The dataset contains chest X-ray images (anterior posterior) from retrospective cohorts of pediatric patients of one to five years old from Guangzhou Women and Children's Medical Center, Guangzhou [3–5]. These chest X-rays were part of routine clinical care of patients.

There are a total of 5,863 X-ray images in the dataset containing 4,273 pneumonia and 1,583 normal images as listed in Table 15.1. The dataset is split into 5,216 images for training, 624 images for testing, and only 16 images for validation purposes during training.

For the analysis of chest X-ray images, all chest radiographs were initially screened for quality control by removing all low quality or unreadable scans. Two expert physicians manually graded and labelled each X-ray image before they were

TABLE 15.1

Classification of Data Samples in Dataset

Classes	Number of Samples
Normal Lungs	1,583
Pneumonia Lungs	4,273
Total	5,856

published for use in training. To account for grading error, an additional third expert manually graded the evaluation set again.

There is a significant class imbalance which may lead to overfitting problem while training. To tackle this class imbalance problem, a class weighted loss function can be used. We can also do data augmentation to increase the instances of the normal lungs' images.

Data Augmentation: Data augmentation is a way to tackle overfitting by introducing variations in the input images and artificially expanding the dataset. When variations such as change in illumination, angle, zoom, orientation of objects, etc. in images are introduced, the model becomes more robust to real-world variations in the data. Some popular augmentation techniques used are grayscale normalization, horizontal flips, vertical flips, random crops, color jitters, translation, and more.

In this chapter, some of the techniques which have been randomly applied to images in the training set for data augmentation are:

1. Randomly rotate some training images in the range of 0 to 180 degrees
2. Apply ZCA whitening randomly to some training images
3. Random shifting of color channel range
4. Randomly zoom some training images
5. Randomly shift images horizontally by some percent of their width
6. Randomly shift images vertically by some percent of their height
7. Randomly flip images vertically or horizontally

15.3 IMPLEMENTED MODELS OF CNN

Two different architecture of CNN models have been developed for the binary classification of X-ray images. The labels for classification task are:

- Class 0: Pneumonia-infected lungs
- Class 1: Normal lungs

15.3.1 MODEL 1 FOR BINARY CLASSIFICATION OF X-RAY IMAGES

The images have been resized to 226 × 226 shape and some data augmentations applied as discussed earlier. Since there is a class imbalance, class weights have been used in the loss function to prevent the model having a class bias. The class weights are inversely proportional to the class frequency.

This model architecture is based on the VGG-16 model architecture [6]. The architecture of the model is described in the below Table 15.2. It consists of two blocks containing two 2D convolution layers and max pooling layers, followed by three blocks containing three 2D convolution layers and max pooling layers. Finally, the outputs are flattened and passed through to the fully connected layers and Softmax layer. In the middle of these layers the inputs are padded with zeros at the edges using "Zero Padding 2D" layer. All over the network, max pooling layer has a pool size of 2 × 2 which reduces the size of activation map by half.

For the first block, the two 2D convolution layers have 64 filters with a kernel size of 3 × 3 and ReLU activation. The output of this block is reduced using max pooling. The second block that follows has convolution layers with 128 filters for high-level feature extraction while the rest of the parameters remain same as the first block.

The next three VGG-16 blocks that follow, each contain three 2D convolution layers with 3 × 3 filter size and ReLU activation. The number of filters gradually increases from 256 to 512 and 512, in order to perform high-level feature extraction. Each block's output is again reduced in half its size by using max pooling.

The output or the fully connected block is relatively simple with 2 dense layers having 4,096 neurons and ReLU activation. Dropout with a rate of 0.5 has been used in between these layers for regularization and prevention of overfitting. The final layer contains two dense neurons with Softmax activation for classification purpose.

The model is trained with an Adam optimizer with a learning rate of 0.0001 and a categorical cross entropy loss for only 4 epochs.

15.3.2   MODEL 2 FOR BINARY CLASSIFICATION OF X-RAY IMAGES

The input images to this model are first resized to 150 × 150 shape, pixel values normalized between 0 and 255. Several data augmentations are applied on these training images like the ones mentioned in earlier sections.

The model architecture used in this example is known as "AlexNet" [7]. The architecture is shown in the below Table 15.3. It consists of five convolution blocks followed by a fully connected output block. All the convolution blocks have a batch normalization layer just after the convolution layer to normalize the activations of the convolution layer which leads to a faster learning. The normalized activations are also passed through a pooling layer which takes the maximum intensity value from a local region and reduces the size of the input map to half thereby reducing the number of parameters in the network. In the fully connected block dropout is performed to do regularization by randomly removing the activations of some neurons in the input to the next layer. There are three fully connected layers present in the output block of the network. Throughout the network ReLU activation is used to introduce non-linearity and prevent vanishing of gradient problem.

The final layer of the model consists of only two neurons with Softmax activation function. The model is trained with Adam optimizer with binary cross entropy loss. The model was trained for 15 epochs with a variable learning rate dynamically decided by monitoring the validation set accuracy.

TABLE 15.2

Architecture of CNN Model 1

Layer (type)	Input Shape	Output Shape	Arguments	Parameters
Zero Padding 2D	(226, 226, 3)	(228, 228, 3)	Padding = (1,1)	0
Convolution 2D	(228, 228,3)	(226,226,64)	Filters = 64, Kernel Size = (3,3), Activation = ReLU	1,792
Zero Padding 2D	(226,226,64)	(228, 228, 64)	Padding = (1,1)	0
Convolution 2D	(228,228,64)	(226,226,64)	Filters = 64, Kernel Size = (3,3), Activation = ReLU	36,928
Max Pooling 2D	(226,226,65)	(113,113,64)	Pool Size = (2,2), Strides = (2,2)	0
Zero Padding 2D	(113,113,64)	(115,115,64)	Padding = (1,1)	0
Convolution 2D	(115,115,64)	(113,113,128)	Filters = 128, Kernel Size = (3,3), Activation = ReLU	73,856
Zero Padding 2D	(113,113,128)	(115,115,128)	Padding = (1,1)	0
Convolution 2D	(115,115,128)	(113,113,128)	Filters = 128, Kernel Size = (3,3), Activation = ReLU	14,758
Max Pooling 2D	(113,113,128)	(56,56,128)	Pool Size = (2,2), Strides = (2,2)	0
Zero Padding 2D	(56,56 ,128)	(58,58,128)	Padding = (1,1)	0
Convolution 2D	(58,58,128)	(56,56,256)	Filters = 256, Kernel Size = (3,3), Activation = ReLU	29,516
Zero Padding 2D	(56,56,256)	(58,58,256)	Padding = (1,1)	0
Convolution 2D	(58,58,256)	(56,56,256)	Filters = 256, Kernel Size = (3,3), Activation = ReLU	59,008
Zero Padding 2D	(56,56,256)	(58,58,256)	Padding = (1,1)	0
Convolution 2D	(58,58,256)	(56,56,256)	Filters = 256, Kernel Size = (3,3), Activation = ReLU	59,008
Max Pooling 2D	(56,56,256)	(28,28,256)	Pool Size = (2,2), Strides = (2,2)	0
Zero Padding 2D	(28,28,256)	(30,30,256)	Padding = (1,1)	0
Convolution 2D	(30,30,256)	(28,28,512)	Filters = 512, Kernel Size = (3,3), Activation = ReLU	11,801
Zero Padding 2D	(28,28,512)	(30,30,512)	Padding = (1,1)	0
Convolution 2D	(30,30,512)	(28,28,512)	Filters = 512, Kernel Size = (3,3), Activation = ReLU	23,598
Zero Padding 2D	(28,28,512)	(30,30,512)	Padding = (1,1)	0
Convolution 2D	(30,30,512)	(28,28,512)	Filters = 512, Kernel Size = (3,3), Activation = ReLU	23,598
Max Pooling 2D	(28,28,512)	(14,14,512)	Pool Size = (2,2), Strides = (2,2)	0
Zero Padding 2D	(14,14,512)	(16,16,512)	Padding = (1,1)	0
Convolution 2D	(16,16,512)	(14,14,512)	Filters = 512, Kernel Size = (3,3), Activation = ReLU	23,598
Zero Padding 2D	(14,14,512)	(16,16,512)	Padding = (1,1)	0
Convolution 2D	(16,16,512)	(14,14,512)	Filters = 512, Kernel Size = (3,3), Activation = ReLU	23,598
Zero Padding 2D	(14,14,512)	(16,16,512)	Padding = (1,1)	0

TABLE 15.2 (Continued)
Architecture of CNN Model 1

Layer (type)	Input Shape	Output Shape	Arguments	Parameters
Convolution 2D	(16,16,512)	(14,14,512)	Filters = 512, Kernel Size = (3,3), Activation = ReLU	23,598
Max Pooling 2D	(14,14,512)	(7,7,512)	Pool Size = (2,2), Strides = (2,2)	0
Flatten	(7,7,512)	(25088)		0
Dense Layer	(25088)	(4096)	Activation = ReLU	10,276
Dropout	(4096)	(4096)	Rate = 0.5	0
Dense Layer	(4096)	(4096)	Activation = ReLU	16,781
Dropout	(4096)	(4096)	Rate = 0.5	0
Dense	(4096)	(2)	Activation = Softmax	8,194

Total parameters: 134,268,738
Trainable parameters: 134,268,738
Non-trainable parameters: 0

15.4   MODEL EVALUATION

Deep learning models used for classification are generally evaluated using the metrics discussed below. All these metrics are defined using a confusion matrix (as shown in Figure 15.4), which is a method to summarize the correct and incorrect classifications for each class [12].

In the above figure, if an instance of a class, say positive class, is predicted as positive than it is called as "True Positive" and if it is predicted as negative than it is called as "False Negative". Various metrics defined using confusion matrix are as follows:

i. Accuracy (ACC): This is the ratio of correct predictions and total number of predictions, accuracy is obtained by Equation (15.1),

$$ACC = (TP + TN)/(TP + TN + FP + FN), \qquad (15.1)$$

ii. Mis-Classification (MC): This is just opposite of ACC, it is simply calculated by Equation (15.2),

$$MC = 1 - ACC, \qquad (15.2)$$

iii. Sensitivity or Recall (RC): This is the ratio of true positive and total predictions in actual positive, it is simply calculated by Equation (15.1),

$$RC = TP/(FN + TP), \qquad (15.3)$$

TABLE 15.3

Architecture of CNN Model 1

Layer (type)	Input Shape	Output Shape	Arguments	Parameters
Convolution 2D	(150,150,3)	(38,38,96)	Filters = 96, Kernel Size = (11,11), Strides = 4, Activation = ReLU	34,944
Batch Normalization	(38,38,96)	(38,38,96)		384
MaxPooling2D	(38, 38,96)	(19,19,96)	Pool Size = (2,2), Strides = 2	0
Convolution 2D	(19,19,96)	(19,19,256)	Filters = 256, Kernel Size = (5,5), Strides = 1, Activation = ReLU	61,465
Batch Normalization	(19,19,256)	(19,19,256)		1,024
Max Pooling 2D	(19,19,256)	(10,10,256)	Pool Size = (2,2), Strides = 2	0
Convolution 2D	(10,10,256)	(10,10,384)	Filters = 384, Kernel Size = (3,3), Strides = 1, Activation = ReLU	88,512
Batch Normalization	(10,10,384)	(10,10,384)		1,536
Convolution 2D	(10,10,384)	(10,10,384)	Filters = 384,Kernel Size = (3,3), Strides = 1, Activation = ReLU	13,274
Batch Normalization	(10,10,384)	(10,10,384)		1,536
Convolution 2D	(10,10,384)	(10,10,256)	Filters = 256, Kernel Size = (3,3), Strides = 1, Activation = ReLU	88,499
Batch Normalization	(10,10,256)	(10,10,256)		0
Max Pooling 2D	(10,10,256)	(5,5,256)	Pool Size = (2,2), Strides = 2	0
Flatten	(5, 5, 256)	(6400)		0
Dense	(6400)	(4096)	Units = 4096, Activation = ReLU	26,218
Batch Normalization	(4096)	(4096)		16,384
Dropout	(4096)	(4096)	Rate = 0.4	0
Dense	(4096)	(4096)	Units = 4096, Activation = ReLU	16,781
Batch Normalization	(4096)	(4096)		16,384
Dropout	(4096)	(4096)	Rate = 0.4	0
Dense	(4096)	(1000)	Units = 1000, Activation = ReLU	40,970
Batch Normalization	(1000)	(1000)		4,000

TABLE 15.3 (Continued)
Architecture of CNN Model 1

Layer (type)	Input Shape	Output Shape	Arguments	Parameters
Dropout	(1000)	(1000)	Rate = 0.4	0
Dense	(1000)	(2)	Units = 2, Activation = Softmax	2,002
Batch Normalization	(2)	(2)		8

Total parameters: 50,888,290
Trainable parameters: 50,867,150
Non-trainable parameters: 21,140

Binary Classification	Predicted Negative	Predicted Positive
Actual Negative	True Negative (TN)	False Positive (FP)
Actual Positive	False Negative (FN)	True Positive (TP)

FIGURE 15.4 Structure of a binary confusion matrix.

iv. Specificity (SP)/(Selectivity or True Negative Rate (TNR)): This is the ratio of true negative and total predictions in actual negative, it is calculated by Equation (15.4),

$$SP = TN/(TN + FP), \tag{15.4}$$

v. Precision (PR)/(Positive Predictive Value (PPV)): This is the ratio of true positive and total predictions in predicted positive, it is simply calculated by Equation (15.5),

$$PR = TP/(TP + FP), \tag{15.5}$$

vi. F1 Score: This is parameter based on previous above parameters, it is calculated as Equation (15.6),

$$F1 = 2 * ((PR * RC)/(PR + RC)), \tag{15.6}$$

In healthcare, there is a focus on increasing the recall of our models so that no positive diagnosis is classified as a being healthy, i.e., a negative diagnosis. This increase in recall is often at the expense of precision, i.e., a decrease in precision, but it is justified by the reasoning that it's better to classify someone as unhealthy and let them consult an expert for rechecking instead of misclassifying an unhealthy person as healthy.

15.5 RESULTS

In this section of the chapter, the outcomes of model training are shown along with a discussion on how to interpret them. The accuracy and loss curves during the model training are shown followed by tables containing the performance measures of the models on testing data and confusion matrices better representing the class-wise performance of the models. The results shown are just for demonstration purposes, the reader can try altering the model hyperparameters and increasing the number of epochs to get better results.

15.5.1 PERFORMANCE EVALUATION OF MODEL 1

In the training and validation accuracy and loss plots (Figures 15.5 and 15.6) for model 1, the validation accuracy is shown in orange while the training accuracy is shown in blue. The validation accuracy is observed to be greater than the training accuracy; this is a clear indication of overfitting and high variance. Such a model will perform poorly on unseen data. Regardless, we have demonstrated the use of a popular and powerful CNN architecture called "VGG-16" for image classification.

In Tables 15.4 and 15.5, classification parameters and results are listed. The recall for pneumonia class is high which is as needed in medical applications, i.e., all positive diagnosis must be detected even if it means that some false positives are

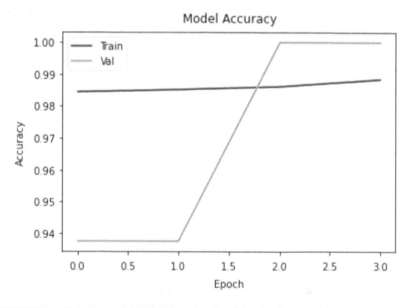

FIGURE 15.5 Training and validation accuracy of Model 1.

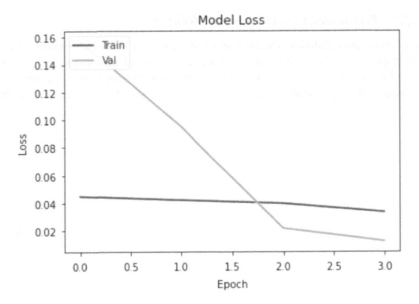

FIGURE 15.6 Training and validation loss of Model 1.

TABLE 15.4
Classification Report of Model 1 on Test Data

Class	Precision	Recall	Specificity	F-1 Score
Pneumonia	0.6394	0.8820	0.1709	0.7413

TABLE 15.5
Result Table for Model 1

	Class Weighted Accuracy	Loss
Training	0.9889	0.0329
Testing	0.7532	2.2214
Validation	1.0	0.0123

generated, or the precision is reduced. As expected from the training and validation accuracy curves, the model overfits the data and the testing accuracy is lesser than the training and the validation accuracy. Such a model performs poor in real world because of high variance.

The overall performance of the model is quite good for demonstration purposes. The summary of predictions can be seen in the confusion matrix.

15.5.2 Performance Evaluation of Model 2

The training and validation accuracy and loss curves are shown in Figures 15.7 and 15.8, respectively. The validation curve has a lot of sudden jumps in it that can be justified by observing that the validation set has only 16 images which a very small size leading to high variations. Despite these variations, it is evident that the both

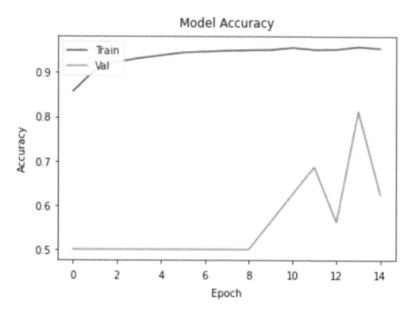

FIGURE 15.7   Training and validation accuracy of Model 2.

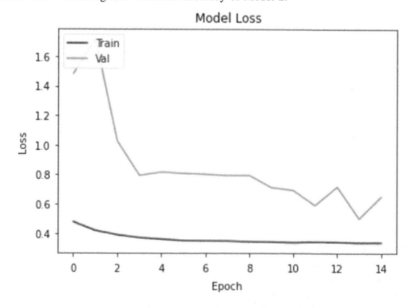

FIGURE 15.8   Training and validation loss of Model 2.

TABLE 15.6
Classification Report of Model 2 on Test Data

Class	Precision	Recall	F1-Score	Support
Pneumonia	0.93	0.96	0.94	390

TABLE 15.7
Result Table for Model 2

	Weighted Accuracy	Loss
Training	0.9555	0.3377
Testing	0.8477	0.4533
Validation	0.6250	0.6519

the validation and training curves are converging which signals that training is going well.

There is clearly an indication of overfitting, i.e., the testing accuracy is lesser than the training accuracy. This is the result of the model having more than 50 million parameters but the dataset having only around 6,000 images.

Tables 15.6 and 15.7 are listed with classification parameters and results of model 2. As required of a model in healthcare, the recall for pneumonia class is quite high. The training and testing accuracies are very close which signals that the model has good generalizability.

We can use this confusion matrix to better understand what biases our model has and what to improve. This chapter has covered both "VGG-16" and "AlexNet" architectures of CNNs which are very popular CNN model architectures and have recently achieved state-of-the art performance in many datasets. These well-known models have successfully demonstrated the power of CNNs in image classification.

15.6 CONCLUSION

In this chapter the need and application of deep learning in automated medical imaging analysis was discussed. We described the functioning of the blocks of a CNN model which is the most prevalent model used in medical image classification. The functioning of CNN model was also demonstrated using a pneumonia detection database as an example and by designing multiple models on this dataset to show the power of CNNs in image classification. The different metrics which are used in image classification tasks were discussed along with how to interpret the results of model training and testing. Some plotting tools were also discussed which help us better understand the performance of the model.

Python Code on Kaggle Note Book:

Step 1: Import Libraries

```python
import numpy as np
import pandas as pd
from matplotlib import pyplot as plt
from glob import glob
import tensorflow as tf
from tensorflow import keras
from tensorflow.keras.models import Sequential
from tensorflow.keras.layers import Dense, Dropout, Flatten,
ZeroPadding2D, Conv2D, MaxPooling2D
from tensorflow.keras.preprocessing.image import ImageData-
Generator
from tensorflow.keras.utils import to_categorical
from tensorflow.keras.optimizers import Adam, SGD, RMSprop
from tensorflow.keras.callbacks import EarlyStopping
from sklearn.metrics import confusion_matrix
from sklearn.metrics import plot_confusion_matrix
import seaborn as sns
from sklearn.metrics import classification_report
```

Step 2: Load Data

```python
#Verifying connection to Kaggle datasets
import os
paths = os.listdir(path="../input")
print(paths)

#specifying paths to train, validation and test folder in
Kaggle Drive storage
path_train = "../input/chest_xray/chest_xray/train"
path_val = "../input/chest_xray/chest_xray/val"
path_test = "../input/chest_xray/chest_xray/test"

img = glob(path_train+"/PNEUMONIA/*.jpeg")  #Getting all
images in this folder
img = np.asarray(plt.imread(img[0]))
plt.imshow(img)

img.shape #Checking the shape of this image

img = glob(path_train+"/NORMAL/*.jpeg") #Getting all images
in this folder
img = np.asarray(plt.imread(img[0]))
plt.imshow(img)

img.shape
```

Step 3: Data Pre-Processing

```python
#Data preprocessing and analysis
classes = ["NORMAL", "PNEUMONIA"]
train_data = glob(path_train+"/NORMAL/*.jpeg")
```

```
train_data += glob(path_train+"/PNEUMONIA/*.jpeg")
data_gen = ImageDataGenerator() #Required Augmentation can be
mention here
# generators for automatic flow and loading of data at runtime
from training and evaluation sets and applying augmentations
train_batches  =  data_gen.flow_from_directory(path_train,
target_size = (226,226), classes = classes, class_mode = "ca-
tegorical")
val_batches = data_gen.flow_from_directory(path_val, tar-
get_size = (226, 226),classes = classes, class_mode = "cate-
gorical")
test_batches = data_gen.flow_from_directory(path_test, tar-
get_size = (226,226), classes = classes, class_mode =
"categorical")

train_batches.image_shape
```

Step 4: Create 2D-CNN Model

#VGG16 Model Architecture
 # Below Code is the implementation of "Karen Simonyan, & Andrew
Zisserman, "Very Deep Convolutional Networks for Large-Scale
Image Recognition", 2015, arXiv:1409.1556." and many copies of
this implementation are available on GitHub and Kaggle. (We
acknowledge all the code developer on GitHub and Kaggle) In
this chapter we are just adding this code for learning purpose
of beginners as a reference after reading above theory of
VGG-16.

```
model = Sequential()
model.add(ZeroPadding2D((1,1),input_shape=train_batches.-
image_shape))
model.add(Conv2D(64, (3, 3), activation='relu'))
model.add(ZeroPadding2D((1,1)))
model.add(Conv2D(64, (3, 3), activation='relu'))
model.add(MaxPooling2D((2,2), strides=(2,2)))
model.add(ZeroPadding2D((1,1)))
model.add(Conv2D(128, (3, 3), activation='relu'))
model.add(ZeroPadding2D((1,1)))
model.add(Conv2D(128, (3, 3), activation='relu'))
model.add(MaxPooling2D((2,2), strides=(2,2)))
model.add(ZeroPadding2D((1,1)))
model.add(Conv2D(256, (3, 3), activation='relu'))
model.add(ZeroPadding2D((1,1)))
model.add(Conv2D(256, (3, 3), activation='relu'))
model.add(ZeroPadding2D((1,1)))
model.add(Conv2D(256, (3, 3), activation='relu'))
model.add(MaxPooling2D((2,2), strides=(2,2)))
model.add(ZeroPadding2D((1,1)))
model.add(Conv2D(512, (3, 3), activation='relu'))
model.add(ZeroPadding2D((1,1)))
model.add(Conv2D(512, (3, 3), activation='relu'))
```

```
model.add(ZeroPadding2D((1,1)))
model.add(Conv2D(512, (3, 3), activation='relu'))
model.add(MaxPooling2D((2,2), strides=(2,2)))
model.add(ZeroPadding2D((1,1)))
model.add(Conv2D(512, (3, 3), activation='relu'))
model.add(ZeroPadding2D((1,1)))
model.add(Conv2D(512, (3, 3), activation='relu'))
model.add(ZeroPadding2D((1,1)))
model.add(Conv2D(512, (3, 3), activation='relu'))
model.add(MaxPooling2D((2,2), strides=(2,2)))
model.add(Flatten())
model.add(Dense(4096, activation='relu'))
model.add(Dropout(0.5))
model.add(Dense(4096, activation='relu'))
model.add(Dropout(0.5))model.add(Dense(2,
activation='softmax'))

#Viewing the architectural summary of the model
model.summary()
```

Step 5: Train Model

```
optimizer = Adam(lr = 0.0001)
early_stopping_monitor = EarlyStopping(patience = 2, monitor
= "val_acc", mode="max", verbose = 2)
model.compile(loss="categorical_crossentropy",    metrics=
["accuracy"],optimizer=optimizer)
history = model.fit(train_batches, epochs=4,callbacks=[ear-
ly_stopping_monitor],
shuffle=True,validation_data=val_batches)

plt.figure()
plt.plot(history.history['accuracy'])
plt.plot(history.history['val_accuracy'])
plt.title('Model Accuracy')
plt.ylabel('Accuracy')
plt.xlabel('Epoch')
plt.legend(['Train', 'Val'], loc='upper left')
plt.show()

plt.figure()
plt.plot(history.history['loss'])
plt.plot(history.history['val_loss'])
plt.title('Model Loss')
plt.ylabel('Loss')
plt.xlabel('Epoch')
plt.legend(['Train', 'Val'], loc='upper left')
plt.show()
```

Step 6: Evaluate Model

```
loss,accuracy = model.evaluate(test_batches)
print('Loss=',loss)
print('Accuracy=',accuracy)
```

```python
P = model.predict(test_batches, steps=100)
print('P=',P)
print('shape of P=',P.shape)

# converting predictions to classes/labels
ypred = np.argmax(P, axis = 1)
print('shape of ypred=',ypred.shape)

ytest = test_batches.classes
print('shpape of ytest=', ytest.shape)
cm = confusion_matrix(ytest, ypred)
np.set_printoptions(precision=2)
print(cm)

cm_df = pd.DataFrame(cm,
columns = ['Predicted Negative', 'Predicted Positive'],
index = ['Actual Negative', 'Actual Positive'])
# Showing the confusion matrix
cm_df
def binary_class_parameters (conf_matrix):
  TP = conf_matrix[1][1]
  TN = conf_matrix[0][0]
  FP = conf_matrix[0][1]
  FN = conf_matrix[1][0]
  print('True Positives:', TP)
  print('True Negatives:', TN)
  print('False Positives:', FP)
  print('False Negatives:', FN)

  # (1) accuracy
  ACC = (float (TP+TN) / float(TP + TN + FP + FN))

  # (2) mis-classification
  MC = 1- ACC

  # (3) sensitivity (Recall)
  RC = (TP / float(TP + FN))

  # (4) specificity
  SP = (TN / float(TN + FP))

  # (5) precision
  PR = (TP / float(TP + FP))

  # (6) f_1 score
  F1 = 2 * ((PR * RC)/(PR + RC))

  print('1. Accuracy:', ACC)
  print('2. Mis-Classification:', MC)
  print('3. Sensitivity (Recall):', RC)
  print('4. Specificity:', SP)
  print('5. Precision:', PR)
  print('6. f_1 Score:', F1)
```

REFERENCES

[1] Hashmi, M. F., Katiyar, S., Keskar, A. G., Bokde, N. D., Geem, Z. W. "Efficient Pneumonia Detection in Chest X-ray Images Using Deep Transfer Learning." *Diagnostics (Basel)* 10(6) (2020): 417. Published 2020 Jun 19. doi: 10.3390/diagnostics10060417.

[2] Ayan, E., Halil, M. Ü. "Diagnosis of Pneumonia from Chest X-ray Images Using Deep Learning." 2019 Scientific Meeting on Electrical-Electronics & Biomedical Engineering and Computer Science (EBBT). IEEE (2019).

[3] Kermany, D., Zhang, K., Goldbaum, M. "Labeled Optical Coherence Tomography (OCT) and Chest X-Ray Images for Classification." *Mendeley Data* 2 (2018). doi: 10.17632/rscbjbr9sj.2.

[4] Kermany, D. S. et al. "Identifying Medical Diagnoses and Treatable Diseases by Image-Based Deep Learning." *Cell* 172(5) (Feb. 2018): 1122–1131e9. doi: 10.1016/j.cell.2018.02.010.

[5] Kaggle Database, https://www.kaggle.com/paultimothymooney/chest-xray-pneumonia [accessed: Feb 2021].

[6] Karen, S., Zisserman, A. "Very Deep Convolutional Networks for Large-Scale Image Recognition." (2015). arXiv:1409.1556.

[7] Alex, K., Ilya, S., Geoffrey, E. H. "ImageNet Classification with Deep Convolutional Neural Networks." *Commun. ACM 60* 6 (June 2017) (2017): 84–90. doi: 10.1145/3065386.

[8] Goodfellow, I. J., Bengio, Y., Courville, A. Deep Learning, MIT Press (2016).

[9] Stanford University Course CS231n: Convolutional Neural Networks for Visual Recognition, http://cs231n.stanford.edu/ [accessed: Feb 2021].

[10] https://cs231n.github.io/assets/cnn/cnn.jpeg

[11] Kaggle Online Platform, https://www.kaggle.com [accessed: June 2020].

[12] Sokolova, M., Lapalme, G. "A Systematic Analysis of Performance Measures for Classification Tasks." *Information Processing & Management* 45(4) (2009): 427–437.

Index